THE ART OF VICTORIAN PROSE

George Levine is Associate Professor
of English at Indiana University, and
Editor of *The Emergence of Victorian
Consciousness*. In 1966 he taught at
the University of London Summer
School in Victorian Literature. William A. Madden is Professor of English and Dean of the Junior Division
at Indiana University. He is the author of *Matthew Arnold*.

THE ART OF VICTORIAN PROSE

EDITED BY

GEORGE LEVINE & WILLIAM MADDEN

NEW YORK

OXFORD UNIVERSITY PRESS

LONDON 1968 TORONTO

CONTENTS

INTRODUCTION

THIS BOOK grew out of the editors' independent experience as students and teachers of Victorian literature, an experience, they discovered, that was generally shared by colleagues elsewhere. Victorian literature is the first for which the claim might reasonably be made that its prose non-fiction surpasses its poetry, not only in bulk but in artistic achievement, and the problem of finding appropriate ways of dealing with this body of non-fiction is therefore peculiarly urgent. The usual explanation given for treating non-fictional prose works in literature classes is that such works provide the indispensable "background" for our understanding of the literature itself. The inadequacy of this explanation is evident: anyone who attempts to teach Mill's *Autobiography,* for example, quickly realizes that he is engaged in discussing a response to experience that differs very little if at all from the kind of thing he has been accustomed to think of as the peculiar activity of poets and novelists. The study of Mill's *Autobiography* or Carlyle's *Past and Present* or Newman's *Apologia* or Ruskin's *Stones of Venice* entails consideration not simply of devices of logic and argument, but of varying forms of self-expression and modes of metaphoric structure: these constitute distinctive styles and express distinctive voices as marked and as identifiable as those, say, of Tennyson or Browning, Dickens or George Eliot.

Although a number of studies in recent years have attempted to treat this problem, to our knowledge there is at present no satisfactory over-all rationale, no adequate method or combination of methods, by which non-fiction might be studied and evaluated as imaginative vision—as art. Despite the large body of existing scholarship about most of the relevant works, relatively little attention has been given to the structure and style of these works, to what in them has caused them to survive while other prose, some of it far more popular in its own day, has been forgotten.

The editors have recognized, both in themselves and in most critics trained in the dominant schools of criticism during the past quarter century, a more or less tacit resistance against regarding non-fiction, and especially literary criticism, as a legitimate art form. After all, literary criticism and art criticism are parasitical, depending for their very existence upon the works on which they feed; and social criticism, autobiography, political oratory, and other less exalted forms of non-fiction are simply emasculated (we think) if students are asked to turn their attention from the substance to mere form and style. Did not T. S. Eliot expose the moral corruption latent in a Saintsburian impressionism? Whether dealing with art or with life, non-fiction—it is assumed—is best when it is most transparent, when it mediates truth without calling attention to the author.

Thus, the obstacles to regarding non-fiction as art seem to be considerable. One central function of this book is to begin, in a tentative way, the exploration of a vast territory for which such maps as we now have are either out of date or bewildering in their self-contradictions. Its primary purpose is to supply a sustained, though obviously incomplete, literary study of Victorian prose. To that end, the editors invited a number of scholars and critics who have had a wide experience in the study of Victorian non-fiction. There are, inevitably, important omissions. In particular, we miss full essays on Newman and on the copious literature of Victorian social criticism (commissioned papers on these topics were not forthcoming). Essays on other important writers and topics—Thackeray, for example, or the great letter-writers FitzGerald and Hopkins, and word-painters like Kilvert and (again) Hopkins—could not be included if the book were to be kept within manageable size. For these omissions the editors must bear responsibility. We can only hope that their absence does not seriously distort the main outlines of the provisional map that emerges.

When planning the book, the editors had no *a priori* theory of their own regarding what was to be found, only the belief that much prose conventionally classified as non-fiction was as imaginative and creative as art proper. We must confess, however, to having entertained the hope that one result of the book might be, if only implicitly, the development of an elementary and general poetics of non-fiction which would interest readers whose main concerns lay outside Victorian literature. The editors think that the essays collected here can in fact imply such a poetics, that they tend to exhibit, despite the variety of writers discussed and the variety of approaches employed, an underlying coherence. The coherence results, we believe, from an impressive similarity in the fundamental assumptions each writer employed when he set to work on the problem of seeing non-fiction as art. It seems appropriate, therefore, to present here our sense of the results of the collective enterprise by way of introducing the reader to the territory he is about to enter.

In his widely read study of poetic diction, Owen Barfield some years ago invoked a fourfold distinction which is germane to the problem with which this volume is concerned. He established, first, a "formal" distinction between *verse* (metrical writing) and *prose* (non-metrical writing), and then added a second, "spiritual" distinction between the *poetic* and the *prosaic*. Barfield's purpose was to demonstrate that just as *verse* may be either *poetic* or *prosaic*, so *prose* may be either *prosaic* or *poetic*. This was not, of course, the first time that the distinction had been made, although the terms used in making it and the motives prompting it have varied greatly—from Wordsworth's distinction between *poetry* and *science*, to Mill's distinction between *poetry* and *eloquence*, through Collingwood's opposition of *art* to *craft*, down to Mr. Norman Holland's contrast, elsewhere in this volume, between *fantasy-projection* and *reality-testing*. For the literary critic, the interest of these distinctions centers on the pole represented by the words "poetic," "art," and "fantasy-projection." This post-Romantic focus, and its radical implications, were clearly defined by the English aesthetician Edward Bullough early in the present century. Bullough isolated what he called the "aesthetic" consciousness, distinguishing it from not one, but three, alternative modes of consciousness—the ethical, the scientific, and the practical—by analyzing "the most elaborate and distinctive form of aesthetic consciousness, namely, that which produces and appreciates a work of art." He wrote,

> *Aesthetically* a work of art has neither antecedents nor final results. Aesthetically the production of an art-object does not go beyond the realisation of the artistic conception in the work, nor is the aesthetic impression a result, to some extent independent of the work which produced it (as the moral consequences of an act assume an importance and live in the strength of their own reality, independently of their proximate causes). Aesthetic response remains centred on the work, drawing its enjoyment from it and reflecting it back upon it. That the other points of view are possible is, of course, a truism: the History of

Art, sociological and ethical studies of Art, aesthetics itself, are evidence of that. But the aesthetic attitude is neither scientific nor ethical. It is, in distinction to the formulas adopted before, neither retrospective nor prospective, but *immanent;* neither explanatory nor final, but contemplative. And this is true not only of Art, but of Nature and Life when these are viewed aesthetically.

Bullough thus regarded the "aesthetic" attitude as relevant to responses to every kind of object. "When we call a thing aesthetic," he concluded, "the reason is to be sought as much, nay even more, in the subjective attitude of the recipient as in the objective features of the thing itself. Everything can, at least theoretically, become for me an aesthetic object, whether it be meant to affect me in this way or not."

This analysis both echoes Keats's earlier statement about the possible loveliness, from a certain point of view, of a quarrel in the streets, and anticipates Mr. Holland's remarks on the importance of a reader's "expectations" in qualifying his response to a literary text. We see—or fail to see—what our expectations have prepared us to look for, and our "impression" of a literary text varies accordingly. Mr. Tillotson's analysis of his response to a brief prose passage describing how one ought to care for a fainting victim illustrates the peculiarly modern capacity to respond aesthetically even to the most "prosaic" prose. Conversely, Mr. Rosenberg's analysis of Ruskin's ethical "reading" of the façade of St. Mark's in Venice discloses a subtle and sophisticated type of "reality-testing" of which less interesting examples can be found in the student who comes to lyric poetry for advice, or in the neurotic viewer who finds salaciousness indiscriminately in all paintings of nudes.

Once it was recognized that we can view everything aesthetically, the question of whether we ought to do so was inevitable. This question appeared comparatively recently in the study of prose, since the capacity to produce artistic prose, evident in English literature as early as Malory, pre-dated by several centuries the conscious capacity to respond to prose aesthetically. The essays by Messrs. Merritt, Stange, and Fraser, in fact, trace the actual emergence of this capacity in English literature during the nineteenth century, and this development of the awareness necessary to respond aesthetically to non-fiction was perhaps one of the most significant phenomena of the century. Such an awareness, conscious of itself and confident of its powers and purposes, was implicit in Wordsworth's juxtaposing of poetry and, not prose, but science, or, to cite another instance, in Hazlitt's account of his enthusiastic discovery of the prose of Burke:

> From the first time I ever cast my eyes on any thing of Burke's . . . I said to myself, "This is true eloquence: this is a man pouring out his mind on paper." All other style seemed to me pedantic and impertinent. . . . Burke's style was forked and playful as the lightning, crested like the serpent. He delivered plain things on the plain ground: but when he rose, there was no end of his flight and circumgyrations.

But, as Mr. Fraser suggests, full consciousness of the flights and circumgyrations of which prose was capable, together with the recognition of the possibility of maintaining the aesthetic attitude in viewing all of experience, seems to have fully arrived only with Pater. Mr. Tillotson points out that even the otherwise modern sensibilities of Matthew Arnold and Arthur Hugh Clough were, in this matter, conditioned by the older, simpler dichotomy between poetry and prose. Arnold, of course, was prepared to give a very high place to the literary critic, yet the critical function remained for him firmly subordinate to the function of the poet, of "genius." It was Pater, significantly, who first advanced the claim that the prose essay was *the* characteristic modern literary genre, and Pater's self-consciousness produced, within a very short time, the overbalance suggested by Saintsbury's remark (cited by Mr. Donagan) that style was "an arrangement of words with meaning subordinate." It was against this kind of dilettantism that the reaction initiated by Eliot and other critics early in this century was directed; but in this reaction, Eliot, and later the New Criticism generally, in effect if not in intent, made the aesthetic attitude toward non-fiction suspect. Although much has been written since Pater, particularly in recent years, on the development of English prose, our instinctive critical habit of mind continues to regard the essayist, the biographer, the social critic, the philosopher as second-class citizens who dwell outside the gates behind which lie the golden realms of poetry.

The question remains: what precisely is entailed in taking up an aesthetic attitude toward ostensibly non-aesthetic objects? At the outset, one might say, very little more than what is entailed in responding properly to "art." Since the "truth" or "fictiveness" of any work is testable only by reference to the outside world, there is nothing intrinsic in non-fictional prose to distinguish it from fictional prose. Our response is usually determined by the context: we assume that a newspaper essay is attempting to report or analyze a reality of the outside world which might be experienced by anyone who happened to be in the right place at the right time. For this reason, our experience of newspaper columnists who are more concerned to be funny than to report the news is usually disorienting until we accept the convention and see them in another context—until we move them, that is, from the editorial page to the amusements section. The importance of context is evident in the frame of the theatrical stage, which serves to make any response but applause, or controlled feeling, inappropriate, even to dramas about murder. There is no point in running on stage to rescue Desdemona.

The aesthetic attitude toward non-aesthetic objects, then, like the aesthetic attitude generally, entails building a frame around the object so as to insulate it from action. Mr. Tillotson's response to instructions on the treatment of fainting can only be primarily aesthetic so long as he is not immediately concerned to apply the information contained in the instructions. Curiously, however, the detachment from immediate experience which is the central quality of the aesthetic attitude does not diminish the significance to the perceiver of the "substance" of the object. The meaning is not ignored; it is, to re-invoke Bullough, regarded contemplatively. Thus, it is widely agreed now that a full response to the "meaning" of a poem is only possible for someone who has willingly put aside his preconceptions and practical commitments and who has left himself open to the full possibilities of the language of the poem. For those refusing to do so, irony will frequently be read as matter of fact, matter of fact as irony; some details will be ignored while others are quietly constructed. All of this has been widely understood since I. A. Richards's *Practical Criticism*. A full response entails a full understanding of the implications of the experience embodied in the language. The meaning is at once tested against reality and deprived of its imperative case.

The correct critical attitude toward an object viewed aesthetically must then be formal rather than ethical or practical, although it may well be concerned with the ethical and practical questions which are the substance of the aesthetic object. So viewed, the object will seem to be flawed insofar as the writer's vision lacks formal coherence. (One of the traditional and, we believe, generally valid assumptions of critics is that the failure of formal coherence implies the inadequacy of the vision itself.) It is not a question of whether the writer finds the best form for the expression of his vision, for this implies a distincton between the vision and the materials he uses to give it expression. The expression itself and the relation among its parts are the object of study.

Obviously, however, some texts seem to require an aesthetic response more insistently than others. If all language, as R. G. Collingwood has said, is art, are we therefore impelled to regard all texts indiscriminately as aesthetic objects? Instructions for first aid are hardly worth our aesthetic attention (except to make an aesthetic point), although it is worth noting that Matthew Arnold was persistently driven toward aesthetic responses even in his social criticism (it will be remembered that his first criticism of the Wragg episode in *Culture and Anarchy* was of the ugliness of the name Wragg). Perhaps, therefore, the first task of the literary critic concerned with discussing non-fiction is to identify those literary texts to which the aesthetic response is immediately appropriate. If our "expectations" are simply "to revive the patient" or "to keep dry," then the expressive element in first-aid instructions or in a building—an element which certainly attends and qualifies our negotiations with these objects —though present is not important. Our mode of awareness is not at the moment responsive to the aesthetic element, or, if it is, then we must suppress that responsiveness—our tendency to regard things contemplatively and formally—in order to realize our prior expectations, which are kinds of action. We do not refuse to shelter ourselves because the only building available for the purpose happens to be ugly.

The aesthetic response might be said to delay or to short-circuit action. How, then, can any non-fiction compel an aesthetic stance? If the aesthetic stance is compelled, how can one discriminate non-fictions that are intrinsically aesthetic from those that are not? For reasons already briefly touched upon, these questions become acute for the student of Victorian literature. As we have already noted, it was in the Victorian age that non-fiction became a central and dominant literary genre. Carlyle, for example, made a reputation as a "poet" through his social and historical writings; indeed, as Messrs. Merritt, Fraser, Tillotson, and Stange show, non-fiction was increasingly invading areas conventionally thought to belong exclusively to poetry. Although Arnold resisted the change in theory, as Mr. Tillotson shows, he nevertheless participated in it in practice. A whole way of seeing was developing which entailed an expansion in the variety and subject matter of prose. As a result, as Mr. Merritt's essay demonstrates, the Victorian age produced an extraordinary variety of important non-fiction and of styles, so that one cannot talk usefully, even in a shorthand way, about *a* Victorian style. John Stuart Mill, beginning from the assumption that truth was ascertainable, came to believe that it was nevertheless beyond the grasp of any single man. His famous essays on Bentham and Coleridge suggest then that discovery of truth entailed a complex and sympathetic exploration of apparently opposed points of view, and we can now see how only an increasingly complex and supple prose could work such a discovery. And with this sense of the personal effort and imaginative leap involved in finding truth, there grew the realization that one is talking more about one's personal experience of an object than of the object itself; in this context even non-fictional prose becomes the man. We are close here to an expressionist aesthetic in which all language is self-expression—that is, art. Mr. Stange traces with clarity and concision the effects of these developments in art criticism, and his diagram of the relations among art-work, writer, text, and reader might stand as a paradigm for the kind of relationship established not only in every non-fictional work but (given the varying nature of the "reality" it describes) in every imaginative work.

"Practical" prose continued to be written in the nineteenth century, of course, and continues to be written in far greater quantities than artistic prose; but our awareness of the expressive element even in "prosaic" prose has meanwhile been enormously heightened. The inseparability of what is said from the way in which it is said might be regarded as one of the major discoveries of modern literary criticism, and this development has created the need to work out a poetics of non-fiction that will enable the critic both to classify the linguistic structures that organize a given literary text and to discover not if, but how these structures function aesthetically. Mr. Milic points out that a writer does have choices—can select from several alternative ways of embodying his thought. Mr. Ohmann, in a previously published essay, "Prolegomena to the Analysis of Prose Style," indicated the essential contradiction in discussing something distinctive called "style" and then asserting that it is no different from meaning. If "style" means anything, it means choice. In his essay in the present volume, Mr. Ohmann develops this point in an interesting and useful distinction between the "deep structure," which holds the meaning, and the surface structure, which is one of many possible choices for the embodiment of the meaning. Mr. Ohmann is correct, we think, in asserting that style can be seen as a pattern of such choices, and that transformational grammar may indeed make possible a coherent theory of style. But we would suggest that the metaphor in "deep structure" is in one sense misleading: an artist does not begin with a meaning which must come to the surface after being formulated in the depths, but the full meaning is only formulated when the artist has found his "surface structure." Mr. Ohmann himself says that the surface structure "implies a characteristic way of viewing," that is, implies another meaning beyond that embedded in the deep structure. Although it is useful for a critic to distinguish the two kinds of meaning, it is important to recognize that the "choice" an artist has is more theoretical than real: until he makes the "choice" he does not fully know what he means. In a sense, that is, the style remains the meaning.

Mr. Ohmann points up another distinction, between writing about the subject and writing about self, which—as we shall argue—more usefully helps to distinguish non-fiction as art from ordinary non-fiction; "the characteristic way of conceiving, and relating, and presenting content" is precisely what makes the great Victorian prose writers interesting after we have long since come to disbelieve in, or be indifferent to, the meaning in their "deep structures." The "choice" that exists, for example, between the passive and active forms, will, however minutely, shape the larger experiential meaning of the work. An essay that persistently uses passive structures, by implying an attitude on the part of the writer toward his subject (self-effacement, objectivity, discomfort requiring self-protection) would be very different from an essay that conveyed the same "ideas" in active structures. The essay by Mr. Stange perhaps most clearly illustrates the distinction we are here proposing. He demonstrates how in Pater's description of a painting, the referent is not, immediately, the painting ("fact") but rather Pater's impression of the painting ("the sense of fact"), and how Pater is aware of this. We may, if we choose, make a "reality-test" of Pater's impression against the original painting, that is, against our own impression of the original painting, but such "reality-testing," indispensable though it ultimately is, comes later. What we get, what we enjoy, when reading Pater is his lucid rendering of his impression. Similarly, what we enjoy in Ruskin's description of St. Mark's are not any supposed facts about the cathedral, but Ruskin's interpretations of the facts, his accounts of how they affected one extraordinarily sensitive and self-conscious individual. Whether or not we ultimately agree with Pater's or Ruskin's impressions, we come to recognize and enjoy in the very texture of their prose the presence of a characteristically Paterean or Ruskinean "voice." In such prose we are close to, indeed we are already within, the poetic realm as described by Robert Frost: "the speaking tone of voice somehow entangled in the words and fastened to the page for the ear of the imagination."

Once we recognize that non-fiction can be interpreted aesthetically, we are in a position to recognize also that for some non-fictional prose the aesthetic response is primary precisely because, like the poet or novelist, the essayist is not "reality-testing," is not involved in "craft" or "rhetoric," but is projecting himself in a created literary work as self-consistent and imaginative as the work of a great poet or novelist. Moreover, it becomes clear that for non-fiction to transcend rhetoric and become art, its producer must make the primary referent of his language his own self or, more precisely, the emotional relation of the self to the object; for the literary critic, the quality of such prose depends not upon its fidelity to some external reality, but upon its unverifiable fidelity to the total impression of reality held in the mind of the writer. The very persuasiveness of a writer's rhetoric is thus carried by the comprehensiveness and self-consistency of his whole linguistic world, not simply by the cogency of his ostensible arguments.

To illustrate this point, we refer the reader to the essays by Mr. Madden on Macaulay, by Messrs. Cannon and Culler on Darwin, and by Mr. Levine on Carlyle. Mr. Svaglic shows how Macaulay's Aristotelian rhetoric (Aristotle himself, significantly, kept his *Rhetoric* separate from his treatise on *Poetics*) points outward to external "reality." Rhetoric, in this sense, whether epideictic, hortatory, or forensic, is "practical" in intent in that its focus is not upon the mind of the producer but upon the mind of the audience. Thus, from the rhetorical point of view, Macaulay's "Milton" can be judged a success. Mr. Madden, on the other hand, shows how, behind Macaulay's ostensible rhetoric and built into the very texture of Macaulay's style, there are complexities and conflicts in Macaulay himself that qualify his rhetoric. Similarly, Mr. Cannon demonstrates how, in general, Darwin's ostensible and outmoded rhetoric is inadequate to express his vision of life, while Mr. Culler shows how the total linguistic structure of Darwin's *Origin of Species* successfully embodies a revolutionary vision. Mr. Svaglic, that is, describes the marvelous "craft" of Macaulay's argument and Mr. Madden describes the breakdown of his "art"; Mr. Cannon locates the failure of Darwin's rhetoric, while Mr. Culler describes the success of his "art." Mr. Levine's essay on Carlyle shows how an artistic prose can be damaged when a hitherto successful external form no longer corresponds to the writer's full vision of experience.

In his essay on political oratory, Mr. Holloway suggests that political rhetoric is, by its very nature, inhibited by the bi-polar simplifications of experience required of the politician if he is to satisfy his objective of persuading his audience to act. His analysis thus suggests one of the criteria for identifying genuinely artistic prose—that it be produced by a disinterested mind, a consciousness that is both open and free, immanent and contemplative, one which, in Keats's phrase, does not have designs upon us but rather is turned back upon itself in such a way that it is capable of the completest possible self-expression. Mr. Holloway's comments are closely related to, indeed in our opinion are inseparable from, Mr. Culler's comments on Darwin, Mr. Madden's comments on Macaulay, Mr. Donagan's strictures upon the "purple passage" in Bertrand Russell's *Free Man's Worship*, Mr. Holland's analysis of several prose passages in the light of the Freudian concept of sublimation, and Mr. Levine's reservations about the late Carlyle. If, as Mr. Donagan argues, following Collingwood, the coming-into-being of a thought and its accompanying emotion is inseparable from the writer's act of putting his experience into language, then from both the philosophical and the psychological points of view, lack of self-awareness on the part of a writer is immediately reflected by the failure of articulation in his language. In such cases, either we do not understand what the writer says, or, so far as we understand him, we are not carried with him because there is a felt discrepancy between the thought and the accompanying emotion; in short, in such cases we understand more about the writer's relation to his subject than the writer does; we understand more than the writer intended to reveal. For an audience of literary critics, at least, that language is most persuasive which most perfectly embodies a comprehensive and self-consistent state of mind fully aware of itself.

The terms of the tentative poetics of non-fiction which we are here proposing thus disclose a hierarchy of kinds of prose, a scale of aesthetic perfection, on which, as we ascend, the distinctions between meaning and language tend to disappear. Those kinds at the bottom of the scale tend, paradoxically, to provide writers with the widest possibility of choice of language, but at a level where the choice is largely irrelevant. This is because writers of this kind of prose are working with pre-established meanings for which they are merely attempting to find approximations in language. The difference, for example, between active and passive voice at these levels would be largely accidental. Thus, at the bottom of the scale may be found the most narrowly practical prose, a prose giving instructions on how to operate a simple machine, or urging us to a simple action, or informing us of a simple fact. Even this language, to be sure, has an expressive element, but for the sake of what needs to be done we ignore or discount this element. Somewhat higher, there is the "factual" prose of ordinary journalism; still higher, the prose of high rhetoric, exhorting or describing, in which the writer's attitude toward his subject becomes for the first time significant; higher still, the prose of "human interest" journalism. As we approach the top of the scale, we find a prose less immediately concerned with action—though perhaps still strongly committed —and more concerned with a clarification of the meaning of the experience considered. It is a prose increasingly marked by a distinctive voice, increasingly self-contained and inward-looking, increasingly shifting its referent from an assumed outward reality to an open consciousness seeking to organize its understanding of a complex experience in language. Such prose makes the "immanent" and "contemplative" stance of the aesthetic attitude indispensable.

In summary, the literary critic of non-fiction must take into account the free awareness of the producer as revealed in the nature of the text produced. An adequate poetics of non-fiction will enable the critic both to classify the linguistic structures that organize a given text and to discover how these structures function aesthetically. In other words, the literary critic must bring to non-fictional prose the same flexibility, the same capacity to discriminate the modes of consciousness that are revealed in the language, as he brings to the drama, to poetry, and to the novel.

It is, of course, impossible, once we are aware that, say, Newman's *Apologia* is not a novel about a man named Newman but a genuine autobiography, to ignore the "practical" significance of the book. Indeed, within the terms we have attempted to establish, our proposed poetic of non-fiction rests on the principle that "practical" prose must be approached practically if the critic is to get at its art. And it would be absurd to pretend that the *Apologia* is all "art" and no "eloquence," no "craft." With Mr. Svaglic, we would not find it difficult to move through the *Apologia* classifying the rhetorical structures and devices Newman employed in order most effectively to create for his readers his sense of self and of the living busy world in which that self moved. The aesthetic "frame" we place around the work is partly provided by time—we are no longer fighting Newman's battles with Kingsley—but largely by our awareness that the fullest expression of Newman's self is engaged in his expression of his relation with his audience. In one sense, to be sure, Newman manipulates his audience; but insofar as the *Apologia* survives, it is as something other than a work of rhetoric. It is, rather, as the expression and clarification of complex attitudes and feelings toward a very complicated experience. And this clarification ends in producing for the reader a vision of experience which is profoundly moving, whether he accepts this vision in his practical world or not. By progressing, that is, through an understanding of the work's meaning, of its professed practical relations to the world, the reader ends by establishing an inevitable and satisfying stance toward the work. The *Apologia* begins in the practical world and ends, as it were, framed, like a novel. This is not to say that it can never be viewed practically again—its practical powers are everywhere evident. But it survives as literature because it can sustain the contemplative and unpragmatic reading.

Criticism of any kind is a perilous enterprise, for the critic tacitly insists upon his capacity to judge another mind. We are arguing only that in evaluating non-fiction as art, the critic is simply approaching Parnassus by another route. Whereas in criticism of fiction he discovers fiction's meaning (rhetoric) through its being (art), he arrives at the non-fictional text's being (art) through its meaning (rhetoric). In non-fictional prose of the highest order, in certain kinds of philosophical speculation or the prose of literary or art criticism, the prose of a Pater, Ruskin, or Newman, we are at the point where practical prose is on the verge of becoming pure fiction in the technical sense, pure story—the imitation of an action which is inward, spiritual, and profound, an action which, as Mr. Fraser notes in concluding his essay on Pater, is the ultimate reality for all men, poets, novelists, and essayists alike.

A word about the organization of the book. The editors' original plan was to have three sections: first, strictly theoretical essays describing possible ways of approaching all prose; second, general studies of kinds of Victorian prose (e.g., art criticism, philosophy, political oratory); and third, particular studies serving as practical applications of theory. These theoretical divisions proved to be impracticable. Mr. Holloway's essay on political oratory, for example, provides a general strategy for approaching polemical (and, by implication, all) prose. Mr. Tillotson theorizes about the status of all non-fictional prose in the process of characterizing Arnold's. Mr. Holland both presents a theory and provides some practical applications of that theory. Mr. Culler carries his discussion over into the realm of fiction. Every essay, in fact, moves beyond the formal limits as originally conceived for programmatic reasons. We believe that the book is richer than it would have been had the theoretical limits been observed.

Nevertheless, the essays as submitted do in fact provide their own structure. The first cluster of essays provides a convenient historical starting point; though concerned also with theory, these essays are centrally concerned with certain aspects of the history of nineteenth-century prose. Mr. Merritt provides a brief general history; Mr. Stange and Mr. Donagan provide short histories for aspects of art criticism and philosophy; and Mr. Tillotson traces the development of a conversational mode from Newman and Arnold. The second group of essays—those of Messrs. Levine, Madden, Cannon, Rosenberg, and Fraser—are all concerned with particular authors, although they frequently touch on matters of history and theory. These essays serve to fill in some of the details of the first historical section and to anticipate some of the larger theoretical problems dealt with in the last essays in the volume. This third group of essays divides itself neatly in two: Messrs. Ohmann, Milic, and Holland approach the theoretical problems by concentrating largely on language—on style in the stricter sense; Messrs. Culler, Holloway, and Svaglic, while engaged in other things also, describe theories of approach which are essentially structural.

It is important, finally, to bear in mind that this volume is deliberately because inevitably tentative, an introduction, hopefully, to further, more extensive studies of Victorian prose and to a more detailed and coherent poetics of the art of non-fiction. It attempts as much to raise questions as to answer them. The editors' speculations are, of course, entirely their own and imply nothing about the attitudes of the contributors. They are aware, moreover, that no theory of approach to non-fiction provides a "formula" for evaluating a work as art. Rather, each theory serves only to describe one possibly useful mode of analysis. It is a commonplace of philosophy that "is" cannot logically produce "ought." Analysis cannot logically produce evaluation, but it can provide evaluation with a more rational, more informed, base. In any case, there is nothing prescriptive about the theorizing in this book.

It is our hope that insofar as these essays begin a debate they will be useful. Moreover, if the editors may for a moment divide the substance from the form, we believe that each essay justifies itself by virtue of its presentation of a valuable body of material. We believe, in short, that the initial case for Victorian prose as an art form—even, perhaps, over the objections of some of the contributors—has been made.

G. L.
W. M.

Bloomington, Indiana
August, 1967

THE ART OF VICTORIAN PROSE

TASTE, OPINION, AND THEORY
IN THE RISE OF VICTORIAN PROSE STYLISM

TRAVIS R. MERRITT

IN 1828 THOMAS DE QUINCEY could say that rhetoric was dead in England.[1] Despite his notorious inconsistency in the use of terms, De Quincey's opinion in such matters is always interesting and usually relevant to the truth; in this case it is particularly so, since the very manner of his discussion pertains directly to the status of prose and prose style during the early part of the nineteenth century. While recognizing that "rhetoric" is a term no longer applicable merely to the arts of oratory, he adopts here a strangely narrow definition, excluding from the rhetorical province not only affairs of "absolute certainty and fixed science," which leave no room for the exercise of persuasion, but also the passions, taken by him as the subject of eloquence, a more poetic mode of utterance.[2] Now if rhetoric is indeed dead, because the conditions in which it flourishes no longer exist, then the prose writer is faced with an extreme choice: he may either use the exact and unpretending language suitable to scientific demonstration, or he may try, like De Quincey himself, to write a "passionate prose" which will embody some of the special powers of eloquence.

But it is here, exactly, that the real problem arises, for by now it is clear that for the outward manifestation of "rhetoric" De Quincey understands something very close to conspicuous beauty of style in prose, and it is clear, too, that he sees the demise of rhetorical style as resulting from a chronic defect in the British temper. Repeatedly in his critical writings he laments the native hostility to style, the exaltation of "matter" over "manner," particularly in prose composition.[3] He finds himself at war, in fact, with a fundamental misconception and confusion of ideas about verbal finish, and it is to clarify this muddle that he draws his distinction between the mechanic and organic aspects of style.[4] If it is the habit of British taste to reject all finery of phrase on the grounds that there should be always a simple, straightforward, and honest projection of thought into words, De Quincey satisfies such a morality with his notion of organic style; but this, he insists, does not absolve the writer of his responsibility to arrange and adjust sentences with the greatest compunction, for the demands of mechanical perfection must be met as well. The fine artifices of grammar and syntax must be preserved or, more appropriately, reclaimed. Finally, though, the British literati must learn that even under the organic conception, ornate style is not necessarily prohibited, for there are subjects and feelings gorgeously ornate in themselves.[5]

De Quincey's exertions on this subject help to confirm two well-established tendencies in early nineteenth-century literary affairs: first, the relation between substance and style was undergoing important redefinition; second, the role, status, and capacity of prose as an artful medium were both more ambiguous and more promising than they had been for a long time. And it is significant that De Quincey himself was troubled by a general lack of enlightened theoretical concern over prose style, as well as by the lack of practical attention to it. He feared that the debased jargon of newspapers might take over by simple default. Fifty years later he would have found quite different troubles to complain of, for toward the end of the century there emerged a great speculative and practical vogue of style—a "stylism" as I shall call it—whose central concern seems to have been the elevation of the prose medium to new heights of expressiveness, distinction, and finesse. How this late-Victorian cult of prose style is reflected in taste, opinion, and theory, and how its peculiar character developed, less exclusively as a product of French influences than is often supposed and more as a complex outgrowth of native causes rooted deep in nineteenth-century intellectual and cultural values, it is the object of this paper to explain. It will be useful to begin by noticing a few characteristics of the criticism of prose style at the start of the century, during the period when neo-Augustan precepts were gradually being replaced. In the process, I hope, the distinctiveness of De Quincey's attitudes will appear more sharply.

I

I suppose it is clear that the so-called Romantic movement might have theorized about and given much more critical attention to prose composition had it not been so preoccupied with poetry. Not that poetry was equated with verse in an exclusive way. The organic processes of poetic creation *might* be released in prose, too, as most serious critics were prepared to admit. And yet it is certain that, for most literary thinkers, the extension comes as an afterthought; one finds few prose passages used in example. My point is simply that, during the time of greatest change in aesthetic value, critical theory did not take the distinctive virtue of prose as an object for definition, and this was because even some of the more advanced opinion-makers tended to preserve the traditional barrier between the province of prose and that of verse. In actual practice, to be sure, the distinction was being broken down, from the one side by Wordsworth, from the other by Lamb and De Quincey. But there was little accompanying revaluation of the peculiar stylistic possibilities through which the art of prose might rank in absolute worth with that of verse.

In other words, criticism was a little slow to derive from its new organicist and expressivist principles an adequate account of what prose is and what it is supposed to be good for. The resulting uncertainty can be felt in critical pronouncements on the most fundamental matters. Take meter versus non-meter, for instance, the prime ostensible distinction between the form of poetry and the form of prose. Meter is something of an embarrassment to Wordsworth. As a practicing poet he will not do without it, but as a defender of his own poetic theory he hardly knows what to do with it. In the Preface to *Lyrical Ballads* he takes up the matter twice, but without much real success: after an unconvincing assertion of his right to "superadd" the "charm" of meter—a procedure obviously not in accord with the spirit of his notions about literary language—he ends by speaking of the effect of regularity in "tempering and restraining" the substantive passion. He is uneasy in granting rights to meter, though, because he fears that its admission may invite other artificial distinctions of language.[6] And it is precisely this habitual opposition of his—that between the natural and the artificial—which lies at the heart of much early nineteenth-century opposition to the stylistic manners (including the rhetorical contrivances suitable to prose) of the preceding age. Coleridge has better success with this problem. Recognizing that meter is, on the face of it, a crucial and not a trivial or "superadded" characteristic of most actual poems, he accounts for its central importance by defining the peculiar office of a poem as "proposing to itself such delight from the *whole*, as is compatible with a distinct gratification from each component part . . . all [the parts] in their proportion harmonizing with, and supporting the known influences of metrical arrangement."[7] This leaves Coleridge still with the bothersome questions whether meter is therefore always necessary in a poem and, if not, why so few poems exist without it. Here he makes use of his distinction between poetry and the poem. Poetry may exist without meter. A long poem will contain some parts that are poetry and some that are not, according to the principle of intensity.

> Yet if an harmonious whole is to be produced, the remaining parts must be preserved *in keeping* with the poetry; and this can be no otherwise effected than by such a studied selection and artificial arrangement, as will partake of *one,* though not a peculiar property of poetry. And this again can be no other than the property of exciting a more continuous and equal attention than the language of prose aims at, whether colloquial or written.[8]

Later, in Chapter xviii of the *Biographia Literaria,* he discusses further the effect of metrical language on the vivacity and susceptibility of the reader's attention, though he is careful again to insist that the measured sound signals a whole ordonnance of language different from that of prose, and not simply an overlaid phonemic pattern. What wants special notice here is Coleridge's criterion of poetic continuity, the evenly uninterrupted skein of the audience's heightened attention and of the verbal beauty which excites it. When the demand for such sustained texture is extended to prose stylistics, toward the end of the Victorian age, the resulting change in critical expectations must be seen as owing much to the force of Coleridge's conception. But he does not make such an extension himself, and so he testifies, at least negatively, to the lesser stylistic capabilities of the prose medium.

I do not wish to suggest that there is some radical novelty in this critical implication that prose language is intrinsically less precious, less susceptible of the highest beauty, than the language of verse, that—to use Wordsworth's phrase—the "regions" of prose "may be gracefully and profitably trod with footsteps less careful and in measures less elaborate."[9] The distinction is, in this sense, about as old as criticism itself, and it had hardly lain dormant during the eighteenth century. Kames, whose ideas so thoroughly influenced the detailed development of psychologically affective rhetoric in the decades preceding *Lyrical Ballads,* admits as a matter of course that the verbal delight of prose is absolutely inferior to that of verse. Beautiful prose may be had—there is no reason why it should be avoided—but we do not "insist" on it: "provided the work convey instruction, its chief end, we are the less solicitous about its dress."[10] And yet it is during the latter part of the eighteenth century that we observe a flourishing of treatises and manuals of rhetoric and style, most of them concerned mainly with prose, not verse, and showing that concern in detailed analysis and precept. Inspired chiefly by the systematic ideas of the dominant elementarist and associationist psychology, these works cover with great care an extensive range of prose technique, from diction to syntax to sound. Their emphasis upon prose composition, in particular, is due to the fact that prose works more generally and obviously involve the didactic relation to an audience, so that they more readily display devices which can be explained in affective psychological terms. If there is an apparent contradiction in critical tendencies here—the assertion on the one hand of the superior conspicuous beauty and elevation of poetic language, the practice on the other of devoting enormous critical effort to the affective niceties of prose language—it can best be explained by recognizing that the eighteenth-century critics conceived of verbal "beauty," "artifice," "refinement," "elevation," and such in two quite different ways. And the underlying causes of this dualistic habit may be seen in the effect of primitivism, and of a concurrent belief in cultural progress, on literary theory.

In the first of his *Lectures*, Hugh Blair surveys with restrained satisfaction the advance of taste within his own age:

> It is an age wherein improvements, in every part of science, have been prosecuted with ardour. To all the liberal arts much attention has been paid: and to none more than to the beauty of language, and the grace and elegance of every kind of writing. The public ear is become refined. It will not easily bear what is slovenly or incorrect.[11]

Blair wonders whether the process of refinement has not indeed gone too far. His predecessor, Kames, is certain it has gone too far, that complexity and profuse ornament are degrading taste in all fields.[12] But they are alike in viewing the "progress" in taste as part of the nature of things; the impulse to refinement which comes with cultural age is, then, in itself a good and proper development. Both men feel that if there is now a corruption of taste it is not so "natural" that it cannot be corrected, for it is only a perversion of things inherently good. When writers (and readers) are reminded of the difference between true and false ornament, all may be well. Thus the art of rhetoric not only is capable of great refinement, but demands the correct sort of refinement, which provides the *raison d'être* for the ambitious critical undertaking of the various manuals.

To this way of thinking may be juxtaposed the familiar eighteenth-century notion of poetry's origin and its historical priority to prose. An important element in this theory, derived from Lucretian and Viconian speculations about primitive society, is the belief that all language must have been in its origins essentially poetic, since it was made by men in whom passion and imagination were pre-eminent. Blair's qualification of this doctrine is important. Surely, he says, the most primitive men did not hold commonplace conversations in "poetry"; they must have had from the start some "very humble and scanty prose" for matters of simple fact and daily exigency. The poetry arose, no doubt, on ceremonial occasions, when men were "roused." And the formal distinctions of the language thus produced are three: syntactical inversion, bold figures, and meter—features which Blair categorically identifies as primitively natural and essentially poetic. Later these are studied, methodized, made artful; but originally they spring from a way of life to which "cool reasoning and plain discourse" are unknown.[13] Thus the rise of discursive language—prose, as modern men know it—is concomitant with a civilizing process which removes the rudeness and some of the liveliness from raw poetry. This accounts for the tendency among critics of the later eighteenth century to regard the nice, the completely wrought, the regular aspect of poetic form in much the same way as they regarded the rhetorical refinement of prose. One is simply *more* elevated than the other. But originally, radically, the difference is more profound. Thus there are really two orders of beauty in language, one inhering in the poetic way of receiving experience, the other developed by careful filing away at the language itself. This goes far to explain the double standard of which I spoke earlier. The conscious craft of versification arises from and improves upon primitive and unconscious heightenings of language derived from the simplest facts of human nature; thus it may properly aspire to elegance and draw attention to itself. The conscious craft of prose composition, on the other hand, while it rightly requires effort at least as particular as that due verse, should have as one of the objects of its care a relative unobtrusiveness, a refusal to draw attention to itself; and this not merely for the obvious reason that we persuade best when our calculation and skill are left to work unobserved—a version of the traditional *ars est celare artem*—

but also because prose refinement, a practice of civilization lacking the sanction of primitive Nature, constitutes when obtrusive *mere* artifice, which is morally repugnant as well as aesthetically displeasing.

Keeping in mind the distinctions just described, it may be worthwhile to summarize in an admittedly condensed and selective way the prescriptive tendencies of the rhetorical school of style criticism. Besides a discernible increase in the campaign for Saxon purity and against "low" words of all sorts, the most important of all the eighteenth-century changes in stylistic taste, as far as diction is concerned, was that which took the premium off Dr. Johnson's "general truth" and put it on particulars, specifics, tangibles, prompted by the reasoning that the human mind, after all, can view distinctly but one object at a time.[14] As for figurative usage, traditionally considered to be the very type of ornament, the reaction of Restoration and Augustan taste against elaborate conceit had made it usual to think of a good metaphor as a device of modest proportions and little internal complication—a construction neat, whole, small, tame, familiar.[15] In grammar and syntax, the basic principles of human understanding govern. The correct order places first the agent, then the act, finally the object, according to "the order of nature and of time," and violent or protracted departures from this decent norm are not to be encouraged.[16] Hence there is mistrust of inversion and especially of periodic structure, though, of course, some exceptions are justified under the principle of Variety. Antithesis is regarded as a centrally valuable, if frequently abused, device. Even in sound, or "melody," associationist principles seemed able to recommend rather specific (and rather silly) rules for the attainment of euphonious combinations and sequences. Broken or harsh collocations are admitted only where mimesis demands them.[17]

Risking bad proportion, I have wanted to say this much about eighteenth-century style criticism, partly because I wish to emphasize the nature of the changes which did follow after 1800, but for another reason as well: much of this body of compositional precept did not die out (though the psychology on which it was founded became obsolete), precisely because no new system emerged to replace it. Thus we can notice that although there is a decided reaction in the Wordsworth-Coleridge camp, for instance, against the idea that certain words belong to the exclusive language of poetry, although metaphor receives new and broader sanction from the revaluing of the imagination as an organically esemplastic power, and although there appears a more determined opposition to antithetical structure because its artifice is patently mechanical, most of the rules and principles promulgated by the rhetoricians of prose seemed as useful for sound composition in 1830 as they had a generation earlier. It is not surprising that, even when associationist principles had ceased to provide serious intellectual justification for their method, manuals of affective rhetoric and style continued to appear—like Richard Whately's enormously successful *Elements of Rhetoric* in 1828—advancing the traditional assumptions and suggestions about the proper management of prose language. And yet preserving, one may add, the very distinct derogation of the beauty and importance of style in prose which Coleridge, Hazlitt, and De Quincey were inclined to qualify if not to reject outright. Good poetry, says Whately, is *"elegant and decorated language, in meter, expressing* such and such thoughts," while good prose is *"such and such thoughts expressed* in good language."[18] His italics are hardly needed to mark the difference.

There is another element in the early nineteenth-century attitude to prose style which must be mentioned before I take up the Victorians themselves, and that is the considerable affection shown for the great prose masters of the pre-Restoration seventeenth century. The reasons for this attachment have a direct bearing on later developments. When Coleridge, Wordsworth, and Hazlitt condemn the characteristic style of much post-Restoration prose for its excessive reliance on balance and antithesis, their motives are partly those of sheer reaction. But there are better reasons, and active alternatives. Most readers nowadays would probably think Renaissance prose "ornate." Coleridge did not judge it so. A clear indication of his values comes in Chapter XVIII of the *Biographia*, where he criticizes the Wordsworthian standard of rustic language as lacking proper arrangement and subordination of parts because of a failure of organization in the minds of those who speak it; it is strongly implied that the form of language, particularly of written language, should proclaim itself as the product of the synthesizing mind.[19] What Coleridge wants is interconnectedness and high structural articulation in prose—qualities of the verbally-embodied thought which may be associated, if only indirectly, with the continuous heightening that he requires of good verse. Balance and antithesis, as connective formulae, are simply not adequate to the expression of rich substance. But in the "thought-agglomerating flood" of Taylor's prose, Coleridge finds an "architectural" structure and unity, "the unity of the subject, and the perpetual growth and evolution of the thoughts, one generating, and explaining, and justifying, the place of another, not, as in Seneca, where the thoughts, striking as they are, are merely strung together like beads, without any causation or progression."[20] Lamb and De Quincey show the same inclination of taste.[21] And the quality which attracts them all is more than just the charm of the antique; it is a fullness and freedom of language—freedom from tidy structural conventions and the full capability to project in style the unintermittent and highly personal activity of intellectual synthesis itself.

This mix of opinion and theory is not easily reduced to main trends, but I think it is at least clear that the advanced critical consensus of the pre-Victorian era favored an increased personal element in the verbal surface, and that this virtue was associated with a loosening of the strictures of decorum in order to achieve a more natural movement of language, whether gorgeous or informally familiar. De Quincey noticed that the more "subjective" branches of thought seemed most conducive to the cultivation of style, and that the more internal and individual the matter treated, "precisely in that degree, and the more subtly, does the style or the embodying of the thoughts cease to be a mere separable ornament, and in fact the more does the manner . . . become confluent with the matter."[22] It was this view, still tempered by vestiges of the traditional notion that verbal craft in prose must work as simply and unobtrusively as possible, which was inherited by the Victorian literary community. One might reasonably expect the next step to be a further liberalizing of opinion about the capacities of prose as an expressive (not just usefully affective) medium, with a concomitant tendency to theorize and practice a more unabashedly "aesthetic" management of style. But this event was in part delayed, in part obscured, by other ones.

It is an irony that in what now appears to have been an age of monumental achievement in prose—the time of Arnold, Ruskin, Carlyle, Newman—the status of the prose vehicle as art should have remained as tenuous as it did. In 1864 Bulwer Lytton can still call prose "brick and mortar" to poetry's "ivory, marble, and cedar."[23] Walter Bagehot explains the subjected condition of prose as an inevitable lack of truly exquisite diction: "The highest excitation of feeling is necessary to this peculiar felicity of choice [in poetry]. In calmer moments the mind has either less choice or less acuteness of selective power. Accordingly, in prose it would be absurd to expect any such nicety."[24] The ranking, of course, has some new implications for the Victorians, whose improved methods in the mass production of books confronted them with an unprecedented quantity of cheap and vulgar prose. Thus David Masson finds prose best suited to the literature of "contemporary fun"; great, serious, and impassioned truths, on the other hand, should be done into poetry, whose style is best suited to the worth of such subjects, while it also "wins independent admiration and is a source of independent intellectual pleasure."[25] Certainly pronouncements of this kind are colored by the general reputation of the novel as a literary form; it had not yet achieved fully respectable status.[26]

II

In understanding the controlling Victorian attitudes to prose style, it is necessary to contemplate some of the dominant social and intellectual movements of the time, and the feelings which they engendered about such things as beauty, ornament, and pleasure. First, there is the pre-eminent doctrine of social utility, whose effect on literary critical practice is instructively various, mainly because it was not informed by a single systematized aesthetic. The Positivist-Utilitarian attack on imaginative literature, for example, may seem more or less stylistically discouraging—not to say prohibitive—depending on whether you read Bentham or Mill.[27] But it is certain that, in a broad view, the Utilitarian habits and values, the no-nonsense frame of mind, did not produce an atmosphere friendly to the flourishing of "pure" literary culture, and still less did they encourage recognition of autonomous formal beauty, as in prose style. This tendency found a correlative in the spread of industrialism itself: as machines continued to improve the material holdings of the nation and to make progress seem an authentic fact, the public acquired a shrewd respect for them, and by association a corollary respect for speed, efficiency, and quantity of output. In yet another area, Evangelical Christianity (though well past its greatest popular height by mid-century) was still exerting profound force in behalf of an artless sort of faith which involved notions both of spontaneity and of enthusiastic sincerity as sufficient authentication in religious experience. It was ever suspicious of mere outward forms. A revived Puritanism could decry the Positivist's material determinism that had replaced Old Conscience, but at the same time it worked, paradoxically, toward the same antagonistic separation of surface from substance, of artifice from true zeal, of graceful execution from meaningful result. Concurrently, in the public sphere, there was a series of political as well as social reforms which allowed a new distribution of wealth and power to complement, in some degree, the rise of literacy and the expansion of the "fit" audience. A combined awareness of (1) the cruder sensibilities and (2) the very numbers of the new readership forced a reconsideration of suasive means even among fairly conservative rhetoricians; writers must bend more to the lower taste and intellect of the more general audience, and this could only conduce to a levelling of stylistic distinction.[28] Finally, but not least important in this odd assortment of causes, there was a deep-rooted anti-intellectualism, bitterness toward the old broken authority and fear of the inquiry which had broken it, which went far beyond the mere mistrust of reason and was now turned, Philistine-like, against the supposed mandarinism of the literary establishment.[29]

Even such a condensed and broadly suggestive account of the age's temper helps to explain how different forces worked together—if not exactly in concert—to form that part of Victorian taste which demands plainness, unadorned language, a new tone of post-Wordsworthian simplicity. But to say that mid-century taste in prose was fixed by an ideal of plain serviceability is to tell much less than half the truth. Although the Utilitarian and materialist impulse seemed to commend functional form stripped of distracting verbal conventions and frills, the effect of simplicity was sought less for its own sake (or because it could be called "natural") than as a way of making possible the true richness of urgent address. It is not far wrong to say that, for the great culture-critics who most affected the advanced taste of the time, the arts of rhetorical heightening and stylistic insinuation were scorned insofar as they might constitute sheer ornamental effect or conspicuous verbal intricacy, but welcomed as they could enhance a usefully didactic tone of earnest conviction and seriousness. Thus Ruskin's pronouncement that "the highest thoughts [in literature] are those which are least dependent upon language," that the real value of a composition is "in exact proportion to its independency of language or expression," must be interpreted in the light of Arnold's opinion that only by the saving virtues of force and sincerity can literary language discard the usual tricks of prettiness and complication to reside in a style "perfectly simple, limpid."[30] It is with these same criteria in mind that Carlyle works out his notion of Symbol and Silence in *Sartor Resartus*.[31]

Correlative with the precept that the style of prose language must be unobtrusive and, at the highest moments, entirely eclipsed from the reader's consciousness, is the recommendation that style not be an object of the *writer's* direct awareness when he is in process of composition. Again, the object is to gain force and conviction. A measure of spontaneity is needed, though the lack of self-consciousness must not lead to loss of power. Carlyle enunciates this particularly well in his essay on Walter Scott: certainly there is great virtue simply in getting a thing said outright, and yet "no great thing ever was done with ease, but with difficulty"; the right way is to meditate, to mature the thought with great care, and then to write it out rapidly.[32] As another critic puts it, there are some kinds of writing, and some occasions which arise in any kind of writing, in which "the matter is so important, that the author cannot attend to the manner."[33] So substantive energy, itself a guarantee of forcible expression, renders all other stylistic concern superfluous; but the style which it leads to is not likely to be simple and unwrought.

It is urgent substance, then, which must be given full primacy; but this substance is empowered and even informed by the verbal manner of a wisely sincere man earnestly arguing and expostulating. The aim is more to be memorable than to be elegant. The kinds of stylistic distinctiveness thus achieved are various, but all of them seem to be marked by strongly mnemonic devices: dictional and phrasal repetition, full scale reiteration of key statements, progressive triadic climax, heavily-set parallel in balance and antithesis. In addition there appeared a special argumentative method, brilliantly surveyed by John Holloway in *The Victorian Sage*, in which the characteristic devices are not wholly classifiable in the categories of traditional rhetoric, but emerge as it were inevitably from the very attitudes being urged, and testify cumulatively to the value of those attitudes.[34]

Throughout the pertinent criticism of prose in the mid-Victorian era, there is relatively little mention of those criteria which neo-classical writers had regarded so highly. Quiet decorum in organization, a nicely proportioned relation of parts, the scrupulous avoidance of excess and the cultivation of urbane civility of surface—these were qualities not particularly sought after or commended in a time when force and utility held such sway. Arnold's prose may be "civilized," but one would hardly say that it has the *politesse* of Addison's. Nevertheless, it is hard to find in the fragmented testimony of reviews and essays anything like a coherent and systematic statement of this tendency and of its cultural and intellectual bearings. Were it not for Herbert Spencer's seminal and wisely praised Positivist manifesto, "The Philosophy of Style," we should be a good deal less certain in what ways stylistic theory was then related to stylistic practice. After De Quincey and before Pater, it is the Spencerian influence which must be called dominant.

It is first necessary to say of Spencer's essay that it contains some difficulties, contradictions, and paradoxes different in kind from the mere duplication and ambiguous pluralism which mar the categorical method of Campbell, Blair, and Whately. Although, unlike those writers, he purports to derive his system "scientifically" from a single irreducible principle, he allows exceptions to erode that principle badly before he is done. But more striking than any internal troubles with methodology is what at first appears to be its plain wrong-headedness, its failure to acknowledge some of the most obvious characteristics of the English language. Spencer contends, for instance, that what has always been thought of as the inverted and less natural order of words in a locution is really the most direct and natural—a contention supported by a clutch of chopped quotations whose selection must have cost him long search. Still, this notion is not as bluntly perverse as it at first appears; looking beyond the local prescriptions to the intellectual predisposition from which they spring, one can find important clues to high Victorian opinion about the nature and office of prose style.

It is instructive to see first how the analogical mechanism of Spencer's psychological account differs, perhaps because of Coleridgean influences, from earlier mechanistic accounts. For one thing, he does not use the categories of the older faculty psychology; it is apparent throughout that he regards reader, like writer, as a whole man with a single reservoir of sensible energy to be tapped. Secondly, he regards verbal realization, language, not as the crown of wit but as "a hindrance to thought, though the necessary instrument of it."[35] Finally, he insists that no system, his own included, is necessary or even desirable to the awareness of real literary genius, which can create, all naturally and spontaneously, not sublimely brilliant departures from economic principle but perfect adherence to it.

Despite these peculiarly expressivist qualifications, Spencer's selection of the machine (rather than the mirror, say, or the growing organism) as his controlling analogue is an important choice. Through it he appeals directly to the practical and materialistic disposition of his age; he procures for his argument at least the ultilitarian appearance of workmanlike local applicability with suggestions of profitable quasi-industrial production; he achieves the outward show of an easy internal consistency. In fact Spencer seems to have chosen the mechanical metaphor more for its affecting sense of generally purposive management than for any real clarification which it may bring to his psycho-stylistics. As an analytic figure, it serves him very badly:

> Regarding language as an apparatus of symbols for the conveyance of thought, we may say that, as in a mechanical apparatus, the more simple and the better arranged its parts, the greater will be the effect produced. In either case, whatever force is absorbed by the machine is deducted from the result. A reader or listener has at each moment but a limited amount of mental power available. To recognize and interpret the symbols presented to him requires part of this power; to arrange and combine the images suggested requires a further part; and only that part which remains can be used for the realization of the thought conveyed. . . . Hence, carrying out the metaphor that language is the vehicle of thought, there seems reason to think that in all cases the friction and inertia of the vehicle deduct from its efficiency; and that in composition the chief if not the sole thing to be done, is to reduce this friction and inertia to the smallest possible amount.[36]

The inconsistency or incompleteness of this account is evident, for it demands that the reader be a user of machine-diminished force which he himself has provided in the first place, and it suggests at the same time that the reader is recipient of a diminished stuff or energy fed into the mechanical conveyance at the "other end" by the writer. There is even some doubt whether the contrivance in question is language or the mind of the reader. In short, the relational dynamics are muddled, pseudo-precise; the analogue only seems to be yielding new understanding of the interdependence of thought, language, writer, and reader. It merely says in a pictursque way what Spencer elsewhere says literally—that there are more and less efficient ways of using language to convey a given meaning, and that these ways may be conceived in more or less specific terms.

But of course Spencer is really trying to make for his reader not a logically persuasive figure but a new frame of mind, a way of regarding the very idea of style. And it is here that the machine becomes centrally important to his thinking: it likens meanings to conveyed objects, things. A survey of his main argument from Economy in "The Philosophy of Style" shows how instinctively and thoroughly Spencer reduces all verbal arrangement to the one principle which in his view makes Economy a meaningful term—the ultimate reality, the exigent primacy, of the world of concrete objects. In diction, preference should be given Saxon derivatives and specific terms, for the reason that these summon most readily the image of the particular physical thing.[37] As for sequence, the adjective or predicate should precede the substantive to which it applies, not because what is primary should be made most conspicuous (as in some earlier grammatical accounts), but because the *thing* must be not even momentarily misconceived; the noun, then, which must always impress us more forcibly, more permanently than a modifier, should fall last, where it may be fully constituted once with no risk of laborious re-constitution compelled by trailing adjectives and predications. Similarly, in whole clauses or propositions the subordinate member should precede the principal.[38] In using figures, it is well to remember that their very reason for being is their specific concretion of meanings; within a metaphor, of course, the modifying element should come before the modified. And so on. The reason for the apotheosis of thing and substance in this systematized grammar-style is that Spencer equates *force* with the sensuous apprehension of things. Economy of composition is no end in itself, nor does Spencer's interest reside either in some severe order of "beauty" or even in fidelity to truth. The sole aim in allowing a reader to use his energy efficiently is to make the communicated thought more forcible, to make the act of cognition take on some of the character of a physical event. It is only slightly surprising to discover that the essay was originally to have been entitled "Force of Expression."

III

The dissatisfaction which some of his contemporaries felt over the insufficiency of Spencerian stylistics may be taken as one of the early signs that a change in taste and theory was in the offing. The reaction follows two paths, one an attempt to liberalize or pluralize the psychological monism of Spencer's account, the other an out-and-out challenge to its basic idea.

Bagehot, Newman, and Bulwer Lytton provide various evidence of the first of these tendencies, but the most telling of all is the case made by

G. H. Lewes in "The Principles of Success in Literature" (1865), a document whose discussion of style actually served, in the main, to popularize and extend Spencer's influence. Lewes acknowledges the unprecedented sanity of the Economical principle, but he seeks to soften its prescriptive effect by citing it as only the first of five principles which govern style. Simplicity, Sequence, Climax, and Variety are the others, and the last three of these open the way for supra-utilitarian characteristics of form. Indeed, says Lewes, "the removal of a trifling superfluity will not be justified by a wise economy if that loss entails a dissonance, or prevents a climax, or robs the expression of its ease and variety. . . . That man would greatly err who tried to make his style effective by stripping it of all redundancy and ornament, presenting it naked before the indifferent public."[39]

Spencer got his stiffest challenge, though, not from the category-juggling of Lewes, but from the increasingly appealing doctrine that style is above all a function of self. In one sense, he did not really deserve the attacks made against him on this score. The remark that got him in trouble—"To have a specific style is to be poor in speech"—is surely intended to advance the cause of thoroughgoing expressivism, not to deprecate it.[40] What Spencer apparently means is that a narrowly "specific style" violates that variety of means which enables a man to say anything and everything he has to say; he does not mean to recommend stylistic impersonality. Even at that, however, the anti-Spencerian movement should not be understood solely as the contrivance of opportunists who chose to quote him out of context, for he is clearly vulnerable on the grounds that he sees reader-psychology, not author-self, as the causal center of things. The quarrel was real enough, and it became more so as the interpretation of Buffon's apophthegm changed. If style is of the man himself, in what sense do we understand "the man"? Under the older critical tradition style was thought of as, among other things, a rather general index to some aspect of the writer as a man, usually either his moral nature or his intellectual capacity—as in the 1845 opinion of *Chambers' Journal* that well-wrought style reflects an order of nobility in the author, shabby style "a certain meanness of mind."[41] But the possibility of a much closer fit had been raised when such influential persons as Wordsworth, De Quincey, and Carlyle insisted that the traditional conception of language as the dress of thought be replaced by the metaphors of "incarnation" and "flesh-garment." And as religious disillusionment and the collapse of established authority brought in the day of philosophical relativism, accompanied by a shrinking away from the chill impersonality of natural science, there came too a different valuation of the self as composer and arbiter of experience—a valuation which could celebrate not just the sanctity of personal emotion and conviction, but the specialness of the personality itself. The new flurry of style-is-the-man-ism was driven by this tendency, going well beyond the traditional claims of stylistic individuation in three ways: (1) the degree of correspondence is assumed to be much greater; (2) the idiosyncrasy, the uniqueness of the creative self and style becomes a quality precious in its own right; (3) the personality of the writer is conceived no longer as merely supplementing but as replacing other agencies which had been supposed to determine style.

The particular assumptions about verbal form which attended this development are of the greatest importance to anyone who wants to understand the late-Victorian vogue of prose style. A good place to start is T. H. Wright's brief but trenchant essay, "Style," which appeared in the *Macmillan's* of November 1877; from the beginning, Wright adopts the tone of one who has made a real discovery, who truly has new light to shed on an old problem. Spencer is commended for establishing that language can have no independent or superadded "beauty" beyond its power of reference; but Spencer is quite wrong about "specific" style. Wright not only affirms the inevitability of the self's verbal projection into style; he makes it a matter of graduated value: the greater the writer, the more individual the style must be.[42] And if the revelation of this "hidden self" is "unconscious," as Wright contends, then style is a secret the less accessible to calculation and deliberate method, less susceptible of analytic rhetorical description. But—and here is the crucial point—"unconscious" does not mean simple or plain. Wright's anti-scientism may try to bury the personal well-springs of style, but it also leads him to specify that style must be by definition an affair of complexity and elaboration, since it transcends mere fact:

> In its powers of direct expression, language is tolerably efficient, and were there nothing but facts, considered objectively, even a simpler vehicle would suffice. . . . In any written composition, the less the author's personality is involved in the matter treated, the simpler the language which suffices. . . . As we ascend the scale of literary composition the author's personality creeps in, and brings with it a corresponding complexity of language, not merely the complexity of structure of

sentences, but of choice of words, use of figures of speech, and all the refinements of elaborate writing.[43]

This may be recognized as De Quincey's argument with a difference; it stipulates a finer and more thoroughgoing correspondence between style and personality than had been proposed before. And its effect is to promote a conspicuous heightening of distinctive verbal effects.

Not all critics were willing to endorse this view of an intimately organic extension of personality in style. Alfred Legge, for instance, takes up a more conservative position in his 1883 essay, "Concerning Style." The inferred relations between man and verbal texture are less specific than those which Wright would admit. "Artistic happiness of diction is the reflection of the author's mind," says Legge, but only to the extent of showing us that the mind has in general the qualities of, say, precision and objectivity—and this serves more to classify than to individuate the writer.[44] Still, individualism as an account of style was producing influential advocates. John Dennis's "Style in Literature" (1885) goes even further than Wright, causally associating style with that most peculiarly personal faculty of the man, his imagination, which synthesizes thought by infusing it with energy and harmony. Thus style is "not merely an outward accomplishment, but the fruit of an inward grace." Dennis is so thoroughly persuaded that this imaginative projection is the sole cause of style, and so anxious to have the exclusiveness of the relation recognized, that he supplies another term, "composition," to cover mere competence in writing and all those other qualities which hitherto have been brought carelessly under the head of "style."[45] John Earle makes the same distinction an important principle in his massive *English Prose* (1890), though he substitutes the term "diction" for Dennis's "composition."[46] Now all this might be dismissed as nothing more than a juggling of terms, except that the shift has implications of rank. "Style" remained the important, the prestigious term, as it had always been. In the earlier part of the nineteenth century, the distinction, when drawn at all, had swung the other way. "Style," as the expert compositional skill of the accomplished writer, was to be distinguished from "manner," the element of mere personal idiosyncrasy.[47]

The theoretical cult of individuality continues into the 'nineties with nearly unabated missionary fervor. In 1892 it is so firmly entrenched that W. H. Mallock finds it hard to believe that the confusion of style and literary skill should persist at all, since it "betrays a complete misconception of facts":

> The foundation of style, its essence, its coloring principle, is not the writer's skill as a writer, but his character as a man; and this shows itself in ways with which technical skill, or even technical genius, has not essentially anything at all to do.[48]

If the cult of prose style had involved only the ascendancy of verbal personalism and notions consonant with it, this essay could now neatly conclude with some pat observation about the logical consequences of Coleridgean theory. The fact is, though, that the phenomenon I have been describing was only one element in a far larger happening. In fact, the most marked characteristics of Victorian stylism come from causes to which individualism is not a prime concern, and which in some ways seem actively to contend against it.

IV

The trend in style-criticism which I am about to discuss may accurately be identified, it seems to me, as one of the important critical functions of the so-called Aesthetic Movement in England. This is not the place to speculate on the social and intellectual causes of Aestheticism—its dependence on relativistic thought, its reaction against the industrial ugliness of the landscape and the moral repulsiveness of the middle class, its association with such earlier phenomena as the Gothic Revival and the Oxford Movement. But it is worth remembering with what insistence the Aesthetic sensibility brought to the apotheosis and redefinition of beauty a spirit of devotional refinement and elevation, fostering a new kind of concern for form. In its fullest development (and viewed from the convenient distance of some eighty years), the principles of the new aesthetic which most affected expectations about verbal form were these: (1) Art is a distinct, special, highly demanding activity, radically different in kind from other activities, and the response to art is similarly unique. (2) The sanctity and autonomy of the artifact are outwardly signalled in its wholeness, proportion, continuity, smoothness, and completeness of surface. (3) The form of the artifact may and indeed should reveal to its audience, albeit quietly, the artist's exercise of exquisite craft in process, and this will constitute a separate source of delight.

It will be clear that, in prescriptive consequences if not in motivation, the second of these formulations, especially, is little more than a variant of the Augustan ideal of stylistic decorum, a concept which had been crucial to the distinction between the Beautiful and the Sublime. And at a more practical level, where prose style is concerned, it relates to the prescriptively "correct" grammar which the earlier century had codified so thoroughly. As the Victorian age progressed, one might hear with increasing frequency an alarm raised against various abuses of the mother tongue, attributed severally to the influence of the newspapers, changes in the educational system, the barbarity of Americans, and the rising jargon of natural science.[49] This reaction is much more than the perversely nostalgic nit-picking of professional grammarians. It subsumes, among other things, an attempt to civilize certain elements in both the emotionally expressivist and morally emphatic strains in the stylistic practice of the preceding generations. In 1860 it was possible to lift an eyebrow with *Leisure Hour* over "New Curiosities of Literature: Peculiarities of Style,"[50] or in 1872, with Taine, contemplate the civility of Thackeray's style in contrast with "our modern temerities, our prodigal imagery, our jostled figures, our habit of gesticulation, our striving for effect."[51] The ecstatic or spasmodic, the exclamatory, the brilliantly eccentric, as well as the insistently repetitious, the obvious, the ponderously rhetorical, all worked against *finesse* in style. When the urge to restrain and subdue these signs of emotive spontaneity and didactic mission was joined with the conception of a discernibly artful surface of words in prose, the style-vogue was ready to flower. A *Fraser's* critic in 1857 had been able approvingly to define the coming ideal quite accurately:

> We do not mean merely the grammatical and proper arrangement of words in each sentence, but the due relation of sentences to each other. A rhythmical structure ought to exist, not only in the separate but in the collective periods; and the warp and woof of the entire texture should be so woven as to preserve continuity of pattern, and produce the effect of an harmonious whole.[52]

At this point—since I have been using words like "politesse" and "finesse" right along—I suppose it will be tactful to admit, once for all, that the Victorian style cult owes much of its impetus to France. At the same time, I hope I may be excused from rehearsing that well-documented story at great length here, since I wish to concentrate as much as possible on the British scene itself. One observation, though, demands to be made. Although it had not been fashionable for some time to appeal to France as unquestioned mistress of culture and the fine arts—nearly three centuries of swelling English nationalism had taken care of that—the Victorian critics still found it easy to celebrate French superiority in the art of prose. At first, the reason for this seems to have been much like that which labels Pope and Dryden "classics of our prose," and it sometimes carries the same sort of backhanded compliment: it is French rationality which causes both their triumphs in prose style and their relative deficiency in poetry.[53] Gradually, though, this essentially intellectual judgment yields to one more patently aesthetic: now it is the art in French prose, the careful attention to pleasing finish, which demands admiration. "*Antics* in style," says Bagehot, "are prohibited" by the French sensibility in prose: "It will not endure that the reader's mind should be jarred by rough transitions or distracted by irrelevant oddities."[54] And twenty years later, in 1898, Frederic Harrison makes the same point still more admiringly, praising the "serene harmony of tone, an infallible nicety of keeping, a brightness and point never spasmodic, never careless, never ruffled."[55] There can be no doubt that this change in attitude derives in part from developments in French criticism and experiment. The emphasis on durable form, given its sharpest impulse by Gautier—"Sculpte, lime, cisele"—in the *Émaux et camées* of 1852, was lent particular application to prose art in Flaubert's doctrine of *le mot juste*. Baudelaire's work with prose poems, too, helped to emphasize the stylistic and expressive possibilities which might be reached in non-metrical language. These developments and others helped to fuel the already sacred flame of English stylism.

In the end, however, it must be acknowledged that the Victorian style-vogue would never have had its fullest sway, would never have applied its aesthetic principles so particularly to the question of prose style, had it not been for the major contributions of several Victorian men of letters, most prominently Walter Pater, George Saintsbury, and Robert Louis Stevenson.

It is indispensable to Pater's steady insights about style that, while he takes as the objects of a critic's proper study "all works of art and the fairer forms of nature and human life," such ambitious breadth of interest does not hold for him any promise of an eventual abstract defining of beauty, but brings him rather to reject such a procedure, depending instead on the recognized uniqueness of each of the orders of aesthetic pleasure afforded by experience, whether literary or not. It is this sense of the special manifestation of beauty, the particular event or medium or artifact judged on its own terms, which, combined with his insistence on the individuality of aesthetic response, defines his characteristic act of criticism. He begins the 1889 essay "Style" by attacking those writers who "have been tempted to limit the proper function of prose too narrowly":

> Critical efforts to limit art *a priori*, by anticipations regarding the natural incapacity of the material with which this or that artist works, as the sculptor with solid form, or the prose-writer with the ordinary language of men, are always liable to be discredited by the facts of artistic production.[56]

He does not mean that analytic differentiation by function must always be nonsense; on the contrary, the trouble is that such differentiation has not been applied thoroughly enough, confused as it is by arbitrary hierarchical assumptions. In other words, criticism has undiscriminatingly assumed that verse and prose can be qualitatively compared because they both try to do the same thing—and it is this misconception which Pater wishes permanently to dissolve. His task is to define, in positive language, the distinctive function of prose, and build his stylistics on that. But a prior distinction is necessary, and for this Pater is able to draw upon both Wordsworth and De Quincey. "The literature of knowledge" and "the literature of power" become in his terminology the literature of fact and the literature of the imaginative sense of fact; in "Style" he proposes to examine the proper qualities of the latter, which "apply indifferently to verse and prose, so far as either is really imaginative—certain conditions of true art in both alike, which conditions may also contain in them the secret of the proper discrimination and guardianship of the peculiar excellences of either."[57] Prose, then, is to be granted its rights as fine art before there can be any accurate estimate of its stylistic propensities, and this requires dismissal of "the arbitrary psychology of the last century."

In 1886, reviewing Saintsbury's *Specimens of English Prose Style,* Pater identifies the "indispensable quality," the "radical merit" of prose as combining order, precision, and directness. But—and this is typical of him—he is anxious lest these terms be misinterpreted to suggest only a "quiet, unpretending usefulness." He patiently speaks of a stylistic character which is neither plain nor ornamental, nor yet merely a compromise between the two, but a "specific and unique beauty."[58] And, he feels, the realization of such beauty can make special contributions to the art of prose at the very moment of its greatest opportunity: the intellectual temper of the time, variously complex and not reducible to "master currents," comes to demand imaginative prose as its expressive vehicle, since its liveliness is not amenable to the restraining law of verse.[59] What is more—and this is the point which distinguishes Pater's view most exactly, and in which is revealed the classical turn of his mind, always seeking reasoned balance—since the natural stylistic spirit of the age runs to eclecticism, affected as it is by the welter of relativistic thought and the endless variety of scientific questioning, the conscientious writer will strive for the stylistic antithesis of this tendency:

> . . . in style, as in other things, it is well always to aim at the combination of as many excellences as possible—opposite excellences, it may be—those other *beauties* of prose. A busy age will hardly educate its writers in correctness. Let its writers make time to write English more as a learned language; and completing that correction of style which had only gone a certain way in the last century, raise the general level of language toward their own.[60]

If this suggests some of the late-Victorian nostalgia for eighteenth-century proprieties which I have mentioned earlier, it does not wholly represent Pater's stylistic ideal. The "order" which he proposes for good style includes, to be sure, both a "scholarly" exactitude in diction and an economy of means, *ascesis*, in phrasing, whose main effect is to restrict severely the use of isolable ornament; yet it is clear that both the avoidance of inexactitude and the *ascesis* are regarded by him less as conspicuous ends in themselves than as practices which clear the way for the assertion of a higher beauty.

The center of Pater's system is what he calls "the necessity of *mind* in style." By "mind" he means not just the pre-eminent sense of the matter conveyed, but that relating faculty which secures an "architectural" structure in the literary work. Coherence, unity, harmony, and integrity are the key notions. There will be of course an organic fusion of matter and form ("The house he has built is rather a body he has informed"), but this is not the relation in which Pater is chiefly interested. What counts most is the perfect integration of verbal parts in the finished piece, a unity co-extensive with that of the author's controlling apprehension of experience.

> With some strong and leading sense of the world, the tight hold of which secures true *composition* and not mere loose accretion, the literary artist, I suppose, goes on considerately, setting joint to joint, sustained by yet restraining the productive ardour, retracing the negligences of his first sketch, repeating his steps only that he may give the reader a sense of secure and restful progress, readjusting mere assonances even, that they may soothe the reader, or at least not interrupt him on his way.[61]

The virtues of stylistic smoothness, delicacy, and continuity—those of stylism's "light touch"—were never more persuasively argued. And Pater complements this view with another that the style-vogue would find attractive: "One of the greatest pleasures of really good prose is the critical tracing out of that conscious structure, and the pervading sense of it as we read."[62]

There is little reason why, in this account of the progress of prose stylism in England, Saintsbury should follow Pater. The two men exerted most of their influence during the same period of time, though Saintsbury survived Pater by many years; their interests, though hardly identical, are remarkably comparable in matters of verbal form; and each respectfully recognizes and approves the efforts of the other. I have put Pater first here because it seems to me that his judgments are the more rooted in a consistent philosophical attitude, and because he makes a subtler and finally more satisfying case in relating style to matter. But it could be argued that Saintsbury kept up the attack more persistently and variously, and that as a result he affected the general stylistic taste of his time more immediately than Pater. Of course I am interested in the "early" Saintsbury here—not the author of the enormous *History of English Prose Rhythm* and the several volumes of generalized history of literature and criticism, whose judgments became more conservative (and perhaps more crotchety) with age, but the young writer of essays and reviews in the 'seventies and 'eighties, discoverer of French *finesse*, lecturer to his countrymen on their neglect of art.

Brought to an awareness of the stylistic shortcomings of English prose by his early acquaintance with Flaubert and, more spectacularly, the *Petits poèmes en prose* of Baudelaire, Saintsbury opens, as early as 1875, his plea for the cultivation of *"écrivains artistes,"* writers—and particularly prose writers—who understand that "writing is an art," and whose secrets demand "the patient energy of sculptors, painters, and musicians." Like Pater, he looks back to the eighteenth century, when "style was not an unknown thing among Englishmen."[63] But Saintsbury's position is more extreme than Pater's and, as one might expect, less defensible. In 1876 his *Fortnightly* essay, "Modern English Prose," makes clear his presiding assumption that style is first of all a certain conscious and continuous structuring of language. What matters is not that a writer have this style or that, but that he have *style,* as opposed to no style. This time the celebration of Augustan virtues is much more tendentious: a hundred years ago, says Saintsbury, the competent prose writer wrought his syntax into certain formal patterns, and, despite some inevitable variation according to his personal taste, "the effort was always present, and was only accidentally if inseparably connected with the intention to express certain thoughts, to describe certain facts, or to present certain characters."[64] This habit of facile though striking distinctions between matter and style—an excess in Saintsbury to which Pater himself objects—is central to the special limitations (and successes) of his stylistic program.[65] His argument provides always the illusion of systematic clarity; though his subject be diaphanous and rare, he is disarmingly easy to understand. Neglect of style is caused by four circumstances, enumerated with a great show of assurance: journalism, the novel, science, and democracy.[66] If this now strikes us as hollow aesthetic snobbery, it had serious appeal for the stylistic establishment of 1880. And there is no denying that in his listing of the characteristic faults of Victorian prose—he finds it easier always to be specific in the negative—Saintsbury is at the center of the cult. He condemns "Diffuseness; sacrifices of the graces of literary proportion to real or apparent clearness of statement; indulgence in cut-and-dried phrases; undue aiming at pictorial effect; gaudiness of unnatural ornament; preference of gross and glaring effects *en bloc* to careful composition."[67]

By the time Robert Louis Stevenson came into his fantastic critical and popular prominence, the new cult of prose stylism was already well established; he can hardly be ranked with Saintsbury and Pater as a reformer of opinion. But it is equally clear that in his combined performance as essayist, novelist, sometime critic, and Scots romantic figure he contributed an authority to the style-vogue which brought it well beyond the confines of academic appreciation. From the earliest review of *An Inland Voyage* in 1878 to the encomiastic rhapsodies at the time of his death,

Stevenson was recognized by the critics as a stylist of the most exquisite type. The graceful handling of language in his light essays seemed impressive enough, but more exhilarating still was his bringing together of stylistic art and narrative instinct in the tales and romances. He was recurrently welcomed as that long-awaited genius, a Walter Scott with style. He would become a "Shakespeare of our prose." And those qualities of his verbal surface which most consistently brought admiration from the reviewers—smoothness, delicacy, sustained syntactical continuity, conscious rhythmic modulation—are precisely those which stylism most jealously promoted. As William Archer puts it in a major appreciative essay of 1885,

> There are fashions in style as in everything else, and, for the moment, we are all agreed that the one great saving grace is "lightness of touch." Of this virtue Mr. Stevenson is the accomplished model. He keeps it always before his eyes.[68]

And indeed the effect was deliberately cultivated by Stevenson. His manuscripts, letters, reminiscences, and critical essays show an unremitting preoccupaton with local technique, an effort to perfect for himself a verbal artifice which might serve him in any circumstance. To be sure, some of his theoretical discussions show a vacillation between this ideal and a plainer allegiance to "matter," and he was especially uneasy about the office of discernibly beautiful language in prose fiction, where, he feared, it might well obscure the subject or destroy the narrative illusion of immediacy, the reader's suspension of disbelief. But for the most part he welcomed his role as stylist, and as his public reputation enlarged itself he became increasingly confident in making theoretical and practical pronouncements. Far and away the most important of the documents thus produced—and the most amazing—is his essay "On Style in Literature: Its Technical Elements," which appeared in the *Contemporary Review* in April 1885. For sheer concentration on verbal method, for a specific interest in the texture of language which seems oddly to anticipate some of the habits of the New Criticism, there is nothing like this piece in all Victorian criticism.[69] In its way, it is the most extreme offering from any of the advocates of prose stylism.

Stevenson's guiding premise is that literature shares with all the other arts, whether "representative" or "presentative," the peculiar activity of pattern-making. On the level of verbal style, literature, like music, contrives its pattern of "sounds and pauses" in time. But Stevenson is not headed into a discussion of rhythmic, alliterative, and assonantal combinations at this point, though he later gives full attention to phonemic effect; what interests him first is the audible interweave of meanings themselves, a sensuous realization of syntax, where "each sentence, by successive phrases, shall first come into a kind of knot, and then, after a moment of suspended meaning, solve and clear itself."[70] Stevenson seems to think that such a figuration of the sentence is achieved where the meaning's completion is deferred through the internal elaboration of one or more of its parts. He is not necessarily recommending periodic structure, but rather any structure or tying-together which is a system of linked elements, each contributing to the sense and each associated with its predecessor (or successor, or both) by some similarity in propositional function or form. Parallelism, both substantive and grammatical, is thus the key to his conception of prose style, because it conduces to moderate elaboration:

> Style is synthetic; and the artist, seeking, so to speak, a peg to plait about, takes up at once two or more elements or two or more views of the subject in hand; combines, implicates, and contrasts them; and while, in one sense, he was merely seeking an occasion for the necessary knot, he will be found, on the other, to have greatly enriched the meaning, or to have transacted the work of two sentences in the space of one.[71]

But in this joining of elements—here is the characteristic touch of late-Victorian stylism—the structured effect, whether of balance or climax, shall not be made heavily obvious. It may be well to throw syntactical resemblances or progressions slightly out of alignment. Artifice, while not quite seeking to conceal itself, must provide slight continuous figuration of the language, without breaking itself into isolable and obtrusive effects.[72] Stevenson extends the same principle to the level of sound, in advancing the scarcely novel idea that prose must be rhythmical but not metrical; a prose writer must exercise the greatest care to avoid "the production of bad blank verse"—bad because it is unintentional and so fails to avail itself of the complicating graces and concealments which, in poetry, redeem the flat regularity of mere meter.[73] His ensuing discussion of purely phonemic qualities, under the head of "melody," contains a great deal of factitious nonsense about the stylistic centricity of P, F, and

V alliterations. But the very fact that Stevenson shows this sort of concern over sylistic minutiae is more important than the opinion itself. Altogether, his pleas for continuity, proportion, co-ordination of parts, control of sound, and continuous rather than separable artifice suit well with his own practice and associate him closely with the efforts of Saintsbury and Pater.

During the last fifteen years of the century, prose stylism fully flowered and withered almost simultaneously. On the one hand, it seemed to many observers that the ultimate perfection of the prose medium was now at last within reach, and there was a great fuss made over it. In sampling the extensive evidence of this fervor, it is necessary only to glance through a work like George Bainton's *The Art of Authorship: Literary Reminiscences, Methods of Work, and Advice to Young Beginners, Personally Contributed by Leading Authors of the Day* (1890), throughout which the conduct of style and the question of "fine writing" in particular are persistently worried, explored, refined;[74] or Earle's *English Prose: Its Elements, History, and Usage,* whose author is so fully aware of (and so perplexed by) the conflicting views on stylistic distinction that he cannot, at last, make up his mind about them;[75] or the critical introductions to individual authors in Craik's five-volume *English Prose Selections,* where the definition of styles is a prominent if not dominating interest;[76] or the studiously careful and extended essays on style by so reputably serious a man of letters as John Addington Symonds;[77] or Walter Raleigh's somewhat precious but symptomatic full-length study, *Style.*[78] The journals, too, got into the act. *Fortnightly Review,* for instance, ran in 1887 a series, "Fine Passages in Verse and Prose: Selected by Living Men of Letters," whose contributors show a marked preference for the more conspicuously artful kinds of verbal surface.[79] In 1900 the *Academy* launched a one-guinea competition among its readers, inviting response to a letter "typical of many which reach this office":

> "Dear Sir,—I am most anxious, as one having literary aspirations, to cultivate *style.* Would you favor me with a few hints, or tell me where I could get the hints?—Yours truly, _____."[80]

A year earlier, the *Edinburgh Review,* the *Academy,* and the American journal *Literature* had conducted a hot three-way squabble over the efficacy of deliberate stylism.[81]

V

If this representative survey suggests an unprecedented celebration of style in prose, there was generated at the same time a powerful reaction against it, and in this one can discern two main elements. In the first place, it was becoming more and more apparent that the two chief impulses behind the movement—the push for stylistic individuality on the one hand, the Aesthetic postulation of the artfully "light" touch on the other—could not be brought into nice accord. The characteristic tendency of much criticism toward the end of the century was to recommend a style artistically finished, but finished in such a way as only subtly to call attention to itself by continuous slight heightening and deft co-ordination rather than by "antics" and strongly marked features which would contort or grotesque the surface. But uniqueness and distinction—the individuating principles of *"le style c'est de l'homme même"*—require precisely that the style make itself obtrusive, and in relatively eccentric ways. The fact that both sides in this contest could cite for supporting authority different aspects of Coleridgean theory did not make the job of reconciliation any easier. I have already shown how the advocates of self-style relegated the less personalized verbal artifices to the category of "diction" or "composition." On the other side, we find the *Spectator* in 1892 deploring the consequences of deliberate individualism: the style of a good writer will of course show some inevitable distinctiveness—"Such distinction of style comes to a man by nature."

> But the other kind of distinction comes by art, and we should call it not a distinctive style, but a distinguished style. To advocate the acquisition of a distinctive style in literature is tantamount to advising the literary aspirant to be original at all costs; surely, rather, a dangerous piece of advice.[82]

In 1899 an anonymous commentator goes so far as to warn that a stylistic "craving for distinction" may be, after all, "a sign of mental or moral weakness."[83] And Symonds, one of the steadiest and sanest of those who entered the controversy, notices that, besides making practical criticism nearly impossible (since it would require "physiological and psychological knowledge which is rarely found in combination with an extensive study of literatures and arts"), the doctrine of extreme stylistic personalism overlooks or ignores an unchanging condition of the literary calling: the very deliberation intrinsic to art must involve circumspection, reservation, selection, suppression, and it is even "compatible" with affectation, dissimulation, and hypocrisy. Thus it is naïve to imagine that the real self either can or ought to be figured forth wholly in the verbal surface.[84] As late as 1904 C. F. Keary continues to press the issue, protesting the tendency of modern "stylists" to cultivate an exotic individuality at the expense of less angular beauties.[85]

The divisive but inconclusive effect of this internal controversy, and the critics' inability to resolve it either practically or philosophically, goes far to account for the disintegration of the style-vogue. But it was only one part of a grander disenchantment. As the critical dialogue wears on, with its discriminations becoming finer and finer, its paradoxes, confusions, and contradictions more obvious, opinion grows wearier and less assured; there is an almost plaintive cry over the lack of settled priorities. "Artistic happiness" of style, ventures one critic, is "generally acquired in an inverse proportion to the labour with which it is sought." And yet

> We are not merely moralists and utilitarians; nor do we demand in literature an ornamental dress and nothing more. We desiderate instruction conveyed in exact and perspicuous language; the union of fine observation and felicity of phrase; the harmonious structure of clear and consecutive ideas . . . free from eccentricities, inelegances, and inaccuracies of expression which inspire antagonism. But it is easy to be hypercritical, and perhaps it may be said that form is little—the basis alone important; that lofty conceptions and just thoughts, appealing at once to the reason and the feelings, are the pearls of great price, which can dispense with the setting of what Lucian called anemone words, "for anemonies are flowers, which, however brilliant, can only please the eye, leaving no fragrance."[86]

The *Spectator* essay of 1892 might affirm that the conspicuous quality of language which we call good style shall be no more ornamental than it shall be slipshod, but rather a certain pleasurable ease and flow, a distinction of utterance that can call attention to itself without jolting the reader's awareness into admiring fits and starts.[87] But it was this very sophistication of the notion of style which seemed to bring after it damning associations with littleness, decadence, indeterminacy, ephemerality. H. M. Stanley complains that style has become "finicky," that England is afflicted with "a race of priggish prosaists . . . superlatively dainty."[88] Another critic regrets the passing of earlier stylistic ideals, particularly as realized in Arnold's prose, which is better than Pater's because it is composed of ideas rather than words, because it is "not so conscious of itself."[89] In its well-advertised readers' competition, the *Academy* awards the guinea prize to a letter asserting that there is no sense in fussing over style, since style has no real existence anyway; power of conception is all that matters. And, despite a hail of protesting letters, the editors uphold their decision in a most strenuously anti-stylistic comment:

> . . . we are oppressed by the worship of style for style's sake, tantalized by the "beautiful secret of beautiful prose," and misled by the fallacy of the "inevitable word." It is an age when young writers seek out choice words and are betrayed by them; when nice harmonies, values, and rejections are pursued beyond reason, as if the irridescent bubbles that float on a strong river would do anything but burst in the hand.[90]

No one sensed the change in critical climate more acutely than the advocates of stylism themselves. Richard Le Gallienne fears that, in their reactionary recoil, critics are no longer able to distinguish euphuism (the only real decadence of style) from "proper organic refinements," a failure which leads them to conclude, absurdly, that "the nearer an instrument approaches perfection . . . the less its value."[91] It seemed most sadly anomalous that the main force of the attack should be directed at stylism in prose, for the artistic claims of prose had been highly affirmed for only a little while. Stevenson himself, surely aware in his last years that his close attentions to language are no longer earning him ungrudged praise, complains to Le Gallienne in 1893:

> The little, artificial popularity of style in England tends, I think, to die out; the British pig returns to his true love, the love of the styleless, of the shapeless, of the slapdash and the disorderly. There is trouble coming, I think.[92]

The cult of prose style could not have survived for long, even under the most favorable conditions. Its inevitable if undeserved association with weakness and decadence was damaging enough, but the final disintegration came from a hopeless internal warring of the several main ideas which had been intrinsic to it, exotically compounded, from the start. While it lasted, though, it helped to produce some genuinely valuable insights to the nature of literary language. And, of course, an understanding of its extraordinarily ambitious though failed ideals is perfectly necessary to any critical estimate of Victorian achievement in prose.

NOTES

1. "Rhetoric," *The Collected Writings of Thomas De Quincey,* ed. David Masson, Edinburgh, 1890, X, 96-9.

2. Ibid., X, 90-92.

3. Of course De Quincey was also capable of putting the blame on environment, and especially the environment of nineteenth-century England; but it is clear, over the long run, that in his view the national temper produces its own unhappy circumstance.

4. "Style," *Collected Writings,* X, 163-4.

5. This is the point of his famous anecdote of the gold coin. Ibid., X, 130.

6. *The Prose Works of William Wordsworth,* ed. Alexander B. Grosart, London, 1876, II, 93-5. Cited hereafter as *Wordsworth Prose.*

7. *Biographia Literaria,* ed. John Shawcross, London, 1907, II, 8-10.

8. Ibid., II, 11. As for the subjective *origin* of meter, Coleridge posits a balance in the mind effected between passion and its self-engendered restraining counter-force; it is worth noticing that this makes better sense than Wordsworth's account, in which the balance of meter itself counteracts the thrust of passion. See II, 49-50.

9. *Wordsworth Prose,* III, 319.

10. Henry Home, Lord Kames, *Elements of Criticism,* ed. A. Mills, New York, 1854, pp. 290-91. The *Elements* was originally published in 1762.

11. Hugh Blair, *Lectures on Rhetoric and Belles Lettres,* Brooklyn, 1812, I, 5. The *Lectures* were originally published in 1783.

12. Kames, p. 107.

13. Blair, I, 82; II, 198-200.

14. Ibid., I, 134-5. See also George Campbell, *The Philosophy of Rhetoric,* new ed. rev., Philadelphia, 1818, pp. 311-12.

15. For an application of this view, see Blair, I, 47-53. A complementary notion is that metaphor belongs in the middle range of sensible interest: up to a certain level of intensity, feeling does not naturally demand figurative expression; beyond a certain higher level, passion is so fierce and absorbing that its urgency makes figuration improbable. See Kames, p. 335.

16. Blair, I, 35, and Kames, pp. 266-73.

17. Kames, pp. 247-50, and Blair, I, 175-6.

18. Richard Whately, *Elements of Rhetoric,* rev. ed., New York, 1869, p. 385.

19. *Biographia Literaria,* II, 44.

20. *The Literary Remains of Samuel Taylor Coleridge,* ed. Henry Nelson Coleridge, London, 1836-39, I, 23.

21. See *Lamb's Criticism,* ed. E. M. W. Tillyard, London, 1923, pp. 68, 72, 80; De Quincey, *Collected Writings,* X, 100-110.

22. *Collected Writings,* X, 229-30.

23. E[dward] Bulwer Lytton, *Caxtoniana: A Series of Essays on Life, Literature, and Manners,* New York, 1864, p. 309.

24. Walter Bagehot, *Literary Studies,* ed. Richard Holt Hutton, London, 1879, II, 183.

25. David Masson, *British Novelists and Their Styles,* Boston, 1859, p. 19. Masson is able, however, to read the signs of prose's encroachment; and since part of his job is to improve the status of the novel, he delivers himself of a visionary peroration which sounds like an attempt to realize its own prophecy: "Need we shrink, either, from anticipating for Prose triumphs even in Verse's own regions of the imaginative and the impassioned, such as yet have hardly been dreamt of? Need we shrink from supposing that, as Prose is still the younger and the invading occupant, and as it already has chased verse from the busy coasts, and the flat and fertile lowlands, so it may encroach farther and farther still, planting its standards along the looming lines of the hills, and even in the mouths of long-withdrawing glens, till at length Verse, sacred and aboriginal Verse, shall take refuge in the remote fastnesses of the mountains, and live, sad, but unconquerable, amid the mists, the cataracts, and the peak-loving eagles?" Pp. 30-31.

26. Much of this can be attributed to an antagonism or neglect by a few very influential figures such as Mill, Arnold, and Carlyle; but that the tendency was more widespread is borne out in Richard Stang's study, *The Theory of the Novel in England, 1850-1870,* New York, 1959, whose vast accumulation of critical opinion shows virtually no concern with questions of verbal style.

It is only fair to add that the essay, as a literary form, affected stylistic expectations regarding prose in quite a different way. It seemed to offer an opportunity for stylistic display and maneuver which the more preoccupied and urgent forms of address did not. Thus Alexander Smith thinks of the essayist as "a kind of poet in prose," a maker of "pure" literature whose success depends pre-eminently on style. See *Dreamthorp: A Book of Essays Written in the Country,* Edinburgh, 1863, p. 25.

27. See, for instance, Jeremy Bentham, "The Rationale of Reward," *Works,* Edinburgh, 1843, II, 253-6; John Stuart Mill, *Dissertations and Discussions,* New York, 1874, III, 306-8.

28. Both Campbell and Whately had made special allowances, in their rhetorical manuals, for means to be adopted in addressing the lower classes.

29. For general discussions of this tendency, see Jerome Hamilton Buckley, *The Victorian Temper: A Study in Literary Culture,* Cambridge, Mass., 1951, pp. 161-206; and Walter Houghton, *The Victorian Frame of Mind,* New Haven, 1957, pp. 110-36.

30. John Ruskin, *Works,* ed. E. T. Cook and Alexander Wedderburn, London, 1903-12, III, 89; Matthew Arnold, *On the Study of Celtic Literature,* New York, 1883, p. 104.

31. Thomas Carlyle, *Works*, New York, 1896, I, 173-80.
32. Ibid., XXIX, 78-80.
33. "Modern Style," *North British Review* [American ed.], XXVI (February 1857), 184.
34. John Holloway, *The Victorian Sage: Studies in Argument*, London, 1953, *passim.*
35. Herbert Spencer, "The Philosophy of Style," *Westminster Review* [American ed.], LVIII (October 1852), 235.
36. Loc. cit.
37. Ibid., p. 234.
38. Ibid., pp. 237-8.
39. George Henry Lewes, "The Principles of Success in Literature," *Fortnightly Review*, II (August-November 1865), 265.
40. Spencer, pp. 246-7.
41. "Style," *Chambers' Journal*, III (May 24, 1845), [321].
42. T. H. Wright, "Style," *Macmillan's Magazine*, XXXVII (November 1877), 78-80.
43. Ibid., p. 81.
44. A. O. Legge, "Concerning Style," *Manchester Quarterly*, II (1883), 58.
45. J. Dennis, "Style in Literature," *Time* [London], XIII (July 1885), 71-2.
46. John Earle, *English Prose; Its Elements, History, and Usage*, New York, 1891, pp. 336-7. "The artifices of composition," says Earle, "belong rather to Diction than to Style. It is desirable to observe the distinction between these two because of their immediate contiguity, and the liability to confusion which is the natural result. For while this term [Style] has gradually risen to an abstract elevation of its own, it has left behind it a surviving trail of earlier and more elementary usage."
47. See, for example, Bulwer Lytton, p. 328.
48. W. H. Mallock, "Le Style c'est l'homme," *Living Age*, CXCI (June 11, 1892), 644. The essay first appeared in the *New Review*, April 1892.
49. Some American critics of this period show a remarkably guilty willingness to place the brunt of the blame on their uncivilized fellow countrymen if not on themselves. A good instance of this sort of thing is Richard Grant White's *Words and Their Uses, Past and Present*, 3rd ed. rev., Boston, 1881, first published in 1867-69, which maintains a remedially chastising tone throughout.
50. "New Curiosities of Literature: Peculiarities of Style," *Leisure Hour*, IX (September 27, 1860), 621-3. In this connection, see the unflattering opinion of Macaulay's style in "Literary Style," *Fraser's Magazine*, LV (March and April 1857), 258; the cry for a return to some semblance of "classical purity" is taken up also in "Modern Style," *North British Review* [American ed.], XXVI (February 1857), 190.
51. H. A. Taine, *History of English Literature*, trans. H. Van Laun, New York, 1872, II, 396. It is worthwhile to compare this with the discussion of Dickens's style by Walter Bagehot, II, 189-91.

52. "Literary Style," *Fraser's*, LV, 250.

53. One of the more influential statements of this distinction comes from De Quincey, *Collected Writings*, X, 157. In "The Literary Influence of Academies" (1864), Matthew Arnold develops at length the dichotomy which associates prose with French intelligence, poetry with English genius. See *Lectures and Essays in Criticism*, ed. R. H. Super, Ann Arbor, 1962, pp. 237-57.

54. Bagehot, II, 132.

55. Frederic Harrison, "On English Prose," *Tennyson, Ruskin, Mill, and Other Literary Estimates*, London, 1899, p. 166. See also John Addington Symonds, *Essays Speculative and Suggestive*, London, 1890, I, 263-4, 309, 330-31.

56. Walter Pater, *Appreciations, with an Essay on Style*, London, 1931, pp. [1]-2.

57. Ibid., p. 4.

58. Walter Pater, *Essays from "The Guardian,"* London, 1910, p. 5.

59. Pater, *Appreciations*, p. 7.

60. Pater, *Essays from "The Guardian,"* p. 15.

61. Pater, *Appreciations*, pp. 20-21.

62. Ibid., p. 21. Pater's attitude on this point can be found unequivocally, if indirectly, expressed again in *Marius*: "*ars est celare artem*—is a saying which . . . has perhaps been oftenest and most confidently quoted by those who have had little literary or other art to conceal." *Marius the Epicurean; His Sensations and Ideas*, London, 1885, p. 99.

63. George Saintsbury, *Collected Essays and Papers, 1875-1920*, London and Toronto, 1923-24, IV, 27.

64. Ibid., III, [62].

65. See Pater, *Essays from "The Guardian,"* p. 15. Pater's reservations about the Saintsbury method appear in his review of the latter's *Specimens of English Prose Style from Malory to Macaulay* (1886).

66. Saintsbury, *Collected Essays and Papers*, III, 69-70.

67. Ibid., III, 75.

68. William Archer, "Robert Louis Stevenson: His Style and Thought," *Time* [London], XIII (November 1885), 583.

69. Unless we count Poe's attempts along similar lines during the 1840's: "The Rationale of Verse" and "The Philosophy of Composition," *Complete Works*, Boston, 1902, X, 193-208, 209-65. But even in the more general essay of the two, Poe used verse, not prose, as his specimen for dissection.

70. Robert Louis Stevenson, *Works*, "Thistle Edition," New York, 1905, XXII, 246-7.

71. Ibid., XXII, 248.

72. Ibid., XXII, 247. A study of Stevenson's own syntactical practice shows how regularly he achieved exactly the effect referred to here: while his prose is loaded with parallel construction on every conceivable scale, the balance between parallel members is almost always made inexact.

73. Ibid., XXII, 257.

74. George Bainton, ed., *The Art of Authorship*, New York, 1890, *passim*.

75. Earle, pp. 150-51, 174-5, 251, 337, 347, 357-8, *et passim*.

76. Henry Craik, ed., *English Prose Selections*, New York, 1896, *passim*.

77. See Symonds, *Essays*, I.

78. Walter Raleigh, *Style*, London, 1897, *passim*.

79. "Fine Passages in Verse and Prose: Selected by Living Men of Letters," *Fortnightly Review*, n.s., XLII (July-December 1887), 296-316, 430-54, 580-604, 717-35.

80. *Academy*, LVIII (June 30, 1900), 559.

81. "Some Tendencies of Prose Style," *Edinburgh Review*, CXC (October 1899), 356-76; "Style and the 'Edinburgh Review,'" *Academy*, LVII (November 18, 1899), 576-7; "Ars Prosaica," *Literature* [New York], V (November 17, 1899), 433-4.

82. "Literary Style," *Spectator*, LXIX (October 1, 1892), 445.

83. "Ars Prosaica," p. 433.

84. Symonds, II, 3-4, 10.

85. C. F. Keary, "Of Style," *Living Age*, CCXLIV (January 21, 1905), 155.

86. Legge, p. 63.

87. "Literary Style," *Spectator*, LXIX, 445-6.

88. H. M. Stanley, *Essays on Literary Art*, London, 1897, p. 163.

89. John Burroughs, "The Vital Touch in Literature," *Atlantic Monthly*, LXXXIII (March 1899), 403-4.

90. "Style," *Academy*, LIX (September 15, 1900), 223.

91. Richard Le Gallienne, *Retrospective Reviews: A Literary Log*, London and New York, 1896, I, 24.

92. *The Letters of Robert Louis Stevenson*, ed. Sidney Colvin, New York, 1911, IV, 268.

ART CRITICISM AS A PROSE GENRE

G .   R O B E R T   S T A N G E

Who cares whether Mr. Ruskin's views on Turner are sound or
not? What does it matter? That mighty and majestic prose of his,
so fervid and fiery-coloured in its noble eloquence, so rich in its
elaborate symphonic music, . . . is at least as great a work of art
as any of those wonderful sunsets that bleach or rot on their
corrupted canvases in England's Gallery; greater indeed, one is
apt to think at times. . . .

Gilbert in *The Critic as Artist*

MY DISCUSSION BEGINS with the assumption that, in the course of the
nineteenth century, there was a radical change in the nature and functions of what we loosely call expository prose. While in the eighteenth
century the primary mode of prose was cognitive, by the middle of the
nineteenth century it had become expressionist. The changes that we are
familiar with in Romantic poetry also took place in prose; but since the
effects of the Romantic ethos are less easily perceived in essays than in
verse, they have tended to go undefined. The practitioners of nineteenth-
century prose, unlike the poets, did not have the benefit of a body of
theoretical formulations, and, because of the very nature of prose, its
modal changes tended to be additive rather than substitutional. Though
it assumed new functions, prose had to continue to perform its ordinary,
utilitarian tasks; the old ways of communicating routine information and
the familiar patterns of sequential discourse are not replaced, but supple-
mented by experimental prose forms which imply a new theory of art.

The conscious prose stylists from, let us say, Lamb to Pater display the
shift of direction I wish to describe. The effect of their work is to break
down traditional distinctions between prose and poetry; logical organization and a conceptual framework are more and more often abandoned in
favor of emotive effects and a perceptual scheme. The serious writers
offer us not systems, but insights, persuasive glimpses of truth. The prose

writer tends to avoid the abstract in favor of the immediate: he will try to imitate a speaking voice, or express the rhythm of the mind as it responds to or perceives concrete experience. Special value is attached to image sequences, to discrete data of precise observation; the emphasis is not so much on the object of imitation as on the medium of expression, on *surface* in both experience and artifact, and, in general, on the representation of particular aesthetic as well as emotional experiences.

I

This congeries of loosely related characteristics could only be illustrated by an analytic history of all nineteenth-century prose. My intention here is not so grand; I want only to look at one of the new kinds of prose —art criticism—and suggest that it provides a convenient and dramatic example of the shift of mode and function which only a long study would fully describe. Art criticism can be defined as a writer's attempt to give a prose account of the aesthetic values and affective qualities of a work of visual art. If we accept this definition we can say categorically that this kind of prose did not exist before the nineteenth century. Earlier writers on the fine arts had concerned themselves with biography and cataloguing or—as in the case of Reynolds and Fuseli—with discussing the general nature of art and the principles of painting. But even when eighteenth-century, or earlier, critics describe a particular painting they do so in order to give technical advice to the painter or to provide the collector with the kind of information that Fuseli called "enumeration."

Art criticism is, then, a new genre, responding to a variety of specifically nineteenth-century needs and impulses. A climate for this sort of enterprise was partly created by the theoretical teachings of the German Romantics. Schelling and Friedrich Schlegel conceived of art as an independent source of value and a means of human liberation. And by a natural extension of these ideas, Schlegel accorded to criticism the status of an art: he envisioned a new "poetic critic" whose function was to go beyond commentary and analysis, to illuminate the work he discussed by creating something equivalent to it. When he set out to write about poetry, Schlegel's critic had, as one German scholar has put it, to "repeat the original performance, re-imagine the original imagery, and then extend and re-form the poem."[1] Poetry, Schlegel said, "can only be criticized by poetry,"[2] and, with intentional ambiguity, he called his essay on *Wilhelm Meister* an *Übermeister*.

Though theoretical prescriptions were not actually given for "poetic" critics of the visual arts, it could be inferred that they had the elevated task of re-creating in words the impressions they had experienced in a non-verbal medium. Lamb and Hazlitt are, I think, the first to practice this kind of criticism. In his essay "On the Genius and Character of Hogarth" (first printed in *The Reflector* in 1811) Lamb startles the reader by comparing *Gin Lane* to Poussin's heroic *Plague of Athens,* and by concluding that Hogarth's "sublime print" shows the greater degree of "imagination." He then supports this judgment by examining the familiar English work with unfamiliar intensity. He analyzes Hogarth's figures in detail, considers the device by which he makes "the very houses seem drunk," and perceptively notes the artist's technique of extending the interest of the print "out of the sphere of the composition."[3]

In spite of his passionate visual sensibility Lamb only described paintings in two other essays. There is a fine treatment of a portrait of Francis the First and then a bravura account of Titian's *Bacchus and Ariadne*[4] which, in its inspired analysis of the painter's treatment of the Ariadne myth (what Lamb interprets as a visual "bringing together of two times"), and in its finely phrased evocation of the aesthetic effect of the painting, is a prototype of the later, more resonant, exercises of Ruskin and Pater. Indeed, in Lamb's two paragraphs on Titian—unfortunately, too long to quote here—one can trace anticipations of almost all the art criticism of the later nineteenth century.

In Hazlitt's essays there are more numerous and more systematic attempts to render in words what he calls "the true and general impression" of a work of art. An excellent example is the description of the central figure of Orion in the essay "On a Landscape of Nicolas Poussin," from which a short passage can be extracted:

> He stalks along, a giant upon earth, and reels and falters in his gait, as if just awaked out of sleep, or uncertain of his way; you see his blindness, though his back is turned. Mists rise around him, and veil the sides of the green forests; earth is dank and fresh with dews, the "grey dawn and the Pleiades before him dance," and in the distance are seen the blue hills and sullen ocean. Nothing was ever more finely conceived or done. It breathes the spirit of the morning; its moisture, its repose, its

obscurity, waiting the miracle of light to kindle it into smiles; the whole is, like the principal figure in it, "a forerunner of the dawn."[5]

Much of the force of Hazlitt's "impression" depends on breaking through the widely accepted Lessing-ite views as to the limitations of the visual arts. He ascribes, for example, movement to the painted figure of Orion and to the landscape: mists *rise,* dawn and stars *dance* in the painting. And, even more significantly, the effects of one medium of sense impression are transposed to another. Hazlitt's description is, like the work of Schlegel's "poetic critic," an independent evocation of feeling; he uses expressive epithets of original poetic description (the ocean, for example, is *sullen*), and reinforces the iconographic significance of Poussin's painting by elaborating on and extending its mythological allusions. One would not say that Hazlitt had written an "Überpoussin," but he has at least manipulated diction and metaphor to produce in the reader a complex sensory response which is equivalent to the impression Poussin's painting might make. Whether Ruskin—and all those who came after him—learned directly from Lamb and Hazlitt is unimportant. These two are, at any rate, the significant innovators. In their modest but genial exercises in criticism they do not use prose as a mere vehicle of distinct ideas, but as an unabashedly expressive language. In their time it was unusual to write at length about a single work of art, and almost unprecedented to find the meaning of the work in the impression that its formal aspects made on a sensitive observer. Lamb and Hazlitt can be said to have made later art criticism possible by challenging traditional ideas about the relations between painting and literature, and thereby extending the possibilities of prose expression.

The neo-classical view of the provinces of the several arts and of the distinct functions of prose and poetry was summed up by Lessing and his followers. Lessing asserted, *tout court,* that "Painting deals with form in space, poetry with action in time."[6] Prose was not even mentioned, presumably because it was not considered one of the fine arts. Those who followed Lessing emphasized the limitations and the immiscibility of the various arts, and tended to affirm what might be called a mechanistic view of language—a view that persists to the present day. Such eminent modern logicians as Rudolf Carnap and I. A. Richards, for example, cannot be called neo-classicists, but their linguistic categories are curiously traditional. Carnap, it appears, believes that there is such a thing as genuinely "representative" language, which is to be distinguished from the "expressive" language of poetry; and I. A. Richards has toyed for years with his famous distinction between "emotive" and "scientific" language (later altered to "influential" and "referential").[7] Whatever their era, those who hold mechanistic views agree in denying that prose may have multiple simultaneous functions, or that it may imitate the processes of other aesthetic media. Art criticism involves an *a priori* rejection of such traditional assumptions as to the nature of prose and the value of systematic, rational sequence. It is a genuinely experimental form of literature, with intentions that contradict both academic and positivistic views of language and art.

Long after the time of Lamb and Hazlitt one finds neo-classical principles being re-stated in the discourses and treatises of Sir Charles Eastlake, an influential director of the National Gallery who became president of the Royal Academy in 1850. Sir Charles sometimes gives the impression of sitting like an uneasy pygmy in the great chair of Joshua Reynolds, but he was a learned and conscientious man, and it is precisely the solid ordinariness of his mind that makes him a useful representative of those views which genius must begin by ignoring. Eastlake makes an orthodox distinction between the visual arts, which are imitative, and literature, which is not. In imitative art, he suggests, the *sense* is actively employed, while language, it would seem, has nothing to do with sense:

> The object of perfected written language is therefore to convey comparatively distinct ideas by forms unmeaning in themselves. . . . Thus in language, whether written or spoken, the sign of the idea is less intelligible (having, in fact, only a conventional meaning) than the idea itself; in the Plastic arts it is the reverse.[8]

According to the traditional theory that Eastlake popularizes, prose is a transparent medium. Eastlake seems to have felt that metaphor, sound pattern, associations, kinaesthetic response and other resources of complex language had nothing to do with prose writing, which—as one might expect—he did not even admit to the hierarchy of the fine arts.[9]

One must be careful, however, not to overemphasize the effect of the views that academicians like Eastlake glibly pass on to their students. The orthodoxies that he represents were a minor tradition, one that could not withstand the high influence of changing literary theories or the more humble one of new social needs. As far as theory went, it can be observed that, from the late eighteenth century, Longinus' influence was as strong as Lessing's, and by the 1820's the effect of the German Romantics was felt all over Europe. In England Hazlitt contributed trenchantly to aesthetic theory: his famous distinction between science and aesthetic pleasure—one being knowledge, the other power—assigned not only to the various literary genres, but to all the arts, the same essential functions. Even the untheoretical Lamb suggested a doctrine of transference of sensation by insisting that the special seriousness and power of Hogarth was in the fact that his "graphic representations . . . have the teeming, fruitful, suggestive meaning of *words*. Other pictures we look at,—his prints we read."[10] The theory and practice of the Romantic prose writers was, however, merely a preparing of the ground. It was left to Ruskin to provide an unexceptionable value base for art criticism, to convince the Victorian public that the experience of the visual arts was not only desirable in itself, but the means to a moral, even religious, exaltation. Because Ruskin could persuade the common reader that aesthetic experience had a transcendental power, art criticism became recognized as itself an artistic enterprise, a form of sustenance for the spiritual man.

The high theoretical notions which led to the development of art criticism were, as is usually the case, supported on a material level by changing social conditions. It would not be extreme to say that in the eighteenth century an English gentleman who took a fancy to a Titian might simply have brought the painting home from Venice with him. In the absence of postcards, Canalettos and Guardis were produced as souvenirs of the travels of the English grandees, and all the members of the cultivated classes had easy access to large private collections of paintings. Nineteenth-century art criticism, however, is addressed to a *parvenu* class, to readers who could visit the newly-opened public collections, but could neither take the grand tour, nor gather up old masters. It is notable that all the practitioners of art criticism have a distinctly cockney flavor: Lamb, Hazlitt, Ruskin, Pater, Arthur Symons are explicitly writing for an urban middle class, offering to enrich their lives by providing them with the culture they so painfully lacked.

It is against this theoretical and practical background that the novelty of Ruskin's and Pater's accomplishments can best be appreciated. It is time now to consider what these two writers did, in their different ways, to advance the new prose of art criticism.

A representative example of Ruskin's practice is his description of Tintoretto's *Massacre of the Innocents* in Volume II of *Modern Painters*. Its context is a discussion of what Ruskin calls the "imagination penetrative," the power of the imagination to reach "by intuition and intensity of gaze (not by reasoning, but by its authoritative opening and revealing power) a more essential truth than is seen at the surface of things."[11] This faculty, Ruskin explains, is to be found at its highest among great artists and poets, but the reader infers that it is also displayed by the sensitive critic of art, and particularly—one might conclude—by Ruskin himself when he embarks on one of the accounts of painting or poetry which adorn *Modern Painters*. Tintoretto, the critic claims, is the only painter who has treated this biblical story successfully; Raphael had lost the effect of terror by particularizing sentiment; other representations of the subject Ruskin finds "false and cold." Tintoretto does not

> depend on details of murder or ghastliness of death; there is no blood, no stabbing or cutting, but there is an awful substitute for these in the chiaroscuro. The scene is the outer vestibule of a palace, the slippery marble floor is fearfully barred across by sanguine shadows, so that our eyes seem to become bloodshot and strained with strange horror and deadly vision; a lake of life before them, like the burning sea of the doomed Moabite on the water that came by the way of Edom; a huge flight of stairs, without parapet, descends on the left; down this rush a crowd of women mixed with the murderers; the child in the arms of one has been seized by the limbs, *she hurls herself over the edge, and falls head downmost, dragging the child out of the grasp by her weight;*—she will be dashed dead in a second;—close to us is the great struggle; a heap of the mothers entangled in one mortal writhe with each other and the swords, one of the murderers dashed down and crushed beneath them, the sword of another caught by the blade and dragged at by a woman's naked hand; the youngest and fairest of the women, her child just torn away from a death grasp and clasped to her breast with the grip of a steel vice, falls backwards, helplessly over the heap, right on the sword points; all knit together and hurled down in one hopeless, frenzied, furious abandonment of body and soul in the effort to save. Their shrieks ring in our ears till the marble seems rending around us, but far back, at the bottom of the stairs, there is something in the shadow like a heap of clothes. It is a woman, sitting quiet,—quite quiet,—still as any stone; she looks down steadfastly on her dead child, laid along on the floor before her, and her hand is pressed softly upon her brow.[12]

We are by now so used to expressionist criticism that we tend not to think how strange it is that Ruskin should describe a two-dimensional plastic form in this way. Though he gives us a certain sense of the spatial aspects of the picture and of the artist's disposition of figures, the principal object of the description—what I would call its referent—is not Tintoretto's painting, but an experience that Ruskin has had. The passage begins by communicating a sense of the painter's "scene," but Ruskin soon shifts to "our" eyes—those of both critic and reader—, which are imagined to "become bloodshot and strained with strange horror." Ruskin does not offer an account of the formal elements of the painting; instead he concentrates on its affective aspects and provides the reader with cues to an emotional response. He pointedly ascribes to the work precisely those features which are impossible to painting: literary comparison, movement in space, extension in time, and even sound. Let me illustrate.

Ruskin's biblical simile of the doomed Moabite provides a rich association that enhances the significance of the painting. Though this kind of allusion is one of the simplest of literary devices, it nevertheless is something that cannot be achieved within the limits of Tintoretto's medium. Then, having set up, by literary means, the affective atmosphere of his description, Ruskin enumerates the figures of the painting and puts them into action. He avoids passive forms of language: there are no "are painted-s," but a series of active verbs (descends, rush, seized, hurls) which suggest a frenzied movement in a space which the writer has supplied to Tintoretto's canvas. Further, by prediction, the frozen events of the painting are projected in time; one of the women will, for example, "be dashed dead in a second." It may be unnecessary to point out that, by concentrating on movement and continuity, Ruskin has endowed a painting with the function that Lessing reserved for poety—the power of depicting action in time. In his expressionistic ardor Ruskin goes so far as to make the painting sound: the shrieks of the mothers "ring in our ears till the marble seems rending around us."

In this passage the transference of sensation is such that Ruskin provides the very composition of the aesthetic experience he describes. He has made his own disposition of Tintoretto's figures, decided what their order of importance should be, and where the weight of expressive emphasis shall lie. Clearly, then, the object of this dazzling paragraph is not an account of the physical properties of a work of plastic art, but the evocation of an aesthetic and emotional experience, deriving from a painting, but originating in Ruskin's prose.

Analysis of Pater's art criticism suggests that, though he is at once more restrained and more consciously "poetic" than Ruskin, the effects he attempts to produce are much the same. In the essay on Botticelli, for example, Pater speaks of a special strangeness in the painter's work, a quality that can be partly explained by the fusion of medieval feeling and the new response to the Greek temper. In *The Birth of Venus* Pater sees "the grotesque emblems of the middle age, and a landscape full of its peculiar feeling." At first, he suggests, the painting may attract us only by a quaintness of design, and we may afterwards

> think that this quaintness must be incongruous with the subject, and that the colour is cadaverous or at least cold. And yet, the more you come to understand what imaginative colouring really is, that all colour is no mere delightful quality of natural things, but a spirit upon them by which they become expressive to the spirit, the better you will like this peculiar quality of colour; and you will find that quaint design of Botticelli's a more direct inlet into the Greek temper than the works of the Greeks themselves even of the finest period.

The preparation for Pater's description of the work itself is extraordinarily effective: it is as if he held a curtain before the painting while he made his generalizations about the character of Botticelli's work, the nature of color and the spirit of Renaissance art and then, having concluded his preliminary remarks, allowed us to see the painting:

> The light is indeed cold—mere sunless dawn; but a later painter would have cloyed you with sunshine; and you can see the better for that quietness in the morning air each long promontory, as it slopes down to the water's edge. Men go forth to their labours until the evening; but she is awake long before them, and you might think that the sorrow in her face was at the thought of the whole long day of love yet to come. An emblematical figure of the wind blows hard across the grey water, moving forward the dainty-lipped shell on which she sails, the sea "showing his teeth" as it moves in thin lines of foam, and sucking in, one by one, the falling roses, each severe in outline, plucked off short at the stalk, but embrowned a little, as Botticelli's flowers always are. Botticelli meant all that imagery to be altogether pleasurable; and it was partly an incomplete-

ness of resources, inseparable from the art of that time, that subdued and chilled it; but his predilection for minor tones counts also; and what is unmistakable is the sadness with which he has conceived the goddess of pleasure, as the depositary of a great power over the lives of men.[13]

More than with Ruskin, one receives from this passage enough data to feel that he would recognize the total assemblage of visual details which make up *The Birth of Venus*. We learn, in a sense, what the limits of the picture are, and the account Pater gives of the relative importance of various aspects of the painting is accurate. But the essence of this description is, like Ruskin's, not an enumeration of the visual features of the painting, but a conveying of the quality of a visual experience through parallel effects of prose rhythm and tone. Pater would have us respond to the minor key of the work, to what he calls its chill, subdued quality. And so his language, elegant and elevated as it is, becomes subdued and even; the long first sentence is cool and quiet, ending in a dying fall that matches the slope of Botticelli's long promontories. The writer turns to the central figure in the next sentence, but generalizes as he does so, by speaking of the labor and sorrow of all men, suggesting the wide sadness which he finds in the face of Venus. Then, as if to indicate a restrained but fierce eroticism, Pater attaches to Botticelli's figure of the wind, his sea and floating roses, a set of oral images which derive from the proverbial notion of the foam being the "teeth" of the sea. Like so many of Pater's effects, the operation is covert, but daring; once recognized, full of sensual implication, but not obvious enough to offend the taste of the Victorian parsonage. The passage ends with what now seems an extraordinarily acute judgment of the insufficiency of Botticelli's painting, and a fine statement of the melancholy which informs it.

It is notable that, in their efforts to provide an aesthetic equivalent for their sense of a work of plastic art, Ruskin and Pater depend heavily on the least analyzable aspects of prose—rhythm and tone. It might be suggested that in these areas of response we do reach a common ground where our reactions to verbal, visual, and aural experience are fused. It is certainly true that we tend to translate effects of rhythm or tone into kinetic activity: rhythm, whether experienced in language, music or the plastic arts, is felt as muscular response and expressed as motion; and often we respond to tone by *feeling* the shape of a sentence or of a musical phrase by an imitative movement of the hands, as if it were a plastic form. Neo-classical formulations, such as Lessing's, are inadequate to explain the complex interconnectedness of aesthetic response. The prose of art criticism suggests a reconsideration of the borderlines between the arts and a movement toward a doctrine of synaesthesia. Without publishing theoretical manifestos, Ruskin and Pater extended the potentialities of prose and led their readers to consider freshly both the values inherent in the various arts and the nature of our responses to them.

II

The historian of prose style can find a special interest in the fact that Ruskin's and Pater's attempts to create a verbal equivalent to painting or sculpture involve a conscious complication of the ordinary procedures of prose description, display a pleasure in complexity for its own sake which is a familiar feature of the Romantic ethos. Gautier, defining the nature of the "modern," or nineteenth-century, style, stressed the quality of the *composite,* a term which usefully suggests not only synthesis, but intricacy.[14] The poetry of Baudelaire—which Gautier used as a touchstone— is, like the poetry of Browning, or the prose of Carlyle or Ruskin, a fusion of the modes and associations of innumerable cultures; the complication of these writers' literary structures is independently interesting and reflects a new sense of the complexity of experience itself.

The art critics' "descriptions" of works of art inevitably complicate the process of ordinary literary description by adding new elements to the reader's response. If we assume that all descriptive prose is concerned to imitate some object to which the writer attaches value and significance, we may call the ultimate object of a prose description the *referent.* We can then conceive a scale of complexity on which the language of direct denotation marks the extreme of simplicity. On such a scale the language of art criticism would represent something close to an opposite extreme. Even the prose of simple denotation involves the four elements of writer, referent, prose text, and reader. A simple diagram could suggest the relationship among these elements and trace the reader's perception, first of the printed page, and then of the referent. However, when we try to diagram the process of response to the prose of art criticism we end up with something quite complicated:

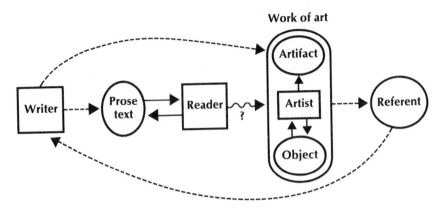

In this diagram the dotted line represents the writer's process of response and creation, the solid line the reader's perception. The referent
which the writer seeks to imitate is, as I have suggested, independent of
the artifact he "describes." The critic responds to a particular work of art,
which is itself perceptible as a process, and from it he produces his referent—an unanalyzably complex fusion of his sensory response to various
features of the artifact, his knowledge of the artist and of his period, and
the values he attaches to his experience of the work of art. This referent
he transforms into prose which is perceived by the reader through a combination of reception and projection. The process, however, does not stop
there, since the reader is able—and, in fact, stimulated—to have recourse
to the original artifact, which is (unlike the objects of natural or emotive
description) available to examination, virtually unchanged and discrete.
This extra step of perception on the reader's part may enhance or modify
his response to the text, but the fact that it is optional gives to the total
process an aspect of open-endedness, of incompleteness, which is characteristic of Romantic art. As long as *The Birth of Venus* still offers itself to
our scrutiny, Pater's description remains active and unfinished.

Since, as this diagram shows, the work of art the critic discusses is itself
a process involving several components, in the total activity of the prose
passage it becomes something extra, a preliminary object which leads to
the referent. Complexity, then, results not only from the presence of an
additional object of description, but from the unprecedentedly intricate
nature of that object. The diagram helps to show that the real referent of
the prose passage is an experience of a sort that writers had not previously
tried to imitate. When we understand that Ruskin and Pater are not con-

cerned merely to describe a work of art, we can see their achievements as representing an essential tendency of Romantic literature, that *Andersstreben* which Pater delighted to discuss. And with this knowledge we can dismiss those modern critics who attack the Victorians for not giving a precise, uncolored account of the purely formal elements of an artifact.

I find it helpful to consider Ruskin's and Pater's descriptive passages as *expressive imitations* of the experience produced by a work of art. After devising this term I came across a discussion of Susanne Langer's, and concluded that she meant much the same thing by the process she calls "transformation."[15] According to Mrs. Langer, transformation is like imitation in that it re-creates the aspects of an object in which the artist finds emotive meaning, but it goes beyond imitation in that it "consists in the rendering of a desired appearance without any actual representation of it, by the production of an *equivalent* sense-impression rather than a literally similar one, in terms of the limited, legitimate material which cannot naïvely copy the desired property of the model." The thing imitated (what Mrs. Langer calls the "model") is transformed into "sensory structures of another sort," and thereby acquires a "heightened import." In this process only the significance of the model is abstracted, and when this significance is "*transformed* into properties of words or of marble, its artistic value shines forth like the intuitively perceived meaning of a metaphor in language—something beyond the expressive medium, stripped of its accidental embodiment by having more than one expression."

Mrs. Langer concludes her discussion of transformation by suggesting that it is a way of "underlining" the abstractive power of art, and finds examples of the process in painting and sculpture, poetry and art criticism. Though Mrs. Langer does not say as much, the effect of her theories is to provide an aesthetic which affirms the special qualities of Romantic art. When her fine insights are applied to the prose I have been discussing they make it possible for us to find a special value in the impulse toward expressionism, and to affirm more confidently the originality of the Victorian prose writers' experiments. To claim that nineteenth-century art criticism is a new genre may, after all, be claiming too little. Perhaps, with further study, we could be bolder, and find in the expressive imitations of Ruskin and Pater not only a culmination of certain theories of Romantic art, but a trying out of new possibilities for the prose that was to come. Certainly their work helped to make possible the intensity, the insights, the new sensibility which had its fullest development in writing that was seemingly unrelated to art criticism—in those complex forms of prose fiction later evolved by Joyce, Proust, and Virginia Woolf.

NOTES

1. Victor Lange, "Friedrich Schlegel's Literary Criticism," *Comparative Literature*, VII (1955), 298. See also, W. K. Wimsatt and Cleanth Brooks, *Literary Criticism: A Short History*, New York, 1957, pp. 376, 493f.

2. Lange, p. 296.

3. *The Works in Prose and Verse of Charles and Mary Lamb*, ed. Thomas Hutchinson, 2 vols., Oxford, 1908, I, 95-6. Hereafter cited as *Works*.

4. See "Reynolds and Leonardo da Vinci," *Works*, I, 191; and "Barrenness of the Imaginative Faculty in the Productions of Modern Art," *Works*, I, 753-4.

5. William Hazlitt, *Criticisms on Art*, Second Series, Edited by his Son, London, 1844, pp. 190-91.

6. See *Laokoön*, XVI, XVII, and *Anhang*, XLIII.

7. See Rudolf Carnap, *Philosophy and Logical Syntax*, London, 1935; and for the most recent summing-up of Richards's (now modified) views, "Emotive Language Still," *Yale Review*, XXXIX (1949), 108ff.

8. "Difference between Language and Art," in *Contributions to the Literature of the Fine Arts*, Second Series, with a memoir compiled by Lady Eastlake, London, 1870, pp. 304-5.

9. See Eastlake's article, "The Fine Arts," originally published in the *Penny Cyclopaedia* in 1830, and reprinted in *Contributions to the Literature of the Fine Arts*, London, 1848.

10. *Works*, I, 92.

11. See *The Works of John Ruskin*, ed. E. T. Cook and Alexander Wedderburn, 39 vols., London, 1903-12, IV, 249-88.

12. *Works of Ruskin*, IV, 272-3. I have restored from the first edition the sentence beginning, "Their shrieks. . . ."

13. Walter Pater, *The Renaissance: Studies in Art and Poetry*, London, 1894, pp. 61-2.

14. Charles Baudelaire, *Les Fleurs du mal, précédé d'une notice par T. Gautier*, Paris, 1868, p. 15.

15. See Susanne K. Langer, *Problems of Art*, New York, 1957, pp. 98-9, 106-7.

VICTORIAN PHILOSOPHICAL PROSE:
J. S. MILL AND F. H. BRADLEY

ALAN DONAGAN

I

PHILOSOPHY is a more ancient form of prose literature than fiction. The classics of ancient Greek and Latin prose are works of history, of philosophy, of oratory. Even of prose written in English, Yvor Winters has contended that, when compared with writers of fiction, "the superiority in achievement to date lies with the historiographers."[1] Probably no literary critic would make such a claim on behalf of philosophy. Yet T. S. Eliot has described the prose style of F. H. Bradley as "for his purposes—and his purposes are more varied than is usually supposed—a perfect style."[2] Whatever its comparative rank among the varieties of prose literature, Victorian philosophical prose deserves more study than it has received.

No serious challenge has been offered to the conventional judgment that English prose was perfected in the classical age begun by Dryden, Temple, and Halifax, and continued by Swift, Addison, and Steele. Yet the chief philosopher contemporary with Dryden and Halifax was Locke, whose style Saintsbury justly deplored as "a disgusting style, bald, dull, plebeian, giving indeed the author's meaning, but giving it ungraced with any due apparatus or ministry."[3] True, the way to the literary achievement of Dryden and his followers had been pioneered by the philosopher Hobbes; and in the fullness of the classical age, Berkeley wrote three philosophical masterpieces which as prose bear comparison with Addison's essays. Berkeley, indeed, was singled out by Saintsbury, who said of him that "he, again with Hume as a second, is as unlikely to be surpassed in philosophical style as Hume and Gibbon are unlikely to be surpassed in the style of history."[4] But Berkeley's prose, admirable as it is, breaks no new ground. From a literary point of view, he is less interesting than Swift;

for nothing he had to say as a philosopher called for a prose different from that of his non-philosophical contemporaries.

By the nineteenth century, philosophy could no longer be written in the prose of Berkeley. There were new things to say, and they could not be said in old ways. Why then did a critic as intelligent as Saintsbury, in 1876—the year in which Bradley published *Ethical Studies*—denounce the "antinomian" decadence of philosophical writing? "Philosophy," he scolded, ". . . has now turned stepmother, and turns out her nurselings to wander in 'thorniest queaches' of terminology and jargon, instead of the ordered gardens wherein Plato and Berkeley walked."[5] Nor did the decade that followed change his opinion: "take almost any living philosopher," he complained in 1885, "and compare him with Berkeley, with Hume, or even with Mill, and the difference is obvious at once."[6]

Saintsbury's strength as a critic is technical. Nobody has better analyzed how Dryden and his successors, paying heed to the genius of colloquial English, reformed the long sentence by expelling imitations of Latin syntax for which an uninflected language is unfit; how they learned to balance and proportion their sentences, and to dispense with rhetorical ornament.[7] His weakness is that his theory is only technical. His literary criticism is criticism of style, and he was capable of defining style as "the choice and arrangement of language with only a subordinate regard to the meaning to be conveyed."[8] Hence he considered "the art of rhythmical arrangement" to be "undoubtedly the principal thing in prose," with "simplicity of language, and directness of expression in the shorter clause and phrase" as the two most important of its "subsidiary arts."[9]

Saintsbury's practice was better than his theory. Many of his critical perceptions were sound. The classical prose he admired was indeed good, and the sins he denounced in Victorian prose—the ugly rhythms of Herbert Spencer, the gaudy epithets of J. R. Green, and the tub-thumping of the journalists—were indeed sins. But it does not follow that the principles he extracted from his perceptions were true. A theory is established by seeking and failing to find unfavorable evidence, not by accumulating evidence that is favorable. Saintsbury's theory was destroyed by the deluge of *belles lettres* at the close of the century, which demonstrated that all his criteria for rhythm and diction could be satisfied by work that was inane, pretentious, and corrupt.

Literary criticism cannot have "only a subordinate regard" to the meaning conveyed. Saintsbury's dictum might even be reversed, and style defined as the choice and arrangement of words having regard *solely* to the meaning to be conveyed. His own examples may be turned against him. Thus, his specimens of bungled rhythm and badly articulated syntax turn out to convey thoughts unformed or ill-formed, and emotions only partly clear.[10] Style, in a word, is expression. Every act of literary composition has its aesthetic side, the writer's effort to grasp something clearly, which is inseparable from his effort to make clear his emotions about it.

The inseparability of the expression of thought from the expression of emotion, which is presupposed by all serious criticism, is seldom fully recognized or clearly understood. Failing to discern the crucial difference between formulating a thought and repeating, perhaps in other words, a thought already formulated, some critics have written as though, even to the man who first arrives at it, a thought can exist before its expression. On the contrary, the stages through which the expression of a thought passes, from clumsy imitation to exact statement, are stages through which the thought itself passes. Finding better words is the same thing as refining a thought. Still other critics have written as though, having arrived at a thought about a certain subject, there is a further process of having emotions about it. They have failed to perceive that a man's emotions about a thing depend on his awareness of it, and of how it is related to other things, himself among them. The way to change his emotions about it is to bring him to think differently of it.

Hence the theory of art as the expression of emotion does not imply that critics can attend to the emotion expressed by a work of art to the neglect of its thought: emotion and thought can only be studied together. Rather, it defines the special nature of a critic's interest in the *thought* a work embodies. He is interested in that thought only as it has to do with the expression of emotion. Genuine art is exploratory. In it, the artist simultaneously becomes aware of something he was unclear about before, and aware of his emotions about it. Bad art is the counterfeit, often not wholly conscious, of genuine art. In it, the artist only pretends to explore; and what he offers is a faked report, designed to present himself as thinking and feeling in some approved way. Its betraying symptom is *cliché*.[11]

This aesthetic theory, or something like it, I take to be embodied in the best work of critics both in the Romantic tradition (like Coleridge and Matthew Arnold) and in the partial post-Romantic reaction from it (like

T. S. Eliot and F. R. Leavis). If it should be true, then it is possible to separate what is true from what is false in a deeply interesting antithesis once proposed by T. S. Eliot.

> I should say [Eliot wrote] that in one's prose reflections one may be legitimately occupied with ideals, whereas in the writing of verse one can only deal with actuality. Why, I would ask, is most religious verse so bad; and why does so little religious verse reach the highest levels of poetry? Largely, I think, because of a pious insincerity.[12]

Eliot's diagnosis of what ails most religious verse was definitive, but he mistook the nature of pious insincerity. It does not consist in being occupied with ideals, but in pretending to ideals you do not really have, or in pretending that your ideals are realities although you do not believe they are. Pious insincerity of these kinds is as fatal in prose as in verse. It is as common in religious prose as in religious verse, and it is far from uncommon in philosophy.

Consider the following passage, fortunately uncharacteristic, from Bertrand Russell, one of the first philosophers of our time.

> Brief and powerless is Man's life; on him and all his race the slow, sure doom falls pitiless and dark. Blind to good and evil, reckless of destruction, omnipotent matter rolls on its relentless way; for Man, condemned today to lose his dearest, to-morrow himself to pass through the gate of darkness, it remains only to cherish, ere yet the blow falls, the lofty thoughts that ennoble his little day; disdaining the coward terrors of the slave of Fate, to worship at the shrine his own hands have built; undismayed by the empire of chance, to preserve a mind free from the wanton tyranny that rules his outward life; proudly defiant of the irresistible forces that tolerate, for a moment, his knowledge and his condemnation, to sustain alone, a weary but unyielding Atlas, the world that his own ideals have fashioned despite the trampling march of unconscious power.[13]

This declamation is philosophically puzzling, because Russell appears in it to embrace an epiphenomenalism that is neither novel nor plausible. How, in his postulated "empire of chance," of "omnipotent matter," could the free minds, whose "ideals" and "lofty thoughts" he celebrates, exist at all? From a literary point of view, it is worse than puzzling. It is piously insincere: "an indulgence," as F. R. Leavis described it, "in the dramatization of one's nobly suffering self."[14] Nor is it characteristic of Russell. The following passage, which expresses his usual attitude, is also better prose:

> In religion, and in every deeply serious view of the world and of human destiny, there is an element of submission, a realization of the limits of human power, which is somewhat lacking in the modern world, with its quick material successes and its insolent belief in the boundless possibilities of progress. "He that loveth his life shall lose it"; and there is danger lest, through a too confident love of life, life itself should lose much of what gives it its highest worth. The submission which religion inculcates in action is essentially the same as that which science teaches in thought; and the ethical neutrality by which its victories have been achieved is the outcome of that submission.[15]

There is not a particle of defiance here; yet here Russell's thought is genuinely courageous.

Suppose an objector were to make the following retort. "Your criticism is as arbitrary as it is unmethodical. Of the two passages you quote from Russell you praise the latter as expressive, and decry the former as insincere, faked, and attitudinizing. But your saying these things does not make them so. How could you show me to be wrong if I were to declare that the former is deeply moving, hard-headed, and nobly written, and the latter timid, commonplace, and flat?"

It would be an easy matter to change ground, and appeal to Saintsbury's technical criteria. The passage from "A Free Man's Worship" might be condemned, as Saintsbury condemned certain passages in Ruskin, for too closely approaching the rhythm of verse.[16] It contains no fewer than five complete heroic verses:

> "The slow sure doom falls pitiless and dark"
> "For Man, condemned today to lose his dearest"
> "The coward terrors of the slave of Fate"
> "Free from the wanton tyranny that rules
> His outward life; proudly defiant of . . ."

Yet this but illustrates an observation already made, that the technical faults analyzed by Saintsbury derive from a deeper non-technical disorder. They are symptoms, not the disease.

If literary criticism is at bottom about success or failure in expression, then no serious critical dispute can be settled by formal demonstration from agreed premises. This fact is sometimes advanced to show that critical differences are matters of taste, concerning which reason can pronounce no verdict. But that does not follow. Not all rational disputes are about what can be formally demonstrated. Literary criticism does not presuppose that all competent judges share the same ultimate premises, but only that they have had the universal experience of trying to express what they feel, and have been aware sometimes that they succeeded and sometimes that they failed. Critical judgments are the fruit neither of demonstration nor logical intuition. They are fallible, but we are reasonably confident that many of them are trustworthy. They can be refined by analysis, and corrected or confirmed by comparing them with judgments of similar successes and failures.

Just as a man learns to understand what others say in the course of learning to speak, so he learns to judge others' successes or failures of expression in the course of learning to judge his own attempts at it. It is impossible to separate either process from the other. Both rest, at bottom, on the same foundation: the comparison of cases that are doubtful with others that are less doubtful. Although questions about the relevance and adequacy of such comparisons can sometimes be settled by analyzing the passages compared, analysis in itself cannot settle critical questions. It clarifies what is to be judged; but it would be pointless if the critic had not the power to judge what his analysis has clarified. T. S. Eliot was, I think, right when he declared that "comparison and analysis . . . are the chief tools of the critic"; and right too, when he added: "They are not used with conspicuous success by many contemporary writers. You must know what to compare and what to analyse."[17]

In reply to the imaginary objector to my harsh judgment of Russell's "A Free Man's Worship," I can say no more than this. That there are those whom its rhetoric may move need not be questioned; whether they are deeply moved by it depends in part on how serious its philosophy is (I do not think it is serious), and in greater part, on what, if anything, it expresses. That the passage is "nobly written," all too nobly written, was part of my reason for saying that it is not expression, but counterfeit. Further comparisons are unnecessary, because every reader can provide them for himself.

II

The work of John Stuart Mill (1806-73) must occupy a central place in any study of Victorian philosophical prose. From the publication of *A System of Logic* (1843) until that of his posthumous *Three Essays on Religion* (1874), his philosophical writings were generally received as the most important appearing in England. And although in the sixty years after his death it was the academic fashion to scorn him, even in writings of that period by philosophers hostile to him, it is common "to find in the Index the acknowledgement which the Preface withholds."[18] At no time did Mill lose his hold on the educated middle class; and he was studied by the academic philosophers he would most have desired as readers: by William James at Harvard (who dedicated *Pragmatism* to his memory); by Henry Sidgwick, Venn and W. E. Johnson at Cambridge; and, on the Continent, by Brentano and his school. As an academic classic in philosophy his position is now unassailable.

As we have seen, Saintsbury contrasted Mill's prose with that of the late Victorian philosophers he denounced, recognizing it as belonging to the classical tradition of Berkeley and Hume: and indeed it has many of the classical virtues. However, I suspect that the passages in Mill's philosophical writings that are remembered most vividly are polemical; and, for all their formal propriety, Mill's polemics betray an influence that is not at all classical. Here he is on Professor Adam Sedgwick's argument that utilitarianism is impossible as an ethical theory, because, in most situations, an agent has no time to make utilitarian calculations as he acts.

> Mr. Sedgwick is a master of the stock phrases of those who know nothing of the principle of utility but the name. To act upon rules of conduct, of which utility is recognized as the basis, he calls "waiting for the calculations of utility"—a thing, according to him, in itself immoral, since "to hesitate is to rebel." On the same principle, navigating by rule instead of by instinct, might be called waiting for the calculations of astronomy. There seems no absolute necessity for putting off the calculations until the ship is in the middle of the South Sea. Because a sailor has not verified all the computations in the Nautical Almanac, does he therefore "hesitate" to use it?[19]

It is evident from this that Mill had studied Macaulay's polemical use of

concrete examples, although he avoids Macaulay's "hard, metallic movement" of which Matthew Arnold complained.[20] Here is Macaulay, in
controversy with Bentham, and with Mill's father, James Mill.

> Mr. Bentham seems to imagine that we have said something implying
> an opinion favourable to despotism. . . . Despotism is bad; but it is
> scarcely anywhere as bad as Mr. Mill says that it is everywhere. This
> we are sure Mr. Bentham will allow. If a man were to say that five
> hundred thousand people die every year in London of dram-drinking,
> he would not assert a proposition more monstrously false than Mr.
> Mill's. Would it be just to charge us with defending intoxication be-
> cause we might say that such a man was grossly in the wrong?[21]

Yet despite the similarity of these passages in structure and polemical
method, the difference they exhibit between Macaulay's and Mill's style
of thought is striking. It is not merely in the contrast between "he would
not assert a proposition more monstrously false than . . ." and "there
seems no absolute necessity for putting off the calculations until . . .";
for Macaulay can be sarcastic, and Mill positive. It is that Mill, whose
opinion of Sedgwick's *Discourse* was no higher than Macaulay's of Mill's
father's *Essay on Government*, entered into Sedgwick's thought in order
to expose it; and so presented the considerations that demolish it, that the
reader has the sense of producing them himself. Macaulay overwhelms;
but Mill converts.

In polemical writing the object primarily contemplated is what your
adversary has said, and the emotions expressed are such as go with exposing it as error. Even when done as well as Macaulay and Mill did it,
sheerly polemical writing can no more be the highest kind of political or
philosophical writing than can sheer satire be the highest kind of poetry.
Philosophers ought certainly to express the emotions with which they remove the rubbish that lies in the road to knowledge; but we look to philosophy for more than that.

Mill's philosophical work was essentially critical. He constructed a
system of logic, but not of metaphysics. In philosophical theology, his
results have been fairly described by Fr. F. C. Copleston as "a rational
scepticism, which is more than sheer agnosticism, but less than firm
assent."[22] Even his theory of the external world as consisting of "permanent possibilities of sensation" was developed in the course of an "examination" of the philosophy of Sir William Hamilton. Yet Mill's best

critical writing is beyond polemics. In his essays on Bentham and Coleridge, in his *Autobiography*, and in less sustained passages in almost all
his later philosophical writings, his purpose in criticizing other philosophers was less to disprove them, than by determining their shortcomings
to define an approach by which philosophy may hope to discover truth. In
fulfilling that purpose, as he largely did, he opened new possibilities for
English prose.

The following well-known passage from the essay on Bentham points
directly to the nature of Mill's achievement.

> Bentham failed in deriving light from other minds. His writings contain
> few traces of the accurate knowledge of any schools of thinking but his
> own; and many proofs of his entire conviction that they could teach him
> nothing worth knowing. For some of the most illustrious of previous
> thinkers, his contempt was unmeasured. In almost the only passage of the
> "Deontology" which . . . may be known to be Bentham's, Socrates, and
> Plato are spoken of in terms distressing to his greatest admirers; and the
> incapacity to appreciate such men, is a fact perfectly in unison with the
> general habits of Bentham's mind. He has a phrase, expressive of the
> view he took of all moral speculations to which his method has not been
> applied, or (which he considered the same thing) not founded on a
> recognition of utility as the moral standard; this phrase was "vague
> generalities." Whatever presented itself to him in such a shape, he dis-
> missed as unworthy of notice, or dwelt upon only to denounce as absurd.
> He did not heed, or rather the nature of his mind prevented it from oc-
> curring to him, that these generalities contained the whole unanalysed
> experience of the human race.[23]

Although external marks betraying the nineteenth century can be re-
moved, like the use of the word "thinkers" for what Berkeley would have
called "philosophers," this passage cannot be rewritten in Berkeley's style.
To Berkeley, as to all the classical English prose-writers, the fundamental
philosophical question to be asked of any opinion is: what reasons are
there for accepting or rejecting it? His style is lucid and pure because it
has but one function: to convey to the reader's intellect an intelligible
object. W. B. Yeats once observed of Berkeley, that "though he could
not describe mystery—his age had no fitting language—his suave glittering
sentences suggest it."[24] In that respect Berkeley outdid not only Addison,
but Mill as well. What Mill was aware of was not a mystery, but an
intelligibility in things that is not directly intelligible to every mind.

If you concede that much of the experience of the human race is un-analyzed, and that no human mind is well-fitted to analyze all of it, when a pronouncement by a thinker of alien approach or tradition seems absurd to you, you cannot escape asking whether it seems absurd because it is so, or because it treats of something not directly intelligible to you. It may, indeed, be mere confusion or insolent bluff. But if it is not? Mill suggested—he was not, of course, the first to do so—that by carefully considering such apparent absurdities, you may come indirectly to recognize and understand things in human experience that are not directly intelligible to you. A philosophical method that in part studies its objects by studying what others have made of them calls for a style more complex than the classical: one that is less direct, and, in its treatment of others' thoughts, more sensitive.

Mill's most extended study of a thinker in an alien tradition is his essay on Coleridge. Unfortunately, specimens of philosophical analysis from it that would not be too short to exhibit Mill's style are too long to quote. Its spirit, however, is shown in the following appraisal of the "Germano-Coleridgean" school.

> Every reaction in opinion, of course, brings into view that portion of the truth which was overlooked before. . . . This is the easy merit of all Tory and Royalist writers. But the peculiarity of the Germano-Coleridgean school is, that they saw beyond the immediate controversy, to the fundamental principles involved in all such controversies. They were the first (except a solitary thinker here and there) who inquired with any comprehensiveness or depth, into the inductive laws of the existence and growth of human society. They were the first to bring prominently forward the three requisites which we have enumerated, as essential principles of all permanent forms of social existence; as principles, we say, and not as mere accidental advantages inherent in the particular policy or religion which the writer happened to patronize. . . . They thus produced, not a piece of party advocacy, but a philosophy of society, in the only form in which it is yet possible, that of a philosophy of history. . . .[25]

Unfortunately, Mill did not perceive how much of his Benthamite inheritance his enlarged philosophical vision required him to renounce; and the greatest of his nineteenth-century adversaries, F. H. Bradley (1846-1924), gained his most enduring victories over him by pointing out what he had overlooked.

III

Not a little misunderstanding of what were the Benthamite errors that Mill failed to jettison can be laid at the door of T. S. Eliot's brilliant essay on Bradley.

> Bradley did not [Eliot wrote] attempt to destroy Mill's logic. Anyone who reads his own *Principles* will see that his force is directed not against Mill's logic as a whole but only against certain limitations, imperfections and abuses. He left the structure of Mill's logic standing, and never meant to do anything else. On the other hand, the *Ethical Studies* are not merely a demolition of the Utilitarian theory of conduct but an attack upon the whole Utilitarian mind. For Utilitarianism was, as every reader of Arnold knows, a great temple in Philistia. . . . And this is the social basis of Bradley's distinction . . . : he replaced a philosophy which was crude and raw and provincial by one which was, in comparison, catholic, civilized, and universal.[26]

That the founder of Utilitarianism was a Philistine, and that Utilitarianism has numbered many a Philistine among its adherents, may be granted; but it does not follow that "the whole Utilitarian mind" was Philistine. Mill and Henry Sidgwick were Utilitarians, as well as Bentham and Frederic Harrison. If Utilitarians provided themselves with a temple in Philistia, so also did Roman Catholics and members of the Church Established.

Neither Mill, nor Henry Sidgwick, his most distinguished successor, was able to make Utilitarianism either theoretically satisfactory, or inoffensive to the "vulgar moral consciousness," which they respected at least as much as Bradley did. That Bradley, writing fifteen years later, should have made telling objections to Mill's *Utilitarianism* (1861) should therefore surprise nobody. Bradley's criticism of Sidgwick,[27] which exposes the inadequacy of Sidgwick's "suppression" of egoism, throws a harsh light on Bradley's own discussion of selfishness and self-sacrifice. Few idealists today would confidently maintain that as an ethical theorist Bradley bettered Sidgwick. In his recent Gifford Lectures, the most distinguished of contemporary American idealists endorsed C. D. Broad's judgement that Sidgwick's *Methods of Ethics* is "on the whole the best treatise on moral theory that has ever been written," and, in an extended discussion of it, found no occasion even to mention Bradley's criticism.[28]

Bradley advanced as "in the main . . . satisfactory," and as decidedly improving on the views of Mill and Kant, the moral theory of "my station and its duties." He never wearied in proclaiming the consonance of that theory with the ordinary moral consciousness: sometimes, as in the following passage, in a style he acknowledge to be "heated."[29]

> If the popularizing of superficial views inclines [the non-theoretical person] to bitterness, he comforts himself when he sees that they live in the head, and but little, if at all, in the heart and life; that still at the push the doctrinaire and the quacksalver go to the wall, and that even that too is as it ought to be. He sees the true account of the state (which holds it to be neither mere force nor convention, but the moral organism, the real identity of might and right) unknown or "refuted," laughed at and despised, but he sees the state every day in its practice refute every other doctrine, and do with the moral approval of all what the explicit theory of scarcely one will justify. He sees instincts are better and stronger than so-called "principles." He sees in the hour of need what are called "rights" laughed at, "freedom," the liberty to do what one pleases, trampled on, the claims of the individual trodden under foot, and theories burst like cobwebs. And he sees, as of old, the heart of a nation rise high and beat in the breast of each one of her citizens, till her safety and honour are dearer to each than life, till to those who live her shame and sorrow, if such is allotted, outweigh their loss, and death seems a little thing to those who go for her to their common and nameless grave.[30]

These sentiments were common enough in the German Empire after the Franco-Prussian War of 1870; and later in the century were to become still commoner. Unquestionably, states in time of war do, with the approval of large majorities, what the explicit theory of scarcely one will justify; but nobody in England before Bradley thought to make a moral theory out of it.

By Saintsbury's formal standards, the passage is magnificent as literature, except perhaps for its last sentence, the iambic-anapaestic rhythm of which is dangerously close to verse. Here again, a formal fault may be traced to a corruption of expression. I believe I will not be alone in finding a difference between the staccato—

> He sees in the hour of need what are called "rights" laughed at, "freedom," the liberty to do what one pleases, trampled on, the claims of the individual trodden under foot, and theories burst like cobwebs—

and the final incantation, moving from ". . . he sees, as of old, the heart of a nation rise high," to its affecting climax. That the former is genuinely felt it is impossible to doubt, however little one may applaud it; but the latter is unashamed, and probably unconscious, pulpit oratory. To try, and fail, to express what few artists have ever expressed is no disgrace. But Bradley allowed his failure to stand, and it infects the whole passage. He offered to express the thought of intellectual scruples being overcome by a higher devotion. In failing imaginatively to realize that devotion, he betrayed his hatred of the scruples themselves: hatred in search of a justification.

How could Eliot have failed to discover the significance of such passages? They are not rare in *Ethical Studies*, although, writing in 1927, Eliot may not have known of things in Bradley's occasional papers even more disturbing: his crude pseudo-Darwinism in "Some Remarks on Punishment,"[31] or his defence of "violence, and even extermination" now and then—for the "good of mankind," of course—in "Individualism and National Self-Sacrifice."[32] Eliot's moral obtuseness in matters political goes some way to explain it: as an admirer of Charles Maurras he may even have found Bradley tame. But there is another reason. Eliot correctly perceived in *Ethical Studies* the influence of the urbane and ironical style of Matthew Arnold's *Culture and Anarchy* and *Friendship's Garland*. The supreme specimen, quoted at length by Eliot, is the criticism of *Literature and Dogma* in the Concluding Remarks. Eliot's contrast between the "crude and raw and provincial" Utilitarians and the "in comparison, catholic, civilized, and universal" Bradley, rests on a delusion to which critics with a horror of provinciality are subject: the delusion that to be non-provincial is to be civilized. Mill and Sidgwick were, in their writings, stiff, earnest, and upright. They could be witty, although in a manner intellectual rather than urbane. These characteristics, no doubt, are limitations; but they are compatible with being catholic and civilized. To be willing to write as Bradley sometimes wrote is not.

IV

It is not impossible that Bradley himself became aware of the flaws, both philosophical and literary, in *Ethical Studies*. Desiring to rewrite it, he withheld his consent to its reprinting; and in the preface to the posthumous second edition there is said to be "reason to believe that, had he been able to carry out his intention of re-writing the book, much would have been softened or omitted."[33] Bradley's acknowledged pre-eminence as a philosophical stylist, however, does not rest on his ethical writings. Nor, admirable though it is, does it lie in his mastery of Arnoldian irony.

The ordinary reader of Bradley's major works, *The Principles of Logic* (1882) and *Appearance and Reality* (1893) probably carries away an impression recorded by his best recent critic, Professor Richard Wollheim, of a "heavy, luxuriant growth of rhetoric and dialectic that is usually allowed to swell and sprawl across the pages often enough obscuring the true lines of the discussion."[34] But Bradley's "rhetoric and dialectic" are vigorously alive, and in *Appearance and Reality* their luxuriance is pruned. The following brief specimen, on the error of Cartesian dualism, gives their flavour:

> The soul and its organism are each a phenomenal series. Each, to speak in general, is implicated in the changes of the other. Their supposed independence is therefore imaginary, and to overcome it by invoking a faculty such as Will—is the effort to heal a delusion by means of a fiction.[35]

This is a little baroque for today's *Bauhaus* taste; but it perfectly expresses Bradley's passionate absorption in his thought. Thinking ought to be a passion in philosophers; and for those in whom it is, Bradley's mature prose will always be worth studying.

It must not be forgotten that, in Berkeley, the eighteenth century produced an unsurpassed rhetorician and dialectician; or that, unlike Mill at his best, Bradley in his treatment of his adversaries reverted to the methods of the eighteenth century. Yet as a writer, Bradley is more than a Victorian Berkeley. To identify his peculiar genius, we must examine another aspect of his relation to Mill.

In his *System of Logic*, Mill contrived to analyze the methodology of nineteenth-century science in terms of traditional British empiricism. Nothing so comprehensive has been done since; and his methodological analyses are still of value. Perhaps that is what Eliot meant when he said that "Bradley left the structure of Mill's logic standing, and never meant to do anything else." Yet it is absurd to say that Bradley's attack on Mill's logic is directed only against "certain limitations, imperfections, and abuses." Adopting Eliot's metaphor, it would be more accurate to say that

Bradley left the wings and extensive outbuildings of Mill's logic standing, but destroyed its central block: its theory of terms and propositions.

Traditional empiricism had great difficulty in acknowledging the existence of anything except what Hume called "perceptions" and Mill "feelings" or "phenomena" or "states of consciousness." In his *System of Logic*, Mill recognized only two kinds of nameable thing besides states of consciousness: substances and attributes. Following the Cartesian tradition, he acknowledged two kinds of substances—minds, which experience states of consciousness; and bodies, the unsentient causes that excite certain of those states. "But," he added, "of the nature of either body or mind, further than the feelings which the former excites, which the latter experiences, we do not, according to the best existing doctrine, know anything."[36] As for attributes, he declared that "if we . . . cannot know, anything of bodies but the sensations which they excite in us or in others, those sensations must be all that we can, at bottom, mean by their attributes."[37] In sum, except for something we know not what that causes states of consciousness, and something we know not what that experiences them, we cannot even think of anything but states of consciousness. A corollary of this doctrine is that philosophical studies like logic and epistemology are fundamentally branches of traditional psychology.

In *The Principles of Logic* (1883), a year before Frege in his *Grundlagen der Arithmetik* attacked psychologism in mathematical theory, Bradley demolished this impossible but tenacious theory.

> In England [he declared] . . . we have lived too long in the psychological attitude. We take it for granted and as a matter of course that, like sensations and emotions, ideas are phenomena. And, considering these phenomena as psychical facts, we have tried (with what success I will not ask) to distinguish between ideas and sensations. But, intent on this, we have as good as forgotten the way in which logic uses ideas. We have not seen that in judgment no fact ever *is* just that which it *means*, or can mean what it is; and we have not learnt that, whenever we have truth or falsehood, it is the signification we use, and not the existence. We never assert the fact in our heads, but something else which that fact stands for.[38]

This is less an argument than a reminder; and it is conclusive. The essential thing in any mental act is what Brentano called its "intentionality":

its reference to an object, not necessarily a real one.[39] No feeling, taken in itself, has intentionality, or means anything. Its meaning, if it has one, is conferred on it. A philosophical theory of mind is therefore a theory, not of psychical facts like Mill's "states of consciousness," but of the meanings conferred on them.

In the empiricist tradition, the fundamental relation that is believed to hold between a word and what it refers to is like that of a label to what it labels. This is not an implausible view of the relation between a proper name, like "John Stuart Mill" or "London," and whatever it names. But, as the empiricists themselves recognized, most words are not proper names. The word "man" does not stand for some individual man, or for anything individual at all, but rather for certain attributes or properties (being a rational animal, perhaps) that all men by nature exemplify. In philosophical jargon, such attributes or properties are *universal:* they can be exemplified by many individuals, but are not themselves individuals.

The precise status of universals is still a matter of contention. One thing, however, it cannot be. Universals cannot be individuals. Yet Mill's doctrine that certain sensations "must be all that we can, at bottom, mean" when we refer to the attributes of bodies, implies that attributes, which are universals, are individuals; for sensations are individual occurrences. It is remarkable that Mill did not see this, because in his theory of denotation and connotation he clearly distinguished proper names from "connotative" or attributive terms.

His failure to see it was disastrous. It led him to hold that all attributes are "grounded" in individual states of consciousness, and that what any proposition ultimately means is that certain individual states of consciousness are "associated" with certain others. This result, as Bradley pointed out, is bankruptcy.

> The ideas which are recalled according to [the] laws [of association] are particular existences. Individual atoms are the units of association. And I should maintain, on the contrary, that in all reproduction what operates everywhere is a common identity. No particular ideas are ever associated or ever could be. What is associated is and must be always universal.[40]

When I say that all men are mortal, I do not mean that the "individual atoms," Socrates, Plato, and the rest are mortal, but that individual *men* are mortal. Individual atoms are here of interest only as having a "common identity" as men; and that common identity Mill's individual states of consciousness cannot provide.

Bradley did not always write with the classical purity of his criticism of associationism. The variety of his prose is unequalled in English philosophical literature. Henry Sidgwick considered the style of *Ethical Studies* to be in bad taste. Bradley, however, refused to tidy up his thoughts to meet Victorian standards of decorum.

> I maintain that all association is between universals, and that no other association exists . . . "And do you really," there may here come a protest, "do you really believe this holds good with emotions? If castor-oil has made me sick once, so that I can not see it or even think of it without uneasiness, is this too a connection between universals?" I reply without hesitation that I believe it is so; and that I must believe this or else accept a miracle, a miracle moreover which is not in harmony with the facts it is invoked to explain. You believe then, I feel inclined to reply, that the actual feelings, which accompanied your vomiting, have risen from the dead in a paler form to trouble you. I could not credit that even if it answered to the facts.[41]

His contemporaries, and most of ours, would have censored this example, and curbed the inclinations to which Bradley gave free rein. But Bradley did not stop at outright black humour:

> What is recalled has not only got different relations; itself is different. . . . If then there is a resurrection, assuredly what rises must be the ghost and not the individual. And if the ghost is not content with his spiritual body, it must come with some members which are not its own. In the hurry of the moment, we have reason to suspect, that the bodies of the dead may be used as common stock.[42]

Bradley's twofold perception that what is essential to mind is not the psychical states that compose it, as they are in themselves, but rather their meanings, and that the meanings it is most important to study are universal, was a turning point in British philosophy. Those who would not, or could not, learn from him forfeited all claim to be considered seriously as philosophers. The opening sentences of an early paper by G. E. Moore, already a formidable adversary, bear ample witness to the importance of his influence:

Now to Mr. Bradley's argument that "the idea in judgment is the universal meaning" I have nothing to add. It appears to me conclusive, as against those, of whom there have been too many, who have treated this idea as a mental state. But he seems to me to be infected by the same error as theirs. . . .[43]

Not even Moore would criticize Bradley except on Bradley's own terms.

Just as Mill could not carry out his indirect investigation into "the unanalysed experience of the human race" in the direct style of the eighteenth-century classics, so Bradley could not write about mind in the style of Mill. Yet it is extremely difficult to state precisely what Bradley's stylistic problem was. If the fundamental problem about mind is the nature of intentionality, philosophers must find a way of speaking about how signs, mental images, and the like can be made to be *about* things other than themselves. Ordinary language, with its devices of quotation and *oratio obliqua,* enables us to talk about what we say, and so, indirectly, about what we think; but it does not enable us to talk about the intentionality in virtue of which something said expresses a thought. The familiar logico-philosophical notion that concepts, propositions, and the like must be postulated as intermediate between words and sentences on the one hand, and things and facts on the other, merely deepens the mystery. The natures of concepts and propositions turn out to be elusive. Frege's discovery that in order to talk about a concept we seem to be obliged to treat it as an object, which it demonstrably cannot be, is only one of the problems raised.

These problems are not merely philosophical; or, if they are philosophical, then solving them will solve a stylistic problem as well. To the present, formalized semantics offers little hope that salvation may be found in some artificial formalism; for the same problem arises about such formalisms as about the natural languages. The passages I have quoted from Bradley's *Principles of Logic* illustrate one of the earliest and most serious attempts to treat of the philosophy of mind, as it is now understood, in natural English prose. Bradley did not succeed, as his successors Bertrand Russell, G. E. Moore, and C. I. Lewis have not succeeded; but he did make progress, and his work continues to reward careful study.

It may be objected that prose that is concerned with the theory of meaning must be too abstract, too remote from any human emotion to engage the attention of students of literature. Even though argument is unlikely to persuade those who have remained unpersuaded by the above quotations from Bradley, I nevertheless recommend to their attention an observation of R. G. Collingwood. "The progressive intellectualization of language, its progressive conversion by the work of grammar and logic into a scientific symbolism, . . . represents not a progressive drying-up of emotion, but its progressive articulation and specialization. We are not getting away from an emotional atmosphere into a dry, rational atmosphere. We are acquiring new emotions and new means of expressing them."[44]

NOTES

1. Yvor Winters, *The Function of Criticism*, Denver, 1957, p. 50.

2. T. S. Eliot, *Selected Essays*, 3rd ed., London, 1951, p. 445.

3. George Saintsbury, "English Prose Style," in *Miscellaneous Essays*, London, 1892, p. 13.

4. Ibid., p. 15.

5. "Modern English Prose" [1876], in *Miscellaneous Essays*, p. 94.

6. "English Prose Style," *Miscellaneous Essays*, p. 24. That this essay first appeared in 1885 is recorded in the Preface, p. x.

7. *Miscellaneous Essays*, pp. 10-18, 27-9.

8. Ibid., p. 84.

9. Ibid., p. 38.

10. Cf. *Miscellaneous Essays*, pp. 17-18, 36-7.

11. My debt here to Benedetto Croce, *Aesthetic*, trans. Douglas Ainslie, 2nd ed., London, 1922, and to R. G. Collingwood, *The Principles of Art*, Oxford, 1938, will be evident.

12. *After Strange Gods*, New York, 1933, p. 27.

13. The concluding paragraph of Bertrand Russell's "A Free Man's Worship," in *Mysticism and Logic*, London, 1917, 46-57. Russell records that it was "written in 1902," and that it "appeared originally . . . in the *New Quarterly*, November 1907" (ibid., p. v).

14. F. R. Leavis, "Tragedy and the 'Medium': A Note on Mr. Santayana's 'Tragic Philosophy,'" *Scrutiny*, XII (1943-44); reprinted in F. R. Leavis, *The Common Pursuit*, London, 1952.

15. *Mysticism and Logic*, p. 31. The quotation is from the essay "Mysticism and Logic," which, Russell records, "appeared in the *Hibbert Journal* for July 1914" (ibid., p. v).

16. *Miscellaneous Essays*, p. 36.

17. "The Function of Criticism" (1923) in *Selected Essays*, pp. 32-3. I have examined the philosophical questions to which this conception of criticism gives rise in my *The Later Philosophy of R. G. Collingwood*, Oxford, 1962, Ch. 5.

18. Reginald Jackson, *An Examination of the Deductive Logic of John Stuart Mill*, Oxford, 1941, p. v.

19. "Professor Sedgwick's Discourse on the Studies of the University of Cambridge," in *Dissertations and Discussions,* 2 vols., London, 1859, I, 146-7.

20. Matthew Arnold, *Friendship's Garland,* 2nd ed., London, 1897, p. 71.

21. "Westminster Reviewer's Defense of Mill" (June 1829), from *The Works of Lord Macaulay,* Albany ed., London, 1898, VII, 349. For J. S. Mill's opinion of this controversy, see J. S. Mill, *Autobiography,* World's Classics ed., London, 1924, pp. 133-6.

22. F. C. Copleston, *A History of Philosophy,* London, 1966, VIII, 90.

23. *Dissertations and Discussions,* I, 350-51.

24. W. B. Yeats's introduction to *Bishop Berkeley,* by T. M. Hone and M. M. Rossi. I owe both quotation and reference to Bonamy Dobrée, "Berkeley as a Man of Letters" in *Hermathena,* LXXXII (1953), 59.

25. *Dissertations and Discussions,* I, 425.

26. "Francis Herbert Bradley," in *Selected Essays,* p. 448.

27. F. H. Bradley, *Ethical Studies,* 2nd ed., Oxford, 1927, pp. 126-8; *Collected Essays,* Oxford, 1935, I, 71-132.

28. Brand Blanshard, *Reason and Goodness,* London, 1961, p. 90.

29. *Ethical Studies,* p. 202.

30. *Ethical Studies,* p. 184.

31. Reprinted in *Collected Essays,* Oxford, 1935, I, 149-64.

32. Reprinted in *Collected Essays,* I, 165-76. The passage in which the quoted phrases occur is on p. 175.

33. *Ethical Studies,* 2nd ed., Oxford, 1927, p. vi.

34. Richard Wollheim, *F. H. Bradley,* Penguin Books, Harmondsworth, 1959, p. 110.

35. F. H. Bradley, *Appearance and Reality,* 2nd ed. corr., Oxford, 1946, p. 296.

36. J. S. Mill, *A System of Logic,* 5th ed., London, 1862, I, 69.

37. Ibid.

38. F. H. Bradley, *The Principles of Logic,* 2nd ed. corr., Oxford, 1928, I, 2.

39. Franz Brentano, *Psychologie vom empirischen Standpunkt,* Leipzig, 1874, I, Book 2, Ch. 1.

40. *The Principles of Logic,* I, 304.

41. Ibid., pp. 307-8.

42. *The Principles of Logic,* II, 306.

43. G. E. Moore, "The Nature of Judgment," *Mind,* n.s., VIII (1899), 177.

44. R. G. Collingwood, *The Principles of Art,* Oxford, 1938, p. 269.

MATTHEW ARNOLD'S PROSE: THEORY AND PRACTICE

GEOFFREY TILLOTSON

I

THE RELATION of mind and written words is a topic of long standing, and Arnold's contribution to it must serve as my excuse for making one of my own. In the process I shall draw on Arnold only here and there, reserving my fuller consideration of his theory and practice till the second half of my essay.

Our response to a piece of literature is both intellectual and æsthetic. What is intellectual in it applies itself to the content—to the matter, the way it is being thought about, the conclusions being drawn from it, the purpose it is being made to serve. If we are the best sort of reader, ready to give the author a fair hearing, the intellect starts by being passive, adjusted to watch and acquire. That state, however, cannot last long, because even the fair reader is a critic, and criticism is mental action. We become combative, for we ourselves might have written the piece —we possess a store of matter more or less similar to that being presented to us; we can think for ourselves; we have our own purposes to serve. And so we make a judgment, our judgment being the culmination of a process: as Arnold noted more than once, judgment forms insensibly as reading proceeds.

All this is in the keeping of the intellect. But already our intellectual response has extended to the æsthetic. For everything in the writer's mind exists coloured by his own individuality, the reader's experience of which colouring is an æsthetic experience. This colouring the intellect either approves or disapproves—Pater approved of the "fine atmosphere of mind" he found in Wordsworth's poetry,[1] and George Eliot disapproved of the atmosphere she found in Pater's *Renaissance* as quite "poisonous."[2] The intellectual and the æsthetic also act together because some part of our æsthetic response is prompted by some part of the matter that is engaging our intellect in the first place, and almost all the matter if the piece is mainly descriptive. To matter that has prompted an æsthetic response when encountered in the course of practical living we respond æsthetically all over again at the sight of the words that recall that practical experience—it seems as if we possess an outfit of shadow senses for the purpose. To take a sentence from Sir Thomas Browne as an instance— an instance brief enough to preclude any noticeable response to his strong personality: "But the iniquity of oblivion blindly scattereth her poppy, and deals with the memory of men without distinction to merit of perpetuity." Our æsthetic response to the matter of this is to a composite picture of the scattering of a liquid opiate and the generalised "idea" of a poppy. Moreover, as that same instance shows strikingly, some part of our total æsthetic response to literature is to its words as words.

When we are discussing prose apart from its content we are discussing our æsthetic response *in toto* and what prompts it. Later on I shall have something to say about our æsthetic response (joined with a response on the part of the intellect) to the colouring supplied by Arnold's personality, but neither that sort of response nor the æsthetic response to the sensuous part of the matter invites any discussion. More tricky, however, is the response we make to the words as words.

I have been using the term "literature" so far, but critics have usually restricted the operation of the æsthetic awareness of words as words to the reader of part of literature only—to literature in verse and to literature as certain sorts of prose. Coleridge so restricted it, specifying "oratory" as a sort of prose that could be ranged with literature in verse. Perhaps others besides myself look back on his remarks[3] as on an era in our education—they illuminated what we had long been fumbling with in twilight. Here is not the place to consider them in detail. All I shall say now is that on maturer thought they throw their light on the whole of literature rather than on a part of it. For the only deep division, as I see it, falls between two sorts of reader—the "literary" readers and the rest— rather than between two sorts of writing. By "literary" readers I mean the readers for whom an author worth the name writes in the first place.

Every literary reader is aware of words on almost all occasions when words are read, and on many when words are spoken. Sometimes he is aware of them as words even when their meaning sharply affects him as a practical person. We have evidence for this in one of Wordsworth's

greatest poems, his "Elegiac Verses in Memory of my Brother." In the
course of the poem he recalls the arrival of the news, conveyed presumably by letter, of John's death by drowning:

> All vanished in a single word,
> A breath, a sound, and scarcely heard.
> Sea—ship—drowned—shipwreck—so it came,
> The meek, the brave, the good, was gone;
> He who had been our living John
> Was nothing but a name.

Perhaps on occasions like these we gaze at words as a temporary refuge
from the things they denote, and perhaps non-literary people gaze in that
way as well as literary. However that may be, literary readers make an
æsthetic response to words so nearly constant that it is strange to find
Coleridge mistaking a difference between degrees of obviousness for a
difference of kind. He instanced the prose of Southey as prose composed
of words that themselves go unnoticed: "In the very best styles, as
Southey's, you read page after page, understanding the author perfectly,
without once taking notice of the medium of communication. . . ."⁴
Surely a literary critic is always aware of words as words. All that varies
as he turns from one piece of literature to another is the nature of the
particular wording, the qualities of his own response to it, and, later on,
his own powers as a worder of that response. To call on the handiest
evidence: If I myself read so humble a piece of prose as one conveying
instructions, I look at its wording as closely as (I hope) I look at its in-
structiveness. On an early page in my pocket diary I read the following:
"FAINTING. If a person faints, lay him flat on the floor or on a couch.
Keep the head low and apply smelling salts or sal volatile on some cotton
wool under the patient's nose. Give him a glass of cold water on recovering consciousness." When I read that, I see that I should have preferred
to read: ". . . Keep his head low and apply smelling salts or sal volatile
on some cotton wool to his nostrils. Give him a glass of cold water when
he recovers consciousness." (I retain the order *salts . . . wool* because
for practical reasons the sooner salts are mentioned the better. There are
several acceptable variants of the last clause including "when he comes
round.") If that instruction had been worded so as not to offend my
æsthetic sense, I suspect I should have taken in its instructions more
deeply (as in any event I should if I were reading it in order to deal with

an actual case of fainting on the carpet before me). Even practical instructions are approached in one way by the non-literary reader, and by the literary reader in another. Certainly, I approach Southey's prose with awareness of its words as words, and so must conclude that Coleridge's account of his own experience was mistaken.

To continue these preliminary remarks, let me try to show how thought exists apart from certain aspects of the wording. The end of writing is to produce the intended effect on the mind of the reader by means of the words used. A writer capable of achieving a thought worth expression—that is, a thought of interest to a reader—has achieved a certain amount of its wording along with it. Thought either comes into being along with words—some of them, if not all—or it very soon achieves them. Some part of the final wording, however, cannot but concern the reader's æsthetic sense. For instance, if the thought is made up of a house and Jack, and their interrelation as builder and thing built, the wording could run in various ways:

> The house that Jack built
> The house which Jack built
> The house Jack built
> The house builded by Jack
> The house erected by Jack
> The house Jack erected

and so on, drawing on "domicile" and even "property," and perhaps using the verb "edify" in a rare sense, or the obsolete "edificate." We could not say that the thought had appreciably changed at any point throughout these changes of its expression. But for the purposes of æsthetic response, changes like these are important.

We can see this by examining the corrections in authors' manuscripts, or as edition follows edition. We know, for instance, that Tennyson changed the order of verb and adverb in the line

> Freedom broadens slowly down

so as to avoid the collision of sound represented by the two s's. Or to take an instance from Arnold: the ending of his essay on Marcus Aurelius gave him trouble. Some of the revision represented in the printed texts—the evidence of which is set out in Professor Super's edition of the prose works—is consequent on an improved clearness of thought. The rest of it was made in the interests of expression. For instance, the text Professor Super has chosen as his copy-text is that of the 1883 edition of *Essays in Criticism*, which received Arnold's last revisions. One of its sentences reads: "And so he remains the especial friend and comforter of all clear-headed and scrupulous, yet pure-hearted and upward striving men, in those ages most especially that walk by sight, not by faith, but yet have no open vision."[5] Both the description of the men and the ages caused Arnold trouble, but I am concerned only with the revisions in the description of the ages. In the *Victoria Magazine*, where the essay was first printed, the last phrase of that description reads: "by faith, that have no open vision." This wording was retained when the essay was included in *Essays in Criticism* (1865), but in the second edition four years later, it became: "by faith, and yet have no open vision." In the new edition of 1880 we find: "by faith, but have, nevertheless, no open vision." A change from "and" to "but" denotes a change in the thinking, but a change from "yet" to "nevertheless" denotes a change in the expression.

Because of this concern with words as words, the critic of prose wording could just as soon be a critic of the wording of poetry. The best qualification for criticising the one is a capacity to criticise the other. The things in the wording of poetry that call for criticism are more striking than those in the wording of prose—more highly coloured, more chimingly musical, more closely packed. They are also more easily recognised and familiar, for there has been much more criticism of the wording of poetry than of prose. But to be a critic of either, one must unite the humble powers that school-children exercise when they triumphantly discover alliteration and the rarer powers of being aware of the whole of the æsthetic response to wording, a whole that exists almost palpably as an object. The critic has to be as much aware of his æsthetic response to wording as Arnold was of his to the shape of a Greek tragedy—in the 1853 Preface to his *Poems* he described it in terms of a group of statuary slowly approached along an avenue until the point comes when it is possessed wholly:

> The terrible old mythic story on which the drama was founded stood, before he entered the theatre, traced in its bare outlines upon the spectator's mind; it stood in his memory, as a group of statuary, faintly seen, at the end of a long and dark vista: then came the Poet, embodying outlines, developing situations, not a word wasted, not a sentiment capriciously thrown in: stroke upon stroke, the drama proceeded: the

light deepened upon the group; more and more it revealed itself to the rivetted gaze of the spectator: until at last, when the final words were spoken, it stood before him in broad sunlight, a model of immortal beauty.[6]

Readers differ in the degree to which they make and are aware of this sort of æsthetic response, but some of them make so strong a response and are so much aware of it that they may give it more attention than they are giving to what is being said. For them the wording of Southey's prose, which like Coleridge they will place with the "very best," achieves an elegance that exists as an object before the mental eye, as the walking gait of a racehorse exists before the eyes of the body. Some readers who happen to be what are called atheists can get much pleasure out of reading Newman, even on those occasions when, to their way of thinking, he is talking nonsense. From these instances it follows that in writing of wording as a thing prompting an æsthetic response we have a firm topic.

Before looking at Arnold's practice, there are one or two further distinctions to draw. The critic of the æsthetic response to wording is not concerned with the accuracy of the words as expression. That accuracy is in the keeping of the thought. I have said that when we achieve a thought, it comes to us in some or all of the words suitable for its expression. If the thought is clear, the words will be mainly the right ones. If not, the process of improvement will usually be a process of clarifying the thought. Like many other critics, Arnold did not see this distinction. Look at his characterisation of good prose as having "regularity, uniformity, precision, balance." In that characterisation, which we shall look into more fully later on, the third term is misused. "Precision" applies to all prose as prose is wording and only to certain prose as prose is thinking. When the wording of prose is unsatisfactory, that wording still has precision. It produces a precise æsthetic impression, but a precise impression of vagueness. To exchange it for a precise impression of light, the writer would have to clear up his thought or the mental picture he is wording. Arnold's asking precision from wording is asking for what no wording can fail to provide, however difficult we should find the describing of it. What he meant to ask for was precision of thought or mental picturing.

On another occasion he fails to make a similar distinction. He is recommending an academy on the grounds that it would reduce what he called "provinciality," and is advancing the idea that "not even great powers of mind will keep [a writer's] taste and style perfectly sound and sure, if he is left too much to himself, with no 'sovereign organ of opinions,' in these matters, near him." Here "taste" is ranged alongside "style," but the instances he gives show that it is not the wording he is objecting to but the matter it is expressing, matter that exists just so because of an alleged deficiency in taste. Take his remarks on Ruskin, for instance. He begins by quoting an "exquisite" passage that shows "Mr. Ruskin exercising his genius":

> Go out, in the spring-time, among the meadows that slope from the shores of the Swiss lakes to the roots of their lower mountains. There, mingled with the taller gentians and the white narcissus, the grass grows deep and free; and as you follow the winding mountain paths, beneath arching boughs all veiled and dim with blossom,—paths that for ever droop and rise over the green banks and mounds sweeping down in scented undulation, step to the blue water, studded here and there with new-mown heaps, filling all the air with fainter sweetness,—look up towards the higher hills, where the waves of everlasting green roll silently into their long inlets among the shadows of the pines.

"Exquisite" as the passage is, Arnold—we may note in passing—raises an objection, an objection he brings forward apologetically:

> All the critic could possibly suggest, in the way of objection, would be, perhaps, that Mr. Ruskin is there trying to make prose do more than it can perfectly do; that what he is there attempting he will never, except in poetry, be able to accomplish to his own entire satisfaction: but he accomplishes so much that the critic may well hesitate to suggest even this.[7]

Surely this is an objection raised by a theorist, one who, to use Johnson's terms, judges by "precept" rather than "perception."

In the past, it is true, the sort of matter Ruskin expressed here had usually gone into metre. Nevertheless it would not be too much to say that Ruskin had left off writing verse simply because the matter he now wished to express—matter that included his mature perception of rocks and stones and trees—could not go into metre without being falsified. Arnold should have seen that the meaning Ruskin had achieved demanded expression in prose. To demand verse of him was like asking Bach to put the matter of a recitative into an aria. Both recitative and aria are beautiful, but the one expresses matter which, being narrative, needs to be kept moving along a line, whereas the other expresses matter which, being meditative, needs to be kept circling. The beauty of the recitative is comparatively informal, and that of the aria formal.

If we look again at the passage Arnold quotes, and especially at its striking last phrase, we see pointedly that the touch of a more regular rhythm would have killed it. Arnold, as I say, must have forgotten. That he well knew about matter choosing its form is clear from his own practice. Some of his verse is formal and some comparatively informal, while some of his prose is informal and some comparatively formal. An instance of formal prose is the invocation to Oxford in the Preface to *Essays in Criticism.* According to the precept he turns on Ruskin, that invocation ought not to have been expressed in prose at all. Prose, however, was demanded by its matter, its thought and feeling combined. Even the comparatively informal verse of "Dover Beach" would have denied it its rightful rhythm.

It is what Arnold goes on to say, however, that contributes most to our discussion—when he turns to a passage that he has no good word for, a passage in which Ruskin considers the naming of some of the characters in Shakespeare's plays:

> Of Shakspeare's names I will afterwards speak at more length; they are curiously—often barbarously—mixed out of various traditions and languages. Three of the clearest in meaning have been already noticed. Desdemona—"δυσδαιμονία," *miserable fortune*—is also plain enough. Othello is, I believe, "the careful"; all the calamity of the tragedy arising from the single flaw and error in his magnificently collected strength. Ophelia, "serviceableness," the true, lost wife of Hamlet, is marked as having a Greek name by that of her brother, Laertes; and its signification is once exquisitely alluded to in that brother's last word of her, where her gentle preciousness is opposed to the uselessness of the churlish clergy:—"A *ministering* angel shall my sister be, when thou liest howling." Hamlet is, I believe, connected in some way with "homely," the entire event of the tragedy turning on betrayal of home duty. Hermione (ἔρμα), "pillar-like" (ἦ εἶδος ἔχε χρυσέης Ἀφροδίτης); Titania (τιτήνη), "the queen;" Benedick and Beatrice, "blessed and blessing;" Valentine and Proteus, "enduring or strong" (*valens*), and "changeful." Iago and Iachimo have evidently the same root—probably the Spanish Iago, Jacob, "the supplanter."

Arnold comments:

Now, really, what a piece of extravagance all that is! I will not say that
the meaning of Shakspeare's names (I put aside the question as to the
correctness of Mr. Ruskin's etymologies) has no effect at all, may be
entirely lost sight of; but to give it that degree of prominence is to throw
the reins to one's whim, to forget all moderation and proportion, to lose
the balance of one's mind altogether. It is to show in one's criticism,
to the highest excess, the note of provinciality.[8]

Here it is not the wording he is objecting to, but the matter, and the
intellect responsible for it. He is not speaking of prose, but of its content.

Arnold's remark about what is proper matter for prose witnesses to a
limitation in his view of the function of prose. He would limit it to
the expression of thinking, or, if to more than thinking, then only to the
simplest narrative and description—he advised Hardy to narrate in the
style Swift had used for *Gulliver's Travels,* overlooking the difference
in the degree of complexity between their respective matter. Arnold
thought of good prose as being one sort of prose only.

That is how Clough had thought of it in his lecture on Dryden, an
excerpt of which had appeared in *Poems and Prose Remains* of 1869.
Clough there had written:

Our language before the Restoration certainly was for the most part
bookish, academical, and stiff. You perceive that our writers have first
learnt to compose in Latin; and you feel as if they were now doing so in
English. Their composition is not an harmonious development of
spoken words, but a copy of written words. We are set to study ornate
and learned periods; but we are not charmed by finding our ordinary
everyday speech rounded into grace and smoothed into polish, chastened
to simplicity and brevity without losing its expressiveness, and raised into
dignity and force without ceasing to be familiar; saying once for all
what we in our rambling talk try over and over in vain to say; and saying it simply and fully, exactly and perfectly.

This scholastic and constrained manner of men who had read more
than they talked, and had (of necessity) read more Latin than English;
of men who passed from the study to the pulpit, and from the pulpit
back to the study—this elevated and elaborated diction of learned and
religious men was doomed at the Restoration. Its learning was pedantry,
and its elevation pretence. It was no way suited to the wants of the
court, nor the wishes of the people. It was not likely that the courtiers
would impede the free motions of their limbs with the folds of the

cumbrous theological vesture; and the nation in general was rather weary of being preached to. The royalist party, crowding back from French banishment, brought their French tastes and distastes. James I. loved Latin and even Greek, but Charles II. liked French better even than English. In one of Dryden's plays is a famous scene, in which he ridicules the fashionable jargon of the day, which seems to have been a sort of slipshod English, continually helped out with the newest French phrases.

Dryden then has the merit of converting this corruption and dissolution of our old language into a new birth and renovation. And not only must we thank him for making the best of the inevitable circumstances and tendencies of the time, but also praise him absolutely for definitely improving our language. It is true that he sacrificed a great deal of the old beauty of English writing, but that sacrifice was inevitable; he retained all that it was practicable to save, and he added at the same time all the new excellence of which the time was capable.

You may call it, if you please, a democratic movement in the language. It was easier henceforth both to write and to read. To understand written English, it was not necessary first to understand Latin: and yet written English was little less instructive than it had been, or if it was less elevating, it was on the other hand more refining.

For the first time, you may say, people found themselves reading words easy at once and graceful; fluent, yet dignified; familiar, yet full of meaning. To have organised the dissolving and separating elements of our tongue into a new and living instrument, perfectly adapted to the requirements and more than meeting the desires and aspirations of the age, this is our author's praise. But it is not fully expressed until you add that this same instrument was found, with no very material modification, sufficient for the wants and purposes of the English people for more than a century. The new diction conquered, which the old one had never done, Scotland and Ireland, and called out American England into articulation. Hume and Robertson learnt it; Allan Ramsay and Burns studied it; Grattan spoke it; Franklin wrote it. You will observe that our most popular works in prose belong to it. So do our greatest orators. A new taste and a new feeling for the classics grew up with it. It translated, to the satisfaction of its time, Homer and Virgil.[9]

The style achieved by Dryden and the eighteenth-century writers generally was the style that Arnold himself wanted to write, after adapting it, of happy necessity, to his own genius. In his Preface to his short edition of *The Six Chief Lives from Johnson's "Lives of the Poets"* he repeated in his own way what Clough had said:

> It seems as if a simple and natural prose were a thing which we might expect to come easy to communities of men, and to come early to them; but we know from experience that it is not so. Poetry and the poetic form of expression naturally precede prose. We see this in ancient Greece. We see prose forming itself there gradually and with labour; we see it passing through more than one stage before it attains to thorough propriety and lucidity, long after forms of consummate accuracy have already been reached and used in poetry. It is a people's growth in practical life, and its native turn for developing this life and for making progress in it, which awaken the desire for a good prose,—a prose plain, direct, intelligible, serviceable. A dead language, the Latin, for a long time furnished the nations of Europe with an instrument of the kind, superior to any which they had yet discovered in their own tongue. But nations such as England and France, called to a great historic life, and with powerful interests and gifts either social or practical, were sure to feel the need of having a sound prose of their own, and to bring such a prose forth. They brought it forth in the seventeenth century; France first, afterwards England.

> The Restoration marks the real moment of birth of our modern English prose. Men of lucid and direct mental habit there were, such as Chillingworth, in whom before the Restoration the desire and the commencement of a modern prose show themselves. There were men like Barrow, weighty and powerful, whose mental habit the old prose suited, who continued its forms and locutions after the Restoration. But the hour was come for the new prose, and it grew and prevailed. In Johnson's time its victory had long been assured, and the old style seemed barbarous. Johnson himself wrote a prose decidedly modern. The reproach conveyed in the phrase "Johnsonian English" must not mislead us. It is aimed at his words, not at his structure. In Johnson's prose the words are often pompous and long, but the structure is always plain and modern. The prose writers of the eighteenth century have indeed their mannerisms and phrases which are no longer ours. Johnson says of Milton's blame of the Universities for permitting young men designed for orders in the Church to act in plays: "This is sufficiently peevish in a man, who, when he mentions his exile from college, relates, with great luxuriance, the compensation which the pleasures of the theatre afford him. Plays were therefore only criminal when they were acted by

academics." We should now-a-days not say *peevish* here, nor *luxuriance,* nor *academics.* Yet the style is ours by its organism, if not by its phrasing. It is by its organism,—an organism opposed to length and involvement, and enabling us to be clear, plain, and short,—that English style after the Restoration breaks with the style of the times preceding it, finds the true law of prose, and becomes modern; becomes, in spite of superficial differences, the style of our own day."[10]

This desirable style Arnold characterises as having "regularity, uniformity, precision, balance."

I have already suggested that "precision" is a property of the thought rather than of the wording. The other three desiderata amount to no more, I think, than what was expressed by Hopkins in one word when he described his own prose (some of the best written in the nineteenth century) as "even flowing."[11]

II

Arnold's call for smoothness had topical point. It came more forcefully in view of Carlyle's explosiveness, and a noticeable contemporary cult of an oracular prose consisting of short sentences constructed according to the simplest of patterns. Perhaps this cult recurs periodically in the history of English prose. Thomas Reid had affected it in the mid-eighteenth century. For example: "A man of sense is a man of judgment. Good sense is good judgment. Nonsense is what is evidently contrary to good judgment. Common sense is that degree of judgment which is common to men with whom we can converse and transact business."[12] I have shown elsewhere that a similar syntax was being favoured as the vehicle for description in verse.[13] In prose it was also being favoured in *Ossian* for this and other purposes. More recently there had been the prose of the belletrist R. A. Willmott, who was much read, it seems, and whose *Pleasures, Objects, and Advantages, of Literature. A Discourse* appeared first in 1851 (and last in 1906). From the start he had formed his sentences, as J. A. Froude did, on the subject-verb-object pattern, but at first so disguised the pattern with additions that it was not noticeable; Froude, by those means, made a style that has been much admired. In the *Discourse,* however, Willmott pared his bi- or tri-partite sentences to the minimum. Here is a sample:

A thoughtful person is struck by the despotic teaching of the modern school. The decisions of the eighteenth century are reversed; the authority of the judges is ignored. Addison's chair is filled by Hazlitt; a German mist intercepts Hurd. Our classical writers daily recede further from the public eye. Milton is visited like a monument. The scholarly hand alone brushes the dust from Dryden. The result is unhappy. Critics and readers, by a sort of necessity, refer every production of the mind to a modern standard. The age weighs itself. One dwarf is measured by another. The fanciful lyrist looks tall, when Pindar is put out of sight.[14]

It is plain that sentences like these, on the barest subject-verb-object pattern, do not provide a staple for extended prose, simply because of the universal law that we soon tire of the repetition of a pattern that is recognisable—the writers who used this oracular style forgot that oracles stop speaking as soon as possible. As I have said, a major writer took up the pattern but made it unrecognisable except to the analyst of wording —there is nothing jerky about Froude's style. One of the greatest, Carlyle, may be said to have made a point of cultivating jerks, but there is no monotony because he multiplied the angles from which they struck the reader.

Like most other nineteenth-century writers, Arnold was fascinated by the strange performance of Carlyle. His brilliant mimicry exists in the letters to Clough, and scraps of it persist till the end—a climax in the late essay on Gray reads as if Carlyle had worded it: "How simply said, and how truly also! Fain would a man like Gray speak out if he could, he 'likes himself better' when he speaks out; if he does not speak out, 'it is because I cannot.' "

Clearly, such prose lacked evenflowingness. The prose Arnold recommended avoided what might be called markedly varying contours, such as characterised oratorical prose. For at least two centuries now the prose written in England had been drawing away from oratory[15] and coming nearer to conversation. In other words, the supposed distance between writer and reader was diminishing. In writing oratorical prose, the writer thinks of himself as dominating his audience from a platform. In writing conversational prose, the writer thinks of himself as on a level with it. And whereas the orator's audience is myriad, the writer of conversational prose has an audience of one. Sterne marked an important point in the history of English written prose when he noted that "Writing, when properly managed (as you may be sure I think mine is) is but a different name for conversation." That remark opens a chapter (Book II, Ch. xi) of *Tristram Shandy,* and in the context "conversation" retains some of its older sense of "social intercourse"—Sterne goes on to warn the reader that he is relying on him to draw on his own experience so as to eke out what cannot be written down in all its completeness. But that the word has also much of its newer, narrower meaning is also plain—it comes in the midst of a book that is almost wholly made up of something as near as possible to the prose we talk together. The preference for written conversational prose meant first of all a looser ordering of the matter being expressed, and secondly a more intimate personal colouring, which might show itself as an addition to the matter, but which would very much affect the wording.

The approach made by written prose to conversation had been embarrassed, as Clough implied in the passage I have quoted, by the age-old habit of imitating the syntax of classical Latin. It may be that in the seventeenth century and earlier this imported syntax was as noticeable in cultivated conversation as a syntax flowing down from Anglo-Saxon. If so, manners, on which conversation depends, were soon to change. An early, and as it happened fictitious exponent of the newer style showed it at its most brilliant. The conversation of Shakespeare's most voluble personage exhibited a prose strikingly different from most of the prose being written at the time. That Hamlet was of the Court went without saying, but to the courtly he added an at least equal amount of the academical— he was also of the University. The prose he spoke and the familiar letter he wrote to Horatio (that to Ophelia belonged to a different kind) was a prose appropriate for writers who were trying to think about the new matter then coming into man's ken, and whose writings were mainly addressed to the aristocracy. We can imagine Dryden writing it, despite his remark that Shakespeare had imitated the conversation of gentlemen less well than Beaumont and Fletcher—a remark that witnesses to the rate at which manners were changing in the seventeenth century. After Dryden came Addison and Pope. Pope's conversation is represented by Spence, and his written prose by the Preface to the *Works* of 1717, of which I quote a paragraph from near the end:

If time shall make it the former, may these Poems (as long as they last) remain as a testimony, that their Author never made his talents subservient to the mean and unworthy ends of Party or self-interest; the gratification of publick prejudices, or private passions; the flattery of the undeserving, or the insult of the unfortunate. If I have written well, let it be consider'd that 'tis what no man can do without good sense, a quality that not only renders one capable of being a good writer, but a good man. And if I have made any acquisition in the opinion of any one under the notion of the former, let it be continued to me under no other title than that of the latter.[16]

Addison and Pope gave way to Sterne, who "managed" his conversational prose so as to make it as graceful as theirs while at the same time giving it all the informality possible. Informality, whether maximum or less, might be welcomed in a novel, but not necessarily in prose of thinking, of which there was so much in the nineteenth century. And yet after Sterne's *tour de force* even the most formal prose shed some of its pomp. In Arnold's day even Herbert Spencer yielded up all he could of his native heaviness: at the conclusion of the Preface to his epoch-making *Social Statics* (1850), he referred to certain "relaxations of style" which may "be censured, as beneath the gravity of the subject," and proceeded:

> In defence of them it may be urged, that the measured movement which custom prescribes for philosophical works, is productive of a monotony extremely repulsive to the generality of readers. That no counterbalancing advantages are obtained, the writer does not assert. But, for his own part, he has preferred to sacrifice somewhat of conventional dignity, in the hope of rendering his theme interesting to a larger number.[17]

I might add that the conversational style had its detractors. Perhaps it was his training among the Jesuits that prompted Hopkins to relegate Newman's prose to an inferior category. In a letter to Patmore towards the close of Newman's long life, he wrote:

> Newman does not follow the common tradition—of writing. His tradition is that of cultured, the most highly educated, conversation; it is the flower of the best Oxford life. Perhaps this gives it a charm of unaffected and personal sincerity that nothing else could. Still he shirks the technic of written prose and shuns the tradition of written English. He seems to be thinking "Gibbon is the last great master of traditional English prose; he is its perfection: I do not propose to emulate him; I begin all over again from the language of conversation, of common life."

> You too seem to me to be saying to yourself "I am writing prose, not poetry; it is bad taste and a confusion of kinds to employ the style of poetry in prose: the style of prose is to shun the style of poetry and to express one's thoughts with point." But the style of prose is a positive thing and not the absence of verse-forms and pointedly expressed thoughts are single hits and given no continuity of style.[18]

In making this criticism, Hopkins may have been asserting his allegiance not only to the Jesuits but to Pater, his Oxford tutor, who was deliberately writing a prose far from conversational—so far that one critic described it as prose lying in state. In a review of *Dorian Gray,* he recommended writers to write English "more as a learned language," which was to revert to the method of the Elizabethans, and in his late essay, "Style," he recommended the removal of "surplusage." That recommendation had pointed reference to a characteristic of conversational prose, which favoured the sort of expressions I shall note as frequent in Arnold's prose. Meanwhile Oscar Wilde was writing in the conversational style that is still so much with us.

Aesthetic considerations bring strange bed-fellows together, and among the disciples of Sterne were Dr. Arnold and Newman. These two take us into the famous Oriel Common Room, to which, in his turn, Matthew Arnold belonged. The prose Dr. Arnold wrote, on occasions at least, is sufficiently indicated by a passage in a letter of Newman's of 1833 in which he sought an opinion about a piece of his own prose from a friend. Having applied the word "flippant" to it (in the older sense of "fluent, talkative, voluble"), he paused to gloss it with "by which I mean what Keble blames in [Dr.] Arnold's writings, conversational."[19] If Newman was uncertain whether or not he had gone too far, it was down a favourite path—he would any day have preferred the flippant to the pompous: there was nothing in him of "stained-glass attitudes," to use Gilbert's brilliant phrase. Froude has left us a picture of Newman's bearing in conversation.

> He, when we met him, spoke to us about subjects of the day, of literature, of public persons and incidents, of everything which was generally interesting. He seemed always to be better informed on common topics of conversation than any one else who was present. He was never con-

descending with us, never didactic or authoritative; but what he said carried conviction along with it. When we were wrong he knew why we were wrong, and excused our mistakes to ourselves while he set us right. Perhaps his supreme merit as a talker was that he never tried to be witty or to say striking things. Ironical he could be, but not ill-natured. Not a malicious anecdote was ever heard from him. Prosy he could not be. He was lightness itself—the lightness of elastic strength—and he was interesting because he never talked for talking's sake, but because he had something real to say.[20]

Newman's manners are the key to his prose, and to that of Matthew Arnold also. For this purpose we need go no further, in amplification of Froude, than to Clough's oblique description of them in a description of Emerson, who was then on a visit to Oxford:

Everybody liked him. . . . He is the quietest, plainest, unobtrusivest man possible—will talk but will rarely *discourse* to more than a single person—and wholly declines "roaring." . . . Some people thought him very like Newman. But his manner is much simpler.[21]

Newman managed his elaborate simplicity with deftness. His grace was crisp. But his horror of being "abrupt" was as strong as his horror of being pompous. His walk was as near to a swift gliding as feet and cassock could make it. We know that he never raised his voice, relying on his audience's intent wish to catch what he was saying for his power of reaching them. Over the course of his long life he said much about writing, and all of it penetrates deep. I need quote only two of his remarks.

When J. B. Mozley was embarking on his first article for the *British Critic*, Newman, his former tutor and editor of the magazine, advised him about the sort of prose he ought to write: "In what you write do not be too essayish: i.e., do not begin, 'Of all the virtues which adorn the human breast!'—be somewhat conversational, and take a jump into your subject. But on the other hand avoid abruptness, or pertness. Be *easy* and take the mean—and now you have full directions how to write."[22] (The last remark is jocular—Newman never liked assuming authority, even when he possessed it *ex officio* or by virtue of his genius.) Then there is his description of the notes to his translation of Athanasius: "They are written *pro re natâ*, capriciously, or at least arbitrarily, with matter that the writer happens to have at hand, or knows where to find, and are composed in what may be called an undress, conversational style. . . ."[23] The metaphor was academic—on ordinary occasions a Doctor of Theology wore an M.A. gown of black instead of his formal scarlet. Newman's style was often in "undress," if we recall how neat and commodious an M.A. gown is. He reserved a more formal style for such occasions as forbade the informal—as when he composed his towering "character" of God.[24] Those occasions were few and far between, but only because he chose to make them so. Most of his writing was *"pro re natâ"* because he could rely on the quality of his thinking whenever pen was set to paper. His thinking was a flowing spring which, in view of its source, justified itself in being just that, not needing to organise and formalise itself into "ornamental waters." Froude tells us how well Newman could think in conversation, but he preferred thinking, pen to paper: "I think best when I write. I cannot in the same way think when I speak. Some men are brilliant in conversation, others in public speaking, others find their minds act best when they have a pen in their hands."[25] When he wrote, however, he wrote as he would have spoken in conversation if he had come up to his own high standards for such speech. And if what he first wrote needed much correction—as it always did and which it always got —the changes were as much for the sake of grace of wording as of the revision of the thought.[26]

We can see the appropriateness of a conversational prose for the nineteenth century. That age looked to its writers for help in understanding the universe as it was then being found to be, and for encouragement to do the good deeds that were urgently required if bloody revolution were to be averted by the narrowing of the gap between the Two Nations. In that age of crisis those many who were puzzled and troubled looked to writers for help. They earnestly wanted to hear the opinions of men they honoured, men of genius, "heroes," and to have received them in prose of a formal style would have been chilling if not insulting. They wanted advice by word of mouth. Literature was constantly spoken of at this time as a voice. At the best it was an actual voice, for many of the great writers performed on platforms as lecturers. Even as lecturers they spoke conversational prose, and when their words were available only in printed pamphlet or book, conversational prose was even more welcome. Conversational prose was the nearest thing to the heard human voice.

III

Newman's sister Harriett noted that those who admired him came to write like him. That was Arnold's double fate—we have recently had a thorough examination of the long master-pupil relationship from Professor DeLaura,[27] on the score both of manner and matter (Professor DeLaura goes into the inspiration Arnold found in Newman's ideas not only on culture but, more strangely, on religion). Arnold himself was proud to acknowledge the two-fold debt, which, he confessed, people had noticed.[28] What mainly concerns us here is his debt for authorial personality since this had its effect on the wording as well as the matter of Arnold's prose.

Arnold tried to be as like Newman as possible without ceasing to be himself. He came to think that he was more like him than Newman could allow.[29] That he could think so showed how little he understood Newman, who was a churchman first and last and wholly, and who had even doubted if Arnold's father was a Christian. Arnold was spared a sharp reply such as Newman made on occasion, when his urbanity was simply so much polish on the blade. Arnold liked wielding the rapier more than Newman did. There was relish in his reference to "the controversial life we all lead,"[30] whereas Newman lamented that the age afforded no time for *"quiet* thought."[31]

And yet Arnold found in Newman's occasional sharpness the inch he extended into an ell. The manner of writing sharply he learned mainly from certain small things of Newman, the chief of which was the series of seven letters printed anonymously in *The Times* during February 1841, and soon collected in pamphlet form as *The Tamworth Reading Room.* They show Newman at the peak of his brilliance—when he found occasion to quote from them in the *Essay in Aid of a Grammar of Assent* thirty years later, he ascribed to them "a freshness and force which I cannot now command."[32] Arnold knew these letters well, as we learn from the quotations from them entered into his notebooks. In them Newman came near to cutting a dash—anonymously, except for those who knew his authorship. Here is the opening of the sixth Letter to serve as a sample of the conversational writing that attracted Arnold: "People say to me, that it is but a dream to suppose that Christianity should regain the organic power in human society which once it possessed. I cannot help that; I never said it could." And which Arnold adopted. This comes towards the close of the "Function of Criticism at the Present Time":

> But stop, some one will say; all this talk is of no practical use to us whatever; this criticism of yours is not what we have in our minds when we speak of criticism; when we speak of critics and criticism, we mean critics and criticism of the current English literature of the day; when you offer to tell criticism its function, it is to this criticism that we expect you to address yourself. I am sorry for it, for I am afraid I must disappoint these expectations.[33]

And so on. The likeness to conversational speech is shown in little by Arnold's preference, which he shared with Newman, for beginning his paragraphs—let alone his sentences—with abrupt monosyllables. In this same essay five begin with "But," three with the conjunctive "For," and one each with "Nay," "Or," "Still," and "Again." In the Academies essay two paragraphs begin with the exclamation "Well," one being a "Well, then," and the other "Well, but." And in the passage about Ruskin I quoted earlier, Arnold's comment, it will be recalled, began with "Now, really, . . ."

Arnold designed his authorial personality to be striking, and his prose to match—a thoughtful critic must have pleased him by describing his style in 1883 as "perhaps, more striking than that of almost any other writer at the present time."[34] In his first prose piece Arnold was striking partly by being superior. He aired his intellectual superiority in such runs of wording as these: "What is *not* interesting, is . . . ," and " 'The poet', it is said, and by an apparently intelligent critic . . ." (in reprinting, Arnold dropped the insulting "apparently"), which is followed by "Now this view I believe to be completely false" (where the "Now" is an aggravation); a little later comes "And why is this? Simply because . . . ," and "No assuredly, it is not, it never can be so"; and again: "A host of voices will indignantly rejoin . . ."; and still again: "For we must never forget . . ." (he uses "we" but the guiltily forgetful reader knows at whom the finger is pointing). These things are more wholly wording than matter—they exhibit the manner of the egoist living in an age of controversy. That manner exists also in the many conversational intensives that Pater would have reckoned "surplusage"—"very," "signal," "very signal," "quite," "really," "profoundly." Along with these intensives go the vivid slang words, chief among which was "adequate," a term he had learned at Oxford.[35] Near to slang are other informalities Newman had given him the taste for—homely expressions like "got talked of" and homely imagery, such as (to draw on the "Literary Influence of Academies"): "that was a dream which will not bear being pulled about too roughly," and "We like to be suffered to lie comfortably in the old straw of our habits, especially of our intellectual habits." I may also note that, like Newman, Arnold prefers that when he strikes out an important phrase it shall be quiet rather than brilliant, as Carlyle's and Ruskin's mainly were—quiet phrases like "the dialogue of the mind with itself" (from the 1853 Preface) and "doing as one likes" (a chapter heading from *Culture and Anarchy*).

Slang, homely and quiet phrases, and homely imagery combine two qualities that Arnold liked to combine—the unassuming and the striking. He liked to blend two opposed æsthetic constituents, which can be variously described. His sentences are both suave and obstructed, smooth and attitudinising, flowing and striking, urbane and barbarous. They have as much of each kind as can coexist in a state of blendedness. They move easily, but among carefully placed obstacles. Newman described the gentleman as one who "never inflicts pain," and who "carefully avoids whatever may cause a jar or a jolt." Arnold's prose has it both ways by alternating long stretches of the gentleman with a flash here and there of the *enfant terrible*. He gives jars and jolts but so deliberately that we accept them as forming part of an individual version of the gentlemanly. To read him is to watch a performance of one who comes near to inflicting pain either without actually doing so, or with ointment so smartly applied that the sting melts away. Later on I shall qualify this description a little, but it is true in the main. The reader is confident that the writer knows where he is going, whatever bundles of sub-clauses, elaborate adverbs and detachable phrases are thrust into his open arms as he moves ahead. It may have been partly this spikiness of Arnold's that led R. H. Hutton to characterise his prose as "crystal," that of Newman's being "liquid."

Take as a handy instance of all this that note Arnold appended to the first paragraph of the "Function of Criticism at the Present Time" when it was collected in his *Essays in Criticism*:

> I cannot help thinking that a practice, common in England during the last century, and still followed in France, of printing a notice of this kind,—a notice by a competent critic,—to serve as an introduction to an

eminent author's works, might be revived among us with advantage. To introduce all succeeding editions of Wordsworth, Mr. Shairp's notice might, it seems to me, excellently serve; it is written from the point of view of an admirer, nay, of a disciple, and that is right; but then the disciple must be also, as in this case he is, a critic, a man of letters, not, as too often happens, some relation or friend with no qualification for his task except affection for his author.[36]

Here there are two sentences with eleven interpolations of one sort and another.

That note also serves to illustrate another characteristic of Arnold's wording. Its flowingness is often secured by the use of the lubricating devices I have already mentioned—"I cannot help thinking," "it is permitted that," and the rest. Spikiness exists in the run of the words in "might, it seems to me, excellently serve," where we not only have the severing of auxiliary from verb but the wide severing across a clause and an adverb—an adverb that is itself spiky because of its smart latinity and ticking polysyllables. In the second paragraph of the same essay we get: "should, for greater good of society, voluntarily doom."

The main means of Arnold's strikingness is this sort of unusual word-order. In the first paragraph of the essay I am drawing my instance from we have the striking word-order of "for now many years," but the expected word-order is often rearranged if not to that degree of strikingness:

Many objections have been made to a proposition which, in some remarks of mine on translating Homer, I ventured to put forth; a proposition about criticism, and its importance at the present day. I said: "Of the literature of France and Germany, as of the intellect of Europe in general, the main effort, for now many years, has been a critical effort; the endeavour, in all branches of knowledge, theology, philosophy, history, art, science, to see the object as in itself it really is." I added, that owing to the operation in English literature of certain causes, "almost the last thing for which one would come to English literature is just that very thing which now Europe most desires,—criticism;" and that the power and value of English literature was thereby impaired.[37]

Sometimes his inversions become ludicrous—sometimes he does *not* avoid paining us! I have noted elsewhere that

his article "The Bishop and the Philosopher" (*Essays, Letters and Reviews*, coll. and ed. F. Neiman, 1960, Cambridge, Mass., pp. 45 ff.) has one paragraph beginning "The little-instructed Spinoza's work could not unsettle . . ." and another beginning "Unction Spinoza's work has not. . . ." If he had been more conversant with Dickens's novels he might have been warned by Mrs. Micawber's example: "'We came,' repeated Mrs. Micawber, 'and saw the Medway. My opinion of the coal trade on that river, is, that it may require talent, but that it certainly requires capital. Talent, Mr. Micawber has; capital, Mr. Micawber has not . . .'" (*David Copperfield,* chapter xvii).[38]

And Arnold can pain us by making a sentence carry too many weights—as in this from one of his ecclesiastical essays:

> But as it is the truth of its Scriptural Protestantism which in Puritanism's eyes especially proves the truth of its Scriptural church-order which has this Protestantism, and the falsehood of the Anglican church-order which has much less of it, to abate the confidence of the Puritans in their Scriptural Protestantism is the first step towards their union, so much to be desired, with the national Church.[39]

A small instance of his deliberate clumsiness comes at the opening of this same essay: "I daresay this is so; only, remembering Spinoza's maxim that the two great banes of humanity are self-conceit and the laziness coming from self-conceit, I think. . . ." Surely it would have been better to write "coming from it" or "that comes of it," better because we stress the ending of a phrase and so here stress the unimportant word, the repeated "self-conceit." Arnold did not make enough use of our pronouns.

This clumsy but deliberate repetition introduces the most notorious item in Arnold's method of wording—his liking for repeating a word or phrase over and over again. For instance, having designed "regularity, uniformity, precision, balance" as a description of the prose achieved by the eighteenth century, he repeats it six times in the course of one (long) paragraph. Such repetition of invented terms is part of his method, but ill-advisedly so. He goes to ungentlemanly lengths in repeating them—his insistence has something of the *entêté* about it. This was a mistake Newman would not have made. Very occasionally Newman did repeat a word mercilessly, as for instance here:

> Again, as to the Ministerial Succession being a form, and adherence to it a form, it can only be called a form because we do not see its effects; did anything *visible* attend it, we should no longer call it a form. Did a

miracle always follow a baptism or a return into the Church, who would any longer call it a form? that is, we call it a form, only so long as we refuse to walk by *faith*, which dispenses with things visible. Faith sees things not to be forms, if commanded, which seem like forms; it realizes consequences. Men ignorant in the sciences would predict no result from chemical and the like experiments; they would count them a form and a pretence. What is prayer but a form? that is, who (to speak generally) sees any thing come of it? But we believe it, and so are blessed. In what sense is adherence to the Church a form in which prayer is not also? The benefit of the one is not seen, nor of the other; the one will not profit the ungodly and careless, nor will the other; the one is commanded in Scripture, so is the other. Therefore, to say that Church-union is a form, is no disparagement of it; forms are the very food of faith.[40]

It is one thing, however, to repeat a monosyllable, and another to repeat a mouthful. Arnold's repeated things are often whole phrases. It may be that his habit was partly encouraged by his love for Homer. He knew the old epics more closely than any other text, except the Bible—in his lectures on translating them he mentions that for two years they were never out of his hands. Homer sometimes repeats a word of great length, and it happens that a note in Pope's translation provides a comment on Arnold's practice. Pope's seventh note on *Iliad* xix reads:

VERSE 197 [of his translation]. *The stern* Aeacides *replies.*] The *Greek* Verse is

Τὸν δ' ἀπαμειξόμενος πζοσέφη πόδας ὠκὺς 'Αχιλλεύς.

Which is repeated very frequently throughout the Iliad. It is a very just Remark of a *French* Critick, that what makes it so much taken notice of, is the rumbling Sound and Length of the Word ἀπαμειξόμενος: [*replies*]: This is so true, that if in a Poem or Romance of the same Length as the Iliad, we should repeat *The Hero answer'd*, full as often, we should never be sensible of that Repetition. And if we are not shock'd at the like Frequency of those Expressions in the Æneid, *sic ore refert, talia voce refert, talia dicta dabat, vix ea fatus erat*, &c. it is only because the Sound of the *Latin* Words does not fill the Ear like that of the *Greek* ἀπαμειξόμενος.[41]

Pope then proceeds to discuss the modern preference for avoiding the repetition of words, especially of polysyllabic words, and decides that

"Either of these Practices is good, but the Excess of either vicious." In Arnold the repetitions are therefore vicious.

There is no offence, however, in what is as common in Arnold as his repeated phrases—his use of long words derived from Greek or Latin, and which if they are repeated, are not noticed as being so. They combine with the other spikinesses to enliven the general flowingness. To draw on a few pages at the beginning of the same essay on Academies we get "prominently," "pre-eminence," "nascent," "instrument," which are sprinkled here and there among the shorter Saxon words that carry the main burden of the thinking. Once Arnold ended an essay with one of these consciously favoured words. In the course of this same essay on Academies he invented a new sense for the epithet "retarding," the sense of slackening the pace of *intellectual* advance, and so can rely on the last word of his essay to come as a climax:

> He will do well constantly to try himself in respect of these, steadily to widen his culture, severely to check in himself the provincial spirit; and he will do this the better the more he keeps in mind that all mere gorifi-cation by ourselves of ourselves or our literature, in the strain of what, at the beginning of these remarks, I quoted from Lord Macaulay, is both vulgar, and, besides being vulgar, retarding.[42]

What was desiderated for the conversational style may be described as "lightness." It may come as a surprise to some that the word "light" was one of those greatly favoured in the mid-nineteenth century. Froude, we recall, called Newman "lightness itself," and Arnold begins one of his greatest poems with

Light flows our war of mocking words . . .

When his *Essays* came out he hoped that Frederick Locker-Lampson would think its Preface "done with that *light hand* we have both of us such an affection for."[43] They were trying to make the English language more like music composed for that still fairly new instrument, the piano. Gide was to describe French prose as like a piano without pedals. We know how much Arnold admired French prose, but there is something about the English language that prevents its sounding like the amputated instrument of Gide's comparison. Newman and Arnold wanted their prose to be like a piano *with* a sustaining pedal, playing music—shall we say as like the favourite parts of Schubert's as possible, light, airy, flowing, wiry, pale-coloured, preferring to tinkle rather than to pound.

I have said that we make an æsthetic response to the personality shown in writing and that we judge it by the exercise of the intellect. Our æsthetic response to Arnold's authorial personality is one of pleasure tempered by intellectual doubt as to whether or not its pleasantness for the twentieth century was pleasantness for the nineteenth. For some nineteenth-century readers it was decidedly that—Arnold had his numerous admirers. Those admirers, however, were already, we guess, in possession of the sweetness and light he was recommending. To the "elphantine main body" of the bourgeoisie that Arnold was out to transform, he cannot have meant very much. He sometimes used the term that Hazlitt had introduced into the critical vocabulary—"tact." But how little of it he himself exercised! *Culture and Anarchy* was met with critics who saw its author as a mere æsthete looking rather out of place in the daily throng of English business: Henry Sidgwick, for instance, ridiculed him as a person "shuddering aloof from the rank exhalations of vulgar enthusiasm, and holding up the pouncet-box of culture betwixt the wind and his nobility."[44] They might have stomached his urbanity if it had been like that of Newman—an, as it were, unconscious urbanity. They could not take the urbanity of one who postured. It seems that he made a big strategical mistake. The writer who had most effect on English culture was William Morris. For him urbanity was fluff and nonsense—unlike Arnold, he was once mistaken for a sea-captain. But if Arnold was bent on being urbane, he ought to have kept his urbanity more like Newman's, which always seemed to exist by right of second nature.

NOTES

1. *Appreciations*, London, 1889, p. 87.
2. *The George Eliot Letters*, ed. G. S. Haight, London, 1954-56, V, 455. My word "atmosphere" covers what she specifies as "false principles of criticism and false conceptions of life."
3. *Table Talk and Omniana*, Oxford, 1917, p. 256.
4. Ibid., pp. 255f.
5. *The Complete Prose Works of Matthew Arnold*, ed. R. H. Super, Ann Arbor, 1960–, III, 156.

6. Ibid., I, 6.

7. Ibid., III, 251.

8. Ibid., III, 252.

9. *The Poems and Prose Remains of Arthur Hugh Clough*, London, 1869, I, 330-31.

10. *The Six Chief Lives from Johnson's "Lives of the Poets,"* London, 1878, pp. xvii-xviii.

11. *Letters of Gerard Manley Hopkins to Robert Bridges*, ed. C. C. Abbott, London, ed. 1955, p. 291.

12. *The Works,* ed. W. Hamilton, London, 1863, I, 421.

13. "The Methods of Description in Eighteenth- and Nineteenth-Century Poetry" in *Restoration and Eighteenth-Century Literature: Essays in Honor of Alan Dugold McKillop*, Chicago, 1963.

14. R. A. Wilmott, *Pleasures, Objects, and Advantages of Literature: A Discourse*, London, 1851, pp. 130f. In the second edition, which followed a year later, Wilmott revised the second of these sentences, replacing the semi-colon after "reversed" by a comma and adding "and" to what followed. It was a generous concession! I might add that his publisher, a Thomas Bosworth of Regent Street, made a pretty thing of the book, employing Caslon Old Face with all its resources of long s's and ornamental ligatures—as Smith, Elder did for Thackeray's *Henry Esmond* in 1852. It is presumably by accident that both Wilmott's book and *Esmond* are bound in the same drab cloth with paper labels. Wilmott's prose is made to look more affected by the get-up of the book, Thackeray's appropriately more Addisonian.

15. Newman recalled that Hurrell Froude considered that the prose Newman was writing as a young man "had a vulgar and rhetorical look about it." *Apologia*, ed. W. Ward, London, 1913, p. 156.

16. *The Twickenham Edition of the Poems of Alexander Pope*, ed. J. E. Butt, London, 1939-61, I, 9.

17. *Social Statics,* London, ed. 1850, p. vi.

18. *Further Letters of . . . Hopkins*, ed. C. C. Abbott, London, 1938, p. 232.

19. *Letters and Correspondence of John Henry Newman*, ed. Anne Mozley, London, 1891, I, 444.

20. "The Oxford Counter-Reformation," in *Short Studies*, new ed., London, 1891, IV, 282-3.

21. *The Correspondence of Arthur Hugh Clough*, ed. F. L. Mulhauser, London, 1957, I, 215.

22. *Letters . . . of . . . Newman*, ed. Mozley, II, 256.

23. *Select Treatises of St. Athanasius . . .* , London, ed. 1888, I, viii.

24. *Discourses on the Scope and Nature of University Education*, Dublin, 1852, discourse II.

25. Letter of 12 March 1871, Edward Bellasis, *Memorials of Mr. Serjeant Bellasis*, London, ed. 1923, p. 151*n*.

26. There is an account of the corrections of the manuscript and printed text of *The Tamworth Reading Room* in an edition of that work in the University of London Library done as an M.A. thesis by Miss Nina Burgiss.

27. David J. DeLaura, "Matthew Arnold and John Henry Newman. The 'Oxford Sentiment' and the Religion of the Future," The University of Texas, *Studies in Literature and Language,* VI, Supplement 1965.

28. Letter to Newman, 29 Nov. 1871, in *Unpublished Letters,* ed. Arnold Whitridge, New Haven, 1923, p. 57.

29. Ibid., p. 59.

30. *Works of Matthew Arnold,* ed. Super, III, 272.

31. *Tracts for the Times,* Oxford and London, 1833-41, No. 41, p. 9.

32. *Essay in Aid of a Grammar of Assent,* London, ed. 1895, p. 91.

33. [Arnold quotation] *Works of Matthew Arnold,* ed. Super, III, 283.

34. Samuel Waddington, *Arthur Hugh Clough,* London, 1883, p. 132.

35. See G. and K. Tillotson, *Mid-Victorian Studies,* London, 1965, p. 134.

36. *Works of Matthew Arnold,* ed. Super, III, 258.

37. Ibid.

38. *Augustan Studies,* London, 1961, p. 118n.

39. "Protestantism and the Church of England," *Cornhill Magazine,* XXI (Jan.-June 1870), 200.

40. *Parochial Sermons,* London, 1834-42, III, 213-14.

41. *The Iliad of Homer,* London, 1715-20, V, 183.

42. [Arnold quotation] *Works of Matthew Arnold,* ed. Super, III, 257.

43. Augustine Birrell, *Frederick Locker-Lampson,* London, 1920, p. 127.

44. "The Prophet of Culture," *Macmillan's Magazine,* XVI (Aug. 1867), 280.

THE USE AND ABUSE OF CARLYLESE

GEORGE LEVINE

THE ATTEMPT to turn Carlyle into an "artist," to preserve his writings as literature, would have been for him the worst of all imaginable fates. Carlyle did not write for all time but for those "latter days" when things seemed to be going from bad to worse, when the whole of his society seemed preparing to shoot Niagara. The history of his reputation during the first half of the twentieth century shows that Carlyle had—in this respect—little to worry about. The mass of doctoral dissertations written about him in the Nazi Germany of the 'thirties suggests that he was admired more for his philosophy than for his art. And in the English-speaking world, the revulsion from him and from the "hero-worship" with which he is so closely linked simply continues a tradition he recognized in his own time—the tradition of rejecting him precisely because of what he stood for. Even some of the recent tentative attempts to restore him to respectability have avoided making claims for him as an artist. Raymond Williams finds in the early essays a sensitivity to the difficulties of English society that partially redeems Carlyle from the failures of his later years. In other words, Carlyle can be saved insofar as we can find in his works intelligent and responsible criticism of society. His tragedy, Williams says, is "that a genuine insight, a genuine vision, should be dragged down by the very situation, the very structure of relationships, to which it was opposed, until a civilizing insight became in its operation barbarous."[1]

It may be that Carlyle can only be saved by finding humanity and freshness of insight in his doctrines. Certainly, it seems a more reasonable and important way than that which so many of his contemporaries took. When they knew they would not listen to what Carlyle had to say but could not ignore how much he had inspired them in their early years, they joined a kind of conspiracy to emasculate him through praise: he may not be right, but he is poetic. Here is Frederic Harrison: "But

though the *French Revolution* is not to be accepted as historical authority, it is profoundly stimulating and instructive, when we look on it as a
lyrical apologue." When Harrison agrees with Carlyle, he tends to play
down the poetry. *Past and Present,* he says, is a great book which would
"impress us much more than it does, were it not already become the very
basis of all sincere thought about social problems and the future condition
of industry."[2] It should be noted, moreover, that where the agreement is
incomplete, Carlyle could always be called "sincere" if not correct.

When the generation that Carlyle had inspired decided he was not to
be trusted, they tended to make the division between the substance and
the style almost absolute. This is already clear in the quotation from Harrison. It can, perhaps, be more precisely seen in John Morley's remarks
about Carlyle:

> the writer who in these days has done more than anybody else to fire
> men's hearts with a feeling for right and an eager desire for social ac-
> tivity, has with deliberate contempt thrust away from him the only
> instruments by which we can make sure what right is, and that our so-
> cial action is wise and effective. A born poet, only wanting perhaps a
> clearer feeling for form and a more delicate spiritual self-possession, to
> have added another name to the illustrious catalogue of English singers,
> he has been driven by the impetuosity of his sympathies to attack the
> scientific side of social questions in an imaginative and highly emotional
> manner. Depth of benevolent feeling is unhappily no proof of fitness for
> handling complex problems, and a fine sense of the picturesque is no
> more a qualification for dealing effectively with the difficulties of an
> old society, than the composition of Wordsworth's famous sonnet on
> Westminster Bridge was any reason for supposing that the author would
> have made a competent Commissioner of Works.[3]

The fate of Carlyle's writing, as suggested here, corresponds to the fate
of literature in general in a practical world of increasing specialization.
Imagination and personal insight are fine for singing, but have nothing
to do with the resolution or even formulation of practical problems. And
since Carlyle was absolutely committed to writing about practical problems, he could only be saved by readers who disregarded what he was
talking about and attended to the way he talked—who regarded him as a
poet.

"Poetry?" he exclaimed in "Shooting Niagara and After?" (1867) "It is not pleasant singing that we want, but wise and earnest speaking:— 'Art,' 'High Art,' etc., are very fine and ornamental, but only to persons sitting at their ease: to persons still wrestling with deadly chaos, and still fighting for dubious existence, they are a mockery rather."[4] What had Carlyle to do with "Art," and what sort of perversity could attempt to rescue him from what he would have to regard now as his honorable failure in order to seat him on Parnassus with his garrulous enemy Macaulay, or on the rather higher levels of the "flimsy, foolish set" of novelists who scribbled while England slipped into the rapids?

In the past it was the perversity of the critic who disagreed with him but could not help admiring him. Now it is the perversity of the academic critic who can see that all along Carlyle did regard himself as an artist— albeit a special kind of artist. For Carlyle there was, after all, a "Genuine Art" to be distinguished from the merely decorative. "Genuine 'Art,' " he said, in that same despairing essay, "in all times is a higher synonym for God Almighty's Facts,—which come to us direct from Heaven, but in so abstruse a condition, and cannot be read at all till the better intellect interpret them.) . . . all real 'Art' is definable as Fact, or say as the disimprisoned 'Soul of Fact'; any other kind of Art, Poetry or High Art is quite idle in comparison" (pp. 24-5).

For the perverse academic critic, this statement about Art, so solemnly old-fashioned and unreasonable, nevertheless might suggest a more useful approach to Carlyle as a single and undivided entity, than the ideologues or aesthetes (both of whom tend to separate matter from manner) have hitherto provided. Obviously there are two central problems in criticism of Carlyle as a writer. The first is that his prose is so violently mannered and extravagant that it seems unjustifiable on any grounds; the second is that once you get past the prose you still have to cope with the ideas and these are now largely untenable. We know how Carlyle answered the first difficulty: "Do you reckon," he wrote in answer to John Sterling's criticism, "this really a time for Purism of Style; or that Style (mere dictionary Style) has much to do with the worth or unworth of a Book? I do not: with whole ragged battalions of Scott's-Novel Scotch, with Irish, German, French, and even Newspaper Cockney (when 'Literature' is little other than a Newspaper) storming in on us, and the whole structure of our Johnsonian English breaking up from its foundations,—revolution *there* as visible as anywhere else!"[5] In a way, this answer is what one would expect from a man who did not care about his "Art." On the other hand, it reveals that craft and deliberation lay behind the style and suggests that the style may, after all, be functional. Whether it is functional is one of the crucial problems with which this essay will be concerned. More important, however, given the amount of work that has already gone into consideration of "Carlylese," it will be necessary to consider the second problem—how to cope with the irrational perversity of Carlyle's ideas.

If Carlyle is right, if Genuine Art is an art of Fact, the answer to the first difficulty will help provide the answer to the second. If as an artist Carlyle did present God's fact—present, that is, a comprehensible vision of a hitherto unrecognized reality—he did it through a genuinely imaginative act of perception and of effectively structuring language. Carlyle's view of the world as thoroughly organic would have made it impossible for him to separate substance from manner; and, indeed, where he speculates about poetry in *Heroes and Hero-Worship* he justifies the music of poetry by saying that it reflects a genuine harmony outside of itself— the music of the spheres, as it were. He justifies his style by arguing that it expresses revolutionary thought in a revolutionary way and is therefore itself revolutionary. It seems that we cannot have Carlyle half way—as writer or thinker. He is the one because he is also the other.

I

The first step in any attempt to come to terms with Carlyle's style is, necessarily, to show that the mannerism is a reflex of the substance, that the style is the best possible means for the expression of the ideas, attitudes, and sensed relation to audience with which Carlyle worked. A defense of Carlyle in this way can be found in an altogether unexpected quarter. Henry James, the stylist of nuance, and artificer of elaborate and —from what would certainly have been Carlyle's point of view—trivial fictions, once said, "Carlyle's extemporized, empirical style seems to us the very substance of his thought. If the merit of style lies in complete correspondence with the feeling of the writer, Carlyle's is one of the best."[6] To be sure, James concludes with an inevitable Jamesian paradox and qualification: "It is not defensible, but it is victorious." But if Carlyle's style is the substance of his thought and feeling, it is more than merely "defensible." James's implicit assumption that Carlyle's style triumphs over the lack of craftsmanship is misguided. Carlyle was a very

careful workman.[7] The extemporized appearance of it (except, one assumes, in the letters) is the product of careful deliberation rather than an
unconsidered dash at paper by a man overheated with passion. The passion one recognizes in the prose is, undoubtedly, genuine, but it is usually
also—and obviously—controlled and directed, at least in his more serious
and ambitious works.

The problem, in any case, is not to examine Carlyle's intention and
preformulated strategies, but to see how the prose works, to see if in fact
James is right and that the style is the appropriate vehicle of the ideas
and feelings that inform it. To do this I want to turn here briefly to a
passage from one of the essays in which Carlylese, though shaping itself
into the form that in the later works became almost a parody of itself, was
not fully formed; by so doing I hope to be able to work out fairly precisely
how important the fully formed style was for the expression of Carlyle's
characteristic attitudes. In "Signs of the Times" (1829), stylistically restricted both because it is fairly early and because it was written for the
same *Edinburgh Review* in which Macaulay was making his name and
for which the spokesman of the Whig aristocracy regularly wrote, we can
see early and mature Carlyle at work together. The ideas are those that
he was to develop for the rest of his career. The manner is, however, less
radical and violent. The essay begins in this way:

> It is no very good symptom either of nations or individuals, that they
> deal much in vaticination. Happy men are full of the present, for its
> bounty suffices them; and wise men also, for its duties engage them. Our
> grand business undoubtedly is, not to *see* what lies dimly at a distance,
> but to *do* what lies clearly at hand. (XXVI, 56)

The pervasive revulsion from theorizing and speculation accompanied
by an alternative insistence on work is immediately recognizable as Carlylean. The form, however, in its extraordinarily neat and rhythmic antitheses, is not what one expects from Carlyle and obviously represents
a continuation of an eighteenth-century mode, a mode spectacularly exploited by Macaulay. Moreover, in its very neatness it implies a rational-
ism that Carlyle spent the best part of his career attacking and that is
implicitly attacked in the passage itself. In one respect, the style here is a
just expression of the vision implied; but in another, the style is in fact
struggling against the ideas and attitudes it is meant to convey.

The central and obvious point of the passage is to set up a dichotomy

between two ways of settling contemporary difficulties. In this respect, it
is all of a piece with the constant tendency of Carlyle's vision—to see the
world as divided between good and evil, right and wrong. Carlyle's essentially dualist position does not change throughout his career. Teufelsdröckh will later exclaim, "Close thy Byron; open thy Goethe"; "Love not
pleasure, Love God." There are, as Carlyle sees it, only two possibilities
for every man and every nation. If you do the one, you must reject the
other. And yet, at his best, Carlyle manages to avoid the impression that
his vision is thus simplistic; the particular passage under discussion does
not in fact equal Carlyle's fully worked out sense of the world and this
because its style is artificially limiting, imposing formal bounds beyond
which Carlyle needed to grow to become the enormously influential
writer he eventually was.

In Carlyle's canon there are certainly hundreds of passages which express, in one way or another, the dualism implicit in this passage. It will
be useful to examine at least one such fully Carlylean passage to see what
Carlylese does that the inherited eighteenth-century form could not do.
Here is a characteristic passage from *Past and Present* (1842):

> Yes, friends: Hero-kings and a whole world not unheroic,—there lies
> the port and happy haven, towards which, through all these stormtost
> seas, French Revolutions, Chartisms, Manchester Insurrections, that
> make the heart sick in these bad days, the Supreme Powers are driving
> us. On the whole, blessed be the Supreme Powers, stern as they are!
> Towards that haven will we, O friends; let all true men, with what of
> faculty is in them, bend valiantly, incessantly, with thousandfold en-
> deavour, thither, thither! There, or else in the Ocean-abysses, it is very
> clear to me, we shall arrive.[8]

The alternatives are once more clearly expressed—the heroic world or the
Ocean-abysses. But the differences in tone, structure, and diction are
immediately apparent. Here we have pure Carlylese.

The qualities of this pasage that draw attention to themselves are
very different from those that make the earlier passage striking. In opposition to intellectual neatness one finds here a passionate and energetic
movement that makes the final antithesis ("There"—"Ocean-abysses")
dramatic rather than witty. Moreover, the antithesis (though Carlyle is
not averse, even in his later career, to using sparingly the balance one

finds in the "Signs of the Times" passage) is clearly not of the balanced kind we expect from eighteenth-century prose. For the sake of the drama of the passage, "Ocean-abysses" carries far more weight in the final sentence than "There." But within the structure of the complete paragraph, the "Ocean-abysses" are outweighed. The paragraph moves with great energy away from the Ocean to the "port and happy haven." It moves, through the central "stormtost" activity of the Ocean, "Towards that haven . . . thither, thither!" This dramatic pattern is repeated, as I shall try to show, in each important sentence. And then, as the strenuous labor of "all true men" seems to have borne us to the haven, the "Ocean-abysses" dramatically remind us of the consequences of not undertaking the struggle.

The dualism, then, is dramatically rather than intellectually presented. The finality of the strangely ordered final sentence pronounces a kind of doom as it makes its threat. Notice what non-Carlylean structure would likely have made of the same words: "It is very clear to me that we shall arrive there or else in the Ocean-abysess." The consecutiveness of the normal English structure deprives the sentence both of the sense of struggle implicit in the original's fragmentation and then of the finality of the last phrase—"we shall arrive." Typically, in this passage the Carlylean inversions of normal word order serve to create a surface tension that reflects the very substance of the passage's meaning. The insistence on *doing,* and on the difficulty of doing, explicit in the penultimate sentence, emerges strenuously in the laboring of the syntax; and the uttter disregard of logical antithesis and balance is justified because Carlyle is not so much thinking as acting. The drama and the passion of Carlyle's style are, then, part of its meaning.

But the drama is only possible because Carlyle sees what he is discussing not in logical but in metaphorical terms. The alternative is not conceived as dictatorship or disorder but as hero-populated harbor or chaotic ocean. Thus, the passage in fact describes a voyage to a harbor, and it envisages what the voyage will be like and what it will require of the crew. The great eruptions of disorder that Carlyle knew actually become the "stormtost seas"; all these eruptions are turned into plural forms to suggest that they are not merely isolated instances. The effort to come through these seas will necessarily be strenuous, and the strenuousness is reflected in the interesting assonating and alliterative line, broken into very small fragments: "let all true men, with what of faculty is in them, bend valiantly, incessantly, with thousandfold endeavour, thither, thither!"

Although I greatly distrust analysis of sound patterns as a guide to meaning (how easy, for instance, it would be to say that the difficulty of pronouncing all those "th's" reflects the strenuousness of the endeavour), it is hard to resist the implication that lines such as this suggest a very conscious artist. And the accumulation of the "e" vowel, the echoing of the "n" sound, and the finally culminating "thi" pattern in "thither" do seem to enforce the sense of direction impelling the voyager forward. The anti-artist Carlyle has needed to resort to the techniques of the artist.

The central components of a poetic mode are here, however gross and lacking in subtlety one may feel that mode to be. The meaning is in the style and the style is fundamentally dramatic, metaphorical, rhythmic, rather than witty and abstract. It should be agreed, moreover, that the rhythms, at least, are much subtler and more functional here than are those of the first passage cited. The eighteenth-century pattern suggests a witty enforcement of a dualist pattern; the subtler pattern complicates while reasserting the dualism dramatically rather than intellectually.

It is worth proceeding further in examining the newly complicated dualism. Carlyle's style characteristically expresses dualism, in a way I have described elsewhere, by elaborating extensively on the aspects of the negative pole and then dramatically and emphatically destroying the elaboration by the assertion of a single, all-potent positive.[9] That basic pattern is present here, although because the passage is engaged in describing a struggle, the annihilation of the negative is not complete. The argument that it should be annihilated is, however, forcefully present in the style itself. The positive pole is presented first—"Hero-kings and a whole world not unheroic"—but the center of the paragraph immediately shifts to the "stormtost seas" which later become "Ocean-abysses." The most characteristic formulation is in the pluralizing, already referred to, of the various manifestations of the age's sickness—the "French Revolutions, Chartisms, Manchester Insurrections." The direction away from this multi-faceted evil is, however, single and insistent: "thither, thither!" Notice how the very sentence that introduces the evils is constructed to conquer them: "there lies the port and happy haven." The sentence moves, then, through the evil and brings us out the other side, assured that there "the Supreme Powers are driving us." The penultimate sentence of the paragraph, already discussed, has a similar shape and ends with the same affirmation of driving toward the haven—"thither." Although the paragraph does not settle for asserting the positive pole once and in one way, the impression of unity holds strongly against the chaos of the negative.

Carlyle's dualism, in fact, tends to be based on a vision of the world which sees evil manifested in endless variety, since evil is merely appearance and always finite, while the good is the single, indivisible, infinite fact of God—the reality that underlies all appearance. Goodness tends to be single, unchanging, and all-pervasive (it is always the port of the Hero-king towards which the passage moves); and Carlyle's favorite symbol for the unchanging single reality is the polar- or lode-star. As, for example, *Sartor Resartus* (1834) progresses towards a wider manifestation of the single underlying fact (the meaning of the "Clothes-philosophy") through the chaos of appearances, the Editor characteristically remarks "nor, let us hope, for all the fantastic Dream-Grottoes through which, as is our lot with Teufelsdröckh, he must wander, will there be wanting between whiles some twinkling of a steady Polar Star" (p. 206). This sentence would yield to almost precisely the same sort of analysis I have used on the passage from *Past and Present,* the "Dream-Grottoes" corresponding to the "Ocean-abysses," the "Polar Star" to the "Hero-kings' " haven. And the pattern here is the paradigmatic one of Teufelsdröckh's whole career, of the structure of *Sartor* (three-fold) and of *Past and Present* as well.

I would suggest, finally, that the *Past and Present* passage is informed by at least one more aspect of Carlyle's mature vision not present in the earlier one—the vision of the world as interconnected energy and movement. One of the clearest and most representatively Carlylean statements of this view comes in the *French Revolution* (1837):

> How true that there is nothing dead in this Universe; that what we call dead is only changed, its forces working in inverse order! "The leaf that lies rotting in moist winds," says one, "has still force; else how could it *rot?*" Our whole Universe is but an Infinite Complex of Forces; thousandfold, from Gravitation up to Thought and Will; man's Freedom environed with Necessity of Nature: in all which nothing at any moment slumbers, but all is forever awake and busy. The thing that lies isolated inactive thou shalt nowhere discover; seek everywhere, from

the granite mountain, slow-mouldering since Creation, to the passing cloud-vapour, to the living man; to the action, to the spoken word of man. (III, 102)

Carlylese regularly "evinces," as John Holloway has remarked, "a wild, passionate energy . . . disorderly and even chaotic, but leaving an indelible impression of life."[10] It is this "wild, passionate energy" that is usually taken to be the most characteristic general quality of Carlylese. But I would suggest that the disorderliness is more apparent than real (at least when Carlyle is working at his best) and that the wild, passionate energy is regularly directed to turn back in on itself and to rest upon the single immutable fact of God. This is so whether, in any given passage, that Fact be the port of Hero-kings, the Polar Star, or Life itself as the ultimate unchanging source of all energy. It is true that since Carlyle's whole way of seeing things rejects logical continuity, his greatest works give the impression of disorder. But if one examines the neatly organized *Edinburgh Review* essays, "Signs of the Times" and "Characteristics" (1831), both expounding in more and more characteristic ways the Carlylean vision, one finds that the organization is less effective in expressing this vision than the apparent disorder of *Sartor* or *Past and Present*.

Carlyle creates the impression of wild and passionate energy in several ways. We have already seen something of the effect of inversion of normal word order, of pluralizing of particular facts and events, of manipulation of patterns of sound. Another obvious device is coinage of compound words, suggesting the need to break through conventional means of expression; we have seen some of the less violent ones: Hero-kings, Ocean-abysses, Dream-Grottoes, cloud-vapour. Such words are usually linked to Carlyle's compulsion to work metaphorically and they seem to imply a kind of compression of large meanings into short compass. Moreover, Carlyle's prose tends to be clogged with allusions to facts, events, things. The passages I have chosen to discuss have many fewer such allusions than are typical, but the kind of thing I mean can be seen in the sequence "French Revolutions, Chartisms, Manchester Insurrections," or "The granite mountain, . . . passing cloud-vapour, . . . living man; . . . action, . . . spoken word."

Within the small compass of paragraphs or chapters it can, I think, be shown that the violence is part of a larger and coherent pattern, frequently a dramatic one. The violence and energy of the passage from the *French Revolution* can be seen to work in much the way the device of Teufelsdröckh's six paper bags works in *Sartor Resartus*. Those six bags, full of the chaos and leavings of Teufelsdröckh's life—notes, laundry-bills, records of dreams, Metaphysico-theological Disquisitions, street-advertisements—are somehow capable of giving in a symbolic or metaphorical way the essence of Teufelsdröckh's character. The bags are a chaos more complete than the chaos of the Clothes volume itself. Yet, "Over such a universal medley of high and low, of hot, cold, moist and dry, is [the Editor] here struggling (by union of like with like, which is Method) to build a firm Bridge for British-travellers" (p. 79). The assumption underlying this bridge-building is that all things are organically connected and that it doesn't ultimately make much difference what aspect of life one focuses on since every fact can be taken as another expression in the world of Space and Time of the great Fact that lies outside that world. In the *French Revolution* passage a similar assumption is at work and can be spotted in the key injunction, "seek everywhere." Wherever we seek—in the rotting leaf, the granite mountain, the cloud-vapour, man, and each of man's actions and words—we find the principle of life and energy. The whole great history makes clear that the source of this life and energy, whatever its violent expression in time, is in the unchanging truth of Carlyle's God. This vision tends to give to Carlyle's larger works a chaotic appearance; but his characteristic structure is that of theme-and-variations because whatever the particular subject he discusses he is always brought back to the single fact which gives life to his subject. The ultimate Carlylean dualism is between appearances and reality. He discusses the appearance, which takes on the qualities of life because of its relation to the reality, in order to get back to the reality. And all the energy of his prose is to bring him back to the still center, where the polar star, apparently only twinkling in the distance, is steadfast and glowing. Over the surging of the waves of the Ocean-abysses can be made out the happy haven of the port of the Hero-kings.[11]

II

The limitations of analysis are, however, obvious. Critics may find it increasingly easy to show by analysis that Carlyle's books and essays have their own justifiable kind of coherence, that Carlylese is not mere mannerism in the service of chaos but the most adequate expression of a particular vision; yet they will be hard-pressed in many instances to make serious claims for Carlyle's works. I would argue that many of the early essays, *Sartor Resartus,* the *French Revolution,* and *Past and Present* can survive on any terms. Analysis on a large scale of the kind I have been suggesting for a few short passages could suffice to demonstrate that these are stylistically and structurally interesting works of art. But what can analysis do for the later Carlyle, for the author of *Latter-Day Pamphlets* (1850), *The History of Frederick the Great* (1858-65), and "Shooting Niagara" (1867)? It may be that one has to settle for Raymond Williams's view that in these later works "a genuine insight" is dragged down, and that what is wrong with them is that the vision which lies behind them is no longer adequate. But in any case, analysis has not demonstrated the adequacy of the early insights, only that the insights are in harmony with the style.

This brings us up against the old problem of the relation between art and belief. But here the problem is compounded because Carlyle writes non-fiction, and particularly because, as we have already noted, what mattered for him was whether people would accept and act on what he said. Is it relevant here even to ask for that willing suspension of disbelief that constitutes poetic faith? I would suggest that as we read the Carlyle of "Signs of the Times," or, more particularly, of *Past and Present,* we do in fact tend to suspend disbelief, to be fascinated with the vision before we begin to question it. The idea, for example, that the early nineteenth-century world was mechanical as opposed to dynamic (the central thesis of "Signs of the Times") is credible only in a special way, only, in fact, if one shares Carlyle's particular angle of vision on his own times. Yet the essay is by and large an impressive one because it makes it possible for us to share the experience of seeing the world in that way. But suppose that we are being asked to share a different view, the view, for example, that Negroes are "Quashee," animal-like blockheads with graceful bodies, and that they, along with all inferior people, should bend their wills to that of some superior being. In fact, we have seen an analogous argument in the passage from *Past and Present* analyzed in the first section, but that passage was so heavily metaphorical and dramatic that it almost escaped into fiction and was thus rescued from the demands of the practical present. Would we find the work acceptable if it made it possible for us to share the experience of seeing the world in that way, all the time knowing that to see the world in that way is to be morally obtuse and potentially dangerous?

The problem hits us squarely and inescapably in "The Nigger Question" (1849), and quickly in one of that essay's opening passages:

> Our beautiful Black darlings are at last happy; with little labour except to the teeth, *which* surely, in those excellent horse-jaws of theirs, will not fail!
>
> Exeter Hall, my philanthropic friends, has had its way in this matter. The Twenty-Millions, a mere trifle despatched with a single dash of the pen, are paid; and far over the sea we have a few black persons rendered extremely "free" indeed. Sitting yonder with their beautiful muzzles up to the ears in pumpkins, imbibing sweet pulps and juices; the grinder and incisor teeth ready for ever new work, and pumpkins cheap as grass in those rich climates. (xxix, 350)

How, in the face of this, are we to suspend disbelief?[12] As Carlyle knew and dramatized in the essay itself, language like this is calculated to evoke very strong feelings. Consciously to suppress those feelings is certainly to falsify. It is true, however, that if we read this essay as an injunction to action the emotional response is far more appropriate than when we read it for a sense of Carlyle and of his times. The anger "The Nigger Question" aroused among intelligent and liberal Victorians was undoubtedly appropriate, and what Carlyle expected. It does not follow that now, from the perspective of years, though bearing always in mind the ultimate seriousness of Carlyle's purposes, we cannot stop to judge the essay on the grounds of whether it makes a coherent and dramatically convincing statement about experience. It would be nice to believe that as Carlyle's position became more and more inimical to what we now regard as humane thought, his writing became increasingly incoherent, and that moral obtuseness is allied to flawed art. It is not immediately clear that things will work out so nicely.

To begin with, however, it might be useful to try to see some of the ways in which the "Occasional Discourse on the Nigger Question" works. Significantly, it exploits one of Carlyle's favorite devices—the use of a fictional character to express the views he is concerned to carry to his English readers.[13] In his 1827 essay, "Jean Paul Friedrich Richter," Carlyle had described how Richter "embaled" every work, "fiction or serious . . . in some fantastic wrappage, some mad narrative accounting for its appearance, and connecting it with the author, who generally becomes a person in the drama himself, before all is over" (xxvi, 12). It is well known that in *Sartor Resartus* Carlyle did the same thing. He had, moreover, before *Sartor* appeared, begun playing with fictional characters in his own quite serious essays. Carlyle usually attempted to preserve some distance—frequently playful, but always important—between himself as a writer and himself as a man, and this distance helped to keep his dogmatic instincts under control. Most frequently he uses the figure of the "Editor," who becomes, as he does in *Sartor,* a fictional character. Often Herr Sauerteig is called upon to speak. Even as late as the *Latter-Day Pamphlets* Carlyle regularly calls upon his friend Crabbe, a writer for the *Intermittent Radiator.* The artist of Fact seemed to have understood that fact could best be communicated through fiction—through art. Carlyle's journalism is amenable to the criticism usually reserved for fiction because it is almost always engaged in building worlds into which his fictional spokesman might fit. Whether the worlds Carlyle created corresponded to any reality except his own would seem to be ultimately irrelevant. Analysis suggests that the task of the critic is to test out those worlds, to see if they have an imaginative reality of the kind we seek in fiction.

"The Nigger Question" seems to require this kind of analysis. It is introduced by just such an "embaling" as Carlyle admired in Richter. The Discourse, he writes,

> comes to us,—no speaker named, no time or place assigned, no commentary of any sort given,—in the handwriting of the so-called "Doctor," properly "Absconded Reporter," Dr. Phelim M'Quirk, whose singular powers of reporting, and also whose debts, extravagancies and sorrowful insidious finance operations, now winded-up by a sudden disappearance, to the grief of many poor tradespeople, are making too much noise in the police-offices at present! Of M'Quirk's composition we by no means suppose it to be; but from M'Quirk, as the last traceable source, it comes to us;—offered, in fact, by his respectable unfortunate landlady, desirous to make-up part of her losses in this way. . . . As the Colonial and Negro Question is still alive, and likely to grow livelier for some time, we have accepted the Article, at a cheap market-rate; and give it publicity, without in the least committing ourselves to the strange doctrines and notions shadowed forth in it (p. 348).

Although this elaborate fiction cannot excuse Carlyle from the implications of the essay as a whole, it does begin by distancing him from the views expressed in the "Discourse." It effectively suggests Carlyle's awareness of the unpopularity of the position the anonymous speaker takes (his "doctrine and notions," the editor says, "we rather suspect, are pretty much in 'a minority of one,' in the present era of the world"); but by so doing it provides a defense against the unpopularity. The fiction, moreover, allows Carlyle a greater freedom to exaggerate, to indulge in grotesque verbal violence he might have felt obliged to temper without the comic framework. It should be noted that the framework is not merely in the introductory statement: the essay proper is punctuated by descriptions of the audience's persistently unfavorable responses to the speaker's remarks, and of the chairman's difficulties in bringing the meeting to order. The framework constantly reminds the reader of the singularity of what is being said; it tends also to undercut his anticipated responses by making them comic. The Sacred Cows of early Victorian thought— Benevolence and Free Trade—are made absurd by suggesting their vulnerability and pomposity. We should, finally, notice that the framework casts all the people involved in presenting the Discourse in a distinctly unfavorable light. Dr. Phelim M'Quirk is a perfect representative of the kinds of defects in contemporary English society against which the speaker rages—he is idle, a charlatan, and a thief. The editor himself pays only a "cheap market-rate" for the discourse, regardless of the difficulties of the landlady. He is a representative modern journalist who exploits newsworthy material without himself being morally committed. Nobody seems to know who the actual composer of the Discourse was.

Any but the natural emotional response to "The Nigger Question" will recognize that it is in many ways very artfully contrived and that much that has been said in defense of Carlylese in the first section of this paper might be said in defense of Carlylese here. If we take the passage with which I began, we can see Carlylese working in its comic mode (and sometimes Carlyle can be very funny, indeed). The analogous form here is the Hollywood comic cartoon of the 1930's, in which the Negro was always depicted as round-faced, with glistening teeth, and his head buried in watermelon. But Carlyle's superiority to this sort of exploitation for the sake of comedy is clear. This passage takes up several of the dominant themes in "The Nigger Question" and in Carlyle's writing as a whole. The Negro becomes a comic symbol of a moral state against which Carlyle is struggling.

The focus on teeth and "horse-jaws" suggests man as a mere consumer, man in pursuit of pleasure and pleasure alone. The constant activity of the jaws is juxtaposed against the utter idleness of the "Black darlings," whose "work" lies entirely in eating. This, as Carlyle sees it, is what freedom really means to those who oppose slavery and look for an extension of democracy: license to pursue personal pleasures regardless of the needs of the community or of the world, license not to work. Moreover, the image of the horse-jaws is part of a larger pattern in which the Negroes are seen as animals, mere grazers in the luxuriant grass of the West Indies, with their "muzzles" buried deep in the "sweet pulps" they find. By reducing the Negro to an animal, Carlyle makes more forcefully his argument that freedom is only meaningful for those who are sufficiently mature and intelligent to recognize it as something other than animal license. Real freedom is freedom to work; animals would prefer to graze, and if given their freedom that is all they would do. And finally, the full context of the essay intensifies the irony implied in seeing the "Twenty-Millions" as a mere "trifle despatched with a single dash of the pen." Indeed, most of the attitudes expressed here are implied in Dickens's portrayal in *Bleak House* of Mrs. Jellybee and of her relation to her daughter, a portrayal that is universally recognized as a comic master-piece.

The essay takes the West-Indian Negro as the comic symbol of an extremely serious problem—no less than the "condition of England." The outrageous passage with which this discussion began is introduced in a way to suggest the larger significance of "The Nigger Question":

> How pleasant, in the universal bankruptcy abroad, and dim dreary stagnancy at home, as if for England too there remained nothing but to suppress Chartist riots, banish united Irishmen, vote the supplies, and *wait* with arms crossed till black Anarchy and Social Death devoured us also, as it has done the others; how pleasant to have always this fact to fall-back upon: Our beautiful Black darlings are at least happy. . . .

Here is the typical Carlylean structure parodied: the struggles within Time and Space, Chartism and so on, juxtaposed against the single Fact. But the Fact here is no positive at all. The happiness of the "Black darlings" is not only not a counter-weight to the difficulties of contemporary life, it is a specially significant manifestation of those difficulties. The preoccupation of Exeter Hall with distant Negroes is, for Carlyle, a sign of the contemporary disease of Sentimentalism, which is itself a function of the fact that contemporary society is *"destitute* of any earnest guidance, and disbelieving that there ever was any, Christian or Heathen" (p. 351).

The condition of the newly liberated Negro, who will only work a half hour a day because that will suffice to keep him in pumpkins, becomes for Carlyle a condition analogous to that of many people closer to home: "Our own white or sallow Ireland, sluttishly starving from age to age on its act-of-parliament 'freedom,' was hitherto the flower of mismanagement: but what will this be to a Negro Ireland" (p. 353). Then there are also the "Distressed Needlewomen" of England, who cannot be got, even for money, to do a workmanlike job of sewing; or the serving-maids, who will not work or obey. All of these people violate the principle of "Mastership and Servantship," without which "there is no conceivable deliverance from Tyranny and Slavery. Cosmos is not Chaos, simply by this one quality, That it is governed. Where wisdom, even approximately, can contrive to govern, all is right, or is ever striving to become so; where folly is 'emancipated,' and gets to govern, as it soon will, all is wrong" (p. 362).

Since all the major Carlylean themes are embodied in this treatment of the Negro, it has been argued that Carlyle is not really a racist: the principles he invokes in the essay are invoked regardless of race. The Negro is more symbol than fact. The speaker in the Discourse specifically expresses his affection for the Negro—in this way:

> Do I, then, hate the Negro? No; except when the soul is killed out of him, I decidedly like poor Quashee; and find him a pretty kind of man. With a pennyworth of oil, you can make a handsome glossy thing of Quashee, when the soul is not killed in him! A swift, supple fellow; a merry-hearted, grinning, dancing, singing, affectionate kind of creature, with a great deal of melody and amenability in his composition. . . . Am I gratified in my mind by the ill-usage of any two- or four-legged thing; of any horse or any dog. Not so, I assure you. In me too the natural sources of human rage exist more or less, and capability of flying out into "fiery wrath against oppression," and of signing petitions; both of which things can be done very cheap.

There is a kind of sense here, a resistance to sentimentality, that one ignores at one's peril. Many sensible people have reacted in a very similar way to anti-vivisectionists.

But this is precisely the point. No matter how elaborately one delves into the strategies of "The Nigger Question," one must recognize that for Carlyle the Negro is sub-human, little more than an animal. His peculiar virtue is that unlike most other sub-human species he can "live among men civilized" (p. 358). The imagery of the whole essay, some of which has already been pointed out, confirms this view.

> If precisely the Wisest Man were at the top of society, and the next-wisest next, and so on till we reached the Demerara Nigger (from whom downwards through the horse, etc., there is no question hitherto), then were this a perfect world. (p. 361)

The ideals of order and hierarchy, of "permanence" as opposed to "nomadism," of adherence to the demands of "Fact and Nature" are the same here as in "Signs of the Times" and *Past and Present*. Yet even though the deliberate excess of the language is modified by the fictional framework, the focus of the essay on actually existing people and actually existing problems makes Carlyle's formulation of this ideal intolerable. There is a kind of coherence to the world of "The Nigger Question" and, if one can repress one's own solemnity about the problem of race, there are some very funny moments in it occasioned by the excessive, almost self-parodying rhetoric of Carlylese. But the problem of the immediate reference to the world outside the art makes laughter difficult. A moral obtuseness and perverse oversimplification of the human condition makes Carlyle's attack on Sentimentality itself sentimental. The passion evoked against the passionate Benevolence of Exeter Hall is in excess of what is necessary. The Negro as symbol is inadequate because the question of the Negro in the West Indies is as real (though less immediate to Carlyle) as the question of impoverished whites in London's slums. Moreover, while the "negative pole" of Carlyle's vision is here imagined with all the particularity of pure Carlylese, the positive is merely an abstraction: "Mastership," "Permanence," "Government," "Wisdom."

But Carlyle's constant habits of quoting from his own writings as from anonymous authorities, of developing a short-hand or slang which he frequently uses in works where the justification of his usage is not present, his persistent development of a small set of themes—all these things and others make it almost impossible to discriminate the late Carlyle from the early by examining excerpts. If one were to attempt to explain why "The Nigger Question" remains, after analysis, so unsatisfactory, one would have to say not that Carlyle's ideas are different here, or even that there is a radical shift in his style, but that there is a slight but extremely important shift which removes from the style a good deal of the tension that sustained it earlier. Carlylese remains the same on the surface, but the emphasis has shifted so that negation persistently triumphs. The minuteness of the shift that finally determines the triumph of the devil might be suggested by the following passage:

> O Anti-Slavery Convention, loud-sounding long-eared Exeter Hall—But in thee too is a kind of instinct towards justice, and I will complain of nothing. Only, black Quashee over the seas being once sufficiently attended to, wilt thou not perhaps open thy dull sodden eyes to the "sixty-thousand valets in London itself who are yearly dismissed to the streets, to be what they can, when the season ends;"—or to the hunger-stricken, pallid *yellow*-coloured "Free Labourers" in Lancashire, York-shire, Buckinghamshire, and all other shires! These Yellow-coloured, for the present, absorb all my sympathies: if I had a Twenty-Millions, with Model-Farms and Niger Expeditions, it is to these I would give it! Quashee has already victuals, clothing; Quashee is not dying of such despair as the yellow-coloured pale man's. Quashee, it must be owned, is hitherto a kind of blockhead. The Haiti Duke of Marmalade, edu-cated now for almost half a century, seems to have next to no sense in him. Why, in one of those Lancashire Weavers, dying of hunger, there is more thought and heart, a greater arithmetical amount of misery and desperation, than in whole gangs of Quashees. It must be owned, thy eyes are of the sodden sort; and with thy emancipations, and thy twenty-millionings and long-eared clamourings, thou, like Robespierre with his pasteboard *Etre Suprême*, threatenest to become a bore to us, *Avec ton Etre Suprême tu commences m'embêter!*—(p. 275)

This is not from "The Nigger Question" but from *Past and Present*.

The difference, I would suggest, is almost unanalyzable. The same superior contempt for "Quashee" and the same villains are immediately recognizable. Here, however, is an intensity of sympathy for suffering which operates partly to redeem the ignorance and consequent brutality about the Negro. The moral indignation generated by the style is partly justified by the world created. Revulsion from the easy benevolence of

Exeter Hall is made comprehensible by the effects of this benevolence on English laborers. Even the perhaps nasty contrast between the blackness of the Quashee and the yellowness of the "Free Labourers" serves to suggest a particular engagement in the sufferings of those laborers. If color matters here, it is the artificial color forced upon honest men by evil conditions, the essence of which is the ignoring of the plight of the sufferers by all that Exeter Hall represents. The pattern of dualism, if still unnecessarily simple, is softened by compassion.

Only seven years separate *Past and Present* from "The Nigger Question," but in those seven years there seems to have been a profound change in Carlyle. The 'forties were the years in which Carlyle became the universally acclaimed sage of Chelsea, but his lionization and new financial security apparently increased rather than diminished his spiritual gloom. He was passing from late middle age and he watched close friends like John Sterling die while his wife persistently weakened into illness. Moreover, the more successful he became the clearer it became to him that nobody was really listening to him. In 1848 he wrote in his journals,

> I am wearied and near heartbroken. Nobody on the whole "believes my report." The friendliest reviewers, I can see, regard me as a wonderful athlete, ropedancer whose perilous somersets it is worth sixpence (paid into the Circulating Library) to *see;* or at most I seem to them a desperate half mad, if usefullish fireman, rushing along the ridge tiles in a frightful manner to quench the burning chimney. Not one of them can or will *do* the least to help me.[14]

The frustration Carlyle felt in this direction was intensified by his newly developed certainty (Froude attributes it to the discoveries Carlyle made in completing his *Cromwell*) that all the democratic reforms of the last decades had done nothing to help England and that what was needed was a strong and wise *man*. Perhaps the most crucial influence on the change recognizable in "The Nigger Question," was Carlyle's bitter disappointment at the fate of Chartism and of the great 1848 revolutions throughout Europe. Froude reports that Carlyle

> had thought that something would have been gained for poor mankind from such a break-down of sham governments. Europe had revolted against them, but the earthquake, alas! had been transient. The sham

powers, temporal and spiritual, had been shaken in their seats; but the shock passed, and they had crept back again. Cant, insincerity, imposture, and practical injustice ruled once more in the name of order (p. 442).

Everywhere Carlyle looked in the real world he found signs of the total failure of all the things he had been striving to achieve and of all that he thought essential to the regeneration of English life. The change that came over him, however, was not so much intellectual as temperamental. Quashee remains Quashee. The central concern is always the condition of England, but the balance has clearly shifted. After *Past and Present* Carlyle's prose almost never admits that strenuous kind of optimism that characterizes all his most mature work between 1829 and 1842. Although it may be difficult to think of Carlyle as ever having been an optimist, each of his important works through *Past and Present* ends on a note suggesting the likelihood of the ultimate triumph of those positives I have analyzed briefly in the first section of this paper: after struggle and suffering we shall come to the Hero-haven. So the last paragraph of *Past and Present* begins: "Unstained by wasteful deformities, by wasted tears or heart's-blood of men, or any defacement of the Pit, noble fruitful Labour, growing ever nobler, will come forth—the grand sole miracle of Man. . . ."

While it was possible for Carlyle to believe in this "coming-forth" in his own or not-too-distant time, he managed to maintain within the structure of his works and in his style a balance of the kind I have earlier described. But the facts of mid-nineteenth-century life drove him increasingly into the position of the Jeremiah whose essential function was to attack. What happens in "The Nigger Question" and in *Latter-Day Pamphlets* is that Carlyle concentrates his attention on particular contemporary problems; and though—as through some instinctive tic—these problems struggle toward the status of symbols, the full energy of his passion is in the attack. The "Nigger" may well be a symbol of a general moral condition, but he is also and primarily the West-Indian Negro whose physical peculiarities are caricatured and brought vividly and incredibly before us. In "The Nigger Question" there really are no "yellow-coloured" white men who evoke the sympathy that counterbalances the violence and brutality of the negation.

I would suggest tentatively here that Carlyle's art fails him in his later years because the dualism that informed his early prose is hardened and simplified: it takes the shape of concrete negation and abstract affirmation. The two poles of the vision now no longer get equal representation. Evil, which is multifarious and finite—"universal bankruptcy abroad," "dim dreary stagnation at home"—is not abolished by some great dramatically realized affirmation, but intensified—as by "the beautiful Black darlings." A style whose essence is the expression of a complicated vision of a dualistic universe and of the constant movement of all things in time from one pole to the other now becomes the vehicle for a proliferating and grotesque vision of evil in the world and of a diminishing and increasingly abstract vision of the ideals necessary to banish that evil.

Perhaps the most convincing sign of this shift of perspective is the flabby and inconclusive ending of "The Nigger Question." The various contortions of the essay do not struggle toward some vision of the good world. Instead, they lead to an almost despairing quiescence, an almost deliberate bathos expressing puzzlement and the flagging of faith:

> O my friends, I feel there is an immense fund of Human Stupidity circulating among us, and much clogging our affairs for some time past! A certain man has called us, "of all peoples the wisest in action"; but he added "the stupidest in speech"; and it is a sore thing, in these constitutional times, times mainly of universal Parliamentary and other Eloquence, that the "speakers" have all first to emit, in such tumultuous volumes, their human stupor, as the indispensable preliminary, and everywhere we must first see that and its results *out*, before beginning any business.—(*Explicit* MS.) (p. 383).

Impressionistically speaking, there is something sadly tired about this. The artist of vituperation settles, in his climactic phrase, for "human stupor." Carlylese here seems to be a series of gestures: the energy of the characteristically fragmented syntax is not really reflected in the diction. Instead of dramatically presenting a movement, it focuses on the "clogging" of movement. No firmly imagined Hero-haven is evoked; the "business"—and notice the uncharacteristic commercial terminology—is still to begin.

"The Nigger Question" ends not with a bang but a whimper, and this despite the fact that we have seen Carlylese to be the perfect vehicle for explosions. The characteristic splintering and accumulation of fragments is not sustained by any tension. The vision of the world is unrelievedly bleak and disillusioned, and the language is as windy as the language of the "tumultuous volumes" Carlyle is attacking. Curiously, the dualism we saw established in the first passage discussed in this essay—between seeing and doing—is here implicitly invoked again. But the invocation is confused and confusing. Since what Carlyle wants is wise action, why is it that he blames the English for being wise in deed, though stupid in speech? The praise is gratuitous, especially in the context of an essay which attacks the English for wrong actions. The passage in a way suggests the inadequacy of the Carlylean insistence on action independent of theory. If the preliminary of right action is getting bad ideas out of the system, it might well be that a further preliminary is arriving at good ideas. Essentially what Carlyle is doing is responding wildly and incoherently—and ineffectually—to all the aspects of his society which repel him. The preliminary to being guided by the Polar Star is absolute annihilation of the conditions which prevail in contemporary society, and Carlylese slips away into a mannered attack on things-in-general and in-particular.

The tendency of Carlylese had always been to work by accumulation. The same explosions go off in sentence after sentence, paragraph after paragraph. At its best, each of its explosions moved toward a richer revelation of the possibilities of the world of Carlyle's vision. Since every drawing room is the crossroads of the infinite, every drawing room might fruitfully be seen in an infinite variety of ways. And since Carlyle's vision is of a world organically coherent, the method of theme and variations makes good sense. We recognize in the contrast, for example, between yellow and black another aspect of the explosion that was created by the confrontation of the idea of democracy and the idea of government by the best, of the law of supply and demand and the law of God. Democracy and laissez-faire imply, for Carlyle, the shirking of responsibility to the rest of the community, and the "yellow" laborers are the result. But by the time of "The Nigger Question" the accumulations tend not to be illuminating. The Negro may be seen in an extraordinary variety of ways, but they are all negative. Connections are not finally made so much by dramatization as by assertion, and only the dreary and ugly aspects of life become vivid. The energy of the "explosions," deriving from curiously precise syntax and diction and relating to Carlyle's extraordinary capacity to see the large implications of the apparently trivial, tends to run off into vituperation or a despairing sort of contempt.

The inevitable stridency of Carlylese leads easily to a blurring of alternative possibilities which can become brutal, just as the exaggerated comic portrait of Quashee is brutal. At times the whole style returns to its eighteenth-century base in aphorism, but to aphorism no longer witty but emotion-laden, no longer balanced but periodic, no longer even dramatic but merely assertive: "I tell you again and again, he or she that will not work, and in the anger of the gods cannot be compelled to work, shall die!" (p. 367). When the exuberance and confidence of the years between 1829 and 1848 finally disappeared, and the optimism of *Sartor Resartus* was being replaced by the eventual near despair of "Shooting Niagara," the alternatives in Carlyle's dualist world increasingly hardened and Carlylese fell away into a sad parody of itself, reflecting an energy and a tension no longer there and incapable of genuinely dramatizing the alternative to multifarious evil. Structurally, the style is frequently identical with the style of the middle years, echoing passages from those years, reiterating old ideas in the old language. But as the dramatic power was replaced by simple assertiveness, the full implications of Carlyle's vision for the here and now become clear. His suggestion for those really interested in abolishing the slave trade is, in "The Nigger Question," to invade Brazil and Cuba. Elsewhere, the haven of the Hero-kings turns out to be a sternly benevolent tyranny where all great problems are resolved by force, where work is done on an unbreakable life contract, where, if Quashee insists on sinking his "beautiful muzzle" in pumpkin, he must die, and where happiness means barely endurable suffering. No style could support this burden.

Carlyle's general confusion and despair are reflected everywhere. The normal insistence on dramatization moves more radically toward the grotesque. The fictions, as in the case of Phelim M'Quirk, serve a primarily defensive function. There is no mistaking in "The Nigger Question" that the anonymous speaker is Carlyle himself. He sees himself almost unequivocally as the "minority of one" mentioned in the introduction to the essay. An implicit self-pity lurks in the mocking ironies, and within the essay the minority of one becomes Christ himself: " 'Crucify him! Crucify him!' That was a considerable feat in the suppressing of minorities; and is still talked of on Sundays" (p. 360). In *Sartor Resartus* the Editor provided sufficient resistance to Teufelsdröckh to humanize the full experience of the book and to soften and complicate the Teufelsdröckhian dualisms. But by the time of "The Nigger Question," only eighteen years later, Carlyle has almost completely identified himself with his creation, and Carlylese becomes the staple mode of expression at the same time as its sustaining tensions and its implicit faith in the possibilities of this world have broken down. Suspension of disbelief becomes pointless because the vision the language bears is incoherent and, finally, barbarous.

NOTES

1. Raymond Williams, *Culture and Society*, Garden City, N. Y., 1960, p. 84.

2. Frederic Harrison, *Studies in Early Victorian Literature*, London, 1895, pp. 58-9.

3. John Morley, *Miscellanies*, London, 1888, I, 148-9.

4. "Shooting Niagara: and After?," *The Works of Thomas Carlyle, Centenary Edition*, London, 1899, XXX, 24. All citations from Carlyle's essays and histories will be from this edition unless otherwise noted, and will be indicated in the text.

5. Quoted in C. F. Harrold, ed., *Sartor Resartus*, New York, 1937, p. 317. Citations from *Sartor* will be from this edition.

6. Henry James, "The Correspondence of Carlyle and Emerson," *The Century*, XXVI (1883), 272.

7. See J. A. Froude, *Thomas Carlyle: A History of His Life in London, 1834-1881*, London, 1885. Froude quotes from Carlyle's Journals describing Carlyle's methods of writing: "Of Art generally (*Kunst*, so-called) I can *almost know nothing.* My first and last secret of *Kunst* is to get a thorough *intelligence* of the *fact* to be painted, represented, or, in whatever way, set forth—the *fact* deep as *Hades*, high as heaven, and written *so*, as to the visual face of it on our poor earth. This once blazing within me, if it will ever get to blaze and bursting to be out, one has to take the whole dexterity of adaption one is master of, and with tremendous struggling, really frightful struggling, contrive to exhibit it, one way or the other" (I, 231). This, at least, does not suggest an extemporized style.

8. *Past and Present*, ed. Richard D. Altick, Boston, 1965, pp. 40-41. Quotations from *Past and Present* are all from Professor Altick's excellent new edition.

9. I hint at this analysis in my "*Sartor Resartus* and the Balance of Fiction," *Victorian Studies*, VIII (December 1964), 140-41. The best analysis of Carlyle's style is in G. B. Tennyson, "*Sartor*" *called* "*Resartus*," Princeton, 1965.

10. John Holloway, *The Victorian Sage*, London, 1953, p. 26.

11. Two other points about the passage might be usefully noted here. First, the invocation of "friends" suggests the alteration of Carlyle's relation to his audience from the *Edinburgh Review* essays to his most mature work. Carlylese characteristically strikes a self-conscious relation to its audience. Usually, the relation is that between "friends," but frequently it will be between preacher and

listeners, or between a contemptuous, badgering Jeremiah and listeners castigated as "fools" or the like. In all cases, however, the style implies an intense self-consciousness about the relation between the speaker and the audience he is trying to convert.

The second point relates to the phrase, "a whole world not unheroic." The use of the double negative form seems merely another mannerism of Carlylese, but it should be noted here that it performs a precise function. Carlyle does not believe that every man can be a hero, but he does believe that by establishing the right relation to the hero himself every man can be "not unheroic," that is, although not actively heroic, consonant with the ideals of heroism. It cannot be said that Carlyle always uses this stylistic "tic" with this kind of precision; but the point surely is that Carlylese can be highly functional in conveying meaning as well as emotion.

12. I assume that for many readers this question will seem naïve, as it may well be. If we once accept the convention that non-fiction may be seen as art, there is no reason—outside of technical failure—to reject any attitudes. There is no subject, the argument runs, outside the province of art. The most recent large-scale attempt to argue that moral failure is the legitimate subject of the literary critic, Wayne Booth's *Rhetoric of Fiction*, Chicago, 1961, was—on this point—received very critically because of the apparent naïveté and Mrs. Grundy-ism of the argument. One reviewer argued that a book which made Nazism look good would, theoretically, be a good book if it were artfully managed. The sentimentalist response to this might be that since Nazism is a distorted vision of experience, such a book could not be artistically satisfying. My own position is not theoretically coherent, but it begins from the assumption that I would personally find any defense of Nazism so repulsive that I could not accept it as genuine art. It is a similar sort of response to Carlyle's later writing which has led to the speculations that follow.

13. For a useful discussion of Carlyle's tendency in this direction, see Tennyson, pp. 121-3. D. L. Maulsby, *The Growth of Sartor Resartus*, Malden, Mass., 1899, has a useful list of Carlyle's self-quotations.

14. Quoted in Froude, I, 421.

MACAULAY'S STYLE

WILLIAM A. MADDEN

Two EARLY COMMENTATORS passed judgments on the writings of Thomas Babington Macaulay which are of interest to the student of Victorian prose style. Sir George Otto Trevelyan, in his authoritative *Life and Letters of Lord Macaulay,* contrasted Macaulay's writings and those of contemporaries like Dickens and Thackeray, arguing that the latter had told their own stories in their books, whereas Macaulay's writings gave "little or no indication of the private history and personal qualities of the author."[1] Gladstone, in reviewing Trevelyan's biography, observed that Macaulay's style was "a thing above the heads of common mortals," but amidst the "blaze of glory, there is want of perspective, of balance, of breadth"; in this, according to Gladstone, Macaulay's style was a "mirror which reflected the image of himself."[2]

These early views, the one separating Macaulay the writer from Macaulay the man and the other separating the content from the form of Macaulay's prose, raise for the critic of prose style the "biographical" question: to what extent is an author "in" his writings? Several recent studies have touched suggestively on this question as it bears upon Macaulay.[3] By exploring the interplay between Macaulay's histrionic temperament, the pressures exerted by his immediate environment, and the style of his prose, they have concluded that Macaulay's style does in fact exhibit clear traces of the personal qualities and the private history of the man himself. In the following remarks I propose to carry this more recent view one step further by discriminating between the basic structure of Macaulay's prose—the stylistic form which embodies his fundamental mode of awareness—and the various surface structures by means of which he adapted his basic style not only to the needs of his Victorian audience but, as I will argue, to urgent private needs as well.

Macaulay's basic conceptions, already fixed by the time he had reached the age of twenty-five, were shaped in large measure by an environment which contained diverse elements not easily reconcilable for those who were exposed to them. In Macaulay's case there was, first of all, the Evangelical atmosphere of his boyhood at Clapham Common, dominated by the strong presence of his father and a moral code which stressed earnest conscientiousness and hard work as correctives to the idle imagination and the indolent flesh. Somewhat later there was the liberal world of eighteenth-century literature and philosophy which Macaulay absorbed through his extensive adolescent readings and which in manner, tone, and ambience were almost the very opposite of Evangelical. Finally, there was the highly charged political and literary climate of England between 1815 and 1825 in which Macaulay came of age. The most important as well as the most obvious consequence of the interaction of these disparate pressures was Macaulay's rejection, while in his early twenties at Cambridge, of his father's Evangelical theology and Tory politics on the one side, and of the democratic politics and religious agnosticism of the Philosophical Radicals on the other.

Details regarding this important event are sparse, but it is possible to isolate at least some of the elements which must have entered into Macaulay's decision. It seems clear, for example, that his rejection of his father's religion was a result of his instinctive reaction against the "sullen" Clapham environment of his childhood, which E. M. Forster has described as lacking a "feeling for poetry."[4] At the same time, Macaulay retained the strict Clapham moral principles as well as the Evangelical distrust of human reason, its suspicion of "fictions" (with the important exception of moral fables), and its indifference to natural beauty. His subsequent readings in the eighteenth century, in addition to helping to undermine his childhood religion, did much to shape Macaulay's literary tastes, to reinforce his identification of reason with "common sense," and to strengthen his attachment to liberty. Finally, the effects of the contemporary climate seem to have been twofold: imaginatively, Macaulay discovered Romanticism very early and assimilated something of its spirit through his reading of Scott's poetry and novels; politically, he reacted against the brutalities of Peterloo and became convinced of the necessity for moderate reform if England were to be saved.

The attitudes to which this combination of pressures led Macaulay combined negative and positive elements. Negatively, he was convinced that ultimate questions of theology, "the grounds of moral obligation or the freedom of the human will," were insoluble enigmas which had puzzled mankind for a hundred generations and would always remain enigmas;[5] that the imagination, *contra* Wordsworth and the other Romantics, was essentially uncreative, having but two functions—either to lie by inventing fictions, or to make more vivid and telling truths already known on other grounds; and that philosophical reason was equally limited, since man was no more granted intuition into ultimate truths through philosophical speculation than he was through imaginative fictions. The positive assumptions that Macaulay adopted, in effect, filled the void left by these negations. For the Evangelical faith in a personal God directly concerned with each man's inmost thoughts and most ordinary acts he proposed faith in the revelatory value of facts; physical, moral, and intellectual events, history in its broadest sense, provided men with their one avenue to truth. In place of imaginative or philosophical intuition he proposed the method of induction working upon observed facts—the "common sense" reasoning used by man from time immemorial (*Works*, vi, 228)—as the single source of knowledge in moral as well as physical science. And for the two great "principles" which had formerly moved masses of men—religious zeal and chivalrous love or honor—he substituted the intellectual and political ideal of liberty, the freedom of every man to think and act without coercion (*Works*, vii, 607). Rejecting tradition and authority as reservoirs of wisdom, Macaulay proposed the free clash of ideas in an open intellectual market as the necessary condition both for truth and for progress. The fruitful results of this clash were guaranteed by the hidden hand of an unseen Providence which regulated it, irrespective of individual hopes and intentions.

These negative and positive assumptions, conventionally included under the rubric of "Whiggism," underlay Macaulay's formulation of a theory of style. The theory entailed three major criteria, the most important of which was that language had first of all to be clear. "The first rule of all writing—that rule to which every other is subordinate—is that the words used by the writer shall be such as most fully and precisely convey his meaning to the great body of his readers. All considerations about the purity and dignity of style ought to bend to this consideration. To write what is not understood in its whole force [is] absurd" (*Life*, ii, 99-100). This emphasis upon clarity was closely related to Macaulay's optimistic view of the simplicity and obviousness of truth. His two other criteria, that of force (referred to obliquely in the above passage) and that of charm, were dictated, on the other hand, by his pessimistic view of human nature as represented by the average audience: if language had to be clear in order to be understood, it had to have charm also in order to attract and hold readers, and force in order to persuade them.

Macaulay's evaluation of the English prose tradition was determined by these basic assumptions. He greatly admired the clarity of eighteenth-century prose, its "everyday language" represented by the tradition running from Addison to Jane Austen, while condemning the embellishments of Augustan "elegance" and of Johnson's "learned" language. At the same time, he admired the simplicity and force of the Evangelical style of preaching, a tradition which went as far back as Bunyan, even though he rejected the theology for which that language had been the traditional vehicle. And he praised the vividness and coloring of Burke, Scott, and Southey while deprecating what he regarded as their suborning of reason by their having let their imaginations run loose. The novelty of Macaulay's own style, which so impressed Lord Jeffrey when he first encountered it ("the more I think, the less can I conceive where you picked up that style"), can be traced to his eclectic assimilation of the quite different Evangelical, eighteenth-century, and Romantic canons of good prose. They appear not only in his theory of style and in his assessment of earlier English prose but also in the varying surface styles which play above the basic structure of his own prose.

The basic structure of Macaulay's style was shaped by his unquestioned faith in the obviousness of truth, and more particularly by his belief that out of the clash of opposing opinions truth and progress irresistibly emerged. A passage in the representative essay "Sir James Mackintosh" (1835), because of its close adaptation of style to theme and the relative absence of the complicating surface styles which elsewhere often veil the basic structure of his prose, may serve to exemplify Macaulay's style as it embodies the characteristic focus and movement of his mind. It is necessary to quote at some length.

> As we would have our descendants judge us, so ought we to judge our fathers. In order to form a correct estimate of their merits, we ought to place ourselves in their situation. . . . It was not merely difficult, but absolutely impossible, for the best and greatest of men, two hundred years ago, to be what a very commonplace person in our days may easily be, and indeed must necessarily be. But it is too much that the benefac-

tors of mankind, after having been reviled by the dunces of their own generation for going too far, should be reviled by the dunces of the next generation for not going far enough.

The truth lies between two absurd extremes. On one side is the bigot who pleads the wisdom of our ancestors as a reason for not doing what they in our place would be the first to do; who opposes the Reform Bill because Lord Somers did not see the necessity of Parliamentary Reform; who would have opposed the Revolution because Ridley and Cranmer professed boundless submission to the royal prerogative; and who would have opposed the Reformation because the Fitzwalters and Mareschals, whose seals are set to the Great Charter, were devoted adherents to the Church of Rome. On the other side is the sciolist who speaks with scorn of the Great Charter because it did not reform the Church; of the Reformation, because it did not limit the prerogative; and of the Revolution, because it did not purify the House of Commons. . . . The former error bears directly on practical questions, and obstructs useful reforms. It may, therefore, seem to be, and probably is, the more mischievous of the two. But the latter is equally absurd; it is at least equally symptomatic of a shallow understanding and an unamiable temper: and, if it should ever become general, it will, we are satisfied, produce very prejudicial effects. Its tendency is to deprive the benefactors of mankind of their honest fame, and to put the best and the worst of men of past times on the same level. The author of a great reformation is almost always unpopular in his own age. He generally passes his life in disquiet and danger. It is therefore for the interest of the human race that the memory of such men should be had in reverence, and that they should be supported against the scorn and hatred of their contemporaries by the hope of leaving a great and imperishable name. To go on the forlorn hope of truth is a service of peril. Who will undertake it, if it be not also a service of honour? (*Works*, vi, 91-2)

In subject, tenor, and mode the passage reveals Macaulay's mind in a style admirably suited to articulate that mind's basic rhythm of predication. The subject is history and politics, the actions of men *en masse*. In tenor it holds to a middle range; there is a slight heightening in the rhetorical "Who will undertake it, if it be not also a service of honour?", but there is not, as often in Macaulay, either high panegyric or low invective. In mode it is expository and refutative in the manner of reasoned debate, neither urgent and highly colored nor entirely dispassionate. The diction is simple and abstract and thus appropriate to the statement of a general principle, yet the proper names alluded to by way of offering inductive support for the generalizations move the style in the direction of concreteness.

The expressed theme of the passage, and the controlling frame of Macaulay's basic mode of thinking, is contained in the proposition that "the truth lies between two absurd extremes." It is doubtful that Macaulay's attachment to this view had a specific source; it was available to him in various contexts and in writers as different from one another as Aristotle, Bacon, Montesquieu, and the Scottish common sense philosophers. What is of interest to the student of style is its effect upon Macaulay's linguistic organization of his experience. The axiom of a philosopher of the opposed school—Coleridge's insistence that "extremes meet"—suggests a world of discourse from which Macaulay was excluded by his aversion to "extremes."[6] This aversion was undoubtedly related to the confused intellectual and political climate in which Macaulay grew up, charged as that climate was by the antagonisms of Evangelical Toryism and Radical atheism in religion and politics and by the counterclaims of Augustan decorum and Romantic enthusiasm in literature. The proposition that the truth lies between extremes, as expressed by Macaulay, represented less a reasoned philosophical position than a pragmatic cast of mind which had been formed and was made permanent by an unstable and sometimes threatening environment working upon an extraordinarily sensitive and retentive temperament. This habit of mind appears everywhere in Macaulay's prose and affects his handling of almost every topic of which he treats.

A style which organizes itself at its deepest level around the proposition that the truth lies between two absurd extremes may be described as antithetical. The stylistic frame which embodies the conception is capable of accepting a wide range of "extremes," and of operating in various ways: logically, to point to a golden mean; dialectically, in analyses of the historic process; ethically, in the recommendation of prudence; and rhetorically both in the black-and-white mode of conventional antithesis and in the shock of paradox ("Mr. Fox wrote debates. Sir James Mackintosh spoke essays" [*Works*, VI, 78]). But whatever the materials to which it is applied or the manner in which Macaulay applies it, the frame preserves a fixed form which might be diagrammed

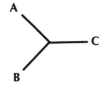

in which A and B represent extremes of thought or feeling or behavior, between which lies truth, poise, or prudence. The form may be used for purposes either of simple contrast, in which case C is muted, or of pointing to a desiderated mean (in the above passage C is muted, but the implied mean between bigot and sciolist is, of course, the author himself). The extremes may be those of the "charm of the past" and the "charm of novelty," pointing to their proper blend in the true statesman; to those of theory and fact, pointing to their ideal blend in true history; or to those of superstition and atheism, pointing to the true religious mean of what might be described as vague and reverent deism. The "distance" separating the extremes may vary. Applied to politics the antithetical form encompasses the broad abstractions of tyranny and anarchy, the more limited ones of King and English people, or the specific ones of Tory and Whig, and thus points to the ever more sharply defined middle ground of constitutional government, the English settlement, or the Trimmer. In religion it can narrow from the wide extremes of superstition-atheism, through Papist-Puritan, to High Church–Low Church Anglican.

The antithetical mode of thought and style was so instinctive for Macaulay that on occasion it proved embarrassing; having yielded to its demands, he had sometimes to ignore its consequences. In the early essay "Dante," to cite just one example, the argument that true religion must satisfy both the mind and heart, like Protestantism, and the imagination, like Greek mythology, points Macaulay to Roman Catholicism as the ideal blend of the "awful doctrines" of the one and what Coleridge called the "fair humanities" of the other (*Works*, vii, 608). But having fallen into the pattern, Macaulay ignores its logic in order to avoid drawing an unacceptable conclusion. The habit was also capable of degenerating into a stylistic tic. The "coarseness" which G. S. Fraser has traced in Macaulay's essays is one result.[7] The rigidity of the form explains also why critics have found Macaulay's prose "metallic," its forever giving, as Matthew Arnold noted, the impression of hitting the nail on the head without the reality. The style is often brilliantly effective in Macaulay's treatment of politics and politicians; in the search for a mean which will be acceptable to parties of the extremes, the compromises reached through practicing the "art of the possible" seem cogent. In his literary essays and the non-political parts of his historical essays, on the other hand, the form can be either falsifying or irrelevant, and sometimes both.

The discussion of poetry in the "Milton" essay not only reveals the limitations of the antithetical style but suggests the existence of a complexity in Macaulay himself which that style could neither disguise nor adequately realize. Having set up the antithesis of reason and imagination and the postulate that as the former improves the latter declines, Macaulay can find no adequate mean, since the triumph of reason is seen as a good. Yet the pull of the antithetical form (as well as the claims of Macaulay's own imagination) results in the curious remark that "perhaps no person can be a poet, or can even enjoy poetry, without a certain unsoundness of mind, *if anything which gives so much pleasure ought to be called unsoundness* (*Works*, v, 5-6), italics added). Here the triumph of the "extreme" of reason over the "extreme" of imagination would not only violate the formula but would also, apparently, do violence to Macaulay's deepest instincts. In a later essay he was to confess that reason and imagination are "powers scarcely compatible with each other," and that their "happy and delicate combination" would require an "intellectual prodigy" whose like we might expect to see even less quickly than we might hope to see "another Shakespeare or another Homer" (*Works*, v, 161). But, the reader may ask, if human progress requires the decline of imagination, why seek a mean at all? Is the pleasure given by poetry sound or it is not?

The inner tension which lay behind Macaulay's evasions in "Milton" appears more broadly in his prose in the interplay between its deep antithetical structure and the various surface-structures by which he amplified, qualified, and, at times, ignored his basic commitments to the proposition that extremes are in their very nature absurd. These surface styles are of three kinds, for which I would suggest the names oratorical, judicious, and histrionic.

The oratorical element in Macaulay's prose reflects the lasting influence of his early Evangelical training within the Clapham circle. In answer to Lord Jeffrey's query about where Macaulay had got his style, G. M. Young suggested that Macaulay picked it up from the pulpit of the preacher Daniel Wilson.[8] Wilson, later a bishop in India, was an Evangelical of the school of Simeon and Venn, the former an adviser to the Clapham circle and the latter the Clapham rector under whose pulpit Macaulay sat as a child. The influence of this school is evident both in the themes of Macaulay's early poetry—"Epitaph on Henry Martyn" (1812), "Sermon in a Churchyard" (1825), a translation of the "Dies Irae" (1826)—and in the style of his prose. The stylistic ideal of Clapham Evangelical preaching, described by Simeon in the handbook which he prepared for young Evangelical ministers, was "scrupulous care in construction—UNITY in the design, PERSPICUITY in the arrangement, and SIMPLICITY in the diction." The objective was not "new and remarkable views," which were merely "self," but "God's truth," and in teaching God's truth the minister had of course to make his personal faith felt by his listeners. Simeon was himself anxious to communicate the intense fervor of his feelings in his sermons: "his whole soul was in his subject and he spoke and acted exactly as he felt."[9]

The Evangelical ideal of personal force combined with intellectual clarity and simplicity was also Macaulay's. His assumption in the remark on style cited above, that there is a "great body" of readers needing to be persuaded, like his preoccupation with "force," suggests the influence of the Evangelical concern with reaching large numbers as well as its belief that fallen human nature was likely to be obdurate to the Word even when it was clearly stated. The truth to be conveyed by a writer, Macaulay observed in his early essay "History," must be "not merely traced on the mind, but branded into it" (*Works,* v, 160). In the open intellectual market of the early nineteenth century, as in the economic, only the strong could survive.

The Evangelical element is evident in Macaulay's preference for "strong plain words, Anglo-Saxon or Norman-French" to a learned diction in which "nobody ever quarrels, or drives bargains, or makes love" (*Works,* v, 535-6); in his frequent use of anecdote and allusion; in the caricatures by means of which he pillories the morally corrupt and enshrines the good; and especially in the constant "presence" of an authorial voice urgent with moral passion—vehement, rapid, repetitive, scornful, and eulogistic by turns. Although Macaulay admired the "energy" of Dante's style in the *Divine Comedy* and the "passionate appeals" of the Earl of Chatham's Parliamentary speeches, the rhythm of his own oratorical style is closest to that of the Evangelical tradition of Bunyan, Whitfield, and Simeon. It may even be that his stylistic addiction to antithesis originated in the long English tradition of the Evangelical sermon:

> While they are singing the songs of the drunkard, you are singing songs and hymns: while they are at a playhouse, you are hearing a sermon: while they are drinking, revelling, and misspending their precious time, and hastening on their own destruction, you are reading, praying, meditating, and working out your salvation with fear and trembling.[10]

The underlying rhythm of this passage from a Whitfield sermon is close to that in which Macaulay writes, for example, of Barère:

> We have had amongst us intemperate zeal for popular rights; we have had amongst us also the intemperance of loyalty. . . . Compared with him, our fiercest demagogues have been gentle; compared with him, our meanest courtiers have been manly. Mix together Thistlewood and Bubb Doddington; and you are still far from having Barère. (*Works*, vii, 202)

Macaulay's oratorical voice normally expresses itself in an abundance of superlatives in diction, in a repetitive clausal structure, in series of short declarative sentences, and in allusions that both color and simplify the meaning. The passage from the Mackintosh essay cited earlier illustrates in a mild way Macaulay's addiction to superlatives (*"boundless* submission," *"very* prejudiced," *"absolutely* impossible," *"always* unpopular"), to an emphatic diction ("dunces," "bigot," "reviled," "scorn"), and to doubling ("a shallow understanding and unamiable temper," "disquiet and danger," "scorn and hatred," "great and imperishable"). Macaulay's oratorical style is sermonic, especially, in the sense of its persuading by character rather than by argument. When most intense the effect is one of almost Pauline earnestness. "Whatsoever things are false, whatsoever things are dishonest, whatsoever things are unjust, whatsoever things are impure, whatsoever things are hateful, whatsoever things are of evil report, if there be any vice, and if there be any infamy, all these things, we knew, were blended in Barère" (*Works*, vii, 203).

Trevelyan reports that as a result of Zachary Macaulay's stern biblical principles, his son's "infant fancy was much exercised with the threats and terrors of the Law [of Sinai]" (*Life*, i, 41). Although Macaulay eventually abandoned the Clapham religion, it seems unlikely that so impressionable a child could ever forget the power or the rhythms of the language in which its theology had first been communicated to him. If the truth had not only to be asserted, but "branded" into the reader's mind, the vividness, force, and diction of Evangelical preachers who converted large, uninformed, inattentive congregations by sheer pressure of style, could hardly be improved upon. It is significant that Macaulay greatly admired Bunyan, of whom he wrote: "In employing fiction to make truth clear and goodness attractive, he was only following the example which every Christian ought to propose to himself" (*Works*, VII, 306). It was an example which Macaulay was to recommend to historians in particular, and one which he followed in his own writings.

A second surface style is reflected in the judicious mode by which Macaulay's prose renders a quite different authorial voice, that of "a cool and philosophical observer" (*Works*, II, 41). In this mode the stylistic canons of clarity and force translate into an abstract diction and an epigrammatic structure, while the heavy oratorical irony gives way to wit. Using the distinction by which Macaulay himself discriminated between the "hanging judge" prose of Hallam and the "mild, calm, and impartial" prose of Mackintosh (*Works*, VI, 81), his own oratorical style is that of the hanging judge and his judicious style that of the detached observer who has calmly weighed the evidence. The essay on Barère illustrates the mordant irony of the former: "We sink under the contemplation of such exquisite and manifold perfection; and feel, with deep humility, how presumptuous it was in us to think of composing the legend of this beatified athlete of the faith, St. Bertrand of the Carmagnoles" (*Works*, VII, 203). Macaulay concluded this vitriolic essay by observing that to attack Barère was "no pleasure" but "a duty," because Carnot's attempt "to enshrine this Jacobin carrion . . . has forced us to gibbet it" (*Works*, VII, 203). The irony of the more dispassionate essay on Gladstone's *Church and State*, on the other hand, is milder and wittier, although still characteristically heavy: "There is no harm at all in inquiring what course a stone thrown into the air would take, if the law of gravitation did not operate. But the consequences would be unpleasant, if the inquirer, as soon as he had finished his calculation, were to begin to throw stones in all directions . . ." (*Works*, VI, 342). The conclusion of the essay is likewise more judicious: "We dissent from his opinions, but we admire his talents; we respect his integrity and benevolence; and we hope that he will not suffer political avocations so entirely to engross him, as to leave him no leisure for literature and philosophy" (*Works*, VI, 380).

Macaulay's frequent use of the epigrammatic structure characteristic of a judicious style gives to much of his prose a pithiness and balance which makes it aphoristic in the Baconian tradition, the seeming fruit of prolonged and searching deliberation. It appears in the Mackintosh passage in the political applications of proverbial lore: "As we would have our descendants judge us, so ought we to judge our fathers"; "The author of a great reformation is almost always unpopular in his own age." Such aphorisms can take a philosophical, moral, or historical turn: "The noblest earthly object of the contemplation of man is man himself" (*Works*, vii, 613); "Where there is elevation of character there will be fastidiousness" (*Works*, v, 117); "A dominant religon is never ascetic" (*Works*, v, 102). The emergence of the epigrammatic "Senecan" style in English prose during the Renaissance has been connected with the new searching into causes, the nervous questioning and probing of Bacon, and with the decline of positiveness in philosophy. Unlike the Ciceronian periods of a Hooker—the style of "those who have a system in which they can trust"—the terse Senecan phrasing of the Baconians expressed the hesitations and the doubts of rationalists, and, in the looser "baroque" complications of its later forms, was much more congenial and persuasive to the average middle-class reader, untrained in the classics, than the learned oratorical style of High Church divines.[11] Yet Macaulay, we know, instinctively disliked the epigrammatic style of Seneca, whose "affectation," he said, he found "even more rank than Gibbon's. His works are made up of mottoes. There is hardly a sentence which might not be quoted" (*Life*, i, 393). This dislike had its source in Macaulay's aversion to doubt, his dislike of mystification in language as well as in thought (he noted in his essay on Pitt that mystification could effectively serve the political orator's purposes, but this was another matter). His own judicious style moves on the surface of his prose, a strategy for presenting the voice of the "cool and philosophical observer" while the underlying antithetical style, the style of a man who has a system in which he trusts, does its work.

The third and the most original element in Macaulay's prose, that which gives it its distinctive "charm," was the creation of what was earlier referred to as Macaulay's histrionic temperament. The biographical evidence indicating that Macaulay's temperament was innately histrionic is impressive, and it is the histrionic element which sets off his prose from the *Edinburgh Review* style with which it has obvious affinities. We know from Marianne Thornton's diary that in his boredom with the scientific toys introduced by the Clapham elders into their children's parties, Macaulay showed very early a distaste both for science and for the earnest practicality of the Clapham circle. The histrionic activities at these parties, on the other hand, the masquerades, magic-lantern shows, dramatic speeches, and games, were Tom Macaulay's delight.[12] What is of interest to the student of style is the fact that this "play" instinct survived in extraordinary strength in the adult Macaulay. The story of his attending as a boy one of Lord Teignmouth's Twelfth Night parties at Clapham Common in the disguise of Napoleon is echoed in Trevelyan's report of his directing the family fun in Great Ormond Street twenty years later: "Macaulay, who at any period of his life could literally spend whole days in playing with children, was master of the innocent revels. Games of hide-and-seek, that lasted for hours, . . . were varied by ballads, which, like the scalds of old, he composed during the act of recitation, while others struck in with the chorus" (*Life*, I, 130). This "play" impulse was related to Macaulay's addiction to novel-reading and his love of imaginatively re-creating and putting into language the worlds which he encountered in his reading. His mother wrote to a friend, when Macaulay was only eight, that her son was "so fired with reading Scott's *Lay* and *Marmion*, the former of which he got entirely, and the latter almost entirely, by heart, merely from his delight in reading them, that he determined on writing himself a poem in six cantos which he called *The Battle of Cheviot*" (*Life*, I, 42). Later, when he began his formal schooling, Macaulay compensated for his intense loneliness by reading "widely, increasingly, more than rapidly," so that he was, in Trevelyan's words, "lost in books" (*Life*, I, 60), and this capacity to "lose" himself in what he read likewise persisted into old age. When over fifty, while reading the *Iliad* during a walk, he reported that he was forced to turn into a bypath "lest the parties of walkers should see me blubbering for imaginary beings, the creations of a ballad-maker who has been dead two thousand seven hundred years" (*Life*, II, 187). Rereading *Clarissa* in this same period, he said that he very nearly "cried his eyes out" (*Life*, II, 237).

Macaulay's histrionic temperament is evident in his prose in two ways.[13] The first involves a simple act of imaginative displacement from the present into the past of the kind illustrated by a passage in the early essay "On the Athenian Orators."

Let us, for a moment, transport ourselves, in thought, to that glorious city. Let us imagine that we are entering its gates, in the time of its power and glory. A crowd is assembled round a portico. All are gazing with delight at the entablature; for Phidias is putting up the frieze. We turn into another street; a rhapsodist is reciting there: men, women, children are thronging round him: the tears are running down their cheeks: their eyes are fixed: their very breath is still. . . . We enter the public palace; there is a ring of youths, all leaning forward, with sparkling eyes, and gestures of expectation. Socrates is pitted against the famous atheist, from Ionia. . . . (*Works*, vii, 666)

Like the "scenes" from novels, memoirs, and histories which he endlessly enacted with his sisters, the passage exhibits a preoccupation with the historical past, with the visually vivid and concrete, and with action, especially the verbal action of dialogue.[14] The second histrionic activity which appears in the prose is mimetic. Here the term "histrionic" is used, in the sense given it by Francis Fergusson in his study of the theater, to designate a temperament characterized by an instinctive tendency to perceive, discriminate, and imitate actions. The most sustained example of this, of course, is Macaulay's *History*.

That the basic impulse behind the *History of England from the Accession of James II* was histrionic in both of the above senses is evident in several ways, most obviously in Macaulay's belief that his most ambitious work would be distinguished from his earlier writings, which he had come to regard as "rubbish fit to be burned," and from all previous histories, by its being as entertaining as the latest novel on the Victorian drawing-room table. It would be "fun" to read. It is likewise evident in the way in which Macaulay went about preparing himself. His "research" consisted chiefly of readings, heavily literary in nature, which brought the lives and times of the past vividly before his imagination, a method that has been attributed to Scott: "to treat every document as the record of a conversation, and [to] go on reading till you hear people talking."[15] I begin to see the men," Macaulay noted in his journal after a day in the British Museum, "and to understand all their difficulties and jealousies" (*Life*, ii, 226). The histrionic intent is evident, finally, in Macaulay's anxiousness to impose a dramatic unity upon his vast materials. "The talent which is required to write history bears a considerable affinity to the talent of a great dramatist," he once wrote, the difference being, in Macaulay's view, that the dramatist "creates" fictions while the historian "disposes" facts (*Works*, v, 144). Even when treating the lives of individuals Macaulay habitually looked for dramatic coherence, although he sometimes found his materials recalcitrant. Writing on Pitt, he complained that "his was not a complete and well-proportioned greatness. The public life of Hampden or of Somers resembles a regular drama, which can be criticized as a whole, and every scene of which is to be viewed in connection with the main action. The public life of Pitt, on the other hand, is a rude though striking piece, a piece abounding in incongruities, a piece without any unity of plan" (*Works*, vi, 37). The more material there was for the historian to "dispose," of course, the greater the opportunity he had to arrange it; the very wealth of the materials involved in writing the *History* was, therefore, from the "dramatic" point of view, an asset to Macaulay as a writer. Precisely because no historian could present the "whole truth," but must, like the artist, unify his materials through the manipulation of "perspective" (*Works*, v, 129-30)—a manipulation evident in the great care which Macaulay exercised in managing his proportions and transitions—the writing of the *History* was for Macaulay essentially an imaginative effort.

As the creator of a plausible drama, Macaulay's first task in the *History* was to draw his readers' attention away from the immediate context— T. B. Macaulay, the well-known Whig politician, addressing the Victorian reader of the 1840's disturbed by fears or hopes of revolution—and focus it upon the "context of situation" necessary for appreciating the "single act" of the drama he is about to unfold.[16] He accomplishes this task in his opening chapters. The first chapter lifts the reader out of his immediate environment to a Pisgah-like eminence and there endows him with a vision like that which Macaulay attributed to Moses: "There we see the great Law-giver looking round from his lonely elevation on an infinite expanse; behind him a wilderness of dreary sands and bitter waters . . . ; before him a goodly land, a land of promise, a land flowing with milk and honey. While the multitude below saw only the flat sterile desert on which they had so long wandered . . . he was gazing from a far higher stand on a far lovelier country . . ." (*Works*, vi, 243-4). Seen from the vantage point of this imaginary Mount Pisgah, the true nature of the action in the *History* comes into perspective. The function of chapter one is to provide a perspective of "centuries" from which to interpret the "single act" which is to form the central matter, and to establish that single act within the larger context of an "eventful drama extending through ages" (*Works*, i, 3).

This larger drama begins in a universal darkness from which, Macaulay tells us in his first chapter, there mysteriously emerged in England's remote past an obscure tribe whose character and way of life in no way indicated the greatness for which they and their descendants were "destined." It is as though an unpredictable mutation had silently introduced mankind to the possibility of a higher form of existence. In a metaphor which, like that of Moses on Mount Pisgah, reminds us of Macaulay's debt to his Evangelical background, he portrays Christianity ("the first of a long series of salutary revolutions" [*Works*, 1, 5]) as a Noah's ark carrying within itself amid the universal darkness the seed of this higher form of life. The Church, we are told, "rode, amidst darkness and tempest, on the deluge beneath which all great works of ancient power and wisdom lay entombed, bearing within her that feeble germ from which a second and more glorious civilisation was to spring" (*Works*, 1, 7). The Victorian reader thus had his attention engaged through a familiar rhetoric, while his point of view was being established: he was to witness, from an Archimedian perspective outside earthly space and time, a cosmic action written by a "hidden hand."

The effect of this perspective upon our response to the famous third chapter, "The State of England in 1685," is worth noting. From what may be called the Clapham point of view, chapter three simply states that human nature does not change, that in the seventeenth as in the nineteenth century power bred bullies, powerlessness sycophancy, courage freedom, balance truth. From the "Whig" point of view, on the other hand, the reader is told that the history of England between 1685 and 1848 was one of continuous physical, moral, and intellectual improvement; the reader canot doubt in which direction the tide has moved. From the histrionic point of view, however, chapter three serves a quite different purpose: the reader is made to feel that although England in 1685 was in part the same as and in part worse than England in 1848, it was above all a more *interesting* place than England either before or since. It was the moment, in fact, when the direction of the tide of history became clear. The reader is prepared, that is, not for an Evangelical sermon or a Whig speech, but for an exciting drama, and chapter three brings the reader down from his Pisgah-like eminence to a seat in front of the stage on which this drama is to unfold.

When subordinated to Macaulay's histrionic powers, the oratorical and judicious surface styles of his prose are subtly transformed. The oratorical pattern becomes dramatic through Macaulay's translation of conventional moral-allegorical abstractions—Sneak and Bully, Moloch and Belial—into the historical figures of Penn and Jeffreys. We are told of the youthful, well-intentioned Penn, for example, that "attacked by royal smiles, by female blandishments, by the insinuating eloquence and delicate flattery of veteran diplomatists and courtiers, his resolution gave way" (*Works*, I, 395), and the reader is thus prepared to find later that Sneak/Penn does not scruple "to use a bishopric as a bait to tempt a divine to perjury" (*Works*, II, 110). The private morality of individual actors and the political bias of the Whigs and Tories are thus firmly subordinated to the central action. Similarly, the judicious style becomes dramatically relevant in the summaries and explanations with which Macaulay brackets individual events and in the imagined deliberations of persons, parties, or the English people rendered in monologues that contain the *dianoia* of Macaulay's drama. Most notable, however, is the alteration in the basic rhythm of predication by which Macaulay organizes his material. What one critic has called the pattern of tension-crisis-resolution[17] gives to the *History* the purpose-passion-perception rhythm of drama proper.

The principal effect of Macaulay's histrionic style, I believe, is to communicate a sense of the inevitability of the action. The reader had been informed in the prologue chapters that Britain became England because the Normans happened to decide not to return to the Continent, that England became great because she happened to be an island, and that at one point the future of the entire nation was determined by an act of "insane bigotry" on the part of a single individual (*Works*, I, 12, 13, 73). Even William III, great though he is, is caught up in an action larger than he. That William should have been at hand at the very moment when the eyes of all England looked about for help "in great perturbation" (*Works*, I, 645) is merely one example both of Macaulay's skill in handling transitions and of the many "rare concurrences" in the *History* by which, in Taine's phrase, Macaulay converted a trial into a drama. "Those who seem to lead the public taste are, in general," Macaulay once wrote, "merely outrunning it in the direction which it is spontaneously pursuing"; without Copernicus there would still have been a Copernican revolution (*Works*, v, 85). In repeatedly calling the reader's attention to "what might have been," Macaulay is not concerned in his *History* to stress the importance of individual choice; on the contrary, its effect is to heighten the reader's sense of the fatality of events which have actually occurred. The effect, that is, to persuade the reader that without William

III there would still have been a Glorious Revolution. We do not, as in the essays, merely pass moral or political judgments upon the characters; rather, we watch them enact their appointed destinies:

> And now the time for the great hazard drew near. The night was not ill suited for such an enterprise. The moon was indeed at the full, and the northern streamers were shining brilliantly. But the marsh fog lay so thick on Sedgemoor that no object could be discerned there at the distance of fifty paces.
>
> The clock struck eleven; and the Duke with his body guard rode out of the castle. He was not in the frame of mind which befits one who is about to strike a decisive blow. The very children who pressed to see him pass observed, and long remembered, that his look was sad and full of evil augury. (*Works*, I, 472)

The end of the action is foreshadowed in the commencement: all is fated, and all is fascinating. In the cohering myth of the action the "errors" of individuals (and the historical inaccuracies of the dramatist) become irrelevant. The play is the thing.

Despite Macaulay's immense learning and remarkable artistry, the consensus of critical opinion is that the *History* remains a flawed literary work. Why this should be so is suggested, first of all, by the need to refer to Macaulay's *styles* rather than to his *style*. Whatever the reasons, he was unable to integrate the various stylistic modes which he had inherited into a coherent and compelling work of literary art; the styles simply coexist in a prose in which the major tensions evident are those between reason and imagination, and between Macaulay's impulse to engagement and his impulse to detachment. These tensions, and the several styles in which they are expressed, might be represented diagrammatically, thus:

	(a) ENGAGED	(b) DETACHED
	oratorical (Clapham)	*histrionic* (Scott)
(A) IMAGINATION	moral	narrative
	forceful—biased	vivid—irrelevant
	antithetical (Whig)	*judicious* (Gibbon)
(B) REASON	dogmatic	relativist
	clear—pre-emptive	impartial—platitudinous

The styles least compatible appear in opposite boxes: the oratorical (imaginative-engaged) and the judicious (rational-detached); the antithetical (rational-engaged) and the histrionic (imaginative-detached). The styles which were relatively compatible are in the vertical columns (a) and (b), while those less so but still capable of reinforcing one another on occasion are in the horizontal columns (A) and (B). The adjectives in each box are meant to suggest the virtue and vice peculiar to each style, and the names in parentheses the prose traditions upon which Macaulay drew.

Viewed chronologically, and in the light of this diagram, the total body of Macaulay's prose falls roughly into three periods: the early writings, in which the histrionic and judicious styles predominate, with the former being limited to occasional displacements of the kind exemplified in "On the Athenian Orators"; the writings of the middle period, roughly from 1825 to 1840, composed during Macaulay's politically active years and dominated by the oratorical "force" and antithetical "clarity" of the fully engaged Macaulay; and the *History* and late essays on Clive and Hastings, in which the histrionic element emerges in strength and spreads over large surfaces of the prose.

In seeking an explanation of why even in his mature period Macaulay did not succeed in integrating the various components of his prose, the critic is brought back to the "biographical" question mentioned at the beginning of our inquiry. It is hardly an exaggeration to say that, despite the excitement which it generates, there are few more redundant, less suspenseful works in English literature than the *History*. Macaulay leaves the reader in no doubt as to either the outcome of the narrative or how he is to feel toward it ("the general effect of this chequered narrative will be to excite thankfulness in all religious minds, and hope in the breasts of all patriots" [*Works*, 1, 2]). But it is not merely foreknowledge that makes the *History* wearisome; audiences frequently know in advance the outcome of dramas which can nevertheless awaken excitement and pleasure each time they are re-enacted. The monotonousness of the *History* can be traced rather to the simplistic moral and intellectual patterns which are embodied in the sustained Clapham "force" and the relentless Whig "clarity" of so much of the writing. The pre-emptive nature of the basic style and the simplifications and irrelevancies which it imposes affect Macaulay's handling of sublime and trivial matters alike. We are told, for example, that "it is only in Britain that an age of fable separates two ages of truth" (*Works*, 1, 5); the antithetical form, operating on momentum, produces a statement which neither relates logically to the matter in hand nor generates a truth—if it is a truth—which has interesting general implications. Macaulay's unexpressed purpose in such remarks is to celebrate England's uniqueness, but the particular virtue of a nation's having two ages of truth separated by an age of fable is hardly self-evident. On a more trivial level the antithetical form operates in such categorical assertions as "inns will be *best* when the means of locomotion are *worst*" (*Works,* i, 301, italics added), a statement which issues, we feel, out of a fixed stylistic habit rather than out of disinterested inquiry. At the same time, accompanying and often working against the grain of the basic antithetical mode are those other styles to which I have referred. At times forceful, at times judicious, at times lucid, and often brilliantly dramatic, Macaulay's style is never all of these at once. Because he cannot bring his various interests together, we are led to the conclusion, not that the style is the man himself, but that the styles are the fragments of the man. Surface clarity and brilliance is belied by an underlying evasiveness.

The biographical clue to Macaulay's inward tensions, and therefore to the unevenness of his performance as writer, is provided by Trevelyan, who documents the close link between Macaulay's life-long interest in games, day-dreaming, play-acting, and books, and his deep emotional attachment to his two sisters, Hannah and Margaret. Hannah, the elder sister, later recalled that Macaulay's notion of perfect happiness "was to see us all working round him while he read aloud a novel, and then to walk all together on the Common, or, if it rained, to have a frightfully noisy game of hide-and-seek" (*Life,* i, 67). As the children at Clapham Common grew older the games became more sophisticated, but they retained their histrionic quality. Trevelyan writes:

> The feeling with which Macaulay and his sister regarded books differed from that of other people in kind rather than in degree. When they were discoursing together about a work of history or biography, a by-stander would have supposed that they had lived in the times of which the author treated, and had a personal acquaintance with every human being who was mentioned in his pages. Pepys, Addison, Horace Walpole, Dr. Johnson, Madame de Genlis, the Duc de St. Simon, and the several societies in which those worthies moved, excited in their minds precisely the same sort of concern, and gave matter for discussions of exactly the same type as most people bestow upon the proceedings of their own contemporaries. The past was to them as the present, and the fictitious as the actual. (*Life,* i, 128)

Towards the end of his life Macaulay attributed a great part of his literary success to the habit of "castle-building" with his sister, a habit, he wrote, "which [Hannah] and I indulge beyond any people I ever knew" (*Life*, II, 380).

Against this background Trevelyan's account of two crises through which Macaulay passed during his thirties is of great interest. Prior to this time Macaulay had confined the exercise of his powerful histrionic impulse almost entirely to the domestic circle provided by his sisters; his public life, like his public prose, was business-like, hard-headed, engaged. Yet, according to Macaulay, it was his private life with his sisters which sustained him in his public role, a role which he came increasingly to dislike.[18] Against the background of this early history, Trevelyan informs us that in 1832, when Macaulay's sister Margaret announced her engagement, the shock to Macaulay was so great that he "never again recovered [his] tone of thorough boyishness"; he was even led to doubt "whether his scheme of life was indeed a wise one; or, rather, he began to be aware that he had never laid out any scheme of life at all" (*Life*, I, 257). Macaulay's initial response to this first crisis was to "lay it on" his political opponent; he felt, he said, "a fierceness and restlessness within me quite new and almost inexplicable" (*Life*, I, 259). His second and more enduring reaction was to revive a plan that had long lain at the back of his mind, to write a history of England that would be read with pleasure for many generations.

If the mere engagement of one sister was so disturbing in 1832, the death of that sister two years later while Macaulay was in India, and the simultaneous engagement of the other sister who had accompanied him there, was certain to create a major psychological crisis. Hannah's engagement first came to Macaulay's knowledge in 1834, and its effect is revealing. He wrote from India to Margaret (of whose death in England meanwhile he was as yet unaware):

> I feel a growing tendency to cynicism and suspicion. My intellect remains; and is likely, I sometimes think, to absorb the whole man. I still retain (not only undiminished, but strengthened by the very events which have deprived me of everything else) my thirst for knowledge; my passion for holding converse with the greatest minds of all ages and nations; my power of forgetting what surrounds me, and of living with the past, the future, the distant, and the unreal. Books are becoming everything to me. (*Life*, I, 343)

When he learned shortly afterwards of Margaret's death, he was staggered. Trevelyan merely notes that he "did what he might to drown his grief in floods of official work" (*Life*, I, 344). According to his letters, however, Macaulay found his salvation not in work, but in literature. "Even now, when time has begun to do its healing office, I can not write about her without being altogether unmanned. That I have not utterly sunk under this blow I owe chiefly to literature. What a blessing it is to love books as I love them—to be able to converse with the dead, and to live amidst the unreal!— . . . I have gone back to Greek literature with a passion quite astonishing to myself" (*Life*, I, 378).

Macaulay's response to his second crisis duplicated the pattern of his response to Margaret's engagement in 1832; an initial fierce aggression, followed by a renewed interest in a long historical work which "may be at once the business and the amusement of my life" (*Life*, I, 388). The aggressive phase appeared in Macaulay's immediate impulse to "strike hard at an assailant of Macintosh" in the first essay which he wrote following the "great blow." "The disgraceful imbecility, and the still more disgraceful malevolence, of the editor have, as you will see," he wrote to a friend, "moved my indignation not a little" (*Life*, I, 338). [19] The attack on the moral character of the editor of Mackintosh's *History* was repeated in the next essay, "Bacon," the first half of which deals with Bacon's moral turpitude and the second half with an extended defense of the thesis that "great and various as the powers of Bacon were, he owes his wide and durable fame chiefly to this, that all those powers received their direction from common sense" (*Works*, VI, 223).

Behind the vehement reassertions of his Clapham moral categories and his Whig "common sense" philosophy in the "Mackintosh" and "Bacon" essays lay, one suspects, a disturbing fear which was closely related to Macaulay's determination in the late 'thirties to turn once and for all from politics to literature, and to give free play to those histrionic powers which he had formerly exercised in private with his sisters. In the course of the Bacon essay he remarked that even in the best living relationships there is something unpredictable and tentative, something therefore unsatisfactory: "fortune is inconstant; tempers are soured; bonds which seemed indissoluble are daily sundered." With the dead, on the other hand, there was no rivalry. "In the dead there is no change. Plato is never sullen. Cervantes is never petulant. Demosthenes never comes unseasonably. Dante never stays too long. No difference of political opinion can alienate Cicero. No heresy can excite the horror of Bossuet" (*Works*, VI, 137). In short, the world of the past, of the dead, of the unreal, held no threat; events, passions, and arguments had been forever decided by men perpetually fixed in their admirable or shameful fates. In his *History*, I would argue, Macaulay was seeking refuge in the past, and in the very act of re-creating that past seeking for himself and vicariously for his sisters the only kind of immortality of which he was sure.

In effect, therefore, the *History* transferred Macaulay's private emotions to the public realm. Intending to record the facts of history as he saw them, he could not see that he saw them through a selective vision rooted in a private need to find meaning and pleasure, now forever lost to him in private life, in the communal life of his country's past, out of the need to integrate the private emotional, moral, and intellectual elements in his experience in a comprehensive public myth. From this point of view Macaulay's life and his greatest work may be read as a reversal of the more usual process described by Péguy: *tout commence en mystique et finit en politique.* In his *History*, as in his public life, Macaulay began in politics and ended in myth. The proper histrionic title of his *History* might be *A Nation's Progress, or Paradise Provisionally Gained: The Epic Story of the Growth of Liberty, Science, and Prosperity.*

Towards the very end of his life, when news of the India Mutiny of 1857 reached him, Macaulay again underwent a symptomatic "unmanning" like that which he had experienced in India in 1834: the thing he most loved in his last years was England itself and that too now seemed to be threatened. In this connection, the fact that the *History* remains a monumental fragment, covering but fifteen of the more than one hundred years of English history which Macaulay had originally intended to treat, is of interest. In losing himself in the past, Macaulay was driven by pressures which he did not understand any better than he had understood why his sister's engagement had made him fierce and restless or why her death had renewed his interest in Greek literature, and these pressures led him to adopt a mode of procedure which assured the defeat of his ostensible plan. To have realized that plan, to have brought the history of England down to the real and threatening present, would have meant leaving that "past and unreal" world in which he essentially lived in his later years and in which his preconceptions were secure, his emotional life unthreatened, and his histrionic temperament free to exercise itself without restraint.

If the juxtaposition of styles in the *History* may be seen as an expression of incompatible impulses in Macaulay himself, it now seems clear that to have organized and integrated these diverse elements would have required on Macaulay's part, not greater intellectual prowess, but a deeper moral, intellectual, and imaginative penetration of his experience. It was Macaulay's misfortune, it might be argued, to have been cut off by the conditioning and pressures of his early years from the sources of those large connecting metaphors drawn from poetry, religion, or the unconscious which have enabled other writers to use histrionic powers less impressive than his for the highest artistic purposes. Privately, we know, Macaulay took great delight in poetry and in what has been described as the great anthology of poetic myths, Plato's dialogues, but publicly he felt obliged to denounce both Plato and poetry. Having rejected religion in the form in which he had first experienced it at Clapham, he refused for the remainder of his life to re-examine the possibility of ever discovering anything by that route; his mature creed, stated in "Bacon," was "much hope, little faith," (*Works*, vi, 235). Finally, the poverty of his private emotional life, severely exposed by the India crisis, made it unsafe for him to turn to that inward life where other writers have discovered linkages provided by the ancestral memory which is the private storehouse of great metaphors. In writing the *History*, therefore, Macaulay's histrionic temperament was inhibited by a style characterized at its deepest level by the connecting of things under the pressure of fear and avoidance.[20]

Finally, it is worth noting that the *History* makes its dramatic quality felt through direct experience of the style, not through reading the synopses in which handbooks of literature attempt to indicate its "meaning." And it is therefore only in a direct encounter with the prose that we can both gauge its intrinsic interest as a work of art and, in addition, through our experience of the tensions expressed in the style, gain some insight into the Victorian sensibility which Macaulay did so much to shape. Like Macaulay's Victorian reader, what we remember when we finish the book is the "going back," the displacement in time, and the re-living of events the most memorable aspects of which have little to do with the history of England's material, moral, and intellectual progress. The complications of the latter story vanish from our memory while the general excitement of the drama and the vivid details linger: the rush of armies, the sneers of courtiers, Monmouth ascending the tower at Sedgemoor, the bravery of Argyll asleep in his death cell as he awaits the rope, the absurdity of Lodowick Muggleton, the smuggling of Father Huddleston into Charles II's death room, the imposing mask of William III, the beseiged defenders at Londonderry shouting, "No surrender!" For these things we can be grateful to Macaulay's histrionic powers, while at the same time we sense that this brilliant and boyish man was crippled by habits of thought and feeling which diminished or dismissed large areas of experience which he chose not to confront. Macaulay is certainly "in" his prose, and nowhere more completely or more revealingly than in his most famous work.

NOTES

1. G. Otto Trevelyan, *The Life and Letters of Lord Macaulay*, New York, 1877, I, 18. Hereafter cited in the text as *Life*.

2. W. E. Gladstone, *Gleanings of Past Years*, New York, 1879, II, 293-4, 300.

3. See *A Review of English Literature*, I (1960), the October issue of which contains several essays on Macaulay. The following were especially helpful in the present study: G. S. Fraser, "Macaulay's Style as Essayist," 9-19; John Clive, "Macaulay's Historical Imagination," 20-28; and Eric Stokes, "Macaulay: The Indian Years 1834-38," 41-50. A recent evaluation of Macaulay's achievement is provided by J. H. Plumb in "Thomas Babington Macaulay," *University of Toronto Quarterly*, XXVI (1956-57), 17-31.

4. E. M. Forster, *Marianne Thorton: A Domestic Biography*, 1797-1887, New York, 1956, pp. 53-4. In a passage which reads like a scene from a Dickens novel, Trevelyan reports that Macaulay all his life remembered "standing up at the nursery window by his father's side, looking at a cloud of black smoke pouring out of a tall chimney. He asked if that was hell: an inquiry that was received with a grave displeasure which at the time he could not understand. The kindly father must have been pained almost against his own will at finding what feature of his stern creed it was that had embodied itself in so material a shape before his little son's imagination" (*Life*, I, 38-9). Hannah Macaulay later recalled her brother's life-long conviction that "the course pursued by his father toward him during his youth was not judicious." She goes on to observe that Macaulay's "faults" were "peculiarly those that my father had no patience with." The great sin was "idle" reading, "a thorn in my father's side that never was extracted" (*Life*, I, 72-3). There is a revealing letter, not printed by Trevelyan, which Macaulay wrote when he was twenty-three to Charles Knight, then editor of an ephemeral magazine to which Macaulay and several undergraduate friends were contributors, announcing the news that his father would no longer permit him to write for the magazine. See Charles Knight, *Passages from the Life of Charles Knight*, New York, 1874, p. 218. Macaulay applied the epithet "sullen" to the Clapham library of his childhood (*Life*, II, 248).

5. *The Works of Lord Macaulay,* ed. by his sister Lady Trevelyan, 8 vols., London, 1873, VI, 226. Hereafter cited in the text as *Works.*

6. An observant contemporary, Sara Coleridge, in remarking the unusual likeness between her father's appearance and conversation and Macaulay's, noted one difference: "The eyes are quite unlike — even opposite in expression — my father's in-looking and visionary, Macaulay's out-looking and objective." Earl Leslie Griggs, *Coleridge Fille, A Biography of Sara Coleridge,* London, 1940, p. 178.

7. "Macaulay's Style as an Essayist," *A Review of English Literature,* I, No. 4 (October 1960), 14.

8. G. M. Young, *Victorian Essays,* London, 1962, p. 154.

9. *Charles Simeon* (1759-1836), ed. Arthur Pollard and Michael Hennell, London, 1959, pp. 168-9.

10. Cited by Horton Davies in *Worship and Theology in England: From Watts and Wesley to Maurice, 1690-1850,* Princeton, 1961, p. 165.

11. Don Cameron Allen, "Style and Certitude," *ELH,* XV (1948), 167-75.

12. The histrionic impulse manifests itself in childhood in the play instinct which expresses itself physically in games and mentally in day-dreaming. At a more self-conscious level it can be exploited for the practical purposes of the preacher or political orator. At the most sophisticated level it combines the functions of play and seriousness in the activity of the dramatist whose imitation of action through language organizes extensive areas of human experience (see Francis Fergusson, *The Idea of a Theater,* Princeton, 1949, pp. 236-40). Although the histrionic impulse has been differentiated both from the poetic and the novelistic impulse, the former being concerned with the emotions and the latter with moral agency (Jacques Maritain, *Creative Intuition in Art and Poetry,* New York, 1955, pp. 286-9), the three modes reinforce one another in the greatest writers. In Macaulay's case, however, the histrionic power seems to have existed in extraordinary strength, totally divorced both from the lyrical impulse and from the novelist's capacity to enter into the inward life of others. I believe that the latter deficiency was related to Macaulay's inability, touched on below, to enter into his own inward life.

13. Because the histrionic temperament is by no means limited to working with historical materials, Macaulay's preference for history over fiction invites some explanation. It originated, I would suggest, in the powerful vogue during Macaulay's formative years of biography and the memoir. One of the most important publications of the Romantic decades was Pepys's *Diary,* which Scott, among others, defended on the grounds that Pepys's very foibles guaranteed his authenticity. The peculiar virtue of a Pepys or Boswell was their suspension of the "meddling" intellect, which enabled them, it was argued, to record everything indiscriminately and therefore accurately. The memorialist's "persevering and omniverous triviality," as one critic has called it, was thus regarded as a *felix culpa.* Macaulay's notorious paradox regarding Boswell, that Boswell was a great biographer *because* he was a fool, is traceable to this vogue, as are his taste for authenticity and for vivid detail, qualities which made the memoir popular (see Francis R. Hart, "Boswell of the Romantics," *ELH,* XXVII (1960), 44-65). Macaulay's remarks to his

sister regarding his habit of "day-dreaming" are relevant in this context: "A slight fact, a sentence, a word, are of importance in my romance. 'Pepys's Diary' formed almost inexhaustible food for my fancy. I seem to know every inch of Whitehall. I go in at Hans Holbein's gate, and come out through the matted gallery. The conversations which I compose between great people of the time are long, and sufficiently animated: in the style, if not with the merits, of Sir Walter Scott's . . ." (*Life*, I, 172). His early essay "History" reveals how important this imaginative approach to historical documents was to Macaulay.

14. Trevelyan reports that Macaulay, who was unable to put on a glove or to shave himself, was physically unhandy "to a degree quite unexampled in the experience of all who knew him" (*Life*, I, 118). This physical disability perhaps explains Macaulay's great admiration for men who could "enact" an argument, whether actors or successful trial lawyers. His description of Jeffrey reveals this admiration: "[Jeffrey] has twenty faces, almost as unlike each other as my father's to Mr. Wilberforce's . . . as soon as he is interested, and opens his eyes upon you, the change is like magic. There is a flash in his glance, a violent contortion in his frown, an exquisite humor in his sneer, and a sweetness and brilliancy in his smile, beyond any thing that ever I witnessed . . . such power and variety of expression I never saw in any human countenance, not even in that of the most celebrated actors. I can conceive that Garrick may have been like him. I have seen several pictures of Garrick, none resembling another, and I have heard Hannah More speak of the extraordinary variety of countenance by which he was distinguished. . . . The voice and delivery of Jeffrey resemble his face" (*Life*, I, 142). Despite the absence of gesture or intonation in his own speeches, Macaulay's verbalizing power was so great that he was able to capture the not easily won attention of the House of Commons.

15. G. M. Young, *Last Essays*, London, 1950, p. 32.

16. On the importance of a writer's shifting the attention of the audience from the "real" context to the "context of situation" appropriate to the reading of his work, see *Linguistics and Style*, ed. John Spencer, London, 1964, p. 101.

17. Clive distinguishes Macaulay's "picturesque and dramatic" mode of narrative from Gibbon's contrastive mode (pp. 20-21).

18. After a particularly well-received Parliamentary speech in 1831, Macaulay wrote to his sister: "It is happy for me that ambition has in my mind been softened into a kind of domestic feeling, and that affection has at least as much to do as vanity with my work to distinguish myself. This I owe to my dear mother, and to the interest which she always took in my childish successes. From my earliest years the gratification of those whom I love has been associated with the gratification of my thirst for fame, until the two have become inseparably joined in my mind" (*Life*, I, 209). For his early disillusionment with politics, see *Life*, I, 280.

19. Macaulay later regretted his vehemence and offered a retraction in an apologetic footnote added to the essay when it was reprinted in 1842.

20. For some of the arguments advanced in this paragraph I am indebted to Jerome S. Bruner's suggestive remarks in *On Knowing: Essays for the Left Hand*, Cambridge, Mass., 1962, pp. 7-14.

DARWIN'S VISION IN *ON THE ORIGIN OF SPECIES*

WALTER F. CANNON

THE MOST INTERESTING PART of writing this essay has been in deciding what the title means, or if, indeed, it means anything at all. I have long wanted to sort out Darwin's own characteristic position, as expressed in his rhetoric, from his theory, his science, his overt philosophy, and the metaphors he inherited from his predecessors. A quick glance at Stanley Hyman's *The Tangled Bank* showed that Hyman has not done this; for him, everything Darwin wrote is part of Darwin's own "imaginative vision." Since Hyman's understanding of Darwin's scientific theory is also incorrect, I ignored the book in making my own analysis.[1] After I had finished, I went back and read Hyman thoroughly. He has indeed seen many important points in Darwin, but in a confusing, fluid, and simplistic context which tends to repel the conscientious historian. As we shall see, the *Origin* fits no pattern of tragic—or for that matter, comic—action. Perhaps my essay should be read as a test case as to whether a close reading of the given text, and a historical knowledge of the period in question, are useful tools in literary analysis. At any rate, I will not, like Hyman, suggest that Jew, Greek, and Christian; tragedians, myth-makers, comedians, and prophets; Shakespeare, Newton, and Darwin; Athens and Kant—have labored all of these years and succeeded in producing only one basic pattern of action.

I

In considering Darwin's *Origin*, it is useful to begin by establishing what kind of book it is. It is obvious that it is not an ordinary scientific work as scientific works were usually written around 1859. Technical scientific monographs of the period, in biology and geology as well as in astronomy and physics, were about as complex and incomprehensible to the layman then as they are now. This had been true for several decades, although it was only in the 1850's that the quarterly reviews gave up on the *Proceedings of the Geological Society* and began confining themselves to more popular works of science; they had given up on the *Philosophical Transactions* long before.

Moreover, the *Origin* is not a "treatise." Treatises, often multi-volumed, were the characteristic Victorian way for a scientist to revise an entire field by presenting it from his point of view. A treatise was directed at changing scientific opinion, and it was as technical as it needed to be to convince one's peers, scientists and educated laity alike. In the case of two of the most famous treatises, those of Charles Lyell on geology and of James Clerk Maxwell on electricity, this was, in sections, quite technical indeed. Lyell eventually found it desirable to eliminate his third volume from the *Principles of Geology* altogether; he turned it into a textbook instead.[2] Clerk Maxwell's treatise was scarcely comprehensible even to mathematically trained physicists.

The *Origin* is not a treatise. It is just what Darwin says it is: an abstract of his theories, undocumented, citing readily understandable examples, written in haste under the unwitting pressure of the absent Alfred Wallace. The *Origin* is only "one long argument" from beginning to end.[3] Darwin used all of the devices readily available to him to make the argument effective. Even so, the book is dull. Darwin was to write much more interesting books than this. But then orchids are inherently interesting; four hundred-odd pages of repetitive argument are not.

The main subject of the book is propagation, and most often sexual propagation at that. We can understand why it was both popular and scandalous in Victorian times. Darwin's theory is not "evolution"; he ignores that word, with its contradictory and ill-fated scientific past, almost completely until the last sentence in the book. "My theory" is "descent with modification" as the cause of the visible analogies and homologies which indicate some kind of relationship among beings in the organic world. Darwin's main argument, which he repeats again and again, is that *there is no known, and probably no conceivable, real relationship among individuals except the one created by reproduction.* This is so extraordinary a position, and yet to Darwin so obvious, that I haven't even begun to speculate as to its origin. Time and again Darwin stresses our profound ignorance of this point or that point; eventually it almost seems that we are ignorant of everything *except* reproduction.

Darwin has no notable verbiage in arguing this position. He uses the words of the breeder—mongrel, hybrid, cross, breed—and sometimes the phrases of ye olde English family—family tree, armorial bearings, unbroken succession of generations—phrases ready at hand for almost any user in almost any context. His real weapon is the repeated use of intense modifiers: "profoundly ignorant," "innumerable transitional forms," "insensibly fine gradations," "countless number," "incomparably less perfect," "extremely cautious," "infinitely complex," "endless," "quite unknown," "utterly inexplicable." On the whole, "profoundly ignorant" and "infinitely complex" are his major phrases in attacking his opposition. In defense, on the other hand, "the inheritance of good and bad qualities is so obvious."[4] His is the natural and obvious explanation.

It should be noted that Darwin's opposition is a straw man which he invented for the purposes of this book. There was no theory of "independent creation" which had all of the properties he desired to refute. At different times he accuses the "usual" theory of postulating separate centers of creation for related species, of holding to the immutability of species, of insisting that an organism has been given organs or powers only for a discernible purpose, of asserting that all organs are adapted specifically for the environment in which the organism occurs, and of believing in instantaneous creation in a magician's puff of smoke. There was no such scientific theory in existence in 1859.[5] What Darwin tries to do is to smear all opposition with the cry of "miracle," or at least of "inexplicable," and he has no compunction about lumping all opposing theories into one grand opposition in order to be able to do so.

The family as a social organism plays little role in the *Origin*, except among ants and bees. It is simple inheritance, not mutual co-operation, which is the key to "my theory." For this reason, Darwin's family rhetoric is simply window-dressing with no strong relation to his argument. It is not a major part of Darwin's vision. The "family tree" of Chapter 4, for example, is not mathmatically a family tree at all.[6] For one thing, in a family tree the oldest generation is at the top of the drawing, the most recent at the bottom. In Darwin's graph the reverse is true; the parent forms are at the bottom and the graph flows and branches upward. This is true of a biological tree but not of a family tree. It seems obvious that Darwin was thinking like a geologist, and was representing organisms imbedded in fourteen levels of strata. For the geologist, the most ancient forms are indeed at the bottom in any cross section of strata, and the more recent are nearer to the top. Equally important is that the horizontal dimension in Darwin's diagram is significant; it indicates the amount of divergence of descendants from the characteristics of the parents. Mathematically, the diagram is co-ordinate geometry, not algebra, plotting time upwards on the vertical co-ordinate and divergence on the horizontal one. This is not true of a family tree, which plots time downwards on the vertical axis but seniority of birth on the horizontal one. This latter is not time but primogeniture; the eldest son of the eldest son may have been born later in time than the eldest son of the second son, but the former has the senior position on the chart.

Third, a family tree is relativistic in the exact scientific sense of the word; that is, its apparent shape but not its basic structure is transformed depending on which person you are interested in. Darwin's diagram is quite absolute, with a definitely implied time zero, and a definite pattern since then (unknown, however, in all details). A family tree can of course be absolute, if you are willing to begin with Adam; as I have pointed out previously, Darwin's universe is structurally Christian, however modern its dynamics may be.[7]

Finally, Darwin's diagram is self-contained in two dimensions; it takes no account of different genealogies for the male and female partners. The usual family tree is *n*-times as complex, where *n* is the number of successful couplings preceding the individual in question. Darwin is quite specific on this point: male and female are for him the same species; whereas in a family tree they are quite distinct families.[8]

These matters are worth noting because it is the diagram itself, and not the analogy to a biological tree or a family tree, to which Darwin returns in later chapters to argue his case. His emphatic and repeated argument —that genealogies "truly give what may be called the plan of creation" —is, as I have said, an insistence on reproduction as the only known relationship among organisms; it is not an emphasis on families, trees, or family trees.[9]

At the next, more specific, level of theory is the "struggle for existence." This concept is not part of Darwin's own vision, and it generates no notable rhetoric. He correctly cites it as an idea borrowed from Lyell and De Candolle—in Lyell it *did* generate rhetoric—and treats it gingerly.[10] He identifies it explicitly as a metaphor and then begins explaining it away. He cannot do without this inherited idea, but he cannot do much with it either. In what sense does a plant "struggle"? Only in a "large and metaphorical" sense, or even in a "far-fetched" sense.[11] In truth, Darwin's theory was much too sophisticated for this idea of direct competition, and he abandoned it verbally almost at the level at which he found it. About all he could do was to try to tame it; his own preferred word for it was "to beat," or to "beat out" in a race. Darwin's tendency is to turn the struggle into a schoolboy's game.

If "my theory" begins by being "descent with modification," it becomes "descent with modification by natural selection." It has often been pointed out that Darwin personifies Nature with the concept of natural selection. But he does so directly and deliberately, as the method of his scientific presentation. Natural selection is meaningless except as an analogue to the artificial selection which had played so important a role in British agricultural history in the preceding century. Darwin does not usually, except in one respect, commit a logical fallacy in his use of this analogue. Its use probably turned some professional scientists against him; but what it tells us is that Darwin was willing to draw upon the old-fashioned British naturalist vocabulary to whatever extent he felt desirable. That tradition had been speaking of "Nature" without believing in her for a hundred years or so. There is no question of Darwin believing in Dame Nature, or of trying to revive her worship. The omnicompetence of natural selection, to which many contemporaries objected, is not presented as the power of a goddess, but quite specifically as that of Darwin's own brain: characteristic phrases are, "I can see no very great difficulty in believing," "we have further to suppose . . . but this is not difficult," "it is an excellent lesson to reflect," "we may cease marvelling."[12] Darwin himself attributed this habit of imaginative extrapolation to his apprenticeship under Charles Lyell, and he was undoubtedly correct. "Speculation" was an approved part of scientific method in Darwin's student days. He has recorded how startled he was as a student when Professor Sedgwick pointed out to him that theory, not a collection of facts, was at the heart of science.[13]

But Darwin also presents the idea taken from natural theology—he cites William Paley, but it was a standard argument—that Nature, far from being omnicompetent, can work only for the good of the individual species.[14] She cannot improve the oyster to make it more succulent for man. In this major aspect, the analogy between natural and artificial selection breaks down. Darwin is nervously aware of this, and, without abandoning the analogy, insists on the point again and again.

What he does do for Nature (although not in a major way) is to make her thrifty. This is interesting, for the obvious description of Darwin's nature, as of that of Lyell, is one of great prodigality and waste, with far more organisms being born than can ever survive. Nevertheless, one of Darwin's favorite words is "profitable." A variation is not so much good as it is "profitable"; and natural selection accumulates all profitable variations, however slight. Natural selection wishes to economize, and lack of waste in the formation of organs profits the individual.[15] Surely this version of the Uniformitarian adding up of small differences has been influenced by: "Save your pennies, and the pounds will take care of themselves." Darwin, we may remember, was very much aware of money; he made himself into a millionaire by careful placement of his own and his wife's inheritances, scrutinizing *The Times*'s financial section at length instead of getting up in the morning. John Maynard Keynes was in this respect only copying Darwin.

It is when we arrive at the actual way in which natural selection works that we arrive at Darwin's own best vision, and best rhetoric. He can *see* plants and animals moving over the face of the earth throughout the years. I have not used the word "vision" as a mere critical reflex. One is seldom asked to hear, taste, touch, smell, weigh, or measure in the *Origin*, although the few examples of these activities which do occur show that they are proper things to do with respect to this theory.[16] In later books Darwin counts quite often; as de Beer has remarked, he becomes very much the experimentalist, and actually had on hand the figures to establish the Mendelian laws of heredity, if his inclinations had led him in that direction.[17] But Darwin's naturalist background had little of arithmetic in it; and his mentor Lyell had actually been opposed to mathematicians in geology: naturally so, as most of them were Catastrophists.[18] Even Mark Twain could make Uniformitarianism look silly, given precise figures to manipulate.[19] The Uniformitarianism procedure of postulating very small changes added up over a very long time was quite vulnerable, once any exact quantities were proposed; and Darwin was in fact soon attacked by the physicist Kelvin and the engineer Jenkin.[20] Darwin's favorite number is therefore "infinity" (as applied to time); and his experiments reported in the *Origin* are little localized ones relating to a given plot of ground or one batch of seeds. They are designed to refute hearsay, not to furnish an experimental justification of the theory.

Darwin prefers to refer to species as "forms." In a Platonist, this would be high praise indeed; but Darwin was thoroughly and deeply anti-Platonic. "Special creation," his rhetorical antagonist, was to him Platonic —that is, stressing formal cause and ignoring efficient cause—and was therefore *not an explanation at all,* but only a confession of ignorance. Darwin feels that he has brought about a revolution, because systematists need no longer be "incessantly haunted by the shadowy doubt whether this or that form be in essence a species." By accepting his theory, "we shall be freed from the vain search for the undiscovered and undiscoverable essence of the term species."[21] The Platonic approach, strangely transmuted through *Naturphilosophie,* was, in the hands of such expert anatomists as Louis Agassiz and Richard Owen, threatening the whole British common-sense tradition in natural history. This is the explanation for a rather odd feature of the *Origin:* Darwin directs his most exact criticism not at his real enemies but at his friend and fellow-Uniformitarian Edward Forbes. Forbes was a bold and brilliant thinker, much like Darwin, but he was also, inexcusably in Darwin's eyes, a Platonist.

For Darwin, a "form" is something unsubstantial, changeable; his own word is "plastic."[22] Forms may be real while they last, but they can flow. Things flow in the *Origin,* as they had earlier in Darwin's geological theories. For a man who has already floated all of South America upwards a few hundred feet or so, what difficulty is there in changing the shape of a pigeon?[23] This plasticity, that is, is clearly derived from Lyell's geology:

> The hills are shadows, and they flow
> From form to form, and nothing stands;
> They melt like mist, the solid lands,
> Like clouds they shape themselves and go.[24]

It is this habit of looking at an apparently rigid structure and imagining it as a plastic one, of "seeing" it flow into another apparently quite different form, which makes Darwin a disciple of Lyell in all of his theories, even though—as I have shown elsewhere—in formal ideology he refuted Lyell's picture of the history of the world.[25] Lyell could not use this vision to explain the existence of *relatively* stable structures; his geological world was indefinitely plastic, but he held fast to an unchanging biology. Darwin, as we shall see, was able to assert both the relative stability of biological species and their changeableness throughout absolute time.

In the *Origin,* most of the time we must "see that" or "look at." This request to use our vision is the overwhelming characteristic that Darwin imposes on anyone who is to understand his theory. This means that the prophetic strain is notably lacking. "I say that," or "Hear, O Israel" does not occur in the book. Only one agency "proclaims," and then only in summary; it is geology, of course.[26] Darwin is very skeptical about hearing, or, more precisely, about being told. In Chapter 13 he deliberately contrasts "I was told" with "but on actually measuring"; and this is what experiments are for: to refute what people say.[27]

This realization inspired me to investigate what words Darwin uses to describe information gained from his most trusted informants: Joseph Hooker, Asa Gray, and Charles Lyell. Not being a research assistant, I simply looked up these men's entries in the index, which is notoriously imperfect. Nevertheless, the results may not be too misleading.

For Hooker the key words in the passages listed are:

> were found
> informs me
> saw maize
> facts are given—hence we see
> informs me
> communicated to me by
> has shown
> *as I hear from*
> as I am informed by
> insisted on by
> stated with admirable clearness by
> has shown that
> as we know from [his] account
> I am assured by[28]

The italicized statement is the only approved kind of hearing I happened to notice in the book, although in Chapter 13, Richardson "speaks."[29] Of course the action with respect to Hooker was not actual hearing, but the reading of a letter.

Asa Gray was much less prominent than I would have guessed:

> tabulated
> are enumerated (by)
> information given me by
> as we hear from[30]

For Charles Lyell, the situation is quite different. Lyell is clearly the hero of the *Origin:*

> [has] largely and philosophically shown
> noble views
> profound remark
> one exception discovered by
> a single glance at [his] table
> found carboniferous beds
> we may read . . . clear evidence
> [he] disputes this [erroneous] conclusion
> entertains grave doubts on [this erroneous opinion]
> has shown
> [his] explanation [is] satisfactory
> according to
> has made similar observations
> wrote . . . to inquire
> in a striking passage has speculated
> informs me
> have communicated to me
> he who can read [his] grand work and . . .
> first insisted.[31]

Foreigners do not rate this kind of treatment. If correct, they have most often "remarked." Sometimes, if quite good, they have "forcibly remarked."

As for himself, Darwin almost painfully projects himself not as a prophet but as a plain man with an obvious argument for all to see, if only he could show the reader all of his facts. "Seeing" means "seeing clearly"; the characteristic use of the word "good" is in the phrase "good and distinct species" as contrasted to an "ill-defined species." And a "fact," for Darwin, is characteristically a high-level generalization. For example, it is a "truly wonderful fact . . . that all animals and all plants throughout all time and space should be related to each other in group subordinate to group. . . ."[32] Darwin could observe an individual mule, but it almost at once becomes part of a theory: "We see several very distinct species of the horse-genus becoming. . . ."[33] It is the law, or the tendency, which normally we are asked to see in the *Origin*; Darwin's vision is perhaps even more abstract than that of contemporary British mathematical physicists such as Kelvin and Clerk Maxwell.

What we must see, above all, is the whole surface of the earth at all times. Europe, now, is too limited. The Malay Archipelago alone is about the size of Europe.[34] Over this expanse of space and geological time we must *see*, for example, that "a considerable number of plants, a few terrestrial animals, and some marine productions, migrated during the Glacial period from the northern and southern temperate zones into the intertropical regions, and some even crossed the equator."[35] *Plants* which *migrate?* Darwin thinks as a zoologist; for him, plants move around just as animals do. This was one of his best insights, for it forced him to explain how seeds could be transported as readily as his vision called for.

Rhetorically, there is no question as to what these migrants are. They are *colonists.* They are so-called, they emigrate, they are naturalized, they beat out "natives" or "aborigines" or "indigenes" and take their places; they find new homes; they become dominant; and their descendants inherit their dominance. Darwin's most original rhetoric, at the heart of his theory, is the rhetoric of the British colonial empire. The nations which typify natural selection are New Zealand and Australia, where the natives—plants, animals, and humans—have been "beaten" by Europeans; for Darwin, a plant is just as much a European as is a human. Note that plants and animals as colonists, like Englishmen, do *not* adapt to local physical conditions to any important extent. This belief is a "deeply seated error."[36] They adapt somewhat to the natives, but more especially to one another. Not only does Darwin's theory owe nothing directly to Lamarck, but his vision is deeply and basically antagonistic to that of Lamarck. It was only apparently valid "evidence" which coerced Darwin into agreeing that use and disuse had any direct validity at all, and then he did so with obvious verbal reluctance. This was not a lack of imagination. Darwin could (notoriously) see a bear becoming a whale by natural selection;[37] but he could not see a giraffe stretching its neck by its own effort and then passing down the longer neck to its descendants. Darwin has no vision of self-help, and no well-developed self-help vocabulary.

As I have remarked before, the British Empire has left behind it more permanent relations than its merely political connections.[38] It brought together for Darwin to "look at," the geography, geology, and natural history not only of the Empire but of all the areas traversed by British surveying ships. In one section we are asked to look at Madeira, the Galapagos Archipelago, Bermuda, New Zealand, the Azores, the Falkland

Islands, Norfolk Island, the Viti Archipelago, Bonin Island, the Caroline and Mariana Archipelagos, the Malay Archipelago, Britain, Australia, the West Indies, the Cape de Verde Islands, Kerguelen Land, and North and South America.[39] In order to invent Darwin's theory, these are the "things" which need to be seen in one vision. And they need to be seen as real physical geography, real physical "barriers" to emigration which must be overcome by physical agencies. In his very first notebook on his theory in 1837-38, Darwin had put it precisely: "Gnu reaches Orange River and says: so far will I go and no further."[40] This may be personification; but it is also good science. In order to invent the theory of descent with modification by natural selection, it was probably necessary to be English in the middle of the nineteenth century. This may not be a justification of Empire; but it is probably its most permanent result.

We have now seen Darwin's own best vision; but there is still one mechanism of his theory to be considered. This is the concept of a niche (or place) in the economy of nature. An organism survives best not by direct competition with its peers, but by escaping the fight and finding an unoccupied niche, or one occupied by a being less efficient than itself in exploiting that niche. Just what a "niche" is, Darwin does not know; it may be anything that confers an advantage; it is one of those undefinables which must exist in order to make the theory work. To describe it, then, he uses a badly mixed-up rhetoric, in which the chain of life, the scale of nature, and the balance of nature are intermingled loosely and imprecisely. "Chains," and "links" in the chain, were a commonplace of scientific verbiage in the previous generation. Perhaps the most impressive use of them was in William Whewell's *Philosophy of the Inductive Sciences* of 1840. Whewell, the Catastrophist who as a matter of fact coined the words "Uniformitarian" and "Catastrophist," spoke of a historical "chain which is extended from the beginning of things down to the present time." For Whewell, this was a chain of which the links were causes, "from those which regulate the imperceptible changes of the remotest nebulae in the heaven, to those which determine the progress of civilization, polity, and literature."[41]

We can see why Darwin was so hesitant in affirming any chain or link philosophy in any consistent fashion. On the whole he most often uses the words "link" and "niche" to indicate discontinuity resulting from continuity, but he never really solves his verbal problem, as, his critics claimed, he never solved his intellectual one. Even though he was supplying the theory which would establish the Catastrophist history of the world, one of progressive development, all of his instincts and all of his loyalties were anti-Catastrophist. Darwin's "chain" is not metaphysical, is not the Great Chain of Being; and he finally defines it in his last chapter as "the chain of ordinary generation."[42] This chain may have links as fine as may be desired (that is, a form may differ from its parent by a very minute characteristic), yet these minor differences can add up over time to a recognizably new species.

Darwin is actually wrestling with the same kind of intellectual problem which seventeenth century geometers "solved" by inventing integral calculus: the summing up of infinitesimals to obtain a significant large-scale result. Newton's method was quite irrational, but it worked; the same can be said for Darwin. He was haunted by the Law of Continuity: that nature does not make jumps.[43] But if varieties arise by insensible variations, and species are only extreme varieties, where are the intermediate forms? Why does paleontology not give us a finely graduated succession of generations? Or, to consider the present, why does the world, when all of the argument about classification and barnacles is over, nevertheless obviously contain more or less distinct structures which naturalists have agreed to call species? Species do exist, in some sense.

Darwin's "procedure," if muddling-through can be characterized by that word, is intimately connected with his confused terminology. He simply lets the old inherited discontinuous "chain" go to the limit of the continuity of "Natura non fecit saltum" by postulating "links" as enough like each other as is conceivable, while merely asserting the necessary existence of the discontinuous "niches" to produce "clear and distinct" species. Each one of these ideas has some comprehensibility, but the whole process does not. One can see what annoyed many scientists about the *Origin* at the time of its publication, those scientists who like their science based on exact and self-consistent nomenclature, not on intuitions expressed in confused and outmoded similes. The critics were quite correct; it took statisticians seventy years to bring mathematics around to Darwin's position.

Darwin was, of course, also quite correct about his "niches." They do exist, biologically and mathematically. He was also quite right in not trying to define them, with consistent rhetoric or in any other way, for they are one of the most complex and interesting of biological problems. It is indeed one of Darwin's great intuitions that, after defining species as only more distinct varieties, he nevertheless insists on his undefined "niches" in order to make species into distinct entities. This is the point at which Darwin could easily have falsified his theory; if he had followed his own logic, or his lack of rhetoric, he would have done so. It is his insistence on the actuality of species, while denying their structural reality (that their physical forms define them) that is Darwin's greatest break with his scientific contemporaries. And he asserts this position without any consistent rhetoric at all.

This point is worth developing, even if it takes us a bit beyond literary criticism narrowly conceived. Rightly or wrongly, the Idealistic approach was being used in the middle of the nineteenth century to find an actually visualizable form, a pattern which could be drawn or plotted. This was immensely successful in physics, in which the development of this approach by Clerk Maxwell, Einstein, Gibbs, and Schrödinger has almost obliterated any other method.[44] But in biology, the attempt to find a basis for form *in* form, after initial successes by such brilliant innovators as Louis Agassiz and Richard Owen, failed badly. In technical terms, we can express this by saying that morphology is not a self-contained science. It is derivative from paleontological ecology. The advantage of expressing it that way is that it isolates Darwin's intellectual position. Paleontology, the study of fossil forms, was the revolutionary science of the early nineteenth century. It wrecked more inherited intellectual structures than, to my knowledge, has any other new study. The Great Chain of Being, Adam, Genesis, Voltaire, the Catholic tradition—all tumbled. Poetry had to revise its habits. "Thou wast not born for death, immortal bird," was true, to Keats's knowledge; it is simply silly to a modern student. Nightingales will be fossils a million years from now.[45]

Ecology, the inter-relationship of living beings in a given environment, although not under that name, was basic to the British naturalist tradition, and was therefore satisfactorily present in British natural theology as well. John Ray in the seventeenth century did not invent this tradition; but what John Ray knew, reproduced by William Paley in the eighteenth century, Darwin knew also.[46] Darwin read and used part of Paley, the part that suited his purposes. That part was the part of Paley which Paley, after reading John Ray, had used for his purposes. And if paleontology posed the problem of the relationship of forms over time, ecology forced a consideration of their relationships to one another; all biologists knew that, but only Darwin and Wallace saw what to do about it, and only Darwin saw both the plasticity of form and the rigidity of niches which were needed to explain it.[47]

Darwin uses two other verbal devices which do not seem to me to be important: that is to say, they are obvious, but I have no good theory to explain them. One is the constant use of words such as "beautiful," "exquisite," and "most perfect" to describe adaptations in nature. Darwin seems to be arguing against any simple theory, such as that of Edward Forbes; he is making sure that he is not accused of minimizing the problem of explaining such adaptations; and he is honestly repeating the words of natural theology: he believes that these adaptations *are* exquisite. Of course, that his theory will explain these adaptations is also good; but I do not believe that he has that primarily in mind.

The second verbal device is Darwin's insertion of a rhetorical paragraph without any over-all consistency in his metaphors. In one case it is the making of a telescope; in another it is Lyell's simile of the earth as a geological museum. At the end of Chapter 11, organisms are compared to "living waters" flowing over the earth.[48] More than once he uses the comparison (common in the previous generation) of human genealogies to language families; this is an important metaphor in the 1830's with Whewell, Lyell, and Herschel, but is merely a stale reference in Darwin in 1859.[49] The book ends with a paragraph which repeats the image of an entangled bank mentioned in Chapter 3, goes on to the war of nature, and ends with the powers "breathed into" a few forms and the earth cycling about the sun. As far as I can see, these are attempts at "fine writing"; they do not affect the argument or express the nature of Darwin's vision. Professor Hyman disagrees with me and finds his principal theme in isolated paragraphs; so, as I have said, the reader will have to choose which procedure he prefers.[50] I can locate each one of these images in the verbal grab-bag of the period; what I cannot do is relate them to one another or to anything important that Darwin was saying.

So far I have been following the structure of Darwin's theory; it has a vision, but it has no consistent metaphor; and it is scientifically most fruitful both when it has its best metaphor—as with geology and geographical distribution—and when it has nothing but verbal confusion, as with niches in the economy of nature.

II

It is also interesting to follow the structure not of the theory but of the physical book itself. The basic structure is quite clear. In Chapters 1–4

Darwin outlines his theory as an intellectual possibility. In Chapters 5–8 he goes to the defensive and tries to explain away objections to the theory. In Chapter 9 he launches into a demonstration of how much his theory will explain which is otherwise inexplicable. These later chapters—9 and 10 on geology, 11 and 12 on geographical distribution—are the most impressive, scientifically and rhetorically, in the book, and had the most obvious influence on Darwin's contemporaries. It should be noted that the immediate impact of the *Origin* on working geologists was probably greater than its impact on working biologists. The *Origin* is the major geological work of the period, regardless of whether the individual geologist agreed with its biology or not.

Chapter 13 is a catch-all for further matters which the theory can explain, but on which Darwin was not himself so certainly an expert. It has been noted that Darwin preferred to go with his antagonist Agassiz in embryology in Chapter 13, even though von Baer's more expert embryology was available.[51] This was simply intellectual laziness, perhaps; Darwin knew little of embryology and chose the easiest authority to reconcile with his own theories. Chapter 14 is the recapitulation of the whole argument. Let us go through the book, chapter by chapter, and see what it is we are asked to "look at."

Chapter 1 is "Variation under Domestication"; what we see are pigeons, but what we are asked to admire are breeders, English breeders who have produced almost magical results as proved by "enormous prizes given for animals with a good pedigree."[52] Darwin will constantly recur to pigeons; they are the most-used example throughout the book. This is rather odd. Darwin's own specialty was barnacles, and as a member of the upper middle class he might have been expected to concentrate on horses, the improvement of whose breed had been spectacular in England since the early eighteenth century. But Darwin had nothing of the county in him; he was not at all the squire. He is not even very productive-middle-class, considering turnips and wheat. His characteristic organisms are not really "class" at all; they are small-boy: birds, worms, weeds, clover, bees, ants, the mud on the feet of sea gulls. The pigeons were a deliberate investigation he undertook to document his theory, and he self-consciously cultivated the lower classes for his information. Otherwise we can recognize his continuity with the young Darwin who collected beetles and birds' nests.

In Chapter 2, "Variation under Nature," we are asked to see a book of biology and "my tables" (neither of which is reproduced). "Seeing," it seems, is going to be an abstract experience.

This is made clear in Chapter 3, "Struggle for Existence." We are given two good concrete examples, cattle which nibble down scotch fir, and the ecology of clover near a village (cats eat field mice which prey on bees' nests whose occupants carry the pollen which fertilizes the clover, so that, as Thomas Huxley observed, the number of old maids with cats influences the flourishing state of the clover in the fields).[53] But we do not really see them. When we "look at the plants and bushes clothing an entangled bank," what we are asked to *see* is that their relationship is not by chance.[54] We see a principle.

Chapter 4, "Natural Selection," features the chart mentioned above. We see an abstract graph which a little verbiage at the end of the chapter concerning the "tree of life" cannot make more comprehensible.[55] But Chapter 4 is notorious for the full-scale introduction, at a central part of his theory, of Darwin's idea of scientific logic. The following seven phrases in seven consecutive sentences are quite literally Darwin's method of arguing the validity of the principle of natural selection:

> Let it be borne in mind
> It may be truly said
> Let it be borne in mind
> Can it, then, be thought improbable?
> If such do occur, can we doubt?
> We may feel sure
> This . . . I call Natural Selection.[56]

I have not exaggerated Darwin's method of argument, or taken only an extreme case. Here is another more extensive example from Chapter 14. Once more I cite consecutive sentences:

> wholly unable even to conjecture how
> yet, as we have reason to believe
> there will always be a good chance
> may often be accounted for by
> it cannot be denied that
> will obviously have
> I have attempted to show
> are as yet profoundly ignorant
> will have been possible

the difficulty . . . is in some degree decreased
must have existed
it may be asked
why are not
we have no right to expect
we have no just right to expect
we have reason to believe
I have also shown . . . will at first probably exist . . .
will be liable to be supplanted . . . will generally be
  modified . . . will be supplanted and exterminated[57]

How one can get from "unable even to conjecture" to the affirmation "will be exterminated" is not logically obvious. Yet Darwin's conclusions were in the main, as in these two examples, correct. His intuitions had outrun any logic available to him. It is apparent that logic and evidence are luxuries which science often abandons in order to make significant progress.[58]

With Chapter 5, "Laws of Variation," Darwin begins his defense, although he pretends that it does not begin until Chapter 6. We look at pigeons, asses, and horses, and pigeons again; by looking at the pigeons, we can understand the horses.[59] Primarily, however, we are informed that we are "profoundly ignorant" of the Laws of Variation. This is Darwin's characteristic position; whenever his theory does not explain a subject, we are told that nothing clear is known about the subject which *any* theory could explain. In Chapter 6 we see abstractions, mostly geographical: "we see the same fact in ascending mountains," "we must see that the range of inhabitants of any country . . . ." We need not look to any one time but to all time; we look at the family of squirrels or the sting of the bee. And we integrate in proper Lyellian fashion: "Let this process go on for millions on millions of years"; and we use our imagination: "And may we not believe that . . . ?"[60]

In Chapter 7 we look above all at the honeycomb, and, next, to the slave-making instincts of ants.[61] I cannot relate these sections rhetorically to anything else in the book, although their propaganda value is obvious. Ants and bees have been famous since the Old Testament; Darwin must deal with them or fail to carry the normal reader with him.

Chapter 8, "Hybridism," is a refreshing change. It has no clear visual picture; rather it features Gärtner, "so good an observer and so hostile a witness," and Kölrauter, "whose accuracy has been confirmed by every subsequent observer."[62] Darwin deftly plays off these experts against each other to obtain the results he wants; he never lets himself emerge as (what he was) a better botanical observer than either one. For once, people and not principles are at the center of the stage.

This brings us to Chapters 9 and 10, on the geological record, and Chapters 11 and 12, on the geographical distribution of organisms. I have already commented on Darwin's vision in these chapters. Here Darwin teaches a whole generation of naturalists the elements of their trade; he is as superior to Lyell, technically, as Lyell had been superior to *his* teacher, William Buckland. Chapter 10 contains the real explanation of the graph printed in Chapter 4; if there is a true center to the *Origin*, it is on page 281, not on pages 90-91. Chapters 11 and 12 contain the most impressive versions of the vision which, as I have stated, is most truly Darwin's own, the vision of the whole earth with all organisms that have ever lived swarming over it. Chapter 13 is a repetitive miscellany. We find pigeons again; the graph of Chapter 4; community of descent as the hidden bond; and abstract vision once more. We do look to the admirable drawings of Huxley, but what we *see* are not the drawings themselves but the *absence* of some principle in them: we see "no trace of the vermiform stage."[63] This negative vision is the mark of the true ideologue. In his slow and creeping fashion Darwin has out-idealized all of the Platonists.[64] He can not only see forms which exist only transiently; he can also see the absence of forms which do not exist. Chapter 14 is the recapitulation, in which many of the principles of the first thirteen chapters are simply summarized.

All of this makes Darwin seem like a dull man, and, at the time he wrote the *Origin* he probably was one. He himself preferred the *Voyage of the Beagle,* when as a young man he could enjoy hitching a ride on the back of a Galapagos turtle, a "form" in whose real existence he was to teach naturalists not to believe—but he enjoyed the ride. I myself prefer the aged Darwin; agonies of the theory over, his orchids and his earthworms seem to me to be among the best of naturalist writing. But it was the intuitions of the *Origin*—the intuitions, not the evidence, for there is none; and not the logic, for it is poor—it was Darwin's intuitions as expressed in the *Origin* which transformed biology and geology. As is now apparent, only rarely did he have language to fit his ideas. He used whatever was available.

There are of course many other rhetorical devices used in a book so long, but I think I have given enough examples to demonstrate my major contention. The *Origin* has no unified rhetorical structure, tragic, comedic, or otherwise. Its structure is science, not ritual; even intellectually, Darwin is vulnerable to the logician. Darwin picked up, for use at each level of his argument, whatever rhetoric was available. When his thoughts were unclear, so were his metaphors. When he was most original, and most sure of himself, as in geographical distribution or geological succession, his language was most modern and most interesting.

Darwin never found an over-all metaphor, or guiding image, which he was willing to affirm. "My theory" is "descent with modification by natural selection"; and there is no more vivid way to put it without falsifying it. A tree, a bank, Dame Nature, a struggle, a chain, a bee-hive: these were all too simple to be taken seriously. Only a vision of the whole world with all things that have ever lived moving over it in space and all time in a complex pattern of intuitively comprehensible principles could be enough; and Darwin was not the poet to create the necessary new language in vivid and unified fashion. The scientific imagination by 1859— and this is true in astronomy also, as I have shown elsewhere—had outrun the resources of inherited myth, ritual, drama, and metaphor.[65] Physics could not even squeeze itself into the metaphors of Isaac Newton, much less the patterns of Sophocles.

Darwin had a vision, but poetry was too simple to express it. Tennyson, by abandoning dramatic structure and going to a loosely integrated lyric form, had been able to put some of Lyell into verse. The much more complex vision of Darwin has never found a poet who could master it; certainly Darwin himself was not that poet. Scientifically, the *Origin* is a classic; biologists have been scrambling for a hundred years to catch up with Darwin's ideas. But verbally it is a rag-and-bone shop. Science took wings in the middle of the nineteenth century, imaginative wings that no other discipline can match even now. Words, logic, evidence, and mathematical consistency tend to strangle the scientist's idea before it ever can be born alive and gasping. Gradually scientists have learned to take words, philosophy, and rhetoric casually, pragmatically. James Clerk Maxwell was perhaps their best teacher, when he deliberately suppressed his physical vision of Faraday's electro-magnetic ideas; that he had used a clear analogy to arrive at his equations, but then had refused to affirm it in his classic presentation, was an open, and scandalous, secret.[66]

Darwin, exposed to the same school as Clerk Maxwell,[67] was more naïve at the conscious level. But then he was English; Clerk Maxwell was from Edinburgh. Darwin's vision is abstract, beyond the vision of Plato.

He sees not forms or ideas, but principles. The *Origin* is not Darwin, but in the *Origin* Darwin shows that it is the *habit of looking at things in a given way* which a master scientist transmits to his disciples. How he does this, rhetorically, is of little importance. If this means that literary criticism as practised by professors of English literature at liberal arts colleges is not of much importance in understanding the important books of the world since 1859, I am sorry. Such people are obviously virtuous. Yet it is true that what is important about Darwin's *On the Origin of Species by Natural Selection* is what he has to show; the way in which he says it is an offense to our logical and rhetorical tradition. Our logical and rhetorical tradition will simply have to change. The scientific imagination will not be confined in these out-worn intellectual structures.

NOTES

1. For example, Chambers's *Vestiges of the Natural History of Creation* does *not* contain "the essence of Darwin's theory": Stanley Hyman, *The Tangled Bank,* New York, 1962, p. 4. After writing this paragraph, I was interested to find that Ralph Ellison has the same objection to Hyman's analysis of Ellison's novel *The Invisible Man:* "My basic quarrel with Hyman is not over his belief in the importance of the folk tradition, nor over his interest in archetype; but that when he turns to specific works of literature he tends to distort their content to fit his theory": Ralph Ellison, *Shadow and Act,* New York, 1966, p. 70.

2. His *Elements of Geology,* London, 1838.

3. Charles Darwin, *On the Origin of Species,* reprint of 1st ed., London, 1950, p. 389; hereafter cited simply as *Origin.*

4. *Origin,* p. 29; cf. p. 297.

5. Walter F. Cannon, "The Bases of Darwin's Achievement: A Revaluation," *Victorian Studies,* IV (1961), 131-2.

6. *Origin,* pp. 90-91.

7. Cannon, "Darwin's Achievement," pp. 109-10 and *passim.*

8. *Origin,* pp. 361, 367, 387.

9. *Origin,* p. 412; contrasted to "some unknown plan of creation," as on p. 368.

10. *Origin,* p. 53.

11. *Origin,* p. 54.

12. *Origin,* pp. 161, 195, 250, 406; contrast Hyman, *Tangled Bank,* p. 38: "She is no less than the earth goddess or Great Mother worshipped everywhere under a variety of names." Is it permissible to use the phrase, "this is just plain silly," about a fellow critic? Hyman, that is, consistently distorts Darwin's emphasis. What for Darwin was simply an available verbalism becomes, in Hyman's account, an expression loaded with symbolic and ritual significance. This proce-

dure has the advantage of making Hyman's analysis *more* exciting than Darwin's book; and that, perhaps, is the point.

13. Charles Darwin, *Life and Letters*, ed. Francis Darwin, New York, 1887, I, 48. On "speculation," cf. John Herschel to Charles Lyell, 12 June 1837: "Convinced as I feel of the great importance of this general view of geological revolution . . . I do, at all events, lay claim to absolute independence of speculation on the subject . . . When I first read your book I was struck with your views of the Metamorphic Rocks, and I began to speculate how & why . . .": reprinted in Walter F. Cannon, "The Impact of Uniformitarianism," *Proceedings of the American Philosophical Society*, CV (1961), p. 313.

14. Paley is cited on p. 172 of the *Origin;* for the general position, see Walter F. Cannon, "The Problem of Miracles in the 1830's," *Victorian Studies*, III (1960), 19-20 and note 20.

15. *Origin*, pp. 53, 128-9.

16. Darwin even *tickles* an ant on p. 181. It is not *his* "anesthetic" or "Freudian" nature which largely excludes these activities from the *Origin;* it is the abstract nature of the book he was writing. In later books he is much more open to suggestions from all of the senses.

17. Gavin de Beer, *Charles Darwin*, London, 1963, pp. 207-8.

18. Cf. Cannon, "Impact of Uniformitarianism," pp. 302-4; and "The Uniformitarian-Castastrophist Debate," *Isis*, LI (1960), esp. 44-6, 49-50, 53-5.

19. Mark Twain, *Life on the Mississippi*, Heritage Press, New York, 1944, Ch. XVII, pp. 114-15.

20. William Thomson is usually called (Lord) Kelvin retroactively, to distinguish him from all of the other Thomsons and Thompsons in the history of science. He was, I believe, the first British scientist to win a peerage for science alone, Lyon Playfair's peerage having been won as a science adviser to the Crown. Of course Thomson was a definite Unionist (Conservative), and Salisbury (Balfour) knew this. Government patronage of scholars was reasonably impartial in scholarship, but openly partial in party affiliation. The best Whig was made Dean of Ely when the Whigs were in power — and was an outstanding success. The best Conservative was made Master of Trinity when the Conservatives were in power — and was an outstanding Master. Had the vacancies appeared in the reverse order, A would have gotten Y instead of X, and B would have had X rather than Y. There was not very much room for mediocrity in the Government's manipulation of patronage concerning clearly scholarly positions in Victorian England. But it would have seemed simply eccentric for a Conservative Prime Minister to give a Liberal scientist a vote in the House of Lords.

21. *Origin*, pp. 410-11.

22. *Origin*, pp. 10, 26, 114.

23. Charles Darwin, "On the connexion of certain volcanic phaenomena, etc.," *Proceedings of the Geological Society of London*, II (1833-38), 654-60; and at length in *Transactions of the Geological Society of London*, 2nd Series, V (1840), 601-30.

24. Tennyson, *In Memoriam,* CXXII.

25. Cannon, "Darwin's Achievement," pp. 128, 132.

26. *Origin,* p. 397. Contrast Hyman, *Tangled Bank,* pp. 35, 36, "the book's prophetic quality"; "what is essentially a new religious message, a new testament or covenant." He gives no convincing examples.

Hyman also observes that the *Origin* does not "ever mention the Second Person of God" (p. 37). But this proves nothing, for or against his position. No respectable work of natural theology used Christ. Christ was a part of revealed theology, and good natural theologians left him out of their books.

27. *Origin,* p. 377.

28. *Origin,* pp. 121, 126, 316, 319, 319, 321, 318, 318, 321, 322, 323, 332, 338, 339.

29. *Origin,* pp. 319, 353.

30. *Origin,* pp. 86, 100, 151, 310.

31. *Origin,* pp. 53, 82, 242, 246, 246, 252, 259, 261, 264, 265, 266, 274, 279, 308, 324, 327, 341, 241, 408.

32. *Origin,* p. 112.

33. *Origin,* pp. 142, 143.

34. *Origin,* p. 255.

35. *Origin,* p. 321.

36. *Origin,* p. 339.

37. *Origin,* p. 158.

38. Walter F. Cannon, "History in Depth: The Early Victorian Period," *History of Science,* III (1964), 33.

39. *Origin,* pp. 331-8.

40. "Darwin's Notebooks on Transmutation of Species, Part I. First Notebook (July 1837–February 1838)," ed. Gavin de Beer, *Bulletin of the British Museum* (Natural History), Historical Series, II (1960), 49.

41. William Whewell, *The Philosophy of the Inductive Sciences,* London, 1840, II, 112, 115.

42. *Origin,* p. 403.

43. The "Law" had been asserted by John Herschel as one which "pervades all nature": *Preliminary Discourse on the Study of Natural Philosophy,* London, 1830, p. 188. On why Darwin stood in awe of Herschel (who is the "one of our greatest philosophers" of the second sentence of the *Origin*), see Walter F. Cannon, "John Herschel and the Idea of Science," *Journal of the History of Ideas,* XXII (1961), 215-39.

44. This rather strong statement perhaps is not true of philosophers of science; but almost all physicists are taught Schrödinger's waves, not Heisenberg's matrix algebra; and they think pictorially, even when they do not affirm the reality of their pictures.

45. Cf. Cannon, "Problem of Miracles," p. 19 and note 19.

46. Cannon, "Darwin's Achievement," pp. 128-9; de Beer, *Darwin,* pp. 16-20.

47. This is the closest I have come to solving the "Wallace problem": that is,

what did Darwin's theory have that Wallace's lacked? It was certainly not evidence — at least, printed evidence. I would be interested to hear from Wallace experts as to whether they think my formulation is at all valid.

48. *Origin*, pp. 162, 412, 324.

49. *Origin*, pp. 358-9; and for a different use of a language analogy, cf. p. 264.

50. Hyman, *Tangled Bank*, pp. 31-3. I cannot resist noting that Professor Hyman has even gotten the title of his own book wrong. Darwin's word is *"entangled."*

51. Jane Oppenheimer, "An Embryological Enigma in the *Origin of Species*," *Forerunners of Darwin: 1749-1859*, ed. Bentley Glass *et al.*, Baltimore, 1959, pp. 292-322; for a more admiring account of Darwin's position by an expert embryologist, see Gavin de Beer, "Darwin and Embryology," in *A Century of Darwin*, ed. S. A. Barnett, London, 1962, pp. 153-72.

52. *Origin*, p. 27.

53. *Origin*, pp. 63-4.

54. *Origin*, p. 64.

55. *Origin*, pp. 90-91, 102-9.

56. *Origin*, pp. 69-70.

57. *Origin*, pp. 391-2.

58. Cf. Cannon, "Darwin's Achievement," pp. 133-4.

59. *Origin*, p. 143.

60. *Origin*, pp. 149, 150, 154-5, 173, 162.

61. *Origin*, pp. 188-202.

62. *Origin*, p. 231.

63. *Origin*, p. 375; on p. 376 we can "see plainly" that we "cannot tell" what will happen.

64. Darwin to Lyell, 16 June 1856: "Why, your disciples in a slow and creeping manner beat all the old Catastrophists who ever lived." Darwin, *Life and Letters*, I, 431.

65. Cannon, "John Herschel," p. 238.

66. Clerk Maxwell's most brilliant disciple, Heinrich Hertz, is usually quoted out of context in this connection. When Hertz said that Maxwell's theory is Maxwell's equations, he did not mean to affirm the validity of a purely abstract physics. Rather he meant that Maxwell's remaining physical ideas were so confused and contradictory that he, Hertz, would have to provide a consistent interpretation for the equations. Heinrich Hertz, *Electric Waves*, trans. D. E. Jones, New York, 1893, pp. 26-7, 195-6.

67. Both men of course went to Cambridge; but by "school" I mean the group of men described in Walter F. Cannon, "Scientists and Broad Churchmen: An Early Victorian Intellectual Network," *Journal of British Studies*, IV (1964), 65-88.

STYLE AND SENSIBILITY IN RUSKIN'S PROSE

JOHN ROSENBERG

AT THE AGE OF THIRTEEN Ruskin apologized to his father for his inability to compose "a short, pithy, laconic, sensible, concentrated" letter. As for the writing itself, he went on, " 'tis nothing, positively nothing. I roll on like a ball, with this exception, that contrary to the usual laws of motion I have no friction to contend with in my mind, and of course have some difficulty in stopping myself, when there is nothing else to stop me."[1] Late in life the friction was to become overwhelming, until Ruskin's mind finally ceased to move at all, or spun at angles which no longer meshed with words. But for some sixty years words came to him with an astonishing aptness and ease.

I

In his very earliest writing, Ruskin the solitary observer occasionally jostles up against Ruskin the precocious mimic of Johnson or Byron. The acuity of vision is uniquely his, but the idiom is stiff and at times fits him like an oversized costume. Publishing *The Poetry of Architecture* while still in his teens, or composing the first volume of *Modern Painters* when scarcely out of them, Ruskin usurps a tone of authority which age or knowledge alone could not confer. The result is intermittent affectation with an obvious straining at effects, show-pieces of literary gesticulation in which phrases too punctually alliterate and cadences too melodiously sing. Here is Ruskin at nineteen attacking the absurdity of imitating the architecture of the past when the conditions which produced the original no longer prevail. The vigor of the verbs, the richness of the metaphor, the Johnsonian syntactical balance heightened by the parallel symmetries of sound, the polysyllabic wedding of adjective to noun at the close—all have an impudence of artistry akin to wit:

> The mistake of our architects in general is, that they fancy they are speaking good English by speaking bad Greek. . . . But imitation, the endeavour to be Gothic, or Tyrolese, or Venetian, without the slightest grain of Gothic or Venetian feeling; the futile effort to splash a building into age, or daub it into dignity, to zigzag it into sanctity, or slit it into ferocity, when its shell is neither ancient nor dignified, and its spirit neither priestly nor baronial,—this is the degrading vice of the age; fostered, as if a man's reason were but a step between the brains of a kitten and a monkey, in the mixed love of despicable excitement and miserable mimicry. (I, 168)

By the time he was twenty, Ruskin had nothing to learn about writing, except to unbend a bit, and let the rhythms of living speech break through those locked, alliterative clauses.

Ruskin's early period is the only one in which he has what is commonly understood as "style"—that is to say, a distinguishable set of mannerisms which overlies his prose like an appliqué. The essence of such a style is that it serves as a shell or container, bearing no organic relation to the thing it contains. It is the hallmark of the minor artist who, through certain recurrent formulæ, achieves the security of an identity. It is a passing phase in the apprenticeship of a great artist, a period of negative identity, as it were, when he fills the void of his uncreated self with the tones of those from whom he is learning his art. Dr. Johnson might have uttered the following sentence in a melancholy moment: "I seem born to conceive what I cannot execute, recommend what I cannot obtain, and mourn over what I cannot save" (VIII, xxix). It was in fact written by the young Ruskin, at work on *The Seven Lamps of Architecture,* as he watched the "restorers" destroying the cathedral of Abbeville.

Although Ruskin has no single style, or, more accurately, shed his style as he became himself, in another sense his styles were as various as the subjects he wrote upon and the audiences he addressed: searingly logical in *Unto This Last,* gracious and courtly in the Inaugural Oxford Lecture on Art, colloquial in *Fors Clavigera,* apocalyptic in *The Storm-Cloud of the Nineteenth Century,* ripplingly lucid in *Praeterita.* He is precious, indeed mincing, in *The Ethics of the Dust,* ten lectures for "little housewives," yet he surpasses the rage of Isaiah in denouncing the British Empire as "a slimy polype, multiplying by involuntary vivisection, and dropping half putrid pieces of itself wherever it crawls or contracts" (XXVII, 451). The idiom of the plays that Shakespeare wrote for the Court differs from the idiom of those first performed before the pit; Ruskin makes precisely the same adjustment, unfailingly and with Shakespearian resourcefulness.

"Style," as I have just used the term is a selection from among the infinite tonalities of language in accord with the matter at hand and the expectations of the audience. But the word has also a rarer and more elusive sense, which everything in this essay is an imperfect attempt to elucidate. I have in mind not an outward adaptation to the exigencies of subject and audience, but an inner manifestation: style as the incarnation of sensibility. Style of this kind has nothing whatever to do with levels of speech; it *is* speech, the unique voice of the writer, the felt presence that hovers over his pages and intones its way into our consciousness. We acknowledge its presence when we say of a very great writer that he "has genius" or is "immortal"; we know that his words, like the books which house them, cannot last forever. But he has succeeded in re-creating *himself*, not in the flesh, as we can do, but in the spirit, and his anima has miraculously passed into our own minds. In this ultimate sense, Ruskin is the greatest prose stylist in English.

Yet Ruskin has always been best known for his most mannered, conventionally stylish passages and less known for the works in which he most intensely lives. He is supposed to have become progressively unreadable; in fact, he was *always* solitary and eccentric, but as his hold on reality became more remote, his style became more and more intimate. In his later works he often seems to stand at an alien's distance from the world, but in almost frightening proximity to the reader. This effect of immediacy is in part due to Ruskin's lifelong labor to avoid all appearance of laboriousness; after a dazzling apprenticeship in which he delighted in making language do splits and somersaults, he discovered he could make it accomplish even more by standing it on its feet. In part the change in tone results from a shift in Ruskin's concerns. In the early volumes of *Modern Painters*, Ruskin focused his superb gifts of observation and articulation upon clouds, seas, and mountains. In middle life, however, the sense of divinity he had felt in nature began to fail him, and his interest shifted from the actual Alps to the mountains of his own mind. To scale those yet more perilous peaks, he perfected a subtler instrument of prose which registers the very pulsations of thought. Reading *Modern Painters* gives one, in Charlotte Brontë's phrase, a new sense, *sight*; reading Ruskin's later works expands one's awareness of consciousness itself.

All through his career, Ruskin's prose remained uncannily responsive to the movements of his sensibility. His style is lyric and overwhelming in his exultant early years. He masses clause upon clause in *Modern Painters* with the same luminous, colossal energy that he observes in nature or on the canvases of Turner. True, at times he postures Byronically upon a mountain peak and paints for us too purple a picture of a sunset. But the heart of the book is a sustained, fanatical hymn to the divinity and force of nature. "Poetic" prose blurs where it should be specific and merely emotes because it cannot enumerate; the prose of *Modern Painters* makes a religion of specificity and a divinity of precision. The command of the Angel of the Apocalypse is heard throughout the book: "Write the things which thou hast seen, and the things which are." *Observe, see, look* recur with obsessive frequency, until the eye becomes exhausted from the sheer multiplicity of things held up before it. Consider, for example, Ruskin's defense of the revolutionary fidelity of J. M. W. Turner's *Snow Storm: Steamboat off a Harbour's Mouth.* The critics had denounced the great, glowing paintings of Turner's last decade as a mess of multi-colored soapsuds, but Ruskin saw in the swirling vortex of the *Snow Storm* a rendering of the cataclysmic forces of nature more impassioned yet more precise than had ever before been captured on canvas. Like some vast, inexhaustible fountain, the passage cannot be compressed, only cut off:

> Few people, comparatively, have ever seen the effect on the sea of a powerful gale continued without intermission for three or four days and nights; and to those who have not, I believe it must be unimaginable, not from the mere force or size of surge, but from the complete annihilation of the limit between sea and air. The water from its prolonged agitation is beaten, not into mere creaming foam, but into masses of accumulated yeast, which hang in ropes and wreaths from wave to wave, and, where one curls over to break, form a festoon like a drapery from its edge; these are taken up by the wind, not in dissipating dust, but bodily, in writhing, hanging, coiling masses, which make the air white and thick as with snow, only the flakes are a foot or two long each: the surges themselves are full of foam in their very bodies, underneath, making them white all through, as the water is under a great cataract; and their masses, being thus half water and half air, are torn to pieces by the wind whenever they rise, and carried away in roaring smoke, which chokes and strangles like actual water. Add to this, that when the air has been exhausted of its moisture by long rain, the spray

of the sea is caught by it as described above, and covers its surface not merely with the smoke of finely divided water, but with boiling mist; imagine also the low rain-clouds brought down to the very level of the sea, as I have often seen them, whirling and flying in rags and fragments from wave to wave; and finally, conceive the surges themselves in their utmost pitch of power, velocity, vastness, and madness, lifting themselves in precipices and peaks, furrowed with their whirl of ascent, through all this chaos; and you will understand that there is indeed no distinction left betwen the sea and air; that no object, nor horizon, nor any land-mark or natural evidence of position is left; that the heaven is all spray, and the ocean all cloud, and that you can see no farther in any direction than you could see through a cataract. Suppose the effect of the first sunbeam sent from above to show this annihilation to itself, and you have the sea picture of the Academy, 1842, the Snowstorm, one of the very grandest statements of sea-motion, mist, and light, that has ever been put on canvas, even by Turner. Of course it was not understood. . . . (iii, 569-71)

Ruskin's greatness as a writer began with his acuity as an observer. He was born with a remarkable capacity to see and to recall, and these gifts were enhanced by every circumstance of his childhood. "Men are made what they finally become," he wrote, "only by the external accidents which are in harmony with their inner nature" (xiv, 385). The biographer is always in danger of attributing to environmental accident the antecedent disposition which gives the accident its importance. Yet Ruskin's whole early experience was "accident-prone," calculated in all its virtues and deficiencies to intensify his "inner nature." The monastic severities of the childhood he describes in *Praeterita*, the paucity of distractions within his affluent but austere home, the influence of benign but remote parents who bared no ugliness to their child yet offered him nothing to love, the serene yet solitary routine of an almost toyless, entirely companionless childhood, forced Ruskin to people his world with the pictures his senses conveyed or his imagination conceived. Patterns in his nursery carpet, like the ants that nested in his walled garden, were the most accessible objects in his world. One imagines him *looking,* where another child would touch: "I had a sensual faculty of pleasure in sight," he once remarked, "as far as I know unparalleled" (xxxv, 619).

Sight and insight were, for Ruskin, a single simultaneous act, the one unfailing pleasure of his life. He once wrote of the painter's gift of "innocence of the eye" (xv, 27), by which he meant a capacity to perceive with a child's immediacy certain pure stains of color, apart from whatever their particular forms might signify. Ruskin retained this gift throughout life, and it gives to his descriptions an almost morbid clarity. The very intensity of his perceptions isolated him in a world from which his countless words and sketches served as a release. "There is the strong instinct in me which I cannot analyse," he wrote in his thirties, "to draw and describe the things I love . . . a sort of instinct like that for eating and drinking."[2]

Words were the reliquary in which Ruskin preserved his experience, and from earliest childhood he approached language with reverence. The subject of his first formal study was the Word itself, in the form of Scripture, which his mother compelled him to commit to memory during their annual progress from Genesis through Apocalypse. In *Praeterita* one feels the deliberate effort he must make to summon up that immense labor. On one occasion, for example, Ruskin and his mother engaged in a three-week contest of wills over the proper stressing of a single word. Yet there is no bitterness in the recollection—only measured gratitude for what he calls "the one *essential* part of my education" (xxxv, 43). Such close scrutiny of the Bible not only shaped Ruskin's values but became part of the texture of his thought. Its influence goes beyond the more than five thousand Biblical allusions in his published works. It underlines the majestic simplicity of his cadences and serves as an anchor of immense moral weight for his social criticism.

Throughout his career, Ruskin approached language as a thing to be tested by tongue and ear. His mother's reading aloud of the Bible, his father's recitations of Shakespeare, Johnson, and Scott exposed him to accuracy of diction and precision of accent that tuned his ear for life. In one of his later works he complains of having to stop writing because the whistle of a passing train prevents him from *hearing* his own words.

The habit of scrutinizing words intently made Ruskin a keen critic of the language of others as well as of his own. Scattered throughout his collected works is a body of close textual criticism of the Bible, Homer, Plato, Virgil, Dante, Spenser, Chaucer, Shakespeare, Milton, Pope, Scott, Byron, and Wordsworth that is unrivalled in the nineteenth century except, possibly, by Coleridge. Ruskin knew the power of language to corrupt intelligence and feeling,[3] and he looked upon his textual criticism as a means of teaching precision of thought by illustrating precision of diction and image. He had a remarkable knowledge of the peerage of words, their sources and connotations, and with his virtual total recall of all that he had ever studied in classical and modern literatures, his mind served him as a kind of universal concordance. One gains insight into Ruskin's own scrupulous use of language from his celebrated exegesis of the "blind mouthes" metaphor in *Lycidas*.[4] He senses his way back into the Miltonic mind and re-creates the learned, literal, impassioned imagination that first coined the phrase:

> I pause again, for this is a strange expression; a broken metaphor, one might think, careless and unscholarly.
> Not so: its very audacity and pithiness are intended to make us look close at the phrase and remember it. Those two monosyllables express the precisely accurate contraries of right character, in the two great offices of the Church—those of bishop and pastor.
> A "Bishop" means "a person who sees."
> A "Pastor" means "a person who feeds."
> The most unbishoply character a man can have is therefore to be Blind.
> The most unpastoral is, instead of feeding, to want to be fed—to be a Mouth.
> Take the two reverses together, and you have "blind mouthes."
>
> (xviii, 72)

II

We demand metaphor in poetry, welcome it in fiction, but fail even to recognize its presence in discursive prose. Of the two greatest creators of metaphor in nineteenth-century English prose, Dickens has long been recognized, but the achievement of Ruskin has passed largely unnoticed because of certain persistent illusions concerning the distinction between poetry and prose. Matthew Arnold exemplifies these illusions in his oddly obtuse essay, "The Literary Influence of Academies." Arnold argues that genius is the defining mark of poetry, intelligence, of prose. The poet may be extravagant or eccentric; the prose writer should be balanced and urbane—Attic rather than Asiatic. Betraying himself by the very vigor of his examples, Arnold holds up for our disapproval sentences by Jeremy Taylor, Burke, and Ruskin. All three, Arnold assures us, are marred by "the note of provinciality"; in each, genius has been too busy and intelligence too quiescent.

Arnold's specious divorce of genius from prose and intelligence from poetry is a sophisticated variant of the vulgar belief that poetry belongs to the province of the heart, prose to the head; that the language of poetry should be fancy and figurative, while the language of prose must be literal and direct. Significantly, each of the excerpts Arnold condemns is highly metaphorical, and this, I suspect, is the cause of his discomfort. The language works in ways that Arnold believes are improper to prose—ways characteristic of "genius": Ruskin is "trying to make prose do more than it can perfectly do; . . . what he is there attempting he will never, except in poetry, be able to accomplish. . . ." In fact, Ruskin's experience was exactly the reverse. He had been brought up to become a bishop or a second Byron, and all through his youth he tried to express in vapid verse what he later discovered he could communicate only in prose—a prose at once infinitely more metaphorical and more precise than anything he had achieved in poetry.

The only useful distinction to be drawn is between figurative and non-figurative language, either in poetry or prose.[5] There is good and bad writing of either kind in either form. The language of the third chapter of *Little Dorrit* or of the chapter on the bird and serpent in *The Queen of the Air,* for example, rewards the same intensity of scrutiny that one gives to the language of *King Lear.*

A passage from *The Stones of Venice* will enable us to test these generalizations against the substance of Ruskin's prose. I have in mind the chapter on St. Mark's, in which Ruskin describes a quiet, English cathedral town, contrasts it with the loud bustle of the streets opening on the Piazza San Marco, stations us before the glittering façade of the cathedral, and then glances at the sullen crowd gathered under its portals. Bits and pieces of the chapter always appear in collections of Ruskin "gems"; the truncation altogether destroys the potent symbolic patterning.

The chapter is a study in stillness and motion, sanctity and depravity. It recapitulates in miniature the larger pattern of *The Stones of Venice,* the three volumes of which constitute a great Christian epic tracing the rise and fall of a Gothic paradise. For a moment we are placed within a modest version of that paradise, all gabled neatness and trim lawns, as Ruskin re-creates the lichened loveliness of an English cathedral close, soundless save for the cry of the birds circling high between the church towers. Ruskin then abruptly turns to the tumultuous streets opening out on San Marco. With a novelist's grasp of sights and sounds, he transforms our flat, postcard recollections of Venice into a rounded substantial thing, a carved architectural space enclosing the magnificent vision he later gives us of the cathedral itself. But first we find ourselves jammed into

> a paved alley, some seven feet wide where it is widest, full of people, and resonant with cries of itinerant salesmen,—a shriek in their beginning, and dying away into a kind of brazen ringing, all the worse for its confinement between the high houses of the passage along which we have to make our way. Overhead, an inextricable confusion of rugged shutters, and iron balconies and chimney flues, pushed out on brackets to save room, and arched windows with projecting sills of Istrian stone, and gleams of green leaves here and there where a fig-tree branch escapes over a lower wall from some inner cortile, leading the eye up to the narrow stream of blue sky high over all. (x, 80)

We pass the narrow row of shops with their prints of the Madonna, their casks of oil and wine, until at last, at the Bocca di Piazza, pushing our way out towards the surge of light, the vast dome of San Marco "seems to lift itself visibly forth from the level field of chequered stones."

The passage modulates from sound to silence and from motion to timelessness as Ruskin pauses to paint for our amazed beholding the façade of the cathedral. He now empties the description of all social content, giving us an aesthete's pure vision of marble and gold:

> . . . Beyond those troops of ordered arches there rises a vision out of the earth, and all the great square seems to have opened from it in a kind of awe, that we may see it far away;—a multitude of pillars and white domes, clustered into a long low pyramid of coloured light; a treasure-heap, it seems, partly of gold, and partly of opal and mother-of-pearl, hollowed beneath into five great vaulted porches, ceiled with fair mosaic, and beset with sculpture of alabaster, clear as amber and delicate as ivory . . . a confusion of delight, amidst which the breasts of the Greek horses are seen blazing in their breadth of golden strength, and the St. Mark's lion, lifted on a blue field covered with stars, until at last, as if in ecstasy, the crests of the arches break into a marble foam, and toss themselves far into the blue sky in flashes and wreathes of sculptured spray, as if the breakers on the Lido shore had been frost-bound before they fell, and the sea-nymphs had inlaid them with coral and amethyst. (x, 82-3)

One feels as though a reel of color film had been suddenly stopped and the eye arrested by the sheer visual impact of a single frame. This is the paradise, Ruskin suggests, that Venice built at the height of her power and faith. Ruskin allows only one living thing to flit across the entire tableau: the doves that "nestle among the marble foliage, and mingle the soft iridescence of their living plumes, changing at every motion, with the tints, hardly less lovely, that have stood unchanged for seven hundred years."

In the final paragraph the dove, with its full weight of Christian association, reappears as a symbol of the contemporary desecration of the square. All classes of mid nineteenth-century Venetian society range before us in Ruskin's portrait of the post-Gothic, fallen city, occupied by Austrian troops, around whose martial bands the menacing crowd *thickens*, like some undifferentiated mass. On the very porch of the church, under the figure of Christ—the one fixed image that presides over this violent bestiality—a dehumanized humanity gambles, as if casting dice for His robe:

> And what effect has this splendour on those who pass beneath it? You may walk from sunrise to sunset, to and fro, before the gateway of St. Mark's, and you will not see an eye lifted to it, nor a countenance brightened by it. Priest and layman, soldier and civilian, rich and poor, pass by it alike regardlessly. Up to the very recesses of the porches, the meanest tradesmen of the city push their counters; nay, the foundations of its pillars are themselves the seats—not "of them that sell doves"[6] for sacrifice, but of the vendors of toys and caricatures. Round the whole square in front of the church there is almost a continuous line of cafés, where the idle Venetians of the middle classes lounge, and read empty journals; in its centre the Austrian bands play during the time of vespers, their martial music jarring with the organ notes,—the march drowning the miserere, and the sullen crowd thickening round them,— a crowd, which if it had its will, would stiletto every soldier that pipes to it. And in the recesses of the porches, all day long, knots of men of the lowest classes, unemployed and listless, lie basking in the sun like lizards; and unregarded children,—every heavy glance of their young eyes full of desperation and stony depravity, and their throats hoarse with cursing,—gamble, and fight, and snarl, and sleep, hour after hour, clashing their bruised centesimi upon the marble ledges of the church porch. And the images of Christ and His angels look down upon it continually. (x, 84-5)

The lizard-like men are at least semi-connected to life; to the children is left the final, Dantesque hardening into lifelessness. Through a brilliant transference of attributes, the metal coins dashed before Christ's image have still the tenderness to be *bruised*, but the children who pitch them curse in *stony* depravity . . . "Suffer the little children to come unto me, for such is the kingdom of God."

Almost invariably the greatest passages in Ruskin's prose are structured around two opposing visions, one of felicity and the other of some form of hell. Composed over a seventeen-year period, *Modern Painters* (1842-60) illustrates this contrast on the grand scale. Parts of the book, of course, can be read as detachable essays, segments of objectively crystallized thought, such as Ruskin's brilliant chapters on the pathetic fallacy or classical landscape; but independent of these essays, although often threaded through them, is an intricate autobiography of the spirit which traces Ruskin's growth from a youthful, ecstatic, evangelical, ego-oriented worshipper of nature to a brooding, guilt-burdened observer of the brutality of man.

In the closing volumes of *Modern Painters* the face of God seems to withdraw from nature and in His stead emerges a "multitudinous, marred humanity" (vii, 384). One feels the whole hinge of sensibility turn from lyric exultation to tragic despair as Ruskin's focus shifts, to use the phrasing of his chapter titles, from "The Mountain Glory" to "The Mountain Gloom." In a passage beautifully poised between sublimity and terror, beauty and despair, Ruskin describes the region of Alps and deep valleys extending from Chamonix into the Swiss canton of Valais. The prose reflects both the contours of the landscape and the inner geography of Ruskin's mind. It opens in a burst of sunshine bathing green fields, but then modulates to saddened shade:

> Green field, and glowing rock, and glancing streamlet, all slope together in the sunshine towards the brows of ravines, where the pines take up their own dominion of saddened shade; and with everlasting roar in the twilight, the stronger torrents thunder down, pale from the glaciers, filling all their chasms with enchanted cold, beating themselves to pieces against the great rocks that they have themselves cast down, and forcing fierce way beneath their ghastly poise. (vi, 387)

We bring to such scenes stock associations of bright beauty, but Ruskin from the start undercuts our expectations with a suggestion of the sinister—"pale . . . cold . . . ghastly"—beneath the sublime. The same balance of juxtaposed elements persists as Ruskin combines in a long, undulating sentence a strange medley of opposites: crimson light and pallor, power and faintness, sunshine and deep melancholy, beauty and the sepulchre:

> Far up the glen, as we pause beside the cross, the sky is seen through the openings in the pines, thin with excess of light; and, in its clear, consuming flame of white space, the summits of the rocky mountains are gathered into solemn crowns and circlets, all flushed in that strange, faint silence of possession by the sunshine which has in it so deep a melancholy; full of power, yet as frail as shadows: lifeless, like the walls of a sepulchre, yet beautiful in tender fall of crimson folds, like the veil of some sea spirit, that lives and dies as the foam flashes. . . . (VI, 387)

The tragic element latent in the landscape intensifies as the perspective shifts from the mountain peaks to the villages clustered on their flanks. "The traveller on his happy journey," Ruskin writes with an intended touch of triteness, as he "gaily" walks along the deep turf, expects to find in the mountain cottages peace and pleasant-fellowship with nature; instead, he comes upon "gloomy foulness" and anguish of soul. The traveller is no mere conventional figure in the foreground of a landscape; he is Ruskin himself, abandoning his Wordsworthian enthusiasm in *Modern Painters,* Volume I, for the somber social concerns of *Modern Painters,* Volume V and of *Unto This Last.* This undercurrent of deeply felt discovery gives to the lines that follow their urgency and eloquent anxiety. As always, what Ruskin describes is rooted in the closest observation of fact; again, as always the fact takes on a reciprocal coloring from Ruskin's mind, so that the world he describes reflects a personally heightened reality. External objects become charged with the inner chiaroscuro of Ruskin's spirit and he gives to inanimate fact, as in *The Queen of the Air* and *The Storm-Cloud of the Nineteenth Century,* the superb force of myth.

Enter one of the village streets, Ruskin writes, and you will find

> torpor—not absolute suffering—not starvation or disease, but darkness of calm enduring; the spring known as the time of the scythe, and the autumn as the time of the sickle, and the sun only as a warmth, the wind as a chill, and the mountains as a danger. . . . Black bread, rude roof, dark night, laborious day, weary arm at sunset; and life ebbs away. No books, no thoughts, no attainments, no rest; except only sometimes a

little sitting in the sun under the church wall, as the bell tolls thin and far in the mountain air; a pattering of a few prayers, not understood, by the altar rails of the dimly gilded chapel, and so back to the sombre home, with the cloud upon them still unbroken—that cloud of rocky gloom, born out of the wild torrents and ruinous stones, and unlightened, even in their religion, except by the vague promise of some better thing unknown, mingled with threatening, and obscured by an unspeakable horror,—a smoke, as it were, of martyrdom, coiling up with the incense, and, amidst the images of tortured bodies and lamenting spirits in hurtling flames, the very cross, for them, dashed more deeply than for others, with gouts of blood. (vi, 388-9)

The passage builds up from weary disillusion to terror. The series of spondees beginning with *bláck bréad, rúde roóf, dárk níght* echoes in its locked, alliterative pattern the imprisoning monotony of the life Ruskin describes, as do the repeated *no's* that follow.[7] There then occurs a remarkable modulation from confinement to the momentary release of "sitting in the sun under the church wall, *as the bell tolls thin and far in the mountain air.*" An iambic rhythm runs in and out of the phrase, echoing the rhythmic tolling of the bell, which peals faintly through eleven attenuated words, ten of them monosyllables. In the final lines the green fields and glowing rocks of the opening paragraph are blotted out by a rising sense of horror in which the idiom of *The Storm-Cloud* makes its first appearance in Ruskin's prose. One recalls an entry that he made in his diary in 1874, after revisiting the very valley he had described twenty years earlier in "The Mountain Gloom": "Exquisite, ineffable beauty and joy of heart for me, all along valley of Cluse. . . . So walked to Bonneville. There—at first—still all sweet; then a cloud seemed to come over my mind and the sky together" (*Diaries*, iii, 817).

It may be that the greatest creative artists are all Manichees in spirit, possessed of a vision of blessedness beyond our grasp of joy and of an inferno more profound and actual than we can fathom. The two worlds stand juxtaposed in a remarkable letter in *Fors Clavigera* entitled "Benediction." Writing from his rooms overlooking the Grand Canal, Ruskin distinguishs between the contrary states of blessedness and accursedness. The measured pace of the prose, with its exegesis of the Biblical text, "out of the same mouth proceedeth blessing and cursing," is suddenly interrupted by the shrill sounds of a Lido steamer and by the cry of a boy selling half-rotten figs at the quayside. The sight of the boy's face brings tears to Ruskin's eyes, "so open, and sweet, and capable it was; and so sad." Ruskin gives the boy some coins but takes no figs, leaving it for the reader to puzzle out the connection between modern accursedness and the impoverished boy selling fruit "that could not be eaten, it was so evil" before the Ducal Palace.

The letter continues with a further series of apparent non-sequiturs, until we realize that the contrary states Ruskin is defining are in fact his own divided consciousness, split into a heightened awareness of felicity and pain. The two states are fused in perhaps the most extraordinary paragraph in all of his works. In the main body of the paragraph, outside the long, violently disruptive parentheses, Ruskin continues his reasoned analysis of blessedness, quoting the passage from Isaiah in which "the lame man shall leap as an hart." Within the parentheses, the piercing whistle of the steamer heard earlier in the letter now cuts like a knife into Ruskin's consciousness and forms a kind of insane, modern counterpoint to the singing of the dumb:

> Again, with regard to the limbs, or general powers of the body. Do you suppose that when it is promised that "the lame man shall leap as an hart, and the tongue of the dumb sing"—(Steam-whistle interrupts me from the *Capo d'Istria,* which is lying in front of my window with her black nose pointed at the red nose of another steamer at the next pier. There are nine large ones at this instant,—half past six, morning, 4th July,—lying between the Church of the Redeemer and the Canal of the Arsenal; one of them an ironclad, five smoking fiercely, and the biggest,—English and half a quarter of a mile long,—blowing steam from all manner of pipes in her sides, and with such a roar through her funnel—whistle number two from *Capo d'Istria*—that I could not make any one hear me speak in this room without an effort),—do you suppose, I say, that such a form of benediction is just the same as saying that the lame man shall leap as a lion, and the tongue of the dumb mourn? Not so, but a special manner of action of the members is meant in both cases: (whistle number three from *Capo d'Istria;* I am writing on, steadily, so that you will be able to form an accurate idea, from this page, of the intervals of time in modern music. The roaring of the English boat goes on all the while, for bass to the *Capo d'Istria's* treble, and a tenth steamer comes in sight round the Armenian Monastery)— a particular kind of activity is meant, I repeat, in both cases. The lame man is to leap, (whistle fourth from *Capo d'Istria,* this time at high pressure, going through my head like a knife) as an innocent and joyful

creature leaps, and the lips of the dumb to move melodiously: they are to be blest, so; may not be unblest even in silence; but are the absolute contrary of blest, in evil utterance. (Fifth whistle, a double one, from *Capo d'Istria*, and it is seven o'clock, nearly; and here's my coffee, and I must stop writing. Sixth whistle—the *Capo d'Istria* is off, with her crew of morning bathers. Seventh,—from I don't know which of the boats outside—and I count no more.)   (xxvii, 341-2)

One expects silence to follow, or articulate madness. Instead, the letter turns back upon itself and Ruskin completes, in perfect control, his discussion of blessedness and damnation.

Perhaps the classic instance of this polarization of reality in Ruskin's writing occurs in the course of a digression in *Deucalion* (1875-83). It is especially revealing of how certain central motifs of Ruskin's experience recur throughout his works, spaced over many decades and independent of the ostensible subject at hand. The first half of the passage has the violent, contorted vigor of an expressionist nightmare; the second half is possibly the noblest evocation of the chiming of bells in English prose. The bells that Ruskin describes, it so happens, were the same ones whose music had tolled "thin and far" through the valley of Cluse and had moved him to record in his diary his "exquisite . . . joy of heart":

I had been, for six months in Italy, never for a single moment quit of liability to interruption of thought. By day or night, whenever I was awake, in the streets of every city, there were entirely monstrous and inhuman noises in perpetual recurrence . . . : wild bellowing and howling of obscene wretches far into the night: clashing of church bells, in the morning, dashed into reckless discord, from twenty towers at once, as if rung by devils to defy and destroy the quiet of God's sky, and mock the laws of His harmony: filthy, stridulous shrieks and squeaks, reaching for miles into the quiet air, from the railroad stations at every gate: and the vociferation, endless, and frantic, of a passing populace whose every word was in mean passion, or in unclean jest.

With an abruptness of transition characteristic of the recorders of visions, Ruskin writes that he found himself "suddenly, as in a dream," walking through the valley of Cluse, unchanged since he first saw it as a boy forty years earlier. The force of that early association drowns out the cacophony of the previous paragraph. We move in tone away from the sinister dissonances of *Fors Clavigera* and *The Storm-Cloud,* back to the ecstatic harmonies of Ruskin's earliest prose, and forward to the cloudless skies of his final work, *Praeterita*:

> As I walked, the calm was deepened, instead of interrupted, by a murmur—first low, as of bees, and then rising into distinct harmonious chime of deep bells, ringing in true cadences—but I could not tell where. The cliffs on each side of the Valley of Cluse vary from 1500 to above 2000 feet in height; and, without absolutely echoing the chime, they so accepted, prolonged, and diffused it, that at first I thought it came from a village high up and far away among the hills; then presently it came down to me as if from above the cliff under which I was walking; then I turned about and stood still, wondering; for the whole valley was filled with the sweet sound, entirely without local or conceivable origin. . . .
> Perfectly beautiful, all the while, the sound, and exquisitely varied, —from ancient bells of perfect tone and series. (xxvi, 150-52)

The passage from *Deucalion* is frankly autobiographical; elsewhere, Ruskin expresses the same polarization of sensibility more indirectly. For example, in "The Two Boyhoods" he combines in a single essay a brilliant critique of Giorgione and Turner, together with an implicit confession of his own changed temper in the long course of writing *Modern Painters.* The chapter opens with a highly mannered account of the Venice that the young Giorgione first saw, a marble fantasy paved with the emerald of the sea, a tidal city whose rhythms, tuned to the moon's, Ruskin repeats in a single perfect sentence: "No foulness, nor tumult, in those tremulous streets, that filled, or fell, beneath the moon; but rippled music of majestic change, or thrilling silence" (vii, 375). At the very verge of excess the prose abruptly modulates to the squalid actuality of the London of Turner's boyhood: dead brick walls, dusty sunbeams over the quays, clusters of half-rotten vegetables in the markets, things "fishy and muddy" and succulently ugly which Turner later reintroduces in the rich *litter* of his foregrounds. Giorgione sees beauty and ceremony everywhere, and paints them everywhere; Turner sees the city's "poverty-struck or cruel faces" and paints a fallen humanity, or seeks refuge in the strength of nature. Of the life of men, he paints only "their labour, their sorrow, and their death." Like "The Mountain Gloom" and "The Mountain Glory," "The Two Boyhoods" is a self-portrait in contrasting styles of two aspects of Ruskin. The closing paragraphs are less a critique of Turner than the bridge between Ruskin's complementary careers as a critic of art and a critic of society.

III

I have stressed—perhaps overstressed—Ruskin's style as the vehicle of his sensibility. In so doing, I am aware of the danger of reducing his books to mere biographical or psychological "evidence," thus eroding their importance as independent works of mind. The fault I suspect in my own analysis differs radically from the fault I would attribute to Ruskin's Victorian critics. Essentially eulogist-disciples, they concentrated on the Master's "message," ignoring his digressions and discounting his eccentricities. The splendid waywardness of Ruskin's genius, the idiosyncratic wrinkles in all that he wrote, were smoothed out to produce the official Victorian portrait of the Prophet: benign, bearded, unshakeably sound. This is the image of Ruskin which bored the generation between the two world wars and which caused his works to go unread.

The critic today, writing in an existential, psychologizing, agony-loving age, almost necessarily overstresses Ruskin's sickness at the expense of his sanity, his psyche at the expense of his thought. An obvious casualty of such a bias is the body of work in which Ruskin, untroubled by private obsession or public concern, writes out of the sheer joy of making words follow his will. Virginia Woolf once commented on this quality of delight in Ruskin's prose: "We find ourselves marveling at the words, as if all the fountains of the English language had been set playing in the sunlight for our pleasure."[8] One feels the exhilaration of absolute mastery over language throughout Ruskin's career, and it defeats any attempt to impose a rigid, sequential pattern of styles or periods upon his prose. It is present in the child's letter which opened this essay; it characterizes each line of the opening essay of *The Harbours of England* (1856), one of Ruskin's sanest, loveliest, and least known books; it recurs most movingly at the very end of his career, when, between incapacitating attacks of madness, he composed this description of the Rhone river:

> For all other rivers there is a surface, and an underneath, and a vaguely displeasing idea of the bottom. But the Rhone flows like one lambent jewel; its surface is nowhere, its ethereal self is everywhere, the

iridescent rush and translucent strength of it blue to the shore, and radiant to the depth.

Fifteen feet thick, of not flowing, but flying water; not water, neither, melted glacier, rather, one should call it; the force of the ice is with it, and the wreathing of the clouds, the gladness of the sky, and the continuance of Time.

Waves of clear sea are, indeed, lovely to watch, but they are always coming or gone, never in any taken shape to be seen for a second. But here was one mighty wave that was always itself, and every fluted swirl of it, constant as the wreathing of a shell. No wasting away of the fallen foam, no pause for gathering of power, no helpless ebb of discouraged recoil; but alike through bright day and lulling night, the never-pausing plunge, and never-fading flash, and never-hushing whisper, and, while the sun was up, the ever-answering glow of unearthly aquamarine, ultramarine, violet-blue, gentian-blue, peacock-blue, river-of-paradise blue, glass of a painted window melted in the sun, and the witch of the Alps flinging the spun tresses of it for ever from her snow. (xxxv, 326-7)

One doesn't "analyze" such prose; one rejoices in it, and recognizes in its reckless abundance of invention the mark of absolute genius.

No one can read Ruskin for very long without feeling the "sudden glory" of language in lighting up reality and revealing interrelations where, without words, there had been only darkness. *Unto This Last* provides an example in the single word *illth*, Ruskin's coinage for what is often called wealth but is in fact superfluous or inimical to the true needs of society. The same gift, akin to wit in its force and felicity, operates in his perception that shadow was treated by the Gothic architect as a "dark colour, to be arranged in certain agreeable masses" (viii, 238), or in his characterization of the darting, chimney-haunting swallow as "an owl that has been trained by the Graces. . . . a bat that loves the morning light. . . . the aërial reflection of a dolphin. . . . the tender domestication of a trout" (xxv, 57).

These are the *divertissements* of a fine mind expending its superflux of energy in play. A graver wit—the play of a mind in deep distress—characterizes *Fors Clavigera* (1871-84), a miscellany of savage social criticism, autobiography, utopian reform, and random observation that Ruskin published in the form of "Letters to the Workmen of Great Britain." "You think I jest, still, do you?" Ruskin asks in a particularly extravagant moment. "Anything but that; only if I took off the Harlequin's mask for a moment, you would say I was simply mad," (xxviii, 513). Ruskin affects the very madness which he fears and which in fact overtook him in the course of writing *Fors Clavigera*. His antic disposition licenses him to follow the thousands of vertiginous thoughts flitting through his mind "like sea-birds for which there are no sands to settle upon" (xxvii, 460). He develops a remarkably colloquial, allusive style, with lightning transitions that propel the reader through the labyrinth of his concerns and the oscillations of his moods. At times the language is so uncannily close in all its rhythms to human speech that one seems to be overhearing a soliloquy within one's own mind. In Cardinal Manning's phrase, the letters are like "the beating of one's heart in a nightmare."[9]

To pass from the intermittent rage of *Fors Clavigera* to the peace of *Praeterita* is to enter another world. Although the book was written in periods of pathological gloom, Ruskin recaptures the past with crystalline lucidity and grace.[10] Stylistically, the book represents the triumph of a deceptively easy style over a painfully complex subject, the growth of a child who numbered chief among his calamities:

> First, that I had nothing to love.
> My parents were—in a sort—visible powers of nature to me, no more loved than the sun and the moon: only I should have been annoyed and puzzled if either of them had gone out; (how much, now, when both are darkened!) . . . (xxxv, 44-5)

The recall is total, yet totally unembittered. In this connection the reader might compare Ruskin's balanced, illusionless account in *Praeterita* of his childhood blessings and calamities with a letter he wrote just before his father's sudden death. He furiously reproaches the elder Ruskins for having thwarted him "in all the earnest fire of passion and life" (xxxvi, 461). Yet the story Ruskin tells in *Praeterita* is not a jot less true for its restraint. Beneath the serenity is a tense and beautifully precise awareness which Ruskin directs equally at his mother, his father, and himself:

> She must then have been rapidly growing into a tall, handsome, and very finely made girl, with a beautiful mild firmness of expression; a faultless and accomplished housekeeper, and a natural, essential, unassailable, yet inoffensive prude. (xxxv, 122)
> The chief fault in my father's mind, (I say so reverently, for its faults

were few, but necessarily, for they were very fatal,) was his dislike of being excelled. He knew his own power—felt that he had not nerve to use or display it, in full measure; but all the more, could not bear, in his own sphere, any approach to equality. He chose his clerks first for trustworthiness, secondly for—*in*capacity. . . . But they stayed with him till his death. (xxxv, 171)

> Nor did I painfully wish, what I was never permitted for an instant to hope, or even imagine, the possession of such things as one saw in toy-shops. I had a bunch of keys to play with, as long as I was capable only of pleasure in what glittered and jingled; as I grew older, I had a cart, and a ball; and when I was five or six years old, two boxes of well-cut wooden bricks. With these modest, but, I still think, entirely sufficient possessions, and being always summarily whipped if I cried, did not do as I was bid, or tumbled on the stairs, I soon attained serene and secure methods of life and motion; and could pass my days contentedly in tracing the squares and comparing the colours of my carpet. . . . (xxxv, 20-21)

Contentedly tracing patterns, not *happily* tracing them, which would have been untrue. Inevitably, one begins and ends with that earliest of Ruskin's activities, seeing. Seeing clearly, and saying with absolute accuracy what he saw, is the heart of Ruskin's achievement. Criticism has only begun to assimilate that achievement into our literature. In time, I believe, Ruskin will assume the place in English prose that Shakespeare holds in our poetry.

NOTES

1. *The Works of John Ruskin,* ed. E. T. Cook and Alexander Wedderburn, London, 1903-12, XXXVI, 4. Subsequent references to this edition will be indicated parenthetically in the text by volume and page numbers.

2. *Ruskin's Letters from Venice 1851-1852,* ed. John L. Bradley, New Haven, 1955, p. 293.

3. Cf. Ruskin's account of "masked words" in *Sesame and Lilies.* His point is as modern as Orwell's in "Politics and the English Language," or as Thucydides' in Book III, Chapter 5, of *The Peloponnesian War:*

> There are masked words droning and skulking about us in Europe just now,—
> (there never were so many, owing to the spread of a shallow, blotching, blundering, infectious "information," or rather deformation, everywhere, and to the teaching of catechisms and phrases at school instead of human meanings)—
> there are masked words abroad, I say, which nobody understands, but which

everybody uses, and most people will also fight for, live for, or even die for, fancying they mean this or that, or the other, of things dear to them: for such words wear chameleon cloaks—"ground-lion" cloaks, of the colour of the ground of any man's fancy: on that ground they lie in wait, and rend them with a spring from it. There never were creatures of prey so mischievous, never diplomatists so cunning, never poisoners so deadly, as these masked words; they are the unjust stewards of all men's ideas: whatever fancy or favourite instinct a man most cherishes, he gives to his favourite masked word to take care of for him; the word at last comes to have an infinite power over him,—you cannot get at him but by its ministry. (xviii, 66)

4. Lines 114-19, in which Milton condemns the corrupt clergy who "for their bellies' sake, / Creep and intrude, and climb into the fold!"

5. Always, of course, one is dealing with questions of degree. Scott's verse narratives might stand as an example of non-figurative poetry and are closer to history as written by Macaulay than to poetry as written by Hopkins. Naturally, literary critics tend to overvalue figurative language, because it gives them more to say, and to undervalue non-figurative language, which, as it were, speaks for itself. Yet an entirely lucid set of instructions for installing a bidet has more in common with great poetry than either has with bad verse or "poetic" prose.

6. "And Jesus went into the temple of God . . . and overthrew the tables of the moneychangers, and the seats of them that sold doves" (Matt. 21:12).

7. Limitations of space prevent me from discussing systematically Ruskin's persistent use of meter, alliteration, and other devices usually associated with poetry. I gather here a crude catalogue of examples that the reader may easily supplement and refine.

Meter: Ruskin uses the cadence of enclosure noted above ("black bread, rude roof . . .") whenever he desires an effect of hopeless confinement. It recurs, for example, in "The Two Boyhoods," where he contrasts Turner's sense of freedom among the Yorkshire hills with his former life amidst the brick walls and blind alleys of London:

> Dead-wall, dark railing, fenced field, gated garden, all passed away like the dream of a prisoner. (vii, 384)

Cf. also the close of *The Storm-Cloud,* where Ruskin conjures before our frightened imaginations an image of the earth rendered desolate and uninhabitable by violence and poisoned air:

> Blanched Sun,—blighted grass,—blinded man. (xxxiv, 40)

Elsewhere Ruskin achieves an effect of perdurability through an unvaried iambic rhythm, which runs with the regularity of the sunset through two pentameter lines:

> . . . far above, among the mountains, the silver lichen-spots rest, star-like, on the stone; and the gathering orange stain up on | the edge | of yon | der wes | tern peak || re flects | the sun | sets of | a thou | sand years ||. (vii, 130)

A quite different effect results from the same meter in a passage in which Ruskin ridicules the sea paintings of the Dutch realists. He manages to enclose their waves in curl-papers through the mechanical, feebly explosively regularity of the alliterating iambs:

> We only are to be reproached, who, familiar with the Atlantic, are yet ready to
>
> accept with faith, as types of the sea, the small waves *en papillote*, and per
>
> uke | like *puffs* | of *far* | i na | ceous *foam*, | which were the delight of Back-
>
> huysen and his compeers. (xiii, 37)

In "The Nature of Gothic" Ruskin uses the hypnotic anapest to suggest the mind-destroying monotomy that degrades the workman into the slave of a machine:

> The men who chop up the rods sit at their work all day, their hands vibrating
>
> with a perpetual and exquisitely timed palsy, and the beads drop | ping be neath |
>
> their vi bra | tion like hail |. (x, 197)

Assonance: Near the end of "The Two Boyhoods" Ruskin describes in a paragraph of immense evocative power the forms of death that have occurred on the streets and in the factories of industrial England. The final phrases are deliberately emptied of clear, articulate meaning, like the muted cries of the starved infants Ruskin describes. In the long, repeated moaning of the vowels—"vague ague . . . bleak amazed despair"—Ruskin creates a kind of grotesque aural shadow, amorphous and terrible:

> Or, worst of all, rotted down to forgotten graves through years of ignorant patience, and vain seeking for help from man, for hope in God—infirm, imperfect yearning, as of motherless infants starving at the dawn; oppressed royalties of captive thought, vague ague-fits of bleak, amazed despair. (vii, 387)

Cf. a similar effect through assonance in *The Seven Lamps of Architecture*. Describing the Gothic ruins strewn along the English coast, Ruskin repeats the mournful open vowel *O*, which seems to blow like a funereal breeze through the fissures of the stones:

> Those rent skeletons of pierced wall, through which our sea-winds moan and
>
> murmur, strewing them joint by joint, and bone by bone, along the bleak
>
> promontories. . . ." (viii, 98)

Alliteration and Consonance: In this example of invective, Ruskin uses repeated consonants, initial and internal, to give his assertions an aura of balance and inevitability:

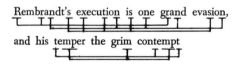

Rembrandt's execution is one grand evasion,

and his temper the grim contempt

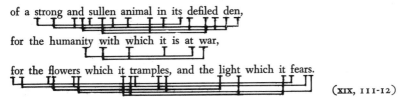

of a strong and sullen animal in its defiled den,

for the humanity with which it is at war,

for the flowers which it tramples, and the light which it fears.

(XIX, 111-12)

Consonance, alliteration, and assonance all function onomatopoetically in the following example, in which Ruskin describes the rising of the dead in Tintoretto's *The Last Judgment*. As so often, the force of Ruskin's writing derives from the peculiar vivacity of his metaphors of decay (cf. the putrid polype on page 178, above). The agonized efforts of the dead to shake off the encumbrance of earth is echoed in the repeated hard *c*'s, and their decomposed, now re-composing, bodies take on a dough-like structurelessness as they *heave* themselves into *half-kneaded* anatomies:

> Bat-like, out of the holes and caverns and shadows of the earth, the bones gather and the clay heaps heave, rattling and adhering into half-kneaded anatomies, that crawl, and startle, and struggle up among the putrid weeds, with the clay clinging to their clotted hair, and their heavy eyes sealed by the earth darkness yet. . . . (IV, 277)

Diction: In a famous descriptive paragraph, Ruskin pictures Western Europe as seen on a bird's flight northward across the burnished Mediterranean to the glaciers of the Arctic. His prose map illustrates the parallelism between the lucent skies and jewelled architecture of the south, and the hostile geography and almost barbarous Gothic of the north. As Ruskin's *locus* shifts, so does his language. The rich, Latinate vocabulary early in the passage yields to a harsher, Anglo-Saxon diction suited to those who, lacking the "redundant fruitage" of the earth, must "break the rock for bread, and cleave the forest for fire." The northern workman

> with rough strength and hurried stroke . . . smites an uncouth animation out of the rocks . . . and heaves into the darkened air the pile of iron buttress and rugged wall, instinct with the work of an imagination as wild and wayward as the northern sea; creatures of ungainly shape and rigid limb, but full of wolfish life. . . . (X, 187-8)

Metaphor: This category is limitless, and hence useless. Metaphor was the habitual mode of Ruskin's thought. He was constantly perceiving the fellowship of the apparently dissimilar, and he used metaphor at once to master and to communicate the relationships he perceived. On a single page, for example, the serpent figures as:

> that running brook of horror on the ground
> that rivulet of smooth silver [which] rows on the earth, with every scale for an oar

a wave, but without wind, a current, but with no fall

one soundless, causeless march of sequent rings, and spectral procession of spotted dust, with dissolution in its fangs, dislocation in its coils

a twisted arrow . . . a cast lance . . . a divine hieroglyph of the demoniac power of the earth

the clothed power of the dust . . . the symbol . . . of the grasp and sting of death. (xix, 362)

8. *The Captain's Deathbed, and Other Essays*, New York, 1950, p. 49.

9. E. T. Cook, *The Life of John Ruskin*, London, 1911, II, 323.

10. These qualities so attracted Proust that, on his own testimony, he came to know *Praeterita* by heart. Unquestionably, he found in the tissue of intertwined motifs — the springs of the River Wandel, the banks of the River Tay — around which Ruskin structured his story a key to his own re-creation of the past. See Marcel Proust, *Lettres à une amie* . . . , Manchester, 1942, p. 14.

WALTER PATER: HIS THEORY OF STYLE, HIS STYLE IN PRACTICE, HIS INFLUENCE

G. S. FRASER

THE ESSAY ON STYLE at the beginning of Pater's volume of critical essays of 1889, *Appreciations*, has been fairly generally considered his most coherent statement about a concept which, throughout his working life, preoccupied Pater. Mr. Ian Fletcher, in his penetrating British Council monograph on Pater, says:

> One comes back, again and again, in discussing Pater, to the idea of style; style as a mode of perception, a total responsive gesture of the whole personality rather than—for all Pater's own very notable stylistic mannerism—a mere way of arranging words. Pater's essay *Style*, an expansion of a review of Flaubert's *Correspondance*, was published towards the end of his life and from its unusual firmness of statement may constitute something of an aesthetic *credo*.[1]

Yet even at his most firm, Pater is what Mr. Fletcher calls an "evasive and tangential" writer.[2] Any summary, though a summary will be attempted here, of this famous essay must fail to do justice to its suggestiveness and elusiveness.

After discussing "Style," I intend to deal with the reaction, not to Pater's theory of style, but to his style in practice, of three contemporaries of his, two of them younger men, one of them as old as Pater but representing a newer movement of thought, Samuel Butler, George Saintsbury, and Max Beerbohm. Butler represented what it is perhaps not unfair to call the reaction of intelligent philistinism against Pater's mannerism. The young Max Beerbohm revered the thought and spirit of Pater's writing, but not the style; the artificiality of the latter lent itself admirably to Beerbohm's gift for stealthy parodic criticism. Saintsbury was a whole-hearted admirer, though the rich pudding-stone or conglomerate of his own allusive style, untidy, rambling, button-holingly intimate, resembles Pater's fastidious prose only in the load of learning it carries. His pages on Pater's prose in his pioneer work of close stylistic analysis, *A History of English Prose Rhythm* (1912), are still the best detailed appreciation of Pater's rhythmical effects, and of some of the qualities of his diction, in the English language.

More briefly, at the end of this study, I want to say something about what Mr. Fletcher calls "Pater's place as an influential writer in a diffused sense," a subject which, he feels, has "yet to be explored."[3] This influence, of course, was not merely due to Pater's style, or his theory of style, but to the attractiveness, to some important writers, of his elusively supple, detached and yet receptive, pious yet sceptical, scholarly and restrained yet ardent attitude towards the contradictory possibilities of life, of art, of religion, of the intense and yet enclosed or private moments of subjective experience. No other writer of the later nineteenth century combines in quite Pater's way the notes of asceticism and the sensuous, severity, the cult of restraint, and an almost alarming covert permissiveness. He gave prose a sort of inwardness, a combination of severe discipline of form with accessibility to the expression of vague, secret, and remote deep feelings, that had previously been associated rather with the art of the poet, though some prose-writers of the romantic period, De Quincey, Landor, Coleridge in the mood of informal self-communion, partly anticipate this inwardness; but with Pater it was constant, deliberate, and controlled. His rhythms are very nearly those of poetry: Yeats, at the beginning of *The Oxford Book of Modern Verse,* reordered the Gioconda "purple panel" (Saintsbury's phrase), turning it very easily into fine free verse. Yeats's own prose, though its natural movement was easier and more spontaneous, though the thought expressed in it was often harder and more systematic than in Pater, though it had often an earthy raciness which Pater lacks, retains to the end Paterian echoes.

But the influence worked also on writers of a quite different kind. It affected George Moore and Oscar Wilde, writers as temperamentally unakin to Pater as might be, fluent, exhibitionist writers with a strong "vulgar streak," as well as a writer very closely akin to Pater, like Lionel Johnson. It worked lastingly on the prose both of Bernard Berenson and George Santayana, both, in their different ways, much harder, much more self-assertive men than Pater, but both, like him, scholar-artists.

It is with the notion of the scholar-artist that Pater's essay "Style" is, in its most intimate passages, centrally concerned. This is a stringent and refining but also in a sense a limiting notion: so many great writers of prose have been more or less than scholars, and so much of the greatest prose is marked by a spontaneity, a transparency which Pater never aimed at or achieved. The central critical question about Pater is whether this concept of the scholar-artist had finally a peculiarly deadening effect (as both Samuel Butler and Max Beerbohm thought) on Pater's own prose; or whether his intense conscious artifice, or art, was for him the only means of conveying a unique and individual appreciation of life, a life in art and ritual and intense inner self-communing, or in the spectator's aesthetic appreciation of these, rather than a broad and open appreciation of the life in life itself. This intense inwardness of appreciation, this painful scrupulousness of response, was certainly part of the secret of Pater's influence on those, like Max Beerbohm, who could not whole-heartedly admire his "arrangement of words." Yet, as we shall see, on Pater's own principles, an attempt to separate the value of what is expressed from the manner of expressing is fallacious, in any discussion about style, if the style in the end clings close to, helps rather than obstructs the import, the deep intention, of a piece of writing. Pater's weaker imitators, those whom Saintsbury called his "apes," can never have mastered Pater's own theory of style.

I

Pater's essay on style begins, concessively, with an acceptance of the established distinction between "the laws and characteristic excellences of verse and prose composition."[4] But, he insists—and this agility and suppleness in handling distinctions is typical of him—it is important not to apply this distinction in too rigid and mechanical a fashion. There is a pleasure in finding in very poetic poetry the latent virtues of prose: "To find in the poem, amid the flowers, the allusions, the mixed perspectives of *Lycidas,* for instance, the thought, the logical structure:—how wholesome!"[5] The characteristic virtues of poetry can similarly have their proper place in prose. Pater cites Dryden as an often very prosaic poet, who made an oddly sharp distinction between verse and prose, though his own prose has some of the virtues of poetry, and is sometimes marred by poetic rhythms: "not only fervid, richly figured, poetic, as we say, but vitiated, all unconsciously, by many a scanning line."[6] Saintsbury, who, as a critic, is in many ways a disciple of Pater, liked prose to be scannable, but thought the frequent presence of detachable blank verse lines, as in Dickens, in Kingsley, in Ruskin, a flaw; he would have agreed with Pater's essential meaning here. Sharp about Dryden, Pater is more in tune with Wordsworth, for whom the two distinctions are the purely technical one between verse and prose and the much more important one between poetry and science, or poetry and matter-of-fact, between "imaginative and unimaginative writing." What Pater, now setting aside the "harsher opposition of poetry to prose," will in the rest of the essay be concerned with is "the literature of the imaginative sense of fact."[7]

Yet even this new distinction between the imaginative and the unimaginative sense of fact has to be handled with suppleness. In a writer like Pascal, what seems at first dry objective argument becomes "a pleading—a theorem no longer, but esssentially an appeal to the reader to catch the writer's spirit. . . ."[8] Something like this is true also of great historians who, even merely by what they select and emphasise, colour fact with their temperaments: "For just in proportion as the writer's aim, consciously or unconsciously, comes to be the transcribing, not of the world, not of mere fact, but of his sense of it, he becomes an artist, his work *fine* art; and good art . . . in proportion to the truth of his presentment of that sense. . . ."[9] What makes the difference between "fine" and merely "serviceable" art is the artist's pleasure in modifying his transcription of mere fact—his presentation not of "mere fact, but of its infinite variety as modified by human preference."[10]

Fine art, in prose, is not, therefore, confined to fiction and *belles lettres;* it can exhibit itself, though with a special economy and restraint, in works of severe thought and strenuous scholarship. In Pater's own day, imaginative prose, in this wide sense, is "the special and opportune art" because of the "chaotic variety" of the interests of the modern world, "the chaotic variety and complexity of its interests."[11] One is reminded here of Matthew Arnold's phrase in "The Scholar-Gypsy" about "Our sick hurry, our divided aims," but the tone is very different: Pater discreetly relishes the chaos and complexity, the hurry and division. They have helped to bring about an "all-pervading naturalism," an enquiring humbleness in the face of fact, which suits "the less ambitious form of literature"[12] better than it suits poetry. Curiosity, humility, naturalism (in the broad sense of exposing oneself to the facts of any situation for what they are) are, of course, the distinguishing marks of the scholar. And, this point made, Pater embarks on the most intimate and moving part of his essay, his description of the temptations with which the scholar-artist has to struggle.

Such a writer is the custodian of "the scholarly conscience—the male conscience": "In his self-criticism, he supposes always that sort of reader who will go (full of eyes) warily, considerately, though without consideration for him, over the ground which the female conscience traverses so lightly, so amiably."[13] Pater is here obviously describing his own struggles with language. He insists on the need for rejections, "rejections demanded by the nature of [the scholar-artist's] medium," on the scholar-artist's "sense of self-restraint and renunciation, having for the susceptible reader the effect of a challenge for minute consideration."[14] Unfortunately, the kind of rejections and renunciations that Pater has in mind is not illustrated very minutely. He tells us that the scholar-artist will "resist a constant tendency on the part of the majority of those who use them to efface the distinctions of language,"[15] and one is reminded of Henry Tilney's strictures on Catherine Morland's use of the word "nice" in *Northanger Abbey*, or of modern attempts to preserve the older sense of the word "disinterested." But the scholar-artist should also revive old and still useful words. He should pay attention to the "physical elements or particles in words like *absorb, consider, extract*"[16]—the ab-, the con-, the ex-, Pater means. Besides reviving old words, he should restore "the finer edge of words still in use: *ascertain, communicate, discover*—words like these it has been part of our 'business' to misuse."[17] In these last points, Pater will seem to most modern readers pedantic; an English word's meaning is its meaning in educated use, not a more edged meaning that might be derived from considering its derivation.

A "frugal closeness of style"[18] is what Pater, as scholar-artist, really admires. At the same time, he sees the need for change and innovation. He praises Wordsworth for breaking away, in *Lyrical Ballads*, from "the consecrated poetic associations of a century" and creating "what was to become in a measure the language of the next generation," but immediately adds, as if to reassure himself: "But he did it with the tact of a scholar."[19] He sees also that the scholar-artist of the nineteenth century must absorb a whole new range of ideas, and with them of words: from science, from metaphysics, from, rather strangely in the nineteenth-century context, mystical theology. But his central emphasis in these intimate passages is on restraint. Yet by this restraint the scholar-artist "is really vindicating his liberty in the making of a vocabulary, an entire system of composition, for himself, his own true manner. . . ."[20]

This almost excessive dread of the otiose and the facile comes out in the most often quoted, certainly the most Paterianly mannered, short passage in the essay: "Is it worth while, can we afford, to attend to just that, to just that figure or literary reference, just then?—Surplusage! he will dread that, as the runner on his muscles."[21] There is a danger, here, of the visualising reader having a picture of a tiny man running up a giant's muscular leg, and almost anybody else would have written: "he will dread that, as the runner would dread it on his muscles." The surplusage in the sentence, if surplusage it was, does seem to have been eliminated almost by an operation of cosmetic surgery: and the effect is all the odder because of the contrast with the at first sight compulsive stammer and repetition, the hammering on the adverb, "just," of the immediately preceding sentence. Read aloud, however, the first sentence justifies its repetitions: they are to hammer in a sense. The second sentence is difficult to read aloud without the tongue, as it were, tripping or slipping and recovering itself (as the runner with surplusage on his muscles might). Mr. Ian Fletcher disagrees with Saintsbury in thinking Pater, in spite of his frequent affectations of colloquial informality, not a writer, like Newman or Arnold, in the high conversational tradition of the Oxford Senior Common Room. Pater usually reads aloud musically; sometimes, as here, though not often, a single sentence will read aloud stumblingly and awkwardly. His tone is intimate, but it is the tone of intimate monologue, addressed very much to the writer's own, and the fit reader's, inner ear. Reading Pater to oneself, one can perceive subtleties often of emphasis and intonation, shadows of implication, which one's speaking or reading-aloud voice, even if well trained, cannot quite reproduce.

I have allowed myself a digression, though in the long run, I hope, a relevant one. This famous sentence about surplusage leads on to some more general considerations about style, which, since they bear less intimately on Pater's own practice, I shall deal with more briefly. All art, for Pater, *is* essentially the removal of surplusage. The true artist composes, he does not accrete. He thinks architecturally. Style is not merely a matter of phrases, sentences, paragraphs, but of the proportions of a whole book, its design. In this aspect of style, architectonics, we recognise the function of *mind,* as distinct from *soul.* The distinction, Pater admits, may be philosophically a vague one (it is, in fact, something like the distinction between thought and feeling): but as unity of design in a literary composition is the work of mind, so "unity of atmosphere"[22] is the work of soul. And there are some readers (Pater, though he does not say so, is obviously among them) for whom the expression of soul in literature, the colour and charm of personality, is the most attractive aspect of literature: "They seem *to know a person in a book, and make way by intuition. . . ."*[23] (In passing, it may be said that, both for instance in *The Renaissance* and in *Imaginary Portraits* the intuitive re-creation or creation of persons, persons felt as embodying some aspect of a culture, was Pater's own critical and fictive method.)

There is a rather abrupt transition here to Flaubert as the hero and martyr of style, a writer with a natural opulence which Pater did not possess, but a writer who restrained it with all the ascetic fervour of a true scholar-artist. Pater comments tactfully, and it might seem evasively, on *le mot juste:*

> The one word for the one thing, the one thought, amid the multitude of words, terms, that might just do: the problem of style was there!— the unique *word, phrase, sentence, paragraph, essay, or song,* absolutely proper to the single mental presentation or vision within.[24]

It would be difficult to say whether the passage italicised represents a dilution of the idea of the *mot juste* almost to meaninglessness, "like gold to airy thinness beat," or a tactful recognition by Pater that the doctrine of *le mot juste* is strictly indefensible unless the phrase is interpreted elastically, and indeed metaphorically. For Pater, the doctrine means in the end simply that language should correspond as closely as possible to thought and intention: what is important in the doctrine is "the idea of a natural economy, of some pre-existent adaptation, between a relative, somewhere in the world of thought, and its correlative, somewhere in the world of language. . . ."[25]

And then Pater adds, very surprisingly, after his earlier account of the scholar-artist's agonies of renunciation and rejection:

> Scott's facility, Flaubert's deeply pondered evocation of "the phrase," are equally good art. Say what you have to say, what you have a will to say, in the simplest, the most direct and exact manner possible, with no surplusage:—there, is the justification of the sentence so fortunately born, "entire, smooth, and round," that it needs no punctuation, and also (that is the point!) of the most elaborate period, if it be right in its elaboration.[26]

That *is* the point, indeed, if Pater is to justify his own style, and his own concept of the scholar-artist: but Scott, though a scholar and an artist, is not a scholar-artist in Pater's sense. Consciously or unconsciously, by this large concession that goodness of style is a mere matter of appropriateness to meaning and purpose, Pater seems to relegate his account of his own wrestling with language to a plane of minor importance.

Pater indeed seems at this stage to be saying that style, considered in the abstract, hardly matters:

> The seeming baldness of *Le Rouge et Le Noir* is nothing in itself; the wild ornament of *Les Miserables* is nothing in itself; and the restraint of Flaubert, amid a real natural opulence, only redoubled beauty—the phrase so large and so precise at the same time, hard as bronze, in service to the more perfect adaptation of words to their matter. Afterthoughts, retouchings, finish, will be of profit only so far as they too really serve to bring out the original, initiative, generative, sense in them.[27]

All kinds of style are, in a sense, permissible, since "the style is the man." But Pater agrees that this may seem "a relegation of style to the subjectivity, the mere caprice, of the individual, which must soon transform it into mannerism."[28] This, in fact, was the sort of accusation—of caprice and mannerism, in moral attitudes as well as style—which is flung against Pater by W. H. Mallock, in his caricature of Pater in *The New Republic*. Even an admirer like Saintsbury thought the charge justly brought against many of Pater's "apes," his minor imitators:

> A sentence of one of the earliest of these, the late Mr Frederick Myers—"to trace the passion and anguish which whirl along across silent squares by summer moonlight amid a smell of dust and flowers," is just a little dangerous in itself. And it was suggested at the time by an urbane critic, that the rhythm would be positively improved, and the sense not materially damaged, if you read "gaze by the moonlight across summer dust and flowers amid a smell of silent squares."[29]

Pater, however, gets out of this trap, adroitly, whether or not convincingly, by asserting that the style is the man not in a capricious mood, "but in absolutely sincere apprehension of what is most real to him. . . . If the style be the man, in all the colour and intensity of a veritable apprehension, it will be in a real sense 'impersonal.'" (This, so far as my own reading goes, is the first use in English literary criticism of the word "impersonal" with the peculiar connotation, or implication, of praise that it was to assume in the early essays of T. S. Eliot and, of course, later very widely in the *Scrutiny* critics.)

Then comes a passage almost as famous as the "surplusage" sentence, the comparison and contrast between music and prose, as key arts of the nineteenth century. Mr. Ian Fletcher rightly finds this passage fascinating but logically puzzling. I italicise, in the quotation, the logically connective words:

> *If* music be the ideal of all art whatever, precisely *because* it is impossible to distinguish the form from the substance or the matter, the subject from the expression, *then,* literature, *by* finding its specific excellence in the absolute correspondence of the term to its import, will be but fulfilling the condition of all artistic quality in things everywhere, of all good art.[30]

The logical worry is this. The indiscernible fusion of form and substance has been postulated as the ideal of all art. The absolute correspondence of the term to its import is then postulated as the specific excellence of prose; but if we can see that the term does absolutely correspond to its import, we must be distinguishing between form and substance very sharply indeed. Pater's logic might be defended if we supposed him to imply that in the very finest prose the term becomes, as it were, transparent, so that we are aware only of the import. Claims like this have, for instance, been made for Tolstoy's writing: "If life could speak, life would speak thus" (Charles du Bos). But transparency of this sort is never the virtue of Pater's own terms, which do very much draw attention to themselves, sometimes at the expense of their import. I do not think the logic of this fine paragraph can be defended, but in bringing in music I believe that Pater may have been half-consciously thinking of one quality of style he much admired, and the quality of his own style on which he worked perhaps even more labouriously than on his diction: rhythmical modulation. The mention of music is perhaps a salute to a quality that meant so much to him, but which the scheme of his essay had not allowed him to isolate for separate consideration.

The final paragraph of Pater's essay on style is often considered as a rather perfunctory concession, by the great aesthete, to conventional Victorian morality. He says that this exact correspondence of language to intention in prose will be the condition "of good art, but not necessarily great art."[31] Great art needs high matter as well as fine form, "alliance to great ends, or the depth of the note of revolt, or the largeness of hope. . . ." As examples of this sort of alliance to great ends, he mentions Dante and Milton and the Bible and, rather strangely in that company to modern ears, Hugo's *Les Misérables;* but the last, at least, is an ambitious book, with a grand humanitarian purpose. Pater is firm, at least, that the great writers express something larger than the individual sensibility. Good art will be, also, great art

> if, over and above those qualities I summed up as mind and soul—that colour and mystic perfume, and that reasonable structure, it has something of the soul of humanity in it, and finds its logical, its architectural place, in the great structure of human life.[32]

One wonders whether he is thinking of his own work, so much shaped and coloured by his own cloistered and meditative life. It is, I suppose, still an open question whether we consider Pater a great writer, the last of the Victorian sages, somehow in the line of Arnold, Ruskin, Carlyle: or whether we think him a good and important minor writer, whose self-absorption, whose labour and artifice of style, somehow cuts him off from "alliance to great ends." It is a little on the side of the possibility of his greatness that it is he himself, here, who raises for us the question.

II

Pater's essay on style may seem, as I have summarised it, a quite reasonably coherent and self-consistent document. The main element of inward strain comes from the contrast between Pater's ideal of himself as the scholar-artist, imposing on himself a special discipline, appealing to a special public, and his critical openness of sensibility which makes him alive to the quite different merits of great, careless popular writers like Hugo and Scott. He puts at the physical centre of his essay, as it were, a type of good writing, his own, which by his final argument (and by his admission that pains and labour in writing, like Flaubert's, are not to be taken account of when we judge a piece of writing's final success) is perhaps only a marginally important kind of good writing: the art, as Saintsbury was to call it, of writing delicately.

If the notion of writing delicately suggests unusual refinement in the writer who does so, it may also suggest a kind of sickliness or invalidism. We look for force, directness, simplicity, concentration in style, before we look for delicacy; we look also first for naturalness, spontaneity, abundance. To many of Pater's contemporaries his pains and labour seemed to produce, in the end, a kind of prose which was not natural, easy, or in the proper English grain; which was, in a sense, dead, like a carefully wrought piece of artificial composition in a dead language.

Samuel Butler put this brutally in his *Note-Books*:

> Mr. Walter Pater's style is, to me, like the face of some old woman who has been to Madame Rachel and had herself enamelled. The bloom is nothing but powder and paint and the odour is cherry-blossom. Mr. Matthew Arnold's odour is as the faint sickliness of hawthorn.[33]

I take it that Butler here is distinguishing, rather than identifying, two styles he dislikes: Pater's style smells like scent out of a bottle, but the cloying smell of Arnold's style is that of living hawthorn blossoms. Arnold's style, for all its mannerisms, is very much more a spoken style than Pater's, the style of Oxford Senior Common Room conversation, with a touch of the professional lecturer's mannerism—the repetitions and the vivacities and the faint condescension, of which Pater is never guilty—added. Butler is reacting, being himself an *enfant terrible,* a master of the plain blunt style, of shock tactics, against what he sees as something narcissistic in Pater's and Arnold's conscious cultivation of charm. He feels, no doubt, that in writing as in life we should be glad if we charm people, but should not too consciously set out to do so. Brutal and one-sided as his statement is, it does not seem to me wholly inept. About both Pater and Arnold, he has a moral and critical point.

Max Beerbohm makes a similar point, in "Diminuendo," the terminal essay of his first book, *The Works of Max Beerbohm,* in a much more courteous, delicate, and balanced way. Pater is one of his heroes but it is not for his famous style that he admires him. Beerbohm describes how as an Oxford undergraduate he had gone into a print-shop and

> there saw, peering into a portfolio, a small, thick, rock-faced man, whose top hat and gloves of *bright* dog-skin struck one of the many discords in that little city of learning or laughter. The serried bristles of his moustachio made for him a false-military air. I think I nearly went down when they told me this was Pater.
>
> Not that even in those more decadent days of my childhood did I admire the man as a stylist. Even then I was angry that he should treat

English as a dead language, bored by that sedulous ritual wherewith he laid out every sentence as in a shroud—hanging, like a widower, long over its marmoreal beauty or ever he could lay it at length in his book, its sepulchre. From that laden air, the so cadaverous murmur of that sanctuary, I could hook it at the beck of any jade.[34]

The grave impudence of the parody in the second paragraph is made all the more effective by contrast with the lively pertness of Beerbohm's own youthful style in the first paragraph, a pertness that reasserts itself with the phrase "at the beck of any jade." In his own characteristic early style, Beerbohm goes directly against Pater's precepts by accepting joyously "many a neology, many a license, many a gipsy phrase."[35] "Moustachio" and the Frenchified "made for him a false-military air" in the first paragraph spring from a taste for Ouida's prose rather than Pater's; though even in the first paragraph there are discreet hints of the parodic criticism to come. "Peering into a portfolio" and "little city of learning or laughter" are examples of a kind of close alliteration within the phrase, drawing too much conscious attention to itself, which Pater's fastidiousness did not reject quite often enough. On the other hand, in the last sentence of the first paragraph, "I nearly went down" (for "I nearly fainted") has a kind of briskness which Pater's own labouriously worked in colloquialisms never possess. Pater praises Tennyson because even when he is aiming at "monosyllabic effect" or "colloquialism," one has a sense of "fine, fastidious scholarship,"[36] and the same rather perverse praise could be applied to his own attempts at the simple and natural.

Beerbohm's second paragraph brilliantly illustrates a number of Pater's tricks: the generation of a sequence and climax of images from an abstraction, "*dead* language," "as in a *shroud*," "like a *widower*," "marmoreal . . . *sepulchre*," "the so *cadaverous* murmur of that *sanctuary*": the careful alternation of Latinate phrases, "redulous ritual," "marmoreal beauty," "cadaverous murmur," with sequences of short, slow-moving words, "or ever he could lay it at length in his book" (note the witty ambiguity of "at length" there, the length of Pater's brooding on a sentence, the physical length of the sentence when laid corpse-like in the book). Beerbohm also illustrates the Paterian use of a dash to prolong a sentence and of a succession of appositional commas to divide it into short phrasal members, and make its rhythm languid and sad. It is a classic parody, if not of Pater's style, at least of his mannerism. It is as glaringly contrived, but also in its own way as memorable, as any of Pater's own "purple panels"; yet the parody seems not unaffectionate. It is a tribute to skill, even if Beerbohm thinks the skill perversely used.

Imitating yet another of Pater's mannerisms, the interspersal of difficult English with fragments of yet more difficult Greek, Beerbohm goes on to say that what has mattered to him has never been Pater's style in itself, but merely that style as the vehicle of Pater's vision of life, his scholarly and philosophical mind, the "couth solemnity" of that mind. (It is difficult to say whether "couth" there is one of Beerbohm's typical pert neologisms, or an archaism that might have appealed to Pater.) It was, Beerbohm explains, his reverence for the couthness of that mind which made the apparition of the actual uncouth Pater so shocking to him.

If Beerbohm's is the best parodic criticism of Pater's mannerism, Saintsbury remains the most sensitive close appreciator of the high art of Pater's style at its best. In *A History of English Prose Rhythm,* he sees Pater as blending the delicacy and precision of Newman with the vividness and strangeness of Ruskin, as fusing amenity and colour. In a sense, James Anthony Froude had already done this, but the blending and fusion was far more "deliberately, extensively, and decoratively" performed by Pater. Saintsbury then notes that Pater's prose is quite free of the restlessness, the shrillness, the occasional harshness and stridency that are Ruskin's defects:

> If there is one thing which, more than another, can be justly urged against Ruskin, it is the absence of quiet. If there is one thing, more than another, that may be put to the credit of Pater, it is the presence thereof. On this apex of English prose, if on no other, there is Rest.[37]

Pater's "quietism," as Saintsbury calls it, seems to him "the instinctive and distinctive character of [Pater's] rhythm." Saintsbury therefore deliberately rejects as an illustrative passage "the usual purple panel . . . of the 'Gioconda' in which . . . there is just the slightest hint of an intention to 'set the trumpet to the lips and blow.' "[38] He chooses a quieter passage from the Leonardo essay, but prefaces his citation of it by a most interesting set of remarks on Pater's "care of the paragraph," or, more broadly, his management of transitions between paragraphs:

> But it must always be remembered that the care of the paragraph was one of Mr. Pater's first and greatest anxieties; when I remarked on this . . . he wrote to me expressing special gratification, and acknowledging

that it had been one of his principal objects. But his paragraph was not, as too many people are under the delusion, that a paragraph must necessarily be, brought to some deeply marked, insistent, peremptorily "concluding" end. He liked—and he had a marvellous faculty in doing it—to drop off at this end with a new sort of modified *aposiopesis,* replacing the actual abruptness of that figure by a gentle glide.[39]

The two paragraphs from the Leonardo essay that Saintsbury examines in detail are chosen partly to illustrate this gift of gently gliding transition. The first paragraph is, for Pater, very plain and expository; the second paragraph is, even for Pater, richly and highly wrought; yet there is no sense of a jarring change of key.

I shall quote these two paragraphs separately (Saintsbury quoted them in sequence) with Saintsbury's own prosodic notation, his marks of "partition and quantification." Saintsbury used the terminology, the feet (though he recognised a native English monosyllabic foot) and the marks for long and short syllables of classical prosody. Syllables of major stress are, in fact, always long for him, though they are by no means his only long syllables; a syllable of major stress, even if in English quantitatively very short, is always treated as long; on the other hand naturally long syllables of minor stress are not very often, though they may be, treated as short. By thus fusing quantitative and stress scansion under one notation, Saintsbury, I think, while trusting us to get the stress right by ourselves, was forcing us to notice subtle alternations of quantity, and the separable units of ryhthm they help to create, more consciously than we usually do. Even so, some of his scansions at first struck me as odd: "sŭr-prises": "nŏtĭces": "of dreams" as a pyrrhic: "of falling" as a tribrach. But I decided after a time that in Oxford in Saintsbury's youth they must have pronounced "surprises" with a short *i* on the analogy of "surplices" and "notices" with a long *i* on the analogy of "devices." The pyrrhic and the tribrach are much more puzzling, for one would think that the vowel sound of "dreams" and the first vowel of "falling" are naturally and incorrigibly long; but I decided that Saintsbury in these two cases used this surprising scansion to indicate a combination of hush and hurry in pronunciation, where, in the context, undue lingering on the naturally long vowels would have unbalanced a complex rhythm. So in the end I have transcribed his notation exactly as I found it.

I suppose no modern writer on the rhythms of prose would use Saintsbury's system. Moreover, the consciousness of quantitative differences in

English, which he took for granted in an educated reader, can no longer
be taken for granted, and a mode of speech which does take account of
these differences will tend to seem today drawling and affected; the sort
of conscious cadencing of prose which fascinated Saintsbury survives
today only in the set speeches of public orators, lauding the honorary
graduands at degree-givings. Saintsbury's book, nevertheless, when I
first read it many years ago, taught me to *listen* to English prose, and to
revive for myself, or to imagine that I was reviving, the very accents and
cadences of great writers long dead. His notation does help me to hear
(and I think it may help other readers to hear) the peculiarly quiet,
grave, and measured glide of Pater's prose. It may help to convince them
that here is art, not merely artifice. So here, with Saintsbury's markings,
is the first Leonardo paragraph:

The movement | of the fifteenth | century | was twofold; | partly |
the Renaissance, | partly | also | the coming | of what is called | the
modern spirit | with its realism, | its appeal | to experience; | it com-
prehended | a return | to antiquity, | and a return | to nature. |
Raffaelle | represents the return | to antiquity | and Lionardo | the
return | to nature. In this return | to nature | he was seeking | to
satisfy | a boundless | curiosity | by her | perpetual | surprises, | a
microscopic | sense | of finish | by her | finesse | or delicacy | of opera-
tion, | that *subtilitas* | *naturae* | which Bacon | notices. | So | we find
him | often | in intimate | relations | with men | of science, | with Fra
| Luca | Paccioli, | the mathe- | matician, | and the anatomist | Marc
Antonio | della Torre. | His observations | and experiments | fill |
thirteen | volumes | of manuscript; | and those | who can judge |
describe him as | anticipating | long before, | by rapid | intuition, |
the later | ideas | of science. | He explained | the obscure | light | of
the unillu- | minated part | of the moon, | knew that the sea | had once
covered | the mountains | which contain | shells, | and the gathering |
of the equatorial | waters | above | the polar.[40]

Saintsbury notes that in its diction and its sentence structure this passage is in a tradition of English expository prose at least as old as Dryden and Sir William Temple. There are no words that from a late nineteenth-century point of view are either strikingly modern or strikingly archaic, and in particular there are no instances of Pater's "peculiar picturesque or imaginative *catachresis* of words—that introduction of them with a slightly new meaning and in slightly unexpected company. . . ." (Readers of Pater, new readers, who prefer the amenities and clarities of a plain though graceful expository style to the beauties of a highly wrought, ornate, and necessarily somewhat opaque style should be referred to *Plato and Platonism*, based on Oxford lecture scripts, and quite the most lucid of his books, both in sentence and paragraph structure, and in general ordonnance.) Saintsbury thinks that the eighteenth-century divine, Conyers Middleton, whom he has earlier introduced as an exemplar of the mid-eighteenth-century formal or academic style at its decentest and dullest, would find in this paragraph no ideas with which he might not have been familiar, no words that he might not have used. Yet to partition and quantify Middleton, though it could be done (Saintsbury thought one could apply "quantitative scansion . . . to almost everything spoken or written by an educated Englishman") would be pointless. In Middleton's dully decent prose there is nothing of Pater's "mysterious consonance or symphony," on account of which "the partition and quantification justify themselves."[41] Greater writers than Middleton in the eighteenth century, Gibbon particularly, were masters of a system of conscious cadencing, and of balancing of parallel rhythms; but Pater did this much more subtly, and Saintsbury illustrates Pater's "undulations, not definitely metrical, but infinitely subtler than those of Gibbon,"[42] by isolating the beautiful last cadence: "and the gathering of the equatorial waters above the polar."

It is this cadence, in fact, which provides the gentle glide from the smooth, expository tone of the first paragraph Saintsbury examines to the "dazzling and wonderful transformation"[43] of rhythmical and verbal elaboration in the second. Here, again with Saintsbury's markings, is the second paragraph, a kind of prose poem:

He | who thus | penetrated | into | the most secret | parts | of nature
| preferred | always | the more | to the less | remote, | what, | seeming

| exceptional, was an instance | of law | more refined, | the construction | about things | of a peculiar | atmosphere | and mixed | lights. | He paints | flowers | with such curious | felicity | that different | writers | have attributed | to him | a fondness | for particular | flowers, | as Clement | the cyclamen, | and Rio | the jasmine; | while at Venice | there is | a stray leaf | from his portfolio | dotted | all over | with studies | of violets | and the wild rose. In him | first appears | the taste | for what | is *bizarre* | or *recherché* | in landscape; | hollow | places | full | of the green | shadow | of bituminous | rocks, | ridged | reefs | of trap rock | which cut | the water | into quaint | sheets | of light— | their exact | antitype | is in | our own | western | seas; | all | solemn | effects | of moving | water; | you may follow | it springing | from its distant | source | among the rocks | on the heath | of the "Madonna | of the Balances," | passing | as a little | fall | into | the treacherous | calm | of the "Madonna | of the Lake," | next, | as a goodly | river | below | the cliffs | of the "Madonna | of the Rocks," | washing | the white | walls | of its distant | villages, | stealing | out | in a network | of divided | streams | in "La Gioconda" | to the sea-shore | of the "Saint Anne"— | that delicate | place | where the wind | passes | like the hand | of some | fine etcher | over | the surface, | and the untorn | shells | lie thick | upon the sand, | and the tops | of the rocks, | to which the waves | never rise, | are green | with grass | grown fine | as hair. It is the landscape, | not | of dreams | or of fancy, | but of places | far withdrawn, | and hours | selected | from a thousand | with a miracle | of finesse. | Through his | strange veil | of sight | things reach | him so; | in no | ordinary | night | or day, | but as | in faint light | of eclipse, | or in some | brief interval | of falling | rain | at daybreak, | or through | deep water.

Saintsbury finds in this second paragraph a "polyphony, as unique and original as anything we have seen."[44] He notes that it moves much more slowly than the first paragraph, partitioning itself into much shorter feet (the succession of three monosyllabic feet, "| rocks, | ridged | reefs |" is a notable example of what he means, as are the four two-syllable feet, three of them spondees, of "| Through his | strange veil | of sight | things reach |"). Enough longer feet, of four and five syllables or more, are thrown in, however, "to prevent the thing from being too languid and too 'precious.'" Saintsbury also notices at the closes of sentences and clauses and sub-paragraph units the presence of "that curious muffled arrest which we have noticed—momentary suspension of movement without a jar—a sort of whispered 'Hush!' "[45] He is expanding there what he had earlier said about Pater's "quietism." He notices also the "immixture" of suggestions of actual verse metre:

And the un-| torn shells | like thick [up]| on the sand . . .
And the tops | of the rocks, [to] | which the waves | never rise, . . .
Are green | with grass | grown fine | as hair. . . .

The bracketed-off small words are, of course, those which would break the verse metre: it would be interesting to know if Yeats had seen this footnote of Saintsbury's before he decided to give the Gioconda passage a free verse setting. Always a little suspicious of pure verse effects in prose, Saintsbury points out that these effects are much more "intricate and nuanced" than similar things in the more loose and open-rhythmed prose of Ruskin or Charles Kingsley.

Saintsbury also takes note here of diction, which can have an effect on rhythm, and remarks that there are several examples of

slight idiosyncratic *diversions* of words (for catachresis, after all, is a bad name to throw at so beautiful a dog) . . . which affect rhythm so powerfully, though so quietly, by the slight shock they give to the understanding—"*green* shadow," "*solemn* . . . water," "*delicate* place."[46]

He points out that these surprises are achieved without "the least touch of such preliminary warning and advertisement" as lead up to De Quincey's or Landor's set pieces of rhythmical bravura or, indeed, to Pater's own longer "Gioconda" passage. The miracle here is the blending of rich polyphony with a prevailing hush: "A new paradox suggests itself, to take place beside Dryden's old one of 'silence invading the ear.'

Silence is blended with sound, and the charms of both invade and soothe the ear together."[47]

Saintsbury concludes his consideration of Pater by a much briefer examination of a paragraph from *Marius the Epicurean*. He does not bother to partition and quantify this, though he says he can see the scansion marks as clearly as if he had written them. It indeed says something for Saintsbury's system of partition and quantification that one finds oneself rapidly learning it, and applying it automatically; writing the scansion marks on the carbon copy of the typescript of this essay, I found I was not copying, but simply applying Saintsbury's method; yet, checked, the carbon markings proved identical with those on the top copy. The *Marius* passage, itself perhaps slightly less interesting for matter, is chosen by Saintsbury as an example of Pater's "middle style," between the plain expository tone of the first Leonardo paragraph and the very highly wrought manner, and exalted mood, of the second. He remarks that in diction (apart from Pater's use of the word "elegant," which Saintsbury thinks irremediably debased by vulgar usage) as well as in movement, the *Marius* paragraph is faultless: "as things in the middle style should be, though those in the very highest need or should not."[48]

Beerbohm in another essay in *Works*, "George IV," contrasts Pater with another very great Victorian stylist, Thackeray, who happened, again, to be one of Saintsbury's very special heroes. Beerbohm again works by parody, but works in the opposite direction to his parody of Pater. Admiring Pater's thought, he deplores, or admires only as a perversely ingenious artifact, his style. Seeing Thackeray, rightly, as a very great natural stylist, he contrives both to imitate the buoyancy and ease of Thackeray's rhythms, and to indicate the element of facile sentiment and moral commonplace in Thackeray's thought:

> He had a charming style. We never find him searching for the *mot juste* as for a needle in a bottle of hay. Could he have looked through a certain window by the river at Croisset or in the quadrangle at Brasenose, how he would have laughed! He blew on his pipe, and words came tripping round him like children, like pretty little children who are perfectly drilled for the dance, or came, did he will it, treading in their precedence, like kings, gloomily.[49]

Pater himself admired Thackeray and more than once cites *Esmond* as an exemplary work of art in prose; but certainly no two great stylists could be more unlike. In his book on prose rhythm, Saintsbury devotes, in fact, more space to Thackeray than to Pater, though he does not partition and quantify so much. He illustrates Thackeray's peculiar natural magic by a very short sentence:

> Take another and shorter—not, I hope, impudently short:
>
> Becky | was always | good to him, | always | amused, | never | angry. Anybody can do that? The Atlantes of the twentieth century could do it, in a posture vernacularly well known [*standing on their heads,* Saintsbury means], but for the peril of disturbing the literature they carry? Perhaps; but please find something like it for me before 1845, and out of Thackeray, if you will kindly do so. *In* him it is everywhere.[50]

And *in* Pater, one might add (Saintsbury suggests the comparison, though he has not made it) it is nowhere. Pater has magic, but nobody would call it natural magic; it is the result of the most labourious spells and incantations, it smells of the wizard's cave; nobody would claim for Pater natural abundance, spontaneity, ease. One would not even quite claim for him opulence, held back by an instinct of restraint, in the sense in which he himself claims that for Flaubert; in the richest passages one has the sense that the gold has been dug and smelted, the gems grubbed out of the earth and painfully polished. All smells of the lamp. And yet Saintsbury perhaps convinces us that this almost excessive labour, of which we seem to feel the strain in the close and minute consideration that Pater's page demands, results in the end not merely in mannerism, not merely in artificiality, but in a high and difficult *art,* the strained but in the end adequate expression of the inner ardours of a noble and lonely soul, of an unsystematic and intermittently self-obfuscating but strikingly original and seminal mind. And, through the painful concentration on subtleties of rhythm, some chord of feeling is struck, new, strange, plangent, and individual, not like anything else in late nineteenth-century English literature.

III

I promised that I would make a few brief final remarks on the influence of Pater's style and his theory of style. I think it is clear that his minor imitators, like Frederick Myers, had never understood the theory; they were captivated by Pater's phrases and cadences without grasping the subtle, often abrupt and elliptical movement of his thought. The sound and shape and colour of words, the manipulation of cadences, would become the main concern of such writers, and they would forget, or would never have taken in, Pater's own insistence that style is of the order of means, not ends: that any style has merit, finally, only in relation to its precise correspondence to a felt truth, a truth grappled with and struggled for. In the sub-Paterians, there is no such felt truth struggling agonisingly into exquisite verbal art; rather, an elaborate verbal mannerism, pursued for its own sake, and creating a kind of phantasmagoria or simulacrum of thought.

On the other hand, there were writers of tougher mental fibre, like, as I have suggested, Berenson and Santayana, who shared with Pater the temperament of the scholar-artist, who shared his learning, or areas of his learning, and who could follow his thought, without being either dazzled or infuriated by his "management of words." But Pater's most interesting influence is that upon the prose of Yeats. It was an influence, of course, of ideas as well as of style: when Yeats talks in a poem of his early middle age about "the fascination of what's difficult" and of how this fascination is in danger of drying up his natural lyrical spontaneity, he might almost be commenting on Pater's essay on style, with its insistence on rejection and renunciation, on the avoidance of the otiose and facile. They were in the end unlike in temperament; Yeats in middle age became a masterful man of action and in spite of his shyness he was, even in youth, what he called himself in his speech of thanks when he received the Nobel Prize, a "very social man." Yet all high creation is germinated in solitude; and one central antithesis of Pater's essay on style, that between the necessary subjectivity of the literary artist and the necessity that he should grapple with objective truth if his style is to become "impersonal," can be seen as central also to Yeats's way of looking at life and art as a tension, a clash, a collision between mutually hostile, but individually inadequate and mutually complementary, opposites. Thoughts that were cloudy and vague in Pater, pregnancies and suggestiveness, became, as Mr. Ian Fletcher has suggested, hard and systematic in Yeats.

More broadly, Pater's influence was obviously partly due to his insistence on the primary importance of art (and not only of art, but of ritual) for the human spirit. Ruskin had uttered a similar message, more dramatically, but more shrilly. What Saintsbury calls the "quietism" of Pater's style made Pater's lessons, less sharp in their immediate impact, sink more deeply in. More broadly still, he made English and American writers aware, as Flaubert and Mallarmé had made French writers aware, that imaginative literary art in modern times, whatever else it may be, is a heroic and perhaps desperate struggle with language. T. S. Eliot's essay on Pater is a cold one; but in the remarks in *Four Quartets* on language, its slipping and sliding, the need for its renewal, and so on, he seems sometimes to me to be echoing the central precepts of Pater's "Style."

NOTES

1. Ian Fletcher, *Walter Pater*, London, 1959, p. 31.

2. Ibid., p. 36.   3. Ibid.

4. Walter Pater, *Appreciations, With an Essay on Style*, London, 1889, p. 1. (Quotations from the reprint of 1931.) Notes 5 through 28 are references to this work; in the citations the page numbers only will be given. Thereafter "Pater" will be used.

5. Ibid., p. 2.   6. Ibid., p. 3.   7. Ibid., p. 4.   8. Ibid.   9. Ibid., p. 6.   10. Ibid., p. 7.   11. Ibid.   12. Ibid.   13. Ibid., p. 8.   14. Ibid.   15. Ibid., p. 9.   16. Ibid., p. 17.   17. Ibid., p. 13.   18. Ibid., p. 14.   19. Ibid., p. 12.   20. Ibid., p. 10.   21. Ibid., p. 16.   22. Ibid., p. 23.   23. Ibid., p. 24.   24. Ibid., p. 27. Italics added.   25. Ibid.   26. Ibid., p. 32.   27. Ibid., p. 33.   28. Ibid., p. 34.

29. George Saintsbury, *A History of English Prose Rhythm*, London, 1912, p. 427. (Quotations from revised edition of 1922.)

30. Pater, p. 35.

31. Ibid.

32. Ibid., p. 36.

33. Samuel Butler, *The Note-Books of Samuel Butler*, ed. Henry Festing Jones (London, 1912) p. 184.

34. Max Beerbohm, *The Works of Max Beerbohm*, London, 1896, p. 129. (Quotations from Heinemann's limited Collected Edition of Beerbohm's prose of 1922, in which Beerbohm, in his preface to this volume, says he made some slight stylistic revisions.)

35. Pater, p. 10.

36. Ibid., p. 13.

37. Saintsbury, p. 420. Notes 38 through 48 are page citations from Saintsbury.

38. Ibid., p. 421.

39. Ibid.
40. Ibid., pp. 421-2.
41. Ibid., p. 423, 424.
42. Ibid., p. 425.
43. Ibid., p. 424.
44. Ibid.
45. Ibid., p. 425
46. Ibid.
47. Ibid.
48. Ibid., p. 426.
49. Beerbohm, p. 52.
50. Saintsbury, p. 388.

THE DARWINIAN REVOLUTION AND LITERARY FORM*

A . D W I G H T C U L L E R

He was a Darwinian for fun.
—*The Education of Henry Adams*

The topic which I wish to pursue in this essay concerns one aspect of the relation between Darwin's theory of evolution by natural selection and the literature of the post-Darwinian period in England. I might have given my remarks the title, "The Influence of Darwin on English Literature," except that the very reason for my undertaking this inquiry is the dissatisfaction I have always felt with studies of this type. These studies trace, with more learning than I could ever summon, the ways in which the substantive matters treated by Darwin provide literary works of the late nineteenth century with their materials or on occasion with their themes. It may be, for example, that a writer will be struck by the Darwinian view of nature as involved in a ruthless struggle for existence, or simply by the idea of evolution itself, or again by the new view of man, who is now dethroned as lord of creation and placed by Darwin firmly in the context of nature, or finally by the fact that Darwin's theory seems to contradict the account of creation as presented in the opening chapters of Genesis and so to cast doubt upon the verbal inspiration of Scripture and ultimately upon the objective truth of Christianity itself. Indeed, at whatever point one takes hold of the Darwinian theory—and this is one of the wonderful things about it—it opens out into large and fruitful considerations which have important consequences for human life. What is more natural than that creative writers should seize upon and develop these ideas? and when they do we are in-

* In a shorter form this essay was originally a lecture delivered at the Ohio State University.

terested. And yet, to trace the way in which these writers derive from Darwin their views of nature, man, God, and society does not seem to me quite to get at the heart of the problem. At least, such is not the task which I set myself in this essay.

The task to which I would address myself is rather to inquire how the form of the Darwinian explanation has influenced, or is analogous to, forms of literary expression in the post-Darwinian world. And here I am obliged to notice the most considerable effort in this direction, Stanley Edgar Hyman's *The Tangled Bank: Darwin, Marx, Fraser, and Freud as Imaginative Writers.* Mr. Hyman's thesis is that the *Origin of Species* through its metaphorical structure reproduces the form of tragedy. "In Gilbert Murray's terms, the basic ritual stages of tragedy are *agon* or contest, *sparagmos* or tearing apart, then *anagnorisis* or discovery and *epiphany* or joyous showing-forth of the resurrected protagonist. Darwin's struggle for existence is clearly Murray's *agon* and *sparagmos*, and his natural selection or survival of the fittest, *anagnorisis* and *epiphany*."[1] One's comment on this is that if Greek tragedy was based upon the process of death and rebirth in nature, then it is no wonder that a modern description of that process will have something analogous to tragedy. Mr. Hyman is reasoning in a circle. But beyond this it is apparent that Mr. Hyman really has no firm conception of the imaginative structure of Darwin's work. In the latter part of his essay he compares the *Origin of Species* to the Bible. As dealing with the origin of life it is a kind of Genesis; as resulting in scientific laws it is a Leviticus. It is also analogous to Paul, to the patristic writings, and to the New Testament; and the *Descent of Man* is a kind of Fall. The central metaphor of the book, according to Mr. Hyman, is the "tangled bank," a bank on which the various forms of life exist in complicated interdependence, and Mr. Hyman rightly sees that this image, in contrast to the traditional images of the Great Chain of Being or the Tree of Life, is disordered and democratic, "essentially a modern vision."[2] But as such it has nothing to do with either Greek tragedy or the Bible. Mr. Hyman's confusion is due to his never being quite clear whether he is dealing with Darwin's metaphors or with the matters they are used to describe, and the main conclusion which emerges from his work is that the metaphors are largely at variance with the form of the Darwinian explanation. It is with this latter in its relation to literary form that I should like to deal.

I

What is the form of the Darwinian explanation? In order to answer this we need to inquire as to the central problem which Darwin was attempting to explain. If we were to judge simply by the title of his book, we would have to say that it was the problem of species, whether species are fixed or mutable or, to put it in philosophic terms, whether they are real or simply convenient fictions of the systematic naturalist. Clearly this is an important problem for Darwin, for it is only when species are regarded in this latter point of view that the fact of evolution or development will appear; but it is also clear—and was so to Darwin—that there is another problem which is logically prior to that of species, namely, the problem of the apparently purposive adaptation of individuals to their environment. Darwin himself in his *Autobiography* speaks of how, on the *Beagle* voyage, although he observed many facts which "could be explained on the supposition that species gradually become modified," "it was equally evident that neither the action of the surrounding conditions, nor the will of the organisms . . . , could account for the innumerable cases in which organisms of every kind are beautifully adapted to their habits of life,—for instance, a woodpecker or tree-frog to climb trees, or a seed for dispersal by hooks or plumes. I had always been much struck by such adaptations, and until these could be explained it seemed to me almost useless to endeavour to prove by indirect evidence that species have been modified."[3] Species, one might say, are the biological equivalent of the Aristotelian formal cause, but they are made necessary by the supposition of a final cause. Or, to employ Biblical language, if God created living things, then it is natural that he should have created them "after their kind," that is, in accordance with his plan or idea of them; but the real question is whether he created them at all.

Darwin's theory of evolution by natural selection, then, while presenting the mechanism whereby species have been modified, is initially concerned with the explanation of why individuals should be adapted. As such it may be considered a reply to the famous argument from design elaborated by William Paley. It is not simply that Darwin studied Paley at Cambridge and, without bothering himself about the correctness of his premises, greatly admired the lucidity of his prose, but rather that Paley's *Natural Theology* is so much the classic statement of the orthodox argument from design that Darwin would almost have to be considered as answering it whether he would or no. Of course, Paley was not primarily concerned with Darwin's problem. His concern was simply to formulate an argument for the existence of God. But in the course of doing this he also gave an explanation of those very adaptations in nature which were Darwin's problem. This explanation was that organisms are so wonderfully adapted to their environment and organs to their function because they were so contrived by an intelligent mind. They were designed *to be* adapted, formed by God so that they would function as they do. This is, of course, at once the simplest and the most complex answer that can be given to this problem—the simplest because it is the most natural thing in the world for human beings to attribute to nature their own intelligent, purposive habits of mind, but also the most complex because it requires a separate purposive act for each separate adaptation. Indeed, one may say that it is no explanation at all, being merely a repetition in religious or idealistic terms of the phenomena to be explained. And yet, being no more than that, it cannot be disproved.

Darwin was not able to disprove it, but he was able to stand it on its head. He said in effect, let's turn this thing upside down, or round about, and look at it from the other end. Perhaps these adaptations are not an end foreseen by an intelligent mind but the chance result of a random process. It is certainly true that individuals of any species vary slightly among themselves. It is also true that such is the struggle for existence among natural forms that not all these individuals can survive to maturity and reproduce themselves. If there are any whose variations give them an advantage, however slight, in the struggle for existence, these will be the ones to survive. Then, if their variations are inherited and if they continue to be advantageous, they will gradually accumulate so as not merely to modify the species but also to adapt it more perfectly to its environment or to continue its adaptation to a changing environment. This is the Darwinian explanation, and it is evident what Darwin has done in proposing it. He has explained adaptations not as an end foreseen by an intelligent mind but as the result of an unintelligent process. He has abandoned the teleological explanation, which looks to the future, for a genetic explanation, which looks to the past. He has appealed not to the formal and final causes of Aristotle but to the material and efficient causes instead. He has given us a new conception of natural law, not as (in capital letters) an antecedent Force or Power which produces harmony in the natural world, but (in small letters) a mere statistical description or formulation of what does in fact take place. Where Paley has taken intelligence to be the cause and adaptation the result, Darwin had shown that adaptation was the cause and survival the result—survival of those fittest to survive.

This dramatic reversal of orthodox thinking is what I take to be the heart of the Darwinian revolution. It is a new manner of conceiving, a new way of looking at things, and it had the impact that it did because, validated in the world of nature, it turned out to be true. Nevertheless, this revolution was not limited to the world of nature, nor was it the unique possession of Darwin. It had already occurred in several other areas of thought, and its repetition, in one sphere after another, must be accounted a central feature of the Victorian age. It is not exactly a watershed in the history of the century so much as a great wheeling round, or re-orientation, of the human mind toward the modern world.

I should be foolish to attempt to exemplify this revolution at length, but merely to substantiate what I have said and to provide further insight into the form of the Darwinian explanation, I should like to give three further examples, that of Malthus in population theory, of Bentham in ethics, and of Hume in general philosophy. Then we shall be in a position to turn to our major example, in literary expression.

It is well known that Darwin got his key insight from reading Malthus's *Essay on the Principle of Population*,[4] but it is not always appreciated, I think, what the true relation of the two men was. Gertrude Himmelfarb, for example, in her study of the Darwinian Revolution, says that the two men were basically at odds because they differed on substantive questions. So they did, but they did not differ in the form of their argument. As Darwin had his Paley, so Malthus had his Godwin, and they argued against their opponents in the same way. William Godwin had developed in the *Enquirer* and earlier in *Political Justice* the idea of a Utopia in which, by the abolition of private property and marriage, the crimes of passion and of theft would be eliminated and man would govern himself purely by reason. At this point, however, he had to meet the question, raised earlier by Robert Wallace, of population. Would it not happen, if man were free to bring children into the world without the restraint of marriage, which forced him to provide for his own, and without the restraint of private property, which forced him to provide for them out of his own pocket—would it not happen that he would breed promiscuously and irresponsibly and that the resulting over-population would more than negative the proposed goods? To which criticism Godwin replied, "There is a principle in human society by which population is perpetually kept down to the level of the means of subsistence."[5] I do not know what Godwin meant, or indeed whether he knew what he meant, by this "principle." But apparently he had in mind some vaguely conceived natural law or principle of cosmic order which saw to it that there never were more people than there was food for them to eat. It was at this point that Malthus, arguing with his pro-Godwinian father, cocked his head on one side and said, No, isn't it just the other way around—not that there is an antecedent principle which effects this harmony but that the harmony is the result of those persons without food dying off? It is true, as Mr. Godwin has observed, there never are more people than there is food for them to eat. But this is not a happy arrangement; it is an unhappy one. They aren't there because they died of starvation some time ago. Such is Malthus's reply to Godwin, and it presents us once again with a teleological explanation replaced by a genetic one, with formal and final causes replaced by material and efficient ones, with the conception of natural law as an agent replaced by the conception of it as a statistical formulation, and with the harmony or adaptation which was once seen as the effect of an event now seen as the cause of quite a different event.

To illustrate this matter with respect to Bentham and the theory of ethics is a somewhat more subtle task, but the Utilitarian analysis is nonetheless precisely parallel to that of Malthus and Darwin. The antagonist in this case is not a particular individual, merely the orthodox ethic of Stoicism or Christianity. The harmony or adaptation to be explained is not that between the organism and its environment, or between population and food supply, but between happiness and virtue. Both sides agree that there is an adaptation, that is, a harmonious relation, to be explained, but whereas the Stoic or Christian says that it is a planned relation, that God has so ordered the world that if you are virtuous you will be made happy, either in this world or the next, Bentham turns it around and says, No, the reason happiness and virtue seem to be related in human life is that we give the name of virtue to those things which make us happy. This is all that the words *virtue* and *vice, good* and *evil* mean; they are simply labels whereby we honor or stigmatize those actions which contribute to our happiness or unhappiness, and they have no other, no independent meaning. Speaking in evolutionary terms, we might say that actions—moral actions—are engaged in a struggle for existence and that those which make us happy thereby show that they are well adapted to their human environment, survive in the world of our approval, and so are denominated good. This it is that creates the harmony which we, having forgotten how it arose, subsequently wonder at.

Behind Malthus and Bentham lies David Hume, who is the true father of this kind of thinking in the nineteenth century. It is not merely that his *Dialogues concerning Natural Religion* crushingly refute the argument from design and all but anticipate Darwin on natural selection. Neither is it that his essay "Of the Populousness of Ancient Nations" does actually anticipate Malthus and that Malthus acknowledged Hume as one of the sources of his ideas. Neither is the well-known relation between Hume's ethics and Benthamite thought the important thing. It is rather that Hume's central discovery, that concerning the origin of our ideas of causation, is the "revolution in philosophy" which is the ultimate source of all these specialized revolutions. Hume observes that when we see two events constantly associated in nature, we assume that one must be the cause of the other. But we are not justified in so assuming, he says, and the true statement would be, not that cause has associated the two events but rather that their constant association has produced in our minds the idea of causation. This reversal, which transforms an objective event into a subjective one, is far more radical than Darwin's, for it asserts that it is not design which implies a designer but the appearance of design which gives rise in our minds to the conception of a designer. In other words, it not only refutes Paley, which Darwin could not do, but it also explains how his error arose.

The importance of Hume for this essay, however, is that he is amused by what he has done. With his elegant sense of form, his exquisite style and delicious irony, he is not only conscious that he has produced a revolution in philosophy but also that this revolution is rather funny. It is in the nature of a sly retort or witty repartee. It is a kind of comic reversal in which the tables are turned upon an opponent to his intense discomfiture and the delight and satisfaction of his enemies. It is no accident that some of Hume's finest works are cast in the form of a dialogue, for his thought would lose half its savour if there were no antagonist to express the overblown, a priori point of view which is then deflated by a sly, insinuating wit. Some of these dialogues, with their brilliantly polished conversation, could almost be transformed into Restoration comedies if they had as their subject a human situation corresponding to their philosophic content. And we do in fact know that Restoration comedy arose out of the libertinism of Hobbes,[6] who is the next earlier philosopher in this particular line, just as the comedies of Menander and Terence arose out of Epicurean thought, the equivalent of Benthamism in antiquity. None of these thinkers was particuarly liked in his own day. In fact, Hobbes, Hume, Malthus, Bentham, and Darwin were probably as hated as it has ever been the misfortune of mild and inoffensive men to be. They were all regarded as some kind of ogre or monster who had set out deliberately to subvert religion, morality, and all that is decent in human life. And in fact they did threaten the established values, and the reason people hated them was that they identified with these values. If they could have achieved a certain detachment by putting the whole matter in art, then they would have seen that the process was rather funny.

Indeed, viewed from this perspective even Malthus and Bentham are funny. Malthus's antagonist, the Godwin of *Political Justice*, is the very type of the utopian philosopher whose head is so much in the clouds that he cannot see what is before him and stumbles and falls in a ditch. Writing of the society of the future, he says, "The whole will be a people of men, and not of children. Generation will not succeed generation, nor truth have in a certain degree to recommence her career at the end of every thirty years. There will be no war, no crimes, no administration of justice as it is called, and no government. . . . Every man will seek with ineffable ardour the good of all."[7] As to the problem of over-population, he quotes Franklin to the effect that "mind will one day become omnipotent over matter," and people "will cease to propagate."[8] In other words, Godwin transforms people into disembodied intellects, and what Malthus does is remind him that they also have stomachs and reproductive organs and that there is a built-in incompatibility between the two. In our actual world this is not funny, but in the world of ideas it is, and the spirit of deep sardonic humor which runs through the first two editions of Malthus's essay suggests that he was perfectly conscious of what he was doing.

Bentham is usually regarded as quite without humor and so in large part he was. And yet in the famous footnote in the *Introduction to the Principles of Morals and Legislation* in which Bentham shows that all the high-sounding phrases which the philosophers have produced to denote the true source of moral value—Reason, Common Sense, the Law of Nature, the Rule of Right, and the Eternal Fitness of Things—all can be reduced to the single arbitrary *ipse dixit,* "I like"[9]—surely this footnote is structurally identical with and almost as amusing as the scene in *Tom Jones* where the philosopher Square, who also believed in the Eternal Fitness of Things, is found "among other female utensils," in Molly Seagrim's closet. The naturalism of Tom Jones (whose activities would surely result in over-population) is the perfect counterpart of the naturalism of Bentham and Malthus.

Only Darwin among these thinkers seems to have had no appreciation of the emotional overtones of his theory. He was, indeed, so bland and colorless a person that a recent writer has made it a major enigma how so brilliant a theory could have emerged from so placid an intellect. In his *Autobiography* he concedes that he had no aesthetic sense and that the only novels he liked were those which presented lovable female characters in a happy ending—in other words, those least likely to have been influenced by his own theory. As a scientist he was the author of the greatest repartee in nature, but as a man he says that he was without wit and that he had a fatality for putting his statements initially in a wrong or awkward form. Surely this is borne out by the form of the *Origin of Species.* Who of us, if we had the opportunity to write such a book, would not begin, as in a drama, by building up Paley and his argument from design with the whole range of existing plausible fact and then, by a quick reversal, bringing it all tumbling down with an explanation so simple and obvious that Huxley would slap his knee and say, "Why didn't I think of that?" and others would wonder and find the new view as satisfying as it was surprising? I do not say that this is the way to get the theory accepted, but simply in order to present it, as a brilliant and paradoxical theory, surely this is the way.[10]

And yet it was not Darwin's way, who thereby added one more to the list of his accomplishments, namely, that he opened up, without himself occupying it, a new, large, and fruitful territory for literary exploitation. T. H. Huxley was Darwin's bulldog, but it was not Huxley who exploited this territory. Rather, I suggest, it was Samuel Butler in his satiric extravaganza *Erewhon.*

II

Whenever I give to graduate students, as I sometimes do, the problem of Darwin's influence on *Erewhon,* I like to find a student who is just naïve enough to go wrong initially but also keen enough not to persist in his error but to find out the truth for himself. Initially he will head straight for the final sections of the work, "The Book of the Machines" (originally called "Darwin Among the Machines") and "The Rights of Animals and Vegetables," for these are full of evolutionary materials. The former presents the extravagant hypothesis that machines are developing so rapidly that they are actually evolving into a higher kind of life and will soon supplant the human race; and the latter tells of an ancient Erewhonian prophet who preached that animals are so nearly akin to man that to eat animal food is a kind of cannibalism, and also of his even more zealous successor who held that vegetables are so nearly akin to animals that to eat them is also a kind of cannibalism, both of these gentlemen being so successful in enforcing their views that the human race very nearly died of starvation. In both episodes the biological argument is extensive and technical, but when my graduate student comes to examine the meaning of the argument he of course discovers that it has nothing to do with Darwinism. The former episode, although using Darwinian materials, is really a satire on modern technology and also on the process of reasoning by analogy as exemplified in Joseph Butler's *Analogy of Religion, Natural and Revealed*. And the latter episode, although again using elaborate biological materials, is a satire on the Old and New Testament asceticism and also on the a priori mode of treating human problems exemplified in Paine, Godwin, and the "rights of man" school. Thus, if my graduate student is not to be out of a subject, or to have a very thin one, he must look elsewhere for his influence.

I will not claim that he always finds it, at least in quite the way I would desire, but he is usually clear that it lies somewhere not in the substance but in the total feeling and structure of the book. *Erewhon* resulted, we know, from the great double emancipation which Butler experienced when in 1859 he went to New Zealand as a sheep-farmer, thus escaping from the oppressive religiosity of England and his clerical father, and simultaneously read the *Origin of Species*. He tells us that his first night on shipboard was the first time in his life that he omitted to say his prayers, and that it was as if a great weight, like a dead albatross, fell from around his neck. A short time later, when he read the *Origin*, he exclaimed, "If this be true, then Christianity is false," and essentially this was his comment upon his new country. Looking about him at the tanned, healthy faces of the New Zealanders, not pasty as in England or cramped by guilt and Evangelical hypocrisy—at people who did not hesitate to admit that they were in a fever over making money—he felt that he really was in the antipodes. In respect to England he was upside down, or England was upside down in respect to him, and he instinctively embodied his upside-down view in a device which I can only call the Darwinian reversal.

It will be remembered that Butler's hero enters Erewhon by means of a mountain pass in which he encounters ten gigantic statues which loom balefully through the mist and moan with an inhuman malevolence. These statues are evidently to be associated with the Ten Commandments, the horrible "thou-shalt-nots" of the Christian religion, which feed upon human suffering, and the suggestion is that in order to reach the sunny land of Erewhon we must travel back across history into the pre-Mosaic era. Once there we find a land which, although not consistently represented, is most frequently conceived simply as England backwards. This is symbolized, perhaps too obviously, by the fact that the names of the principal Erewhonians are English names spelled backwards or with their syllables reversed, and that Erewhon itself, of course, is "Nowhere" (the English for Utopia) spelled as nearly backwards as euphony will permit. It is quite wrong, I think, to say that Erewhon is an anagram of "Nowhere." It is "Nowhere" backwards with a single concession to pronounceability.

The reversed names, however, are little more than a symbol of the reversal of situation which Butler makes the basis of his satiric technique. The two most famous such situations are those of the Musical Banks and the extraordinary treatment of crime and disease. In the former the roles of bank and church are exchanged, and in the latter criminals are treated medically whereas sick men are punished. In neither reversal, we should notice, does the technique quite fit the matter which Butler has it in hand to say. The bank-church reversal, for instance, is really only one-half of a reversal, for whereas the church is represented as a bank (although one dealing in a very fraudulent spiritual coin), the bank is not represented as a church. One can imagine such an episode, in which the worshippers would kneel down before an altar which had all the aspects of a teller's cage, but for Butler to have done this would be to have satirized the very position which he wished to sustain, namely, that the worship of money is one of our healthiest habits of mind and ought to be indulged in more frankly. Then, when we turn to the other episode, we discover that that is a complete reversal but that both sides of it curiously mean the same thing. On the one hand, we see Mr. Nosnibor, who is suffering from a bad fit of embezzlement, being visited by his friends and the family straightener, who inquire solicitously about the state of his morals. And on the other hand, we see the narrator innocently mentioning to the jailor's daughter that he has a bad cold and being bewildered to see her flounce out of the room as if he had made an indecent proposal. Obviously, both of these episodes illustrate the same idea, only the one by a positive and the other by a negative example. Negatively, we are told that it is no more foolish to be angry with a man for having a bad cold, which he can't help, than it is to be angry with him for having bad intentions, which presumably he can't help either; and positively, we are told that it is quite as sensible to try to cure a man of embezzling as it is to cure him of tuberculosis. That Butler should have reversed his situation, but not his idea, is illuminating, and it prepares us for the many other reversals which he employs. When he wishes to satirize the belief in a life after death, he instinctively does it by attributing to the Erewhonians a belief in a life before birth; and when he wants to satirize the parent-child relation, he explains that in Erewhon children "have" parents instead of parents having children, with all the unholy consequences which that idea entails. These, he says, are examples of those extraordinary "perversions of thought"[11] which characterize the Erewhonians, a people so impish and mischievous that they speak not of the "seven deadly sins" but of the "seven deadly virtues," and their text of Alexander Pope (or should one call him Pope Alexander?) has become so corrupt that it reads not, "And those who came to scoff remained to pray," but, "Those who came to pray remained to scoff."[12] A good deal of Butler's wit is of this kind, both in *Erewhon* and *The Way of All Flesh*, simply the impish, mischievous reversal of some commonplace or proverb in order to see, as he says, if it is not really one of "those cant half-truths of which the other half is as true or truer."[13] Doubtless most of these were of his father's manufacture, but if so, it was the *Origin* which gave Butler the courage to play Darwin to his father's Paley and, if not exactly to turn him upside down, at least to reverse his collar and see if he did not look a little more human in that guise.

III

I do not know any other work of English literature which illustrates quite so clearly as does *Erewhon* the influence of the Darwinian explanation upon literary form. But having established this as the kind of thing for which we ought to be looking, it is not difficult, I believe, to extend our analysis into a wide range of more remote but perhaps no less fundamental examples. Let us begin with a work closely related in substance, George Bernard Shaw's *Man and Superman*. It is well known that Shaw inherited his philosophy of creative evolution from Butler after the latter had parted company with Darwin and had reverted to a modified form of Lamarckism. Indeed, it is clear that Shaw and Butler, for all their appearance of modernity, really re-introduce through the back door the very teleology which Darwin had succeeded in expelling. Shaw makes fun of Paley's watch, but the only difference between him and Paley is that whereas the latter placed the element of purpose outside of nature, in God, Shaw and Butler placed it within nature, in life itself. It is the Life Force which, erratically but with a sure instinct, achieves those adaptations which Darwin had attributed to a random process and which Paley had imputed to God. And yet, would anyone say that this New Teleology, as we may call it, gives the true flavor of such a play as *Man and Superman?* True, Tanner, the hero, is the mouthpiece of that philosophy, and his blustering opponent, Roebuck Ramsden, is characterized as "an Evolutionist from the publication of the *Origin of Species.*" and yet the whole spirit of the play, it seems to me, is impudently, brashly Darwinian. It is heart-and-soul given over to the subversion of established values, and its iconoclasm operates by the technique of direct reversal. This is true both in the Hell scene and in the surrounding comedy. In the Hell scene the humor depends on the paradoxical situation that Hell, far from being a place of torment, corresponds pretty closely to the conventional idea of Heaven, and is a Hell precisely for that reason. Conversely, Heaven, a place where the masters of reality strive for a higher and higher self-consciousness, corresponds pretty closely to the ordinary man's idea of Hell. In the comedy the reversal is between roles of the sexes in finding a mate. Ricky-Ticky-Tavy naïvely believes that man is the pursuer and woman the pursued, whereas Tanner sees with great clarity that it is just the other way around, the only thing that he does not see being the fact that he himself is the intended victim. Naturally, as his realistic vitalism is substituted for Ricky-Ticky-Tavy's romantic sentimentalism, the two characters themselves undergo a transformation, the romantic amorist being seen as basically the bachelor type and the libertine as your only true moralist and propagator of the species. The libertine is, in addition, the jester of the play, and his paradoxes, which follow the Butlerian form of the inverted commonplace, are simply an expression on the verbal level of those same "perversions of thought" which constitute the central situation of the play.

If this be so, if the work which Shaw calls "a Comedy and a Philosophy" be Darwinian not by virtue of its philosophy but by virtue of its comic form, can we not generalize this fact and suggest a fundamental analogy between the Darwinian explanation and the whole comic, satiric tradition? Can we not say that the Darwinian reversal does in the realm of evolutionary thought precisely the same thing as is done in the realm of comedy by that reversal of situation which we call the *peripeteia?* Can we not say that the discovery by Darwin of the true explanation of adaptations in the natural world is analogous to what in comedy we also call a "discovery" (or recognition scene or *anagnorisis*), in which characters learn for the first time their true relation with each other and with their world? Certainly both worlds are vastly ironic. It is no more ironic that Tanner should warn Ricky-Ticky-Tavy against the danger by which he himself is imperilled, or that Volpone should attempt to overreach his enemies by a device through which he himself is overreached, than it is that Paley should seek the explanation of adaptations in precisely that area in which they are not to be found. He is as blind as Volpone, and Darwin as cunning as Mosca. Indeed, it is clear that Darwin and Paley, Malthus and Godwin, Bentham and the traditional moralist stand in precisely the same intellectual and emotional relation to one another as do those two stock figures, the *eiron* and the *alazon,* in comedy. The *eiron* is that low, cunning figure who pretends not to know but does, the *alazon* that strutting, blustering figure who pretends to know but does not. In the beast fable the one is the rooster, the other the fox. Not that Paley, of course, as an individual has the bluster and self-conceit of the *alazon* or that Darwin in any way affects the sly humility of the Socratic underdog or *eiron.* But the former does embody a view of the world which is complex, inflated, pretentious, and wrong, and the latter is able to undercut that view by another which is simple, unpretentious, obvious, and right. Put them on the stage and give them an outwitting situation in which to act and they would be perfectly recognizable as good comic drama.

We may develop this point by observing that the Paley-Darwin conflict reproduces very closely the form of comedy as it has recently been analyzed by critics like Susanne Langer, Northrop Frye, Helen Gardner, and Alvin Kernan.[14] All these writers emphasize that comedy centers about a conflict between an older generation which is life-denying in its attitude and a younger which is life-asserting. The older generation (of husbands and fathers) have devised a social order which is rigid, arbitrary, a priori, and closed. It is usually based on some kind of law which is essentially a law against lovers. The action of the play is the outwitting of these people and the circumventing of their law so that in the end the young lovers come together in a new society which is open, flexible, pragmatic, and free. Comedy is biological in that it expresses the will to live, the irrepressible sexual energy which bursts through the false barriers erected by society and fulfills itself in love. It does this by many a lucky coincidence, for chance, as Schlegel observes, occupies the same place in comedy that is occupied by destiny in tragedy.[15] Tragedy focuses upon the death of the individual and is the expression of the denial of the will to live. Comedy asserts that will and, through its stock characters and happy ending, focuses upon the continuation of the species.

It is obvious that Darwin's random process corresponds to comic chance, and that Paley's design is the expression in natural forms of that pattern which in events we call destiny. Paley's immutable species are the rigid categories which in Darwin's fluid individuals are confounded. Paley's law, indeed, is essentially a law against lovers in that it forbids species to intermingle, whereas Darwin's merely observes the pragmatic fact that —they already have. Historically, the conflict between Darwin and his antagonists was one aspect of the conflict between the generations, and also, as Professor Darlington has pointed out, between the social classes.[16] So, too, comedy champions the sons against the fathers and the lower orders against the higher. Both comedy and Darwinism are a part of that great outburst of nature against society which is both very funny when it happens and also socially disturbing.

This explains, of course, why there was so little comedy in England during the hundred years from about 1770 to 1870. The Evangelical revival, followed by the Tractarian movement, the transcendental idealism of the Romantic poets together with the earnestness of the Victorian critics, the great political reaction against the French Revolution, and the intellectual synthesis of the high Victorian authors, all produced a series of moral, social, and religious absolutes which were doubtless very necessary at the time but which had the effect of suppressing laughter. Ultimately they came to be felt as a burden, and after they had been battered by Hume, Malthus, Bentham, and Darwin, they crumbled and fell apart. Some found this very tragic and moaned about "nature red in tooth and claw." But the younger generation found it funny and breathed a sigh of relief. It is no accident that the two late nineteenth-century thinkers who are most closely associated with evolution, Meredith and Bergson, should have written essays on the Comic Spirit and on Laughter. The former saw very clearly that the absence of the Comic Spirit from England was due to the prevalence of Puritan morality, but he did not see that his own requirement for its return, a society which gives a high place to women, is essentially biological. Bergson does make this connection, but in using the language of mechanism to describe the rigidities of the comic butt— rigidities which in the character's eyes derive from a high moral absolute— he obscures the reductive element which is present in his own examples. Both essays are defective as analyses, but they testify by their existence to the phenomenon we are describing.

IV

Comedy, of course, was not the only reaction against the moral abso- lutes of the Victorian period: the aesthetic movement was another. The connection between the two, which meet in Oscar Wilde, is their com- mon preoccupation with form. For whereas tragedy tends in the direction of philosophy and religion, comedy really tends in no direction at all. It inclines to be naturalistic, but the only thing essential to it is its form— its style, its conventions, its artificiality. As the only thing essential to the Darwinian explanation is also its form, this suggests that if we are to look further for Darwin's influence we may find it in the aesthetic movement and the related "nonsense" literature—in writers like Lewis Carroll, Pater, and Wilde. Let it be understood, of course, that by "influence" we do not mean that Darwin was consciously present to the mind of any one of these writers but merely that he (and Malthus, Bentham, and Hume) created a climate of opinion without which their work could not have been written.

It is very difficult to say what *Alice in Wonderland* means, and I do not wish to deny either the psychological interpretation or that which sees in the various episodes allusions to contemporary events. Indeed, both are quite consonant with my view which is simply that in *Alice* we are taken down through a rabbit-hole into a world which is quite as strange and preposterous as that of *Erewhon*. Like Erewhon it has some elements of a backwards world, although this idea is more fully developed in *Through the Looking-Glass*. But in general, it is an adult world of rigid, anti-natural manners as seen through the essentially sane and kindly eyes of a child. The pompous moralistic poems, which some devil in Alice prompts her to parody, the travesties of justice and of a tea-party, of education and religion, are all brought down to earth either by their own inherent absurdity or by the relativistic and destructive devices of the book. For Alice's frequent changes in size, which make her now a child to the animals' adulthood, and now an adult to their childishness, not only emphasize the relativism of all these manners and morals but also emphasize on what basis of physical force society is founded. For when at the end of the book Alice sweeps away the cards in disgust, she does what any child would like to do in an England so constituted. But primarily these things are swept away by their own inherent absurdity, for the final basis of Carroll's nonsense is the fact that in the mathematical, logical, and linguistic sciences we have disciplines which can move, in perfect consistency with their own rules, from premises which are not unreasonable to conclusions which are insane in terms of the real world. For whereas the real world consists of certain facts or values which are fixed, the purely formal worlds of mathematics, logic, and language do not. Darwin's world is such a world of biological forms. Here there is no basis for saying that a man is "better" than a chimpanzee or a deer than a wolf. It is only that different forms come into existence and are validated by their own survival. Obviously, such a system is vastly reductive. In Darwin it is reductive by submitting biological design to a world of flux, in Carroll by submitting the fixities of an ethical society to the whimsies of mathematics, logic, and linguistic play. Thus, I do not say that *Alice in Wonderland* is a part of the post-Darwinian world because it contains evolutionary materials (as in abundance it does) nor despite the fact that its author is known to have detested Darwin (as he certainly did), rather because, like Darwin, he subjects the rigidities of an ethical, social, and religious world to the fresh natural vision of a child and to the destructive analysis of formal chance.

Alice was published in 1865, Pater's *Renaissance* in 1873. The famous Conclusion to the latter work is anomalous (for an aesthetic study) in that it takes its departure from the latest conclusions of modern science. We are told, says Pater, that both our outward physical life and our inward mental life are but the momentary concurrence of atoms which come into being only to pass away again. Thus, all is flux, and what we call the fixities of ethics, philosophy, and religion are merely the forms of thought thrown up by the history of culture and fossilized into realities. To them both art and science are opposed. They are opposed in that they want any form which succeeds simply by virtue of its form to be recognized. The artist does not wish aesthetic forms to be burdened by a didactic content any more than the biologist wishes evolutionary forms to be ranked on an anthropomorphic scale. Neither does he wish the individual work of art to be bound by conceptions of genre, which are the "species" of the aesthetic world. As Pater sees it, art has evolved in the sense of freeing itself from matter. Specifically, it has evolved from architecture, which is a kind of dinosaur emerging from the primeval mud of its practical functions; to sculpture, which is still bound by intractable materials; to bas-relief, which is emergent and therefore suggestive; to painting, poetry, and music. "All art aspires to the condition of music" in the sense that it aspires to pure form, but once any degree of formal perfection has been reached then it is impossible to prefer one school to another. "All periods, types, schools of taste, are in themselves equal,"[17] and the task of the critic is not to assign works to schools (that would be the old-fashioned biology of Linnæus), rather to discriminate the unique quality which differentiates one work of art from another. Thus, of preference Pater chooses transitional figures or intermediate forms—the early French stories which mingle the sweetness of the Middle Ages with the strength of the Renaissance, the Pico della Mirandolas who hover between paganism and Christianity, the Botticellis whose middle world takes no sides in conflicts but makes the great refusals, the minor, poetic medium of a painter-sculptor like Michelangelo, the bas-reliefs of Della Robbia, the strange mixture of artist and scientist in Leonardo, and so on. There are, of course, elements of stability in Pater, especially in the Winckelmann essay, and it would be wrong not to notice that much of his effort was to disengage himself from flux. Still, what struck his contemporaries about him was that he set art over against morality, philosophy, and religion and that he did so in conjunction with science. The basis of their association was, of course, the relativism, the atomism, the materialism of both fields—ultimately, their dependence upon sensation. "There is no such thing as a moral or an immoral book," said Wilde. "Books are well written, or badly written. That is all."[18] "There is no such thing as a moral or an immoral organism," Darwin might have said. "Organisms are well adapted, or badly adapted. That is all."

The one element that we miss in Pater is the element of the reversal—he is conscious of no Paley—but this is supplied for us in Oscar Wilde, not merely in his comedies but also, and very strikingly, in *The Picture of Dorian Gray*. In that work the painter Basil Hallward creates so living a likeness of his young friend Dorian Gray that it is as if the very soul of the youth had been put on canvas, and this enables Dorian to make a kind of Faustian compact with his Mephistophelian friend, Lord Henry, whereby he and the picture shall change places. He shall live in art, experiencing all things with the heightened intensity and freedom from practical consequences which is possible only in art, whereas his portrait shall live in life, bearing in its changing pigments all the hideous disfigurements which belong more properly to the face and soul of its subject. This idea of a kind of antithesis or paradoxical relation between art and life, so that what is true of one is distinctly not true of the other, is worked out in several ways in the novel. The characters, for example, are divided into two groups, those who are (what we might call) artists-in-life and those who are artists-in-art. Basil Hallward is a fine painter but a dull man, and Lord Henry elevates this fact into a general truth: "A really great poet," he says, "is the most unpoetical of all creatures. But inferior poets are absolutely fascinating. The worse their rhymes are, the more picturesque they look. The mere fact of having published a book of second-rate sonnets makes a man quite irresistible. He lives the poetry that he cannot write. The others write the poetry that they dare not realize."[19] Sibyl Vane, the actress to whom Dorian was attracted by her magnificent performance as Juliet, cannot play that role after she falls in love. She finds that she could mimic a passion that she did not feel, but she cannot mimic a passion that burns her like fire. Conversely, Lord Henry, who is not an artist in any usual medium, makes a work of art out of his own life, and this too is the ideal of Dorian Gray. All these artists-in-life live dramatic forms—the Vane family that of conscious melodrama, Lord Henry that of Restoration comedy, and Dorian that of a decadent French novel by Huysmans or by Oscar Wilde himself. Thus, life imitates art, as Wilde said it should, instead of art imitating life, and this paradoxical situation is extended through the book by the bewildering verbal paradoxes whereby Lord Henry creates his own world of aristocratic elegance out of the simple negation or reversal of the bourgeois morality of Basil Hallward.

Hallward is Paley to Lord Henry's Darwin, just as Dorian is Darwin to his picture's Paley. As the novel unfolds, the antithesis is widened, the tension strained, by the greater and greater oscillation of Dorian between exquisite art and gross orgy, as he attempts to cure the soul by means of the senses and the senses by means of the soul, until at last the reversal reaches the limits of absurdity and, with Dorian's stabbing of the portrait, surges back across itself, reverting all his sins upon his own soul, all his deformities upon his own person. The ending is anti-Darwinian, of course, but even if it be not considered purely conventional, there is still the figure of Lord Henry, who continues, unpunished and unperturbed, maintaining the supremacy of form over matter, and, like Ernest in *The Importance of Being Earnest*, of style over substance, in the true Darwinian way.

At this point I have come to the end of my subject, but, in the manner of my subject, I would now like to do an about-face and say that I do not think that ultimately the Darwinian technique is susceptible of very profound or satisfying literary exploitation. The reason for this is essentially the same as that which limits the possibilities of the Freudian technique, namely, as Charles Lamb said, that the "poet dreams being awake."[20] Paraphrasing him we might say, the "poet attacks design with design." It is inconceivable that he could be against design itself. He may be against old designs, antiquated designs, ugly designs, stupid designs, but he cannot for very long be against design itself. I recall a fantasy, devised I believe by Sir James Jeans and then made the basis of a story in the *New Yorker*, wherein several chimpanzees were placed at typewriters and by typing purely at random for generation after generation they at last produced all the books in the British Museum. I am very glad that this task was entrusted to chimpanzees, because these little creatures are just the ones to express the true evolutionary significance of the fable. Surely if we are looking for the pure literary counterpart of Darwinism, this is it —chimpanzees typing at random through the ages and producing, perhaps once a decade some recognizable word, perhaps once a century some intelligible sentence, and once an eon the great American novel. So it is that our technique of automatic reversal would work if it were applied automatically—and it may be that we feel the paradoxes of Butler and Wilde do have a certain automatic, mechanical character. So too with the larger structural reversals. One reason why a satire like *Gulliver's Travels* is greater than *Erewhon* is that Swift is always writing in the name of a perfectly ordered and supremely controlled philosophy, whereas Butler is writing in the name of a device. This device sometimes works and sometimes does not. By and large I think it works, and rather brilliantly, and it happens to say pretty much what Butler wants it to say; but of its nature it is equipped to say anything. Chesterton can utter paradoxes in behalf of Christianity because by his day Christianity had become sufficiently disestablished to be paradoxical. On the other hand, in Lord Henry's society the paradox has become so much the established thing that he who would be original has to utter truisms. "I can . . . say," declared Lord Henry in reference to getting out of a dinner, "that I am prevented from coming in consequence of a subsequent engagement. I think that would be a rather nice excuse: it would have all the surprise of candour."[21] It is obvious that the Darwinian-Wildean reversal means something only against the background of a world that is sufficiently firm and established to be reversed. When all is flux, the reversal cannot be distinguished from any other position, and one thing is quite as meaningless as another.

It is the recognition of this fact which leads, in the second generation of all these movements I have described, not to a reversal of the reversals but to a subtle falling away or gravitating back into the older world of design. And yet it is not the same world: it is a world with the same values but reinterpreted in some form more acceptable to the modern spirit. Thus Shaw and Butler turned away from Darwin because, as they said, he "banished mind from the universe," but they did not turn back to Paley. They combined Genesis with geology in Creative Evolution. And the neo-Malthusians, agreeing with their master that there is no principle whereby the population is perpetually kept down to the level of the means of subsistence, nevertheless saw in birth-control the means of creating that principle for themselves. Finally, John Stuart Mill did a comparable thing in respect to Bentham. Raised a Benthamite, he nevertheless reinterpreted the Utilitarian philosophy in a way absolutely at variance with his master's principles, even to the point of reasserting those absolute values which Bentham had been at such pains to deny. It is a great puzzle as to how Mill, the author of a textbook on logic, could have done so illogical a thing, but the truth is that this whole Darwinian-Benthamite-Malthusian view is so antithetic to the purposive cast of the human mind that it is very difficult to keep it firmly in focus. And when we come to express it, then we discover that language, as an instrument of the human intelligence, is simply not adapted to express unintelligence. This, I believe, is why Paley got away for so long with his argument that "design implies a Designer," for people did not see that the word *design* begs the question. Of course if there is design in nature, there must be a designer, but this is the very question, whether there is. And yet any word that Paley might have used would have similarly begged the question. And conversely, when Darwin came to express the idea of undesign, he found that he could hardly talk about his subject without employing expressions such as "Natural Selection," which, as he noted, imply the very opposite of what he was trying to prove, namely, that there is no such thing as Nature and that it doesn't select. But if Darwin had trouble in a scientific treatise, what would a poet do? I suggest that we get our answer in Hardy's "Hap," where the poet is trying to assert that the world is not governed by design, not even by malignant design, but purely by chance. Unfortunately, being a poet, he personifies chance. He calls it "Crass Casualty" or "dicing Time"; in other words, he makes it into a gambler with the normal purpose of a gambler, namely, to win. In this way both the character of language and the conditions of artistic representation have militated against the accurate expression of the Darwinian world-view.

Nevertheless, when that view is taken in conjunction with Paley, as I believe it was in the nineteenth century, then we have a dramatic encounter or confrontation which *is* perfectly intelligible—is indeed replete with meaning—and so is capable of varied and successful literary exploitation.

NOTES

1. New York, 1962, p. 28.

2. Ibid., p. 33. The references in the preceding sentence are to pp. 34-5, 40-42, 49. Theodore Baird's article, "Darwin and the Tangled Bank," *The American Scholar*, XV (Autumn 1946), 477-86, from which Hyman takes his departure, actually has a quite different thesis.

3. *The Autobiography of Charles Darwin*, ed. Nora Barlow, New York, 1959, p. 119.

4. Loren C. Eiseley has recently cast doubt on this, suggesting that Darwin got his key insight from Edward Blyth, a druggist and naturalist, who published two articles in *The Magazine of Natural History* in 1835 and 1837 which clearly

state the principle of natural selection, though giving it a conservative force. There is also some evidence that Darwin did not read Malthus till 1863. Eiseley, "Charles Darwin, Edward Blyth, and the Theory of Natural Selection," *Proceedings of the American Philosophical Society,* CIII (1959), 94-158. Obviously, the question of historical influence does not affect the intellectual relation of the two books.

5. *An Enquiry Concerning Political Justice and Its Influence on General Virtue and Happiness,* London, 1793, II, 813.

6. Thomas H. Fujimura, *The Restoration Comedy of Wit,* Princeton, 1952, Ch. II.

7. *Political Justice,* II, 871-2.

8. Ibid., II, 862, 871.

9. See Ch. II.

10. C. D. Darlington, *Darwin's Place in History,* Oxford, 1960, contends that Darwin deliberately softened the issue between himself and his antagonists in order to get his theory accepted. It should be clear that in this essay I am not referring to the historical Darwin who in successive editions increasingly adopted a compromise position but to an abstract "Darwinism" which says sharply what he ought to have said.

11. *Erewhon,* Modern Library edition, p. 71.

12. *Letters between Samuel Butler and Miss E. M. A. Savage,* London, 1935, p. 22.

13. Samuel Butler, *Further Extracts from the Notebooks,* ed. A. T. Bartholomew, London, 1934, p. 294.

14. Susanne Langer, *Feeling and Form,* New York, 1953, pp. 327-8; Northrop Frye, *Anatomy of Criticism,* Princeton, 1957, pp. 163-87; Helen Gardner, "As You Like It," in *More Talking of Shakespeare,* ed. John Garrett, London, 1959; Alvin Kernan, *The Plot of Satire,* New Haven, 1965, pp. 185-99. The first three works are cited in Kernan.

15. *Lectures on Dramatic Art and Literature* (1808), Lecture XIII, reprinted in *Theories of Comedy,* ed. Paul Lauter, Anchor Books, New York, 1964.

16. *Darwin's Place in History,* p. 30.

17. Walter Pater, *The Renaissance,* London, 1893, p. xii. Cf. Morse Peckham's suggestive remarks on Darwin and Pater in "Darwinism and Darwinisticism," *Victorian Studies,* III (September 1959), 38-9.

18. Oscar Wilde, *The Picture of Dorian Gray,* Preface.

19. Ibid., Ch. IV.

20. "The Sanity of True Genius," *The Last Essays of Elia.*

21. Wilde, *The Picture of Dorian Gray,* Ch. II.

LOGIC, FEELING, AND STRUCTURE
IN POLITICAL ORATORY: A PRIMER OF ANALYSIS

JOHN HOLLOWAY

[The proposition-number layout I have adopted in the following essay, which is somewhat theoretical in nature, has the advantage of conciseness, and has enabled me to say what I had to say in the space allowed me: which I felt doubtful of doing otherwise. Essential to the operation was to establish that the logical analysis of Part II of the essay was strictly in analogy with literary analysis as generally understood (if one may so speak). The layout adopted at least presents the claim for analogy in sharp definition, with the points of reference clearly shown; and if readers find that they cannot accept that claim, they will at least find it easy to locate their exact point of divergence. The symbolism of Part II is in essence simple, and not abstruse at all: though others, better qualified than I, might be able to make it so. I found myself using it spontaneously in trying to come to grips with the underlying structure of exact argument in the speeches. I retained that symbolism not only because of its spontaneity, but also because the essence of the operation was to show that not simply rhetoric or literary expression, but pervasive logical structure, was one with what might loosely be termed the patterns of attitude and feeling developed by speakers, and therefore, surely, one with the imaginative and literary form of what they produced. — J.H.]

I

1.0 This essay proposes:

    i. to identify and elucidate some of the things in parliamentary or public oratory, during the chosen period, which to a greater or lesser extent endow it with literary quality and cause it to invite a response such as is given to examples of the literary art.

    ii. from findings under (i), in certain respects to posit for review the general nature of the literary work.

2.0 Is the most conspicuous and perhaps distinguishing quality of the oratorical work, *eloquence*? "Eloquence," insofar as that word has loose association with "rhetoric" (modern, broad sense) and "oratory," is well understood: at least, well enough for present limited purposes. "Eloquence," so understood, is what Dickens satirized in Mr. Serjeant Buzfuz. It can be defined in intention. Probably it can be identified and determined only in extension (as with other terms for special language, like "vernacular," "poetic diction," etc.). That is to say, reference must ultimately be to a historically specific list of eloquence-structures, and the eloquence-terms that can complete them.

2.1 The Copernican Revolution occurs in the literary study of oratory when eloquence is recognized as a side issue. It is not the achievement but the convention of oratory. Statements 2.2 and 2.3 propose parallel cases which help to bring this out. In the interests of brevity, they are related to local literary quality only.

2.2 While literary quality in Pope's verse, or Johnson's, was seen as in a category such as "perfection of the couplet," convention was mistaken for achievement. Today the virtual starting-point for analysis of literary quality as locally manifested in their verse would be verbal texture, figurative structure, quality of statement, argument structure, etc.

2.3 The argument of 2.2 applies to the verse of Shelley, Keats, or Tennyson viewed in terms of a category like "music."

2.4 In all cases, there will be an initial achievement (which may be called the achievement of competence) simply in sustained conformity to the chosen convention. Decisive achievement lies in the creation, within the convention, of a reality which invites apprehension through one or other of the fundamental literary modes.

2.5 The assertion in 2.4 is argued for, in respect of the present subject, to the degree that the remainder of this essay identifies, within the oratorical work, achievement in one or other of the fundamental literary modes. This is its major purpose. To say that achievement is in a fundamental mode *is to say* that it excels any achievement of competence.

3.0 Form is among the fundamental modes.

3.01 Statement 3.0 does not define its subject-term.

3.1 A literary work may be endowed with form in more ways than one. In the present context (but see 12.5), nothing is being said against views such as that form is characteristically, regularly, always, or best generated through the creation of value structures, or the posing, stressing, pondering, wrestling with, or solution of questions, problems, issues, and so on. I note this to avoid confusion with views I have expressed elsewhere. The present argument requires, however, the postulates listed in 3.2 and 3.3.

3.2 *General Postulates of Criticism (N.B., A Select List):*

P_1–Self-consistency is *prima facie* a desirable quality in a work of literary art. (Note: for "prima facie," "necessarily" may be read if wished.)

P_2–It is standard critical practice to *propound* causal connections between a given emotional-imaginative response and a "feature" which the critic connects with that in interpretation, and not to prove their existence after the manner of a scientist.

P_3–Literary apprehension is not confined to what the text expresses explicitly and overtly.

P_4–In literary works of certain major types (drama, novel, etc.), imaginative form is regularly related to developing patterns of sympathy and antipathy for individual characters.

P_5–In literary works of perhaps all types, imaginative form is regularly related to developing patterns of endorsement or non-endorsement of entities which may at least to a limited extent be formulated as propositions.

Lemma to P_5: P_4 may or may not be reducible to P_5.

P_6–Every literary work has a "theme" (or themes) which is embodied in its details. (N.B. This is a conventional postulate: in the present writer's opinion it is probably reducible to P_5.)

3.3 *Axioms of the Criticism of Oratory:*

A_1–Literary form is not identical in quality with, nor apprehended in the same way as, logical form. This axiom will be accepted on inspection of complexes having *either* literary *or* logical form, but not both.

A_2–Literary form is charactistically related to sequential order. This axiom will be accepted on inspection of complexes having literary form, alongside complexes composed of the same parts (stanzas, lines, sentences, etc.) re-arranged in another sequential order; when it will be found that characteristically the form is changed.

> *Lemma 1 to A₂:* In principle, re-arrangement may *improve* literary form: that this could not be so of logical form and, moreover, that re-arrangement of the parts of a complex having logical form is properly speaking not re-arrangement but dis-arrangement are necessary propositions.
> *Lemma 2 to A₂:* Lemma 1 to A₂ may be used to elucidate A₁ if required.

4.0 The work of oratory may have literary form, distinguishable from its logical form (its argument structure) and illustrative of A₁ and A₂.

5.0 EXAMPLE ONE OF 4.0 The first oratorical work proposed for detailed examination is (A) George Canning, *Speech on Parliamentary Reform Given at a Public Dinner in Liverpool, 18 March 1820.*[1] Polemics of this kind are often impressive for sustained and versatile covert denigration of the speaker's opponents. This denigration can rise to the level of notable verbal dexterity and command of language, though to speak in this way is in itself to imply that it is barely among the fundamental modes of literary achievement. But I find very little of such insinuation and innuendo in A. Again, in the closing pages of the present essay, there is a brief review of the literary impact of sustained interaction of the general and the particular in works of oratory. Canning's dependence, in general, on something like a Burkeian conception of the state is plain enough in A, but that dependence is of a straightforward and indeed rather pedestrian, kind; and is also not fully self-consistent. Therefore, (by 3.2, P₁) less than nothing has been done so far to establish A as a work of literary art.

5.1 Nevertheless, A unquestionably strikes the reader, on reflection, as having some great persuasive quality which is intangible, and barely related to the cogency of the speech as a piece of argument. It seems to have some almost poetic power to convince, and to invite response by what must be called the literary imagination.

5.2 *I propound*, as cause of this (refer to 3.2, P₂), a *basic rhythm of alternation* which may be traced almost throughout the speech. This alternating pattern is between two generic ideas. They take many different local forms, varying with the immediate context; they alternate almost continuously throughout, regardless of whether they themselves are under discussion or not; and they enact, but do not necessarily state, Canning's fundamental ideas on his subject. (Therefore see 3.2, P_3.) Speaking loosely, the effect is a little like that of a *passacaglia* in music. (Therefore see 3.3.)

5.3 Canning is opposed to general parliamentary reform of the kind under discussion in 1820. He sees it as likely to bring only pervasive unrest and disorder. The two alternating ideas are (A) destructive and disastrous activity and movement and (B) the stable, the static, the orderly.

5.4 In 5.5 an attempt is made to sketch this complex structure, on a manageable scale, diagramatically. Page references are given, followed by decimal points that divide the page by eye into tenths (thus 369.7 means seven-tenths of the way down page 369). Even without reference to the full text, these bring out the virtual continuity of the alternation. This brings out in its turn the fact that the fundamental choice that Canning wishes his audience to see and to make is implicitly present to them by enactment, regardless of what is for the time being under explicit discussion (3.2, P_3). The table sets out the alternation in two columns. Three remarks in the speech, conspicuously inviting attention to a developing contrast, are centered and italicized in the schema below. So is the opening paragraph, which does the same. Four such invitations are a significant recurrence. But it should be noted that the speech does not begin by discussing the general question of reform at all. What Canning has to say on that subject is already transpiring, by the *passacaglia* enactment, while he deals with something of much more limited scope.

5.5 *Illustrative Scheme for 5.4.*

(GENERIC IDEA OF TYPE A)   (GENERIC IDEA OF TYPE B)

Part I: Defence of the recently imposed restrictions on public meetings (the "Six Acts," 1820)

Opening Paragraph

Gentlemen, short as is the interval since I last met you in this place on a similar occasion, the events which have filled up that interval have not been unimportant. The great moral disease which we then talked of as gaining ground on the community has, since that period, arrived at its most extravagant height; and, since that period also, remedies have been applied to it, if not of permanent cure, at least of temporary mitigation.

TYPE A	TYPE B

370.7 *whether any country . . . ever presented such a contrast.*

371 Crown in danger . . . anxiety and dismay . . . irresistible diffusion of doctrines hostile to the very existence of Parliament

372.5 tendency to root the attachment to monarchy deeper in the hearts of the people

372.6 restoration of peace throughout the country

373.3 menace . . . charge (i.e. accusation)

373.4 answered [by Canning's own overwhelming majority in his own constituency]

373.6 British liberty was established [Note: Canning means long *before* the Gordon Riots, not as their immediate sequel]

374.2 Lord George Gordon [of the "Gordon Riots"] . . . demolition of chapels and dwelling-houses, the breaking of prisons and the conflagration of London

374.9 countless multitudes . . . without reference to the comfort . . . of the neighbourhood

375.2 I have a right to quiet in my house . . . I call upon the laws

375.7 turbulent . . . tumult

375.8 orderly meeting

376.3 multitudes . . . irresponsible
. . . caprice

376.5 . . . a spirit of corporation

376.5 . . . *the spirit of the laws goes
directly the other way*

377.3 collect a mob . . . set half Manchester on fire . . . French Revolution

377.8 the law prescribes a corporate
character

378.5 a multitude . . . no common
tie . . . wrought up to mischief

378.7 How different are the genuine
and recognized modes of ascertaining
national opinion

378.8 untold multitudes

378.8 No! corporations in their corporate capacity . . . recognized bodies
of the state

379.3 tyranny . . . despot . . . mob
. . . inflamed and infuriated population . . . reign of terror

379.9 responsibility

379.9 degrade into multitudes . . .
what security have you . . .

380.5 lawful authority . . . respectable community . . . authority

Part II: Argument against radical electoral reform

384.5 sweep away
385.6 . . . the leap is taken . . . did
not stop there
386.5 in a few weeks the House of
Peers was voted useless. We all know
what happened to the Crown (i.e. in
the 1640's)

389.8 again destroy . . . dispossess

387.3 I for my part will not consent to take one step . . .

391.8 . . . I fear to touch that balance

392.6 brink of a precipice . . . fall . . . hurry . . . irretrievable destruction

392.9 stake in the country . . . Government under which he lives . . . steadfastly

5.6 For clarity, 5.6 recapitulates 5.2.

6.0 EXAMPLE TWO OF 4.0. The second oratorical work proposed for detailed examination is (B) Robert Lowe, *Speech in the House of Commons, 26 April 1866, on the Second Reading of the Representation of the People Bill.*[2] B is perhaps Lowe's most celebrated speech, as A is Canning's. What is now to be discussed is its claim to distinctively literary status as under 3.0.

6.1 Literary form (refer to 3.3, and for the purpose of the present paragraph to 3.2, P_2) is manifested in B not as a rhythm of alternation, but insofar as (1) by its organization of material and (2) by its changing tone it enacts and embodies, from beginning through to end, the sort of development which its speaker envisages over future history if the House passes the measure to which he is opposed. (Page-decimals are used as before.)

6.2 *Organization of Material.*

Lowe asserts that the principle of the Bill has not been stated by its proponents. It may be (1) that the franchise ought to be given to *all* those who in themselves are fitted for it; this would then be done as an end in itself. Or (II) that the franchise ought to be given *only* to those to whom giving it is a means to ends other than itself (viz., good government, as defined on p. 105.3). The main argument of the speech opens when Lowe asserts ("and so the thing comes round again": p. 126.9) that the Bill is based on I, and that this false principle must inevitably open the floodgates and bring national destruction.

6.3 Thenceforth, the material of the speech has an organization that enacts this kind of process. Lowe opened with a topic—the semantic distinction between one formulation of principle and another—which invites and indeed demands the sharpest focusing of attention. Progressively, throughout the whole work, the attention of reader/audience is extended more widely. The principle of the Bill, Lowe first notes, is admitted by his opponents (p. 125) to call for the enfranchisement of 204,000 persons. But really it calls for the enfranchisement of the whole working class. His opponents talk merely of a difference of one pound sterling; the reality behind that is on another scale: 100,000 men (p. 128). Moreover, universal education requires to be surveyed, not universal enfranchisement alone (p. 136). Beyond that, it is necessary to look back to 1848, the year of Revolutions; to take into account the teachings of Fourier and Saint-Simon (p. 138) and the trades union movement and its restrictive practices—as these are noted in Birmingham, say, or Edinburgh (p. 140); or to look to France and America "where Democracy may be said to have run its course and arrived at something like its ultimate limits" (p. 146); or to the "terrible . . . power" of Democracy for war (the American Civil War), and then to the Crimea, Turkey, Hungary in 1849, Poland, the Australian colonies, Canada (p. 149). The whole line of thought must lead to the end of the House of Peers—the Church—the Judiciary—the Commons itself—probably the Throne. But finally: we learn better if we survey "history" and "the stream of time" (p. 168)—going back to Virgil and the sack of Troy, or the Book of Judges. After the Book of Judges, only seventeen words remain of a speech of seventeen thousand.

6.4 *Tone.*

Gathering acerbity of tone is a common practice in oratory: its presence in *B* is noted briefly as a second embodiment, in texture and implicitly, of the developing non-logical structure. The following quotations sketch out the appropriate schema:

> *page*
> 102 "it is not inopportune to ask"
> "rather pale and colourless" [N.B. This is said of his opponents' views: as *assertion* the phrase sharpens tone, but merely as *diction*, its tendency is to mollify it.]
> 131 "why shouldn't we call it by its right name at once?"

132 "the member for Westminster has come out in a new character"

140 "no one can tell where it will stop" [i.e. the destructive movement of events, once it sets in]

142 "like men contending with a maelstrom into which . . . eventually they will be sucked"

157 "absolutely tramples down"

(closing "History may tell of other acts as signally disastrous, but of sentence) none more wanton, none more disgraceful"

By the end of the speech, Lowe's rhythms (e.g., the superb sentence just quoted) enact his thought, and so does the final image: "we are about to pluck down on our own heads the venerable temple of our liberty and glory." What can be, at one and the same moment, both Samson and the whole host of the Philistines? Only "the Multitude united in one Person . . . that great Leviathan or rather (to speak more reverently) that *Mortall God.*" Lowe's term for the Hobbesian state is "Caesarianism," and on p. 163 of the text he envisages its coming.

6.5 Recapitulates, for clarity, 6.1.

II

7.0 P_4 (3.2) regularly has its analogue in the oratorical work.

7.01 The patterns referred to in 7.0 regularly develop as between the speaker *and his opponent.*

7.02 These patterns develop in the course of manipulated argument. They are therefore related to logic, and it is a differentiating aspect of the literary quality of the oratorical work that its analogue to P_4 so develops. For these reasons it is both possible, and desirable, to formalize such patterns in a rudimentary notation. But if these patterns were patterns of true/false or agreement/disagreement only, they would not present an analogue to P_4. Therefore their expression in a notation requires symbols additional to those employed in the logic of implication. In fact, the notation now to be proposed differs essentially in function from that of implication logic.

7.1 Argument and criticism of argument create patterns of emotional response in the audience and in respect of, especially, the speaker's opponent(s). If the following analyses demonstrate this, then 7.0 is valid, and the discussion is relevant to the purpose enunciated in 2.5.

7.2 The Notation (I).

The following are definitions ($\overset{Df}{=}$):

$S[p] \overset{Df}{=}$ the speaker believes proposition p.[3]

$O[p] \overset{Df}{=}$ the speaker's opponent believes proposition p.

I employ p, q, etc., for propositions in general, but in the worked examples these are replaced by Roman numerals, which represent, as shown in each case afresh, statements paraphrased from the texts. Since I, II, etc., are semantically determinate, it is sometimes useful to employ $\frac{c}{p}$ or $\frac{c}{I}$ to mean "the logical converse of p (or I)." Thus p, q, $S[p]$ and $O[p]$ represent typical propositions in the notation. In addition to these symbols, brackets, the signs $\sim$ (not), $\vee$ (or), $\cdot$ (and), and occasionally the modifications of $\cdot$ to substitute for brackets (i.e. $:$, $:\cdot$) are employed as in the logic of implication. It should be noted that $\rightarrow$, where it occurs, is a genuinely semantic relation when it relates the Roman numerals: i.e. I $\rightarrow$ II may be seen to be true or false from the meanings of I and II as given in the paraphrases. "Establishes" is a better term for it than "entails," because what it frequently (though not always) represents is a probable argument.

7.3 The Notation (II): Emotion symbols (see 7.02).

The following are definitions:

$\approx p \overset{Df}{=}$ p is a ridiculous or disreputable proposition

$\downarrow O \overset{Df}{=}$ O is discredited

The sign ! is used to mark the termination of an argument in a discrediting. It should be noted that $\sim (\approx p \cdot = \cdot \sim \sim p)$. The symbols $\approx p$ often correspond approximately to the expression "doubly false" (therefore self-evidently false to those not blinded by stupidity or prejudice).

This is why the commonest form of argument is probably:

$$\approx p \cdot O\,[p] \cdot \rightarrow \cdot \downarrow O\,!$$

p could sometimes be expressed in notation:

$$\approx p \cdot = \cdot p \rightarrow q \cdot \sim (q \rightarrow p) \cdot \sim q$$

meaning something like "even the implications of p, weaker than itself, are false." E.g. "All members of the Republican Party are Communist" is a ridiculous proposition, since not even any sub-class of the Republican Party is Communist (or so I believe). The force of $\approx p$ in certain arguments seems to be best brought out by subsequently duplicating the other emotion symbol, or the "argues for" sign. Thus:

$$\approx p \cdot O\,[p] \cdot \rightarrow \cdot \downarrow\downarrow O\,!$$

or　$\approx p \cdot O\,[p] \cdot \underset{\rightarrow}{\overset{\rightarrow}{}} \cdot \downarrow O\,!$ ("one cannot possibly escape the conclusion that . . .")

7.4 It is no part of the present essay's purpose to construct a calculus in the notation. Nevertheless, it may be the case that this can be done, since it seems clear that certain propositions could be taken as primitive. E.g.:

(i)　$\sim p \cdot O\,[p] \cdot \rightarrow \cdot \downarrow O\,!$
　　(Whoever believes a false proposition is discredited.)
(ii)　$O\,[p] \cdot p \rightarrow q \cdot \rightarrow \cdot O\,[q] \vee \downarrow O\,!$
　　(Whoever does not believe, or disbelieves, the implications of what he believes, is discredited.)
(iii)　$O\,[p] \cdot O\,[\sim p] \cdot \rightarrow \cdot \downarrow O\,!$
　　(Whoever believes a self-contradition is discredited; but this presumably follows from $\approx p \cdot O\,[p] \cdot \rightarrow \cdot \downarrow O\,!$, since all self-contradictions are ridiculous propositions.)

7.5 EXAMPLE ONE OF 7.01. The first speech analyzed is (C) W. E. *Gladstone, Speech on Moving the Second Reading of the Representation of the People Bill, 12 April* 1866.[4] This speech contains (among much else, of course) the following argument: First, (I) the working classes make a full contribution (through taxation, which is based directly or indirectly on income) to the expenses of government. Therefore, (II) the working classes should contribute correspondingly, through the franchise, to the constitution of government in the House of Commons. But it may be said that (III) property and not income is the correct basis on which to assess eligibility for the franchise. (Some Opposition members

were obliging and incautious enough to cry "Hear, hear!" at this point.)
But if so, one must "take the consequence" (p. 107.8). It is that (IV)
property should provide thirteen-fourteenths of the national budget, instead of income as at present. Since it is clear that to advocate IV was in
no way part of Gladstone's purpose, one can see already that something
other than a proposition is the "target" of the argument. That something
is O.

7.6 There are two implicit (but acceptable) premises in Gladstone's
own position, which is, of course, I → II. The first premise is (V) partici-
pation in the expenses of government qualifies a man for enfranchisement. (This is simply "No taxation without representation!") The second is the logical converse of V; or more precisely perhaps, $\approx$ ($\sim$
$\frac{c}{V}$), i.e. the denial of "no representation without paying some tax" is a
disreputable proposition.

7.7 The argument paraphrased in 7.5 may now be expressed in notation
as follows:

a.   O [V] : I $\cdot$ V $\cdot$ → $\cdot$ II (All British politicians in 1866 must [V])
b.   O [$\sim$ I] $\cdot$ O [III] (By the debate, and the cries of "Hear, hear!")
c.   but III → IV $\cdot$ V $\cdot$ $\sim\frac{c}{V}$ ("if $\sim$ [III → IV], it could be just to have
     a vote and pay no taxes")
d.   therefore O [IV] $\cdot$ V $\cdot$ O [$\sim\frac{c}{V}$]
e.   but O [$\sim$ IV] $\cdot$ $\approx$ ($\sim \frac{c}{V}$) ("it could be just . . . (etc.)" is a
     disreputable proposition)
f.   therefore: O [IV $\cdot \sim$ IV] $\cdot$ V $\cdot$ O $\left[\sim\frac{c}{V} \right] \cdot \approx \left(\sim\frac{c}{V} \right) : → : \downarrow$ O !

That is to say, Gladstone's opponents are discredited by believing either
a self-contradictory proposition or a disreputable one.

8.0 EXAMPLE TWO OF 7.01. In the same speech occurs the following rebuttal of opponents' argument. (Note that in each example worked
the Roman numerals take fresh meanings.) Those opponents assert that
(I) where the working class has a majority it will vote as a class. But (II)

"municipal franchises are in a predominant degree working men's franchises," and (III) municipal elections are not fought on a class basis. Moreover, (IV) Parliamentary borough constituencies in which there are already working-class majorities now return more Opposition (i.e. Conservative) than Gladstonian (Liberal) members.

8.1 There is again an implicit premise, treated as axiomatic: it is that (V) a working-class majority could not return a Conservative MP if it voted on a class basis. The argument may then be expressed in notation:

a. II · III : II · III · → · ~ I (the true propositions II and III disprove I)
b. IV · V : IV · V · → · ~ I (the true propositions IV and V independently do the same)
c. therefore ≈ I
d. but O [I]
e. O [I] · ≈ I · → · ↓ O !

That I is a ridiculous proposition, not merely a false one, transpires in the text (p. 108.3): "is there any shade or shadow, any rag, even, of proof . . . ?" The question is rhetorical. The depreciatory force of the conclusion is especially clear from b above, in that Gladstone's opponents know *only too well* that these propositions are true: IV is to their most immediate advantage, V follows from their very identity. (Note: a modern reader is likely, perhaps, to understand V too strongly and therefore to see IV as itself beginning to discredit Conservative MPs, at least those so elected. But there is nothing of this in the speech: one must remember that neither Gladstone nor his opponents would have called themselves democrats or said that they advocated democracy. Gladstone's position would certainly have been that a Conservative member did not represent the true interest of a working class electing him, *only* because as a Conservative he did not represent the true interest of the country. Neither side saw class interests as they are widely seen now.)

8.2 It should be noted that in the full text (p. 111), the paragraph expressing IV · V · → · ~ I (i.e. b in 8.1) closes by putting the idea of "the Opposition" before the reader/audience as emphatically as it possibly can. Once more, it is the implication of the train of thought in respect of them, not merely of a proposition, which is the nerve of it.

9.0 EXAMPLE THREE OF 7.01. "Sir, I must now beg leave to deny" that (I) ". . . (a) general transfer of power, either in counties or boroughs, is contemplated by this Bill" (p. 118). This conclusion is valid because (II) majorities determine results (this means, a majority of a certain class elects a candidate to serve that class: O [II] from proposition I *of the last example*); and (III) there are no county constituencies in which the working class have a majority. But furthermore, (IV) they will have a majority only in fewer than half of the boroughs, even when the Bill passes. But, Gladstone says, if his opponents stress the influence of the working class in the counties, despite their minority position, "I shall be obliged to put the proposition in a manner much more unfavourable to my opponents" (p. 120). It would then be proper to stress middle- and upper-class influence where those classes, in their turn, do not command a majority: all the more so, in fact, since wealth and position are intrinsically more influential than the lack of those things.

9.1 Depreciation of the opponents, in contrast to argument simply against a proposition, is plain here not only from the last quotation (9.0), but also from Gladstone's opening words: "We are met too much . . . not by reasoning, but by suspicions and fears." The notation, as before, brings out how intimately depreciation is involved with the logical structure:

a. $\text{III} \cdot \text{IV} \cdot \rightarrow \cdot \sim \text{I} \vee \sim \text{II}$

b. O [I]

c. therefore, $\text{O } [\sim \text{II}] \vee \text{O } [\text{I} \sim \text{I}]$ (from which $\downarrow \text{O }!$)

d. but $\sim \text{II} \rightarrow \sim \text{I}$ (if majorities do not determine results, it follows without more ado that not even a working-class majority is necessarily going to bring in its own candidate)

e. moreover, $\text{I} \rightarrow \text{II}$ (this should be taken semantically; but it follows from $p \rightarrow q \cdot \rightarrow \cdot \sim q \rightarrow \sim p$ in the logic of implication)

f. therefore, $\text{O } [\text{I} \sim \text{I} \cdot \text{II} \sim \text{II}]$ from which $\downarrow\downarrow \text{O }!$

Gladstone's opponents commit themselves to two self-contradictions: clear evidence for the quotation above ("We are met . . .").

10.0 The purpose of the discussion from 7.0 may now be recalled. It has been to show that the oratorical texture carries a constant, and indeed (review the page references) not far short of continuous, creation of patterns of thought culminating in *depreciation and negative feeling-response (antipathy) for the speaker's opponent*; and therefore, by implication, approval and sympathy for the speaker. There is, we may say, a more or less permanent texture *of dramatization and characterization.* Then see 3.2, P_4 and 2.5.

10.1 The occurrence of these patterns, at least here and there in a text, could have been demonstrated merely by quoting disparaging or ironical references to opponents which occur from time to time. Why then the notation? Because such evidence would have been evidence of *intermittent and non-essential* dramatization and characterization. The notation, however, shows succinctly that these are intrinsic to structure because they are set up by the logic itself of one argument after another. Remove that from which they of necessity result and the oratorical work disappears as a whole. That the polemical activity, insofar as it is conducted by argument and the rebuttal of argument, creates patterns is a necessary and not a contingent proposition. Thus the notation brings out how the analogue of the oratorical work to the literary-imaginative one, under P_4, is not intermittent but pervasive, and not incidental but carried by its structure and therefore characteristic. Refer then to 4.0 and 3.0.

11.0 P_5 regularly has its analogue in the oratorical work.

11.1 That the work of oratory regularly and characteristically creates structures of attitudes to propositions is indeed self-evident: that it does so follows from its being polemical and argumentative in character, and to say this is jejune. To examine, however, the closeness between the analogue to P_4 and the analogue to P_5 is not jejune. One example must suffice.

11.2 Disraeli, on the *First* Reading of the 1866 Bill, had asserted that (I) it was wrong to introduce a representation of the people bill without introducing a re-distribution of seats bill to go with it and make the government's whole intention explicit. *John Bright,* in his *Speech on the Second Reading of the Representation of the People Bill, 23 April 1866*[5] (D), replied to this argument as follows: (II) to introduce a re-distribution of seats bill such as conforms to (I) means to introduce a bill which may reasonably be expected to last as long as the representation of the people bill is expected to last. But (III) in 1859 Disraeli had himself introduced a sweeping representation bill, and at the same time a re-distribution of seats bill which affected fifteen seats only. (IV) Such a bill could not possibly be expected to satisfy (II). Therefore in 1859 Disraeli himself had not believed I.

11.3 Ignoring the distinction between 1859 and 1866, the notation gives:

a. $O[I]$

b. $II \cdot III \cdot \rightarrow \cdot O[\sim I] \vee \downarrow O!$ (by 7.4 (ii))

c. i.e. $O[I \sim I] \cdot \vee \cdot \downarrow O!$

d. i.e. $\downarrow O! \vee \downarrow O!$

Disraeli, either unconscious of the implications of his actions or inconsistent in his views, is discredited. *But:* if the opening assumption of 11.3 is not made, the position is that Disraeli has changed his mind, and that a proposition about which a man can change his mind is very much open to question.

11.4 The logic-and-feeling complex is thus more complex than has previously been argued: there is a kind of unstable balance and equipoise between the tendency of the argument to $\downarrow$ Disraeli, and its tendency to call I in question. One need not, therefore, be in the least surprised that Bright's references to Disraeli in this part of his speech are (though ironical) to some extent sympathetic. "Gentleman opposite . . . would be a great deal wiser if they remembered some of the things which the Member for Buckingham tells them" (p. 359a); "he distributed [the seats] in a way which I am willing to admit was very fair and reasonable" (p. 360b).

11.5 The example has as its purpose to show how the analogue in the oratorical work to P_5 is regularly and characteristically "co-adunative" with the analogue to P_4: just as P_4 and P_5 themselves refer to co-adunatives in the literary work.

III

12.0 P_6 regularly has its analogue in the oratorical work.

12.1 P_6 makes two assertions (about the presence of themes, about their being present in a distinctive manner, viz. their embodiment in details); and that an analogous postulate holds in respect of the oratorical work is self-evident. It will therefore be supported only in brief and for a particular purpose.

12.2 In the oratorical work, the analogue to "theme" is "principle." It is this which the speech as a whole is based upon, and which controls its development and its treatment of detail. The guiding principle or principles of the speech need barely be explicit, and certainly they may also be embodied implicitly in the train of thought and enacted in the local detail of how it is conducted.[6] Sometimes, however, they become fully explicit; and this is no contrast with literary-imaginative works (critics regularly stress the implicitness of the theme in these, but usually also find quotations which state it). Examples are:

i/ Gladstone, *Speech in the Amphitheatre at Liverpool, 6 April 1866* (E) : "I ask what *justice* it is that we can ask the working population to pay us from two-sevenths to three-sevenths of the taxation, and to pay them in return with . . . one-seventh of the representation?"

ii/ D : "Sir, I think that this House should be a *fair* representation of the people of this country . . . so arranged that every person of every class will feel that his interests are fairly represented."

iii/ B : "I want to show that this measure is not founded upon any *calculation of results,* but in broad sweeping principles, having their rise in the assumed rights of man!"

iv/ Disraeli, *Speech on the Second Reading of the Representation of the People Bill,* 27 April 1866: "I hold it [the English (sic) constitution] to be a polity founded on distinct principles . . . I hold our Constitution to be a monarchy, limited by the *co-ordinate authority* of . . . the Estates of the Realm."

12.3 Needless to say, the embodiment of principles in the detail of illustration and argument is the major principle of organization of material in the oratorical work (refer to 6.1) and the most definite and conspicuous aspect of its self-consistency (refer to 3.2, P_1, but also to 3.3, A_1). But although this is to begin with a matter of logic, it is certainly not rigidly confined to logic, as may be seen in the examples (12.2). "Justice," "fairness," practical calculation, and sense of balance (especially of balance co-ordinated over a period of time since "the Plantagenets," which is Disraeli's base-line) are easily traced in tone, characterization, descriptive detail, irony, and other distinguishable dimensions of the feeling structure of the oratorical work.

12.4 The more suggestive line of thought lies actually in the opposite direction: in considering whether, in view of the overwhelming prominence and centrality in the oratorical work of the analogue to P_6, and in view furthermore of the fact that what has been said hitherto does not obscure the fact that *there is a major distinction still to be made* between the oratorical and the literary-imaginative.

12.5 P_6 has perhaps been over-stressed in respect of the literary work. (Refer to 1.0 (ii).)

12.6 No assertion has been made in 12.4 and 12.5; they put forward an idea for review. But it is worth reviewing, in the light of the "major distinction still to be made," which was referred to in 12.4. This major distinction is as follows: in spite of the existence of the analogues between oratorical and literary-imaginative already discussed, such oratory as has been discussed here, and perhaps parliamentary oratory at all times, may have substantial, or even something approaching major, literary interest, but is very clearly not among the supreme literary forms. Yet if this is so, it is unlikely that what seems to be its characteristic principle of organization should be very like (even if not identical with) any characteristic principle of organization (see P_6) in the supreme literary forms.

13.0 I now speculate, briefly, as to what it may be in parliamentary oratory that precludes its reaching supreme greatness as literature. It cannot well be its involvement simply in *detail*. This may be unavoidable for it, but on the other hand the novel makes no attempt to avoid detail. It might be that the kind of detail involved in oratory requires special study if it is subsequently to be mastered, and that therefore even supremely great parliamentary oratory is of necessity a comparatively recondite literary taste. But that is not the point at issue. Nor does it seem adequate to suggest that it is the wrong kind of detail, in that it is generally found boring or becomes irrelevant. These would be facts too contingent to serve as bases for saying that a certain *genre* seemed to be essentially precluded from greatness; and could also be applied only too easily (indeed, have been sometimes applied) to authors like Dante and Homer. I therefore note, in particular, two other features of the oratorical work as follows.

13.1 *The work of parliamentary or public oratory is circumscribed by involvement in controversy.*

13.2 In the oratorical work, characterization, dramatization, logic-and-feeling structure, and perhaps much else, tend *necessarily* (not contingently) toward a limiting and crudifying *bi-polarity*. They need not, of course, be exclusively such: in E, for example, Gladstone has a substantial development both of his opponents, and of his principal topic, which is the working class. But the tendency is necessarily not contingently there; and once made, the point is plain and pervasive enough to invite pondering without being elaborated. The inadequacy of anything like bi-polarity in criticism of supreme works should be recalled at this point. *Othello* is not all light and dark, and not even *Pericles* is all storms and music.

13.3 Moreover, organization upon the particular bi-polarity of controversy introduces a restriction of attitude and emotional range which cannot be called contingent, even if it is not clearly necessary. It is hardly right to say that the fact that there tends not to be controversy in charity, or in rapture, is a contingent fact.

13.4 The second of the two features (refer to 13.0, end, and 13.1) is that the work of oratory is circumscribed by involvement in "the actual," in reality.

13.5 It should be noted that "involvement in reality" is not the same thing as "involvement in detail" (13.0). Treatment of reality may avoid detail (philosophy, metaphysics), and clearly some detailed products of imagination, though doubtless not all, are unrelated to reality. But the point is that for Lowe, say, but also for his opponents too, "calculation of results" can never be very far away. The point is analogous to the distinction Aristotle made between poetry and history. The great work of literary art is more than a *speculum vitae*: but beyond that, it is also more than an *organon vitae*, an organization of reality comprehended and structured into its principles. To see Aristotle's "what could be," "what might be," fully expounded, means to see human reality within the larger and stranger perspective of human possibility, potentiality, even mystery. Put it another way: the House of Commons, doubtless, is realist; but the novel, even the novel, is ultimately not.

> *Lemma to* 13.5: There is a sense in which possibility, potentiality, and mystery, as "going beyond" reality, are also "part" of reality.

NOTES

1. George Canning, *Speeches*, 6 vols., London, 1828, VI, 369-93.
2. Robert Lowe, *Speeches and Letters on Reform*, London, 1867, pp. 102-70.

3. Contrast Jaakko Hintikka's notation, B_{ap} (*Knowledge and Belief*, Cornell, 1962). But relegation of the believer to a subscript is not helpful in the present context.

4. W. E. Gladstone, *Speeches on Parliamentary Reform in 1866*, London, 1866, pp. 91-130.

5. John Bright, *Speeches on Questions of Public Policy*, London, 1869, pp. 354-70.

6. A particularly clear example is Disraeli's speech entitled "Conservative and Liberal Principles" in *Speeches*, ed. T. E. Kebbel, London, 1882, II, 523-36. I discuss this in detail in a forthcoming essay.

CLASSICAL RHETORIC AND VICTORIAN PROSE

MARTIN J. SVAGLIC

I

FOR SOME YEARS now there has been a movement under way to revive
the study of rhetoric, a discipline central to education from antiquity
through the Renaissance but which thereafter slowly lost its vigor, its
original meaning, and ultimately its place in the curricula of English and
American universities. By the early twentieth century the subject commonly survived in the United States only in the attenuated form of
courses usually entitled "Composition and Rhetoric," in which the principal concern was three of the four "modes of discourse," argumentation
being relegated to departments of speech. As the years went by and
university enrollments burgeoned, the quality of student writing dete-
riorated; and these courses, in consequence, came to be devoted more
and more to the simplest fundamentals of English.

The decline of classical rhetoric, foreshadowed in England as early as
the seventeenth century in Samuel Butler's jibe that "all a rhetorician's
rules / Teach nothing but to name his tools," was part of the general
reaction against all rigidities of code and prescription, whether in life or
in art, which is so fundamental a trait of the modern temper. And no
doubt there is much to be said for no longer having to commit to memory
the nearly two hundred tropes and schemes eventually discriminated by
Renaissance rhetoricians—tropes which too often suggest only the effete
refinements of a decadent scholasticism.

It is one thing to deplore such abuses of the old rhetoric, however, or
to suggest that the whole subject needs broadening in the light of modern
developments in psychology and linguistics, as do I. A. Richards, Kenneth
Burke, and other more recent proponents of rhetoric; but it is quite another to dispense entirely, as is commonly done in higher education, with

the study of an art which all of us daily practice and are molded by and the basic techniques of which were outlined centuries ago by Aristotle, Cicero, Quintilian, and Longinus. Perceiving the folly of neglecting such an inheritance, speech teachers and others at Cornell University began many years ago to attempt a revitalization of classical rhetoric. They were later joined in effect by literary specialists, particularly those in the Renaissance, who showed how profoundly Sidney and Shakespeare and Bacon and Donne and Milton were indebted to the rhetoricians. The work of these scholars has now penetrated the field of composition: courses in rhetoric are being developed in colleges and summer institutes for teachers, and hardly a month goes by that we do not come across a new article or even a new textbook on the subject.[1]

Since classical rhetoric has so long been neglected, however, it is not surprising that even well-educated readers today commonly do not know what the subject involves. They are likely to think of it as being concerned principally with the improvement or, even worse, the mere ornamentation of style, a conception that began to grow common (for unfortunate if understandable reasons) during the late Renaissance. Some may think of it in terms of its ancient abuse: deceptive appeals to the uneducated or the unwary, as in Matthew Arnold's occasional contrast of "rhetoric" with *"vraie verité."* The primary concern of rhetoric in the classical sense of the word, however, is not style, much less mere ornamentation; nor is it an art of sophistry, though sophists may use it. Its true and principal aim is the discovery of the available means of persuasion on any subject, an art presumably as useful in modern democratic societies as the ancients found it centuries ago. According to Aristotle, rhetoric is an offshoot of dialectics—hence closely related to the study of logic; the better a logician a speaker or writer is, the more successful a rhetorician he will prove, *ceteris paribus.* As Cardinal Newman, one of the greatest of Victorian rhetoricians, put it, rhetoric is properly "the reduction of reasonings, in themselves sound, into the calculus of the tastes, opinions, passions, and aims of a particular audience."[2]

There are three main types of classical rhetoric: deliberative or hortatory, whose aim is persuasion to or dissuasion from a course of action or point of view; forensic or judicial, concerned with the guilt or innocence of past actions, as in a law court or public forum; and epideictic or ceremonial, whose object is the praise and commemoration of great men and deeds. In every type of the art the rhetorician concerns himself with three things: finding in the subject proofs or reasons likely to seem most cogent to his particular audience or reading public (*inventio*); arranging these proofs in the most effective order (*dispositio*); and expressing them as forcefully as his command of language will permit (*elocutio*). There are common topics or "places" that supply proof for every kind of rhetoric: e.g., the possible and the impossible, comparison, circumstance, size, testimony, and so forth. And there are places or topics more or less special to each kind: e.g., the worthy or the expedient to deliberative rhetoric; the noble or the base to epideictic; and the just and the unjust to forensic. Each of these topics has, of course, many subdivisions.

Whatever his subject may be, the rhetorician has three main sources of appeal: the rational or logical, which derives from his mode of reasoning; the ethical, from his personal character; and the emotional, from the feelings or mood of his audience. All three types of appeal are exerted to at least some degree in almost every piece of rhetoric; but in general, the ethical is likely to prove most telling in deliberative discourse; the logical (often in the form of enthymeme or example) in forensic; and the emotional in epideictic.

The essential parts of a rhetorician's speech or essay will normally be three or four: the introduction, preparing the audience for what is coming and attempting to win their sympathetic attention: e.g., the first discourse of Newman's *Idea of a University*, written to allay the doubts of an influential Dublin audience about the wisdom of founding a Catholic university in Ireland, and to elicit their support for the project; the statement of the question, which may or may not be part of the introduction: e.g., Arnold's explanation in "Literature and Science" of precisely where he parts company with Thomas Huxley and other advocates of a scientific education; the proof: e.g., the double enthymeme that Arnold employs in the same essay to argue that the exponents of a scientific education for the majority should not and will not prevail; and the conclusion or peroration, restating the argument or underscoring the writer's point of view in heightened language marked by strong ethical or emotional appeals: e.g., the "Conclusion" of Walter Pater's *Renaissance*, with its memorable summons to a life of refined epicureanism.

Rhetoricians later than Aristotle came to divide a work of rhetoric (then almost invariably a speech) into six or seven parts: exordium, narration, proposition, partition, confirmation, refutation, and peroration; but not all of these conventional divisions of the classical oration need be present in every piece of rhetoric, and there is no valid reason for insisting on them. An otherwise illuminating critical analysis may easily be marred by a determination to reveal every one of them in the work being discussed.[3]

What all of this has to do with the art of Victorian prose should by now be fairly obvious. All the great Victorian prose writers are rhetoricians, practicing at one time or another every mode of rhetoric, but most commonly the deliberative or hortatory, which is why they are so often called prophets. They are usually engaged in trying to persuade their readers that the crucial problems of a deeply troubled age may best be solved by adopting a particular course of action or creed or temper of mind, be it a scientific education, renunciation of the claims of the ego, Christianity, natural supernaturalism, humanism, epicureanism, or what have you. Thomas Carlyle's *Sartor Resartus* and *Past and Present*, Macaulay's essays on Southey, Hallam, and James Mill, Newman's *Apologia*, Ruskin's *Unto This Last*, J. S. Mill's *On Liberty*, Thomas Huxley's "Science and Culture," even Pater's "Coleridge" are all *au fond* works of rhetoric, whatever else they may be; and they can be only imperfectly understood or appreciated without some consideration of their rhetorical aims and technique.

It is true that the formal study of rhetoric had gradually declined in the universities, as Richard Whately laments in his *Elements of Rhetoric;* and hence that most Victorian prose writers were in all probability a good deal less consciously guided by rhetorical theory than their predecessors of the sixteenth and seventeenth centuries had been. Nevertheless, the subject of rhetoric in the older sense of the word was far from dead in Victorian England. Not only were eighteenth-century rhetoricians like Blair and Campbell still well known; but there were highly influential advocates of classical rhetoric at the universities, like Whately at Oxford and later R. C. Jebb at Cambridge. The *Rhetoric* of Aristotle had long been one of the most basic texts of the *litterae humaniores* program at Oxford and was thus very well known by such avid classicists as Newman, Matthew Arnold, and Pater, and to some degree at least by Ruskin.[4] Documentary evidence appears to be lacking for Macaulay and Carlyle; but we do know that Macaulay was all his life a reader of the classics, and hence it would be more reasonable to assume that he was familiar with classical rhetoric than that he was not. As for Carlyle, we know that he aspired to the chair of rhetoric at Edinburgh, a post for which the authorities preferred Macaulay, who did not seek it.[5] And we know that even a non-university man like John Stuart Mill was compelled in childhood by his father, who had been deeply impressed by its knowledge of human nature, to study the *Rhetoric* of Aristotle "with peculiar care, and throw the matter of it into synoptic tables."[6]

There is good reason to assume, therefore, that much the same kind of light may be thrown on Victorian prose by a study of its rhetorical technique as has already illuminated major works of the Renaissance. And this would be true even if there were no evidence that the great Victorians knew their Aristotle and Cicero as well as they appear to have done; even if it could be shown that in writing their essays, they never once thought of the *Rhetoric* of Aristotle or of anyone else. The fact remains that since they were all indisputably rhetoricians, they could not help illustrating the types and observing the principles of rhetoric, whether they did so consciously or intuitively.

To take a parallel case, many a good dramatist either never read Aristotle's *Poetics* at all or, if he did so (as Ibsen did), can rarely be proved to have been conscious of its principles when writing his plays. Yet the artistic effect of his work, whether written in the fifth century B.C. or the nineteenth A.D., remains dependent on his skill in treating those "qualitative" parts of a drama (plot, character, thought, diction, spectacle, and frequently song) the nature of which Aristotle through careful induction first isolated and analyzed with enduring relevance. In the same way, every rhetorician (even a Ruskin, who knew but disliked Aristotle) will find himself concerned with *inventio, dispositio,* and *elocutio;* and he will seek out his arguments in those common or special places of which Aristotle has given us what is still the most comprehensive and acute discussion available. As the student of drama can increase his appreciation of every play by making himself conscious of the playwright's technique in manipulating the qualitative parts, so can the student of Victorian prose by bringing himself to analyze its rhetorical methods.

It may be true in a sense, as Carlyle argues in "Characteristics," that the sign of right performance is unconsciousness. At the same time, it would be hard to think of a more carefully and minutely organized essay than "Characteristics" in the whole body of Victorian prose, a fact which makes one wonder about the soundness of the analogy between the criteria of physical and mental health which is the informing principle of that nonetheless profound work. In any event, Carlyle's dictum, whatever truth it might hold for a writer whose skill had become second nature to him, would not apply to a reader. From a good analysis of any work of rhetoric, the latter may reasonably expect to learn something enlightening about its origin, its purpose, the provenance of its arguments, its structure, its style, and (to some degree) its value as a contribution to thought. And it would be a remarkable reader indeed who could become aware of all of these things by a process of intuition.

II

As almost no extended rhetorical analyses of Victorian prose texts appear to have been published, it is difficult to cite examples of what I have in mind.[7] Accordingly, I propose now, in the limited space at my disposal, to test at least some of the claims I have made for the value of rhetorical analysis by considering one well-known essay from this point of view: Macaulay's "Milton." It is not, to be sure, one of Macaulay's best essays. It was written, he later said, "when the author was fresh from college . . . contains scarcely a paragraph such as his matured judgment approves," and is "overloaded with gaudy and ungraceful ornament."[8] Still, it is the essay which made him suddenly famous, much as *Childe Harold* had done for Byron; it assured his place on the *Edinburgh Review*, eliciting the only literary compliment he was ever heard to repeat at home, Jeffrey's awed "The more I think, the less I can conceive where you picked up that style";[9] and it is often reprinted, at least in part, to this day. Most important for our purposes, it illustrates all three types of classical rhetoric: though primarily a work of the ceremonial or panegyrical kind, its longest section is forensic; and its ultimate purpose, as so often with Macaulay, is hortatory.

Perhaps the most striking thing at first about the essay on Milton is that although its immediate occasion was the publication in 1825 of the recently discovered *De doctrina christiana*, it concerns itself with that weighty treatise for hardly a page or so: just long enough to assure us that it is of no lasting importance and used here only as the Capuchins might employ the relic of a saint to awaken "the devotional feelings of the auditors" before preaching on him. His real purpose, Macaulay says, is "to commemorate, in all love and reverence, the genius and virtues of John Milton, the poet, the statesman, the philosopher, the glory of English literature, the champion and martyr of English liberty" (v,3).

One might say that there is nothing surprising about this, as it was common for Victorian reviewers to use the book at hand as hardly more than a jumping-off place for an essay on a wider subject. How many readers ever remember that Carlyle's "Characteristics," for example, was a review of James Hope's *Essay on the Origin and Prospects of Man?* The difference, however, is that Carlyle's essay is at least a "metaphysical" one, concerned with the same kind of questions Hope was raising; whereas Macaulay's essay has almost nothing to do with the subjects of *De doctrina christiana,* although the book was causing a real stir at the time he was writing. The reviewer in the *Quarterly,* in contrast, talked about *De doctrina christiana,* not about something else.

It may be that Macaulay chose to pass over *De doctrina* in such haste because he had no great interest in theological disputation. It seems more likely that he deliberately minimized its importance, however, because that heterodox book could hardly be cited for most of Macaulay's predominantly Christian readers as a happy example of Milton's "genius and virtues." It was, in fact, just the kind of thing that might further damage a reputation already chequered, and this is what soon came to pass: "It is said that the discovery of Milton's Arianism, in this rigid generation, has already impaired the sale of *Paradise Lost.*"[10] Accordingly, Macaulay dismisses the subject of Arianism quickly, praising the book only for its digests of scriptural texts and its evidence of a temper dear to Whigs: "a powerful and independent mind, emancipated from the influence of authority."

What had previously hurt Milton was his alliance with the regicides and Cromwell; and the most influential source of the indictment was Dr. Johnson's "Life of Milton" in his *Lives of the English Poets,* selections from which were still being reprinted in Macaulay's day as introductions to new editions of *Paradise Lost.* The more closely one examines the essay on Milton, the more evident becomes the conclusion that Macaulay conceived and framed it as a refutation of the dominant Tory view of Milton —the view of Johnson above all, as the most eminent of those critics "of great name, who contrive in the same breath to extol the poems and to decry the poet." It is an essay of some twenty-four thousand words, only slightly shorter than Johnson's; it treats of Milton's poetry and his character, as did Johnson; it discusses the poetry chiefly in answer to Johnson's rather minor objections and defends the man against the substance of Johnson's almost vitriolic attack; and it was welcomed by those close to Macaulay as "a relief from the perverted ability of that elaborate libel on our great epic poet which goes by the name of Dr. Johnson's Life of Milton."[11]

Having employed *De doctrina christiana* as an introduction and dismissed it quickly for good reason, Macaulay passes on to his first major subject, the praise of Milton's poetry. Here he reverses Johnson's order because his principal purpose was not so much to praise Milton the poet, whose merits had been generally acknowledged, as to absolve Milton the statesman from the Tory indictment and to canonize him as a Whig saint, "the champion and martyr of English liberty."[12] He therefore naturally reserves the discussion of Milton's public conduct for the climactic part of his essay.

In discussing Milton's poetry, Macaulay faced a real challenge. He was ill at ease as a literary critic and never showed any talent for examining in detail a narrative or drama in the traditional terms of its fable, character, sentiments, and diction, as Johnson had done with *Paradise Lost*. Furthermore, Johnson had treated Milton the poet with great respect, hailing *Paradise Lost* as first in design and second in execution "among the productions of the human mind" and affirming that its moral sentiments "excel those of all other poets." Unless, then, he could think of something significant to add to Johnson's commendation, Macaulay would have to find another approach to the praise of Milton's poetry, preferably one that would allow him to refute something in Johnson along the way.

According to Aristotle, the topic of size or magnification is most closely associated with epideictic rhetoric; and the rhetorician may magnify his subject's achievements in various ways: "For example, he should make it clear if the man is the only one, or the first, to have done the deed, or if he has done it almost alone, or more than anyone else; for all these things are noble. Then there are the circumstances of time and occasion, when a man's performances exceed what we might naturally expect."[13] Macaulay evidently found this approach congenial, perhaps because it suited his penchant for sweeping generalizations and paradoxes. He would soon base his commendation of John Bunyan, for example, on the assertion that he was "almost the only writer who ever gave to the abstract the interest of the concrete"; and of Boswell on the even more startling claim that in virtue of his folly, "to which it is impossible to find a parallel in the whole history of mankind," he became a great writer.

In the first of the three main parts of his discussion of Milton's poetry, then, Macaulay attempts a general estimate of Milton's achievement, basing it largely on the rhetorical topic of "circumstances of time and occasion, when a man's performances exceed what we might naturally expect." To do this, he must establish the striking paradox that "no poet has ever had to struggle with more unfavourable circumstances than Milton"; and he attempts to do so by arguing that "as civilisation advances, poetry almost necessarily declines," language becoming more generalized and abstract to the detriment of the sense of particularity on which the poet's images depend. Thus, "the most wonderful and splendid proof of genius is a great poem produced in a civilised age." Macaulay may have picked up this notion in part from Thomas Love Peacock, whose then recent tongue-in-cheek *Four Ages of Poetry* contained such assertions as that poetry was "the mental rattle that awakened the attention of intellect in the infancy of civil society; but for the maturity of mind to make a serious business of the playthings of its childhood, is as absurd as for a full-grown man to rub his gums with coral, and cry to be charmed to sleep by the jingle of silver bells."[14] In the same vein, Macaulay assures us (v,6) that "No man, whatever his sensibility may be, is ever affected by *Hamlet* or *Lear* as a little girl is affected by the story of poor Red Riding-hood" because of "the despotism of the imagination over uncultivated minds."

Wherever he got his theory, however, Macaulay's real target here is not the critics who said that in estimating Milton's achievement we should make deductions for the advantages conferred on him by his education and the civilization of his time. These critics may have existed, but they are left unnamed. The one who is named, and with asperity, is Johnson, for his comments on Milton's own fear lest he had been born "an age too late," obviously the notion that provoked Macaulay's whole discussion at this point.

> For this notion Johnson has thought fit to make him the butt of much clumsy ridicule. The poet, we believe, understood the nature of his art better than the critic. He knew that his poetical genius derived no advantage from the civilisation which surrounded him, or from the learning which he had acquired; and he looked back with something like regret to the ruder age of simple words and vivid impressions (v,4).

Macaulay is so anxious to score a point against Johnson that he is led to misrepresent both Johnson's argument and his tone, however, as anyone can see who looks impartially at Johnson's words. Milton the poet is not made "the butt of much clumsy ridicule." On the contrary, he is treated quite gently, with a measure of sympathy for his feeling that his poetic powers were more active in springtime than at other seasons. What Johnson does take exception to, with a little good-natured irony, is Milton's fear (not perhaps very serious—see *Paradise Lost,* IX, 41-7) lest the "climate" of his country might be "too cold" for flights of imagination; and especially that he was writing in "an age too late" for heroic poesy. This last is presumably an allusion to the common late Renaissance notion of a world in decay, but Macaulay does not recognize it as such, and he never does face up to Johnson's precise objection:

> Milton's submission to the seasons was at least more reasonable than his dread of decaying Nature or a frigid zone, for general causes must operate uniformly in a general abatement of mental power; if less could be performed by the writer, less likewise would content the judges of his works. Among this lagging race of frosty grovellers, he might still have risen into eminence by producing something which they should not willingly let die.[15]

Having indicated the general nature of Milton's poetic achievement, Macaulay now goes on to define the peculiar characteristic of the poetry, illustrating it from various works. This characteristic is said to be "the extreme remoteness of the associations by means of which it acts on the reader." It is a poetry of incantation, producing its effects by what it suggests more than by what it actually expresses, as in the muster-roll of names which evoke now "the splendid phantoms of chivalrous romance" and now "the dog-eared Virgil, the holiday, and the prize." To be sure, this tells us more about the essayist's reading habits than it does about the poet's style; but it follows logically from Macaulay's earlier deliberately restricted definition of poetry as "the art of employing words in such a manner as to produce an illusion on the imagination, the art of doing by means of words what the painter does by means of colours." Illusion or suggestion, then, is what Macaulay looks for as he examines the poems.

Thus, "L'Allegro" and "Il Penseroso" are seen merely as "collections of hints from each of which the reader is to make out a poem for himself." (It is appallingly thin criticism by comparison with Johnson's remarks on the same poems.) *Comus* is adjudged superior to *Samson Agonistes* because the former preserves the illusion, being essentially lyrical and dramatic only in semblance; whereas the illusion in the latter is broken by the futile attempt to combine the subjectivity of the lyric and the objectivity of drama. Since *Paradise Regained* is virtually impossible to discuss favorably in terms of illusion, Macaulay gives it less than a paragraph, pausing only to assure us after his fashion that though Milton was mistaken in preferring it to *Paradise Lost,* "we are sure that the superiority of *Paradise Lost* to the *Paradise Regained* is not more decided than the superiority of the *Paradise Regained* to every poem which has since made its appearance."

This brings Macaulay to *Paradise Lost,* and now he can expatiate *con brio* on illusion or suggestiveness as the essential quality of Milton's poetry. He does so while observing another of Aristotle's suggestions, that the epideictic rhetorician compare his subject "with men of note: this will tend to magnify the subject of the speech, and if you make him seem better than men of worth, that will ennoble his deed."[16] Here the man of note is Dante.

The contrast between the two poets is first made in terms of the "exact details" of Dante versus the "dim intimations" of Milton, the value of the former resting on what they represent, of the latter on what they suggest. In view of his definition of poetry, we might expect Macaulay to award the palm to Milton at this point, but he does not do so at first: on the contrary, he remarks quite sensibly that he will not take upon himself "the invidious office of settling precedency between two such writers," each having followed the method that best suited his subject. The reader would "throw aside" Dante's poem "unless it were told with the strongest air of veracity . . . with the greatest precision and multiplicity in its details."

Macaulay then turns around and proceeds to settle the precedency after all on the basis of an enthymeme whose apparently quite arbitrary major premise is that "Poetry which relates to the beings of another world ought to be at once mysterious and picturesque." Milton's is so; whereas Dante's is "picturesque to the exclusion of all mystery." In a burst of illogic he concludes: "this is a fault on the right side, a fault inseparable from the plan of Dante's poem, which, as we have already observed, rendered the utmost accuracy of description necessary. Still it is a fault. The supernatural agents excite an interest; but it is not the interest which is proper to supernatural agents."

How did Macaulay arrive at a major premise that involved him in this obvious self-contradiction? Clearly again through the desire to refute

Johnson, whose argument must be quoted at some length so that the reader may judge Macaulay's success:

> Milton saw that immateriality supplied no images, and that he could not show angels acting but by instruments of action; he therefore invested them with form and matter. This being necessary was therefore defensible; and he should have secured the consistency of his system by keeping immateriality out of sight, and enticing his reader to drop it from his thoughts. But he has unhappily perplexed his poetry with his philosophy. His infernal and celestial powers are sometimes pure spirit and sometimes animated body. . . .
> The vulgar inhabitants of Pandaemonium, being "incorporeal spirits," are "at large though without number," in a limited space; yet in the battle, when they were overwhelmed by mountains their armour hurt them, crushed in upon their substance, "now grown gross by sinning."[17]

This confusion of matter and spirit "pervades the whole narration of the war of heaven," Johnson asserts, "and fills it with incongruity."

Macaulay does not discuss the effect on the reader of the war in heaven, which Johnson thought difficult for adult readers to take seriously, but limits himself to generalities. He admits that Milton has left himself open to Johnson's charge of inconsistency but insists that he was poetically in the right, it being impossible to persuade readers "to drop immateriality from their thoughts" of spiritual beings, any more than they could conceive of them as completely disembodied spirits. Milton's way was accordingly the proper *via media*, since "beings of another world ought to be at once mysterious and picturesque." Johnson's point, of course, is that they are at one time seen as "mysterious," at another as "picturesque," and hence that it is sometimes difficult to reconcile one image of the supernatural characters with the other. Whether or not this is a sound objection, Macaulay does not really face up to it.

In the third and final part of his discussion of Milton's poetry, which serves also as a transition to the discussion of Milton's statesmanship, Macaulay indicates the source of Milton's poetic achievement in his personal character: he was not an egotist—hence (by implication) there was no danger that he would dispel the illusion of his readers by obtruding his "idiosyncrasies" on them in the manner of those modern "beggars for fame" who "extort a pittance from the compassion of the inexperienced by exposing the nakedness and sores of their minds." In this respect he was like Dante; but he was superior to Dante in that his troubles did not render him melancholy and sullen. On the contrary, he retained a "singularly equable spirit," a "sedate and majestic patience," which kept him aware also of the brighter side of the world. Macaulay cites the sonnets to illustrate what he sums up as Milton's "sobriety and greatness of mind."

Macaulay now proceeds to his second and final major subject, which is treated at greater length than the first because more important for his purposes: the defense and praise of Milton's public conduct. In this part he examines first the behavior that Milton shared with other supporters of the Rebellion; then that which was distinctively his own; and finally he traces Milton's conduct to its source in his character.

Macaulay admits that "a large portion of his countrymen" still think Milton's public conduct unjustifiable, no doubt because most of the better accounts of the resistance to Charles have been Tory in sympathy. He singles out "the most popular historical works in our language, that of Clarendon, and that of Hume," the latter especially as a "fascinating narrative" from which "the great mass of the reading public are still contented to take their opinions." Accordingly, Clarendon and especially Hume take a place alongside Johnson as the opposing counsel in this forensic and longest subdivision of the essay. It is essentially a defense of Whig principles viewed as synonymous with "the freedom of the English people"—"those mighty principles which have since worked their way into the depths of the American forests, which have roused Greece from the slavery of two thousand years, and which, from one end of Europe to the other, have kindled an unquenchable fire in the hearts of the oppressed, and bowed the knees of the oppressors with an unwonted fear" (v,23). Knowing that he had an uphill fight, with even many Whigs quite dubious about Milton's public conduct, Macaulay makes occasional use of such obvious emotional appeals in this section; but his principal approach is a rational or logical one, and the style is on the whole simpler and more effective than in the overwrought earlier and final sections of the essay.

The magnitude and severity of the Tory indictment that Macaulay was attempting to demolish may be gathered from Clarendon's impassioned description of 1649 as "a year of reproach and infamy above all years which had passed before it; a year of the highest dissimulation and hypocrisy, of the deepest villainy and most bloody treasons, that any nation was ever cursed with or under; a year in which the memory of all the transactions ought to be erased out of all records, lest, by the success of it, atheism, infidelity, and rebellion should be propagated in the world. . . .[18]

Hume had insisted that the "illusion, if it be an illusion, which teaches us to pay a sacred regard to the person of princes, is so salutary, that to dissipate it by the formal trial and punishment of a sovereign, will have more pernicious effect upon the people, than the example of justice can be supposed to have a beneficial influence upon princes, by checking their career of tyranny." In any event, the virtues of Charles I "predominated extremely" above his vices or rather faults, Hume argued; and the events of the time "furnish us with another instruction, no less natural, and no less useful, concerning the madness of the people, the furies of fanaticism, and the danger of mercenary armies."[19]

Johnson had dismissed Milton's republicanism as "founded in an envious hatred of greatness, and a sullen desire of independence . . . he hated monarchs in the state and prelates in the church; for he hated all whom he was required to obey . . . he felt not so much the love of liberty as repugnance to authority." And for his association with Cromwell, Johnson accused Milton of betraying liberty: "Nothing can be more just than that rebellion should end in slavery: that he, who had justified the murder of his king, for some acts which to him seemed unlawful, should now sell his services and his flatteries to a tyrant, of whom it was evident that he could do nothing lawful."[20]

Macaulay first defends the rebellion itself; then, though regarding it as a mistake, he defends the execution of the king and exculpates Milton for his relation to it; and finally, he defends Milton's association with Cromwell. In the first of these defenses, he is at his most persuasive, being as restrained as his opponents were impassioned, eschewing emotional appeals, and advancing a simple argument difficult to answer. In forensic rhetoric a common "non-artistic" topic is precedent—"non-artistic" because dependent on matters of fact more than on the art of the rhetorician. Macaulay could find no precedent in English history for this type of rebellion, but he does make use of the topic of comparison to advance an argument which he calls now "the analogy of" and now "the parallel case of" the Revolution. It is the same kind of argument that underlies the crucial sections of Newman's *Apologia*.

Macaulay knew well that Englishmen in general, Tory as well as Whig, acclaimed the Revolution of 1688. Even Johnson, who detested William of Orange and rather admired James II for everything except his attempt to enforce Catholicism, reluctantly approved. (He does not discuss the matter in his "Life of Milton.") Hume was much less guarded. James II, he said, lacked a "due regard and affection to the religion and constitution of his country. . . . When it was wanting, every excellency which he possessed became dangerous and pernicious to his kingdom." And so the Prince of Orange was saluted by Hume as one who "effected the deliverance of this island."[21]

Macaulay casts his analogical argument in the form of an enthymeme whose major premise is that "Every man . . . who approves of the Revolution of 1688 must hold the breach of fundamental laws on the part of the sovereign justifies resistance." He then asserts that Charles had clearly broken the fundamental laws of England, there being not "a single article in the Declaration of Right, presented by the two Houses to William and Mary, which Charles is not acknowledged to have violated." The reader is left to draw the inevitable conclusion that Macaulay points to: "If these things do not justify resistance, the Revolution was treason; if they do, the great Rebellion was laudable"(v,26).

After minimizing the excesses of the Rebellion in a burst of analogies and maxims to the effect that the "only one cure for the evils which newly acquired freedom produces . . . is freedom," Macaulay proceeds to what was commonly regarded as the worst excess of all: the execution of the king. The act itself is palliated by the same analogical argument: "What essential distinction can be drawn between the execution of the father and the deposition of the son? . . . To discharge cannon against any army in which a king is known to be posted is to approach pretty near to regicide"(v,32). Still, Macaulay disapproves of the execution on the ground that it injured the cause of freedom, the king's heir being at large and the people opposed to the act. Milton's part was not blameable, however—trying to render the evil as small as possible, defending it against "the ravings of servility and superstition," and especially against the attack by Salmasius on "the fundamental principles of all free governments."

Macaulay's third and final defense is of Milton's service under Cromwell. Forensic rhetoricians concerned themselves with three principal questions: whether a thing happened (*an sit*); what it was that happened (*quid sit*); and the quality of what happened (*quale sit*).[22] In the previous two defenses, Macaulay was concerned primarily with *what* had been done: i.e., defining the nature of Charles's offenses and of Milton's deeds; in this one he is concerned with the quality of the act or the motives of Milton's alliance with Cromwell, motives being the principal sub-topic of this kind of rhetoric. To appreciate why Macaulay spends so much time on this question and relies heavily at one point on an emotional appeal, one should remember that he was writing before the apotheosis of Cromwell by Carlyle and others; and that not only Tories like Johnson but even Whigs like Addison had deplored Milton's association with "a military usurper":

> Oh, had the poet ne'er profaned his pen,
> To varnish o'er the guilt of faithless men,
> His other works might have deserved applause;
> But now the language can't support the cause;
> While the clear current, though serene and bright,
> Betrays a bottom odious to the sight.[23]

Macaulay defends Milton for choosing the lesser of two evils. Though "a good constitution is infinitely better than the best despot," Milton's choice "lay, not between Cromwell and liberty, but between Cromwell and the Stuarts." Cromwell's guilt is minimized by a thrice-repeated appeal to the circumstances of the time, another common topic in this kind of rhetoric: "he was driven from the noble course which he had marked out for himself by the almost irresistible force of circumstances," the Parliament having "deserted its duty." And the guilt of the Stuarts is maximized by one of the most emotional appeals in the entire essay, *ore rotundo*. It is an epitome of Macaulay's early style at its most florid, employing antithesis, apposition, polysyndeton, alliteration, assonance, and climax among the schemes, and among the tropes metaphor, synecdoche, analogy, and oxymoron. Too long to quote in full, it begins: "Then came those days, never to be recalled without a blush, the days of servitude without loyalty and sensuality without love, of dwarfish talents and gigantic vices, the paradise of cold hearts and narrow minds, the golden age of the coward, the bigot, and the slave." And it ends in the cadences of a Hebrew prophet or a Puritan divine: "Crime succeeded to crime, and disgrace to disgrace, till the race accursed of God and man was a second time driven forth, to wander on the face of the earth, and to be a byword and a shaking of the head to the nations" (v,35-36).

Having completed his defense of the public character Milton shared with others, Macaulay now praises him for the qualities "which distinguished him from his contemporaries." This is the occasion for his description of Puritan and Cavalier, which is too well known to dwell on here. Milton is presented in good Aristotelian fashion as a mean between these extremes, uniting the virtues of each and avoiding their vices. (There is a third class, the freethinkers; but they are passed over very quickly as a small group difficult to distinguish from "their devout associates." Macaulay seems no more anxious to stress their unique virtues, which Milton is also said to have possessed, than he was earlier to discuss *De doctrina christiana*.) His mode of procedure in praising Milton here reminds us of the young man who only a few years before the essay on Milton had chosen Whiggery as a *via media* between the Toryism of his father's circle and the radicalism of his own college friends.

At the end of the first major part of his essay, Macaulay had traced Milton's poetic achievements to their source in his serenity and freedom from egotism; now, with the nice symmetry which has marked the entire essay,[24] he concludes the second and final major part by tracing Milton's achievements as a statesman to their source in his devotion to the most valuable of all freedoms—"the freedom of the human mind." It is the peroration of the essay, which here clearly becomes hortatory rhetoric, relying heavily on ethical and emotional appeals to arouse the readers of 1825 to an emulation of Milton's behavior in a time of political crisis. There is nothing surprising about this, of course, because epideictic rhetoric has a natural tendency to shade over into hortatory, and because Macaulay always wrote with one eye on his own time. The historian of England in 1685 could vividly describe, for instance, a projector's scheme for lighting up London; but his ultimate purpose was to instill in his readers a point of view: "There were fools in that age who opposed the introduction of what was called the new light as strenuously as fools in our age have opposed the introduction of vaccination and railroads, as strenuously as the fools of an age anterior to the dawn of history doubtless opposed the introduction of the plough and of alphabetical writing"(1,283).

Recurring to the imagery of the introduction, which had likened the essayist to Capuchins who display the relic of a saint before preaching on his virtues, Macaulay now venerates Milton as the patron saint of Whiggery. He lingers near Milton's "shrine." Could he do so, though "not much in the habit of idolising either the living or the dead," he would kneel to kiss Milton's hand "with passionate veneration." Milton's thoughts "resemble those celestial fruits and flowers which the Virgin

Martyr of Massinger sent down from the gardens of Paradise to the earth, and which were distinguished from the productions of other soils, not only by superior bloom and sweetness, but by miraculous efficacy to invigorate and to heal" (v,45).

Who can doubt that such praise of Milton for his "hatred . . . to bigots and tyrants," for his courage in supporting unpopular courses, was a protest against George IV and a plea for various reforms such as Catholic Emancipation, supported by leading Whigh but opposed by the King, and defeated to the exultant ringing of church bells only weeks before Macaulay completed his essay?[25] Reform was in the air as Macaulay wrote. Bentham had supported Catholic Emancipation, for example, in expectation that O'Connell would eventually give his backing to a variety of reforms. And when Macaulay tells us that Milton crusaded "less against particular abuses than against those deeply seated errors on which almost all abuses are founded, the servile worship of eminent men and the irrational dread of innovation," he is clearly doing his best to hasten the day when even a Wellington might be conquered by the forces of reform.

In this brief analysis of Macaulay's essay, I have deliberately concentrated on *inventio* and *dispositio,* on the origin, nature, and arrangement of the arguments, discussing the style only *en passant.* I have done so, not because the style is an unimportant aspect of the essay; for many readers it was no doubt the feature that most forcibly struck their attention. But the early style of Macaulay is one whose principal traits are obvious to the point of flamboyance, and they have been well discussed elsewhere.[26] What I have wished to emphasize is the fact that classical rhetoric is not primarily the study of style; that style is, in fact, subordinate to *inventio* and *dispositio* in the same way that in drama for Aristotle, diction is subordinate to plot.

What I have presented here is thus hardly more than a sketch of a rhetorical analysis; but I hope it may prove sufficient to indicate the value of this commonly neglected approach in opening up prose texts and in the process developing reading skills of which there is never a surplus, either in the university or out of it. The analysis of rhetoric is, of course, no substitute for other, perhaps more exciting, modes of criticism. But then neither are other modes of criticism any substitute for it—for the disinterested effort to see the object as it literally is before analogizing it to some other thing, viewing it as only one element of a significant pattern, or evaluating it in relation to contemporary thought or at least to the critic's own set of values. Here, too, it would seem, Arnold's words apply: "Whoever sets himself to see things as they are will find himself one of a very small circle; but it is only by this small circle resolutely doing its own work that adequate ideas will ever get current at all." The student of Victorian prose, which so impressively sets forth a variety of approaches to problems still very much with us, can do something to encourage that small circle and perhaps even to enlarge it. And that is no mean task.

NOTES

1. For a brief survey and bibliography of recent developments, see Edward P. J. Corbett, "Rhetoric and Teachers of English," *The Quarterly Journal of Speech,* LI (December 1965), 375-81. See also Donald L. Clark, *Rhetoric in Greco-Roman Education,* New York, 1957, and *John Milton at St. Paul's School,* New York, 1948; *Historical Studies of Rhetoric and Rhetoricians,* Ithaca, N.Y., 1961; *Essays in Rhetoric,* ed. Dudley Bailey, New York, 1963; *The Province of Rhetoric,* ed. Joseph Schwartz and John A. Rycenga, New York, 1964; Edward P. J. Corbett, *Classical Rhetoric for the Modern Student,* New York, 1965; and *Rhetoric: Theories for Application,* National Council of Teachers of English, Champaign, Ill., 1967.

2. *Essays Critical and Historical,* I, 288-9, in *The Works of John Henry Cardinal Newman,* 39 vols., London, 1898-1903.

3. This is what happens in part, I think, to Kenneth O. Myrick's valuable study of *The Defense of Poetry* in his *Sir Philip Sidney as a Literary Craftsman,* Cambridge, Mass., 1935, pp. 46ff. What Myrick insists on calling *narratio,* for instance, seems rather to be the first part of the *confirmatio* or proof, as Sidney's own summary would indicate.

4. On reading the *Rhetoric* again in the sixth form at Rugby, Thomas Arnold wrote in 1841: ". . . its immense value struck me again so forcibly that I could not consent to send my son to [a] University where he would lose it altogether." From a letter of June 26 to Mr. Justice Coleridge, quoted in *The Rhetoric of Aristotle,* trans. Lane Cooper, New York, 1932, p. xiii.

5. See James Anthony Froude, *Thomas Carlyle: A History of the First Forty Years of His Life,* 2 vols., London, 1882, II, 399.

6. *Autobiography of John Stuart Mill,* New York, 1924, p. 8.

7. A very perceptive study partially along these lines is John Holloway's *The Victorian Sage,* London, 1953; but Mr. Holloway does not analyze works as wholes, and he says (p. 11) that he is not studying techniques of persuasion so much as the view of life mediated through "the whole weave of a book."

8. Preference to his *Critical and Historical Essays,* in *The Works of Lord Macaulay,* ed. by his sister Lady Trevelyan, 8 vols., London, 1879, V, xii. All fur-

ther citations of Macaulay will be from this edition and incorporated in the text.

9. G. O. Trevelyan, *The Life and Letters of Lord Macaulay,* 2 vols., London, 1876, I, 117-18.

10. Henry Hallam, *Introduction to the Literature of Europe,* 4 vols., London, 1837-39, IV, 418. Quoted by G. B. Hill in his edition of Samuel Johnson's *Lives of the English Poets,* 3 vols., Oxford, 1905, I, 156.

11. G. O. Trevelyan, *Life and Letters of Lord Macaulay,* I, 117.

12. For some time before the appearance of Macaulay's essay, Jeffrey had been hoping that a talented young man might turn up who would write from Whig or "liberal" principles and thus provide a counterbalance to all the bright young Tories. Macaulay probably knew this before he wrote "Milton," but his advent was in any case a providential response to Jeffrey's *"exoriare aliquis!"* (See Trevelyan, *Life and Letters,* I, 116-17.)

13. *Rhetoric,* 1.9, trans. Cooper, p. 54.

14. *Peacock's "Four Ages of Poetry," Shelley's "Defense of Poetry," Browning's "Essay on Shelley,"* ed. H. F. B. Brett-Smith, Oxford, 1923, p. 18. See also the first of Hazlitt's "Lectures on the English Poets," *The Complete Works of William Hazlitt,* ed. P. P. Howe, 21 vols., London, 1930, V, 9-10.

15. "The Life of Milton," in *Lives of the English Poets,* ed. G. B. Hill, I, 137-8.

16. *Rhetoric,* 1.9, trans. Cooper, p. 54.

17. *Lives of the English Poets,* I, 184-5. In an informative article showing that in the essay on Milton, Macaulay sometimes echoes his own earlier essays in *Knight's Quarterly Magazine* and sometimes Hazlitt, P. L. Carver attempts to defend Macaulay against W. J. Courthope's objection to his comparison of Milton's descriptive technique with Dante's. Carver argues that "the point for which he [Macaulay] is contending is not, as Courthope lightly assumed, that Milton's method is superior to Dante's, but only that it differs from it." ("The Sources of Macaulay's Essay on Milton," *Review of English Studies,* VI [1930], 51.) Carver is clearly incorrect, however, since Macaulay twice uses the word "fault" in referring to Dante's method. It is true that Macaulay normally preferred Dante to Milton, as Carver shows by referring to an earlier essay in *Knight's,* and as can also be proved from one or two of Macaulay's later letters. But the rhetorical purpose of the essay on Milton led Macaulay against his natural instinct to weigh the comparison in favor of Milton, with the result that he ends up by talking out of both sides of his mouth at the same time.

18. Edward, Earl of Clarendon, *The History of the Rebellion and Civil Wars Begun in the Year 1641,* ed. W. Dunn Macray, 6 vols., Oxford, 1888, IV, 511.

19. David Hume, *The History of England,* 8 vols., Oxford, 1826, VII, 128 and 131-2.

20. *Lives of the English Poets,* I, 157 and 116.

21. *The History of England,* VIII, 269-70.

22. See Corbett, *Classical Rhetoric for the Modern Student,* pp. 137-8.

23. Thus Addison, after praising *Paradise Lost.* He is referring to Milton's prose works. See "An Account of the Greatest English Poets," *The Works of the*

Right Honourable Joseph Addison, ed. Henry G. Bohn, 6 vols., London, 1885, I, 25.

24. Macaulay was usually very conscious of structure. As late as 1854, he could write in his journal, "arrangement and transition are arts which I value much, but which I do not flatter myself that I have attained." (Quoted by John Clive, "Macaulay's Historical Imagination," *A Review of English Literature,* I, No. 4 [Oct. 1960], 21.) Anyone who has analyzed the famous third chapter of his *History of England,* however, to cite only one example of his architectonic skill, must consider him far too modest in this respect at least.

25. For some of the contemporary historical background of Macaulay's essay, see G. I. T. Machin, *The Catholic Question in English Politics,* Oxford, 1964, esp. Ch. III, "The Catholic Association and the Crisis of 1825," pp. 42-64.

26. See, for example, G. S. Fraser, "Macaulay's Style as an Essayist," *A Review of English Literature,* I, No. 4 (Oct. 1960), 9-19.

A LINGUISTIC APPRAISAL OF VICTORIAN STYLE

RICHARD OHMANN

HERE IS EDMUND BURKE, responding with feeling to the notion that the state dances when the mob calls the tune:

> To avoid, therefore, the evils of inconstancy and versatility, ten thousand times worse than those of obstinacy and the blindest prejudice, we have consecrated the state, that no man should approach to look into its defects or corruptions but with due caution; that he should never dream of beginning its reformation by its subversion; that he should approach to the faults of the state as to the wounds of a father, with pious awe and trembling solicitude.[1]

The sentence has enough thickness and weight to contain not only the core of Burke's political thought, but the core of his style as well. One knows some of the devices from long acquaintance: the periodic opening, with the long infinitive phrase positioned before rather than after the verb it modifies; the neat marshaling of parallel forms—"faults of the state"/"wounds of a father," "evils of inconstancy and versatility"/"those of obstinacy and the blindest prejudice"; the duration of the single syntactic flight (77 words); the generality, and the dependence on abstract nouns like "prejudice" and "subversion." These we consider touchstones of eighteenth-century prose, and of Burke's in particular. Other contours of the sentence are less apparent, though no less typical. Among the abstract nouns, many (e.g. "inconstancy," "solicitude," "obstinacy") derive from adjectives, which is to say that the deep structure of the sentence contains a number of rudimentary structures in the form Noun + Be + Adjective, each of which has undergone a grammatical transformation that couches the adjectival content in nominal form.[2] Again, Burke has a habit of using the possessive mold, so that instead of "reform the state" and "subvert the state" we have "its reformation" and "its subversion," by a series of transformations. More generally, we might mark how co-ordination works in the interest of compactness, how little repetition there is. We should also note the lack of impedance to syntactic movement: only once does a construction halt midway for another construction to intrude and run its course. Finally, the mood of the sentence is distinctly declarative. To be sure, these observations do not nearly exhaust the makeup of the sentence, much less of Burke's style. But they at least touch the characteristic peaks of expression.

Burke, or some other writer by the same name, *might* have said what he wanted to say in a different manner, for *a* style implies alternative styles. How can we shift the underpinnings of Burke's sentence to give the same material another shape? By letting constructions interrupt each other. By shaking the phrases out of their tidy parallels. By transplanting the initial phrase to eliminate the periodic element. By expanding some of the constructions that are pared down in co-ordination. By converting one clause, say, into a rhetorical question. We must also find alternatives to some of the nominalized adjectives, and phrases like "its reformation" will have to assume another form. Taking these editorial liberties, and a few smaller ones, we arrive at a passage, no more than slightly barbarous, that sounds like this:

> To be inconstant, to be versatile, are evils—evils ten thousand times worse than being obstinate or being most blindly prejudiced. Inconstant and versatile! we have consecrated the state to avoid these evils. Although it has defects, therefore, although it is corrupted, no man but a duly cautious one should approach to look into its defects. And should he dream, ever, of beginning to reform the state by subverting it? No, I say, but approach trembling, solicitous, to the faults that it has, and with pious awe, as he would approach to a father's wounds.

Something besides the style has escaped, of which more later; but the stylistic alteration alone takes the passage away from Burke, takes it quite out of the eighteenth century, and in fact, to my ear, places it rather near to this specimen from the 1860's:

> Children of God;—it is an immense pretension!—and how are we to justify it? By the works which we do, and the words which we speak. And the work which we collective children of God do, our grand centre of life, our *city* which we have builded for us to dwell in, is London!

London, with its unutterable external hideousness, and with its internal
canker of *publice egestas, privatim opulentia,*—to use the words which
Sallust puts into Cato's mouth about Rome,—unequalled in the world!
The word, again, which we children of God speak, the voice which
most hits our collective thought, the newspaper with the largest circulation in England, nay, with the largest circulation in the whole world,
is the *Daily Telegraph!* I say that when our religious organizations,—
which I admit to express the most considerable effort after perfection
that our race has yet made,—land us in no better result than this, it is
high time to examine carefully their idea of perfection. . . .[3]

This is Arnold, of course, and it is interesting to notice that he writes
in a frame of mind not unlike Burke's: both deplore what only Arnold
could call "machinery"—external reforms; both are appalled by a rootless
vulgarity, though the one sees it in France and the other in England;
both, in fact, are responding to noises made by the mob;[4] both argue for
gradualism and tradition; both try to discredit the fanaticism of the hour
by imposing a broad historical perspective. So the differences that any
reader sees between the two passages cannot be laid to a contrast in allegiance or purpose. And plainly no such contrast can account for the difference between Burke's sentence and my revision, for these have virtually identical content. Style is the discriminator.

I should like to suggest that the contrast between Burke's style and the
quasi-Arnoldian style of my revision is a matter of different choices made
in expressing the same content and, if I am right in thinking my revision
Arnoldian, that the contrast between Burke and *echt*-Arnold, or between
almost any two writers, is of a related kind.[5] To conceive style thus is no
more than critics normally and rightly do, except when they pause to
theorize about style; and the point would hardly be worth making but for
the way criticism, in those theoretical interludes, puts on its Sunday best
and proclaims that style and content are inseparable.[6] In any case, for the
practical critic who is interested in style the serious questions go well beyond this issue. Of these serious questions, the two main ones are: how
can we best describe the choices that make up a style? and, what importance do styles have?

I think that we are on the edge of some better answers to the first question than we have had. But in order to explain why, I must intrude some
remarks about linguistic theory (to be omitted, please, by readers already

familiar with generative grammar) before returning circuitously to the main theme.

A grammar should be taken as an attempt to model a man's knowledge of his language, to make explicit what he *tacitly* knows about its structure. Given this intent, a grammar of English will have to represent and explain such things as the ability of a speaker or hearer to tell which sequences of sounds or words are English and which are not; his ability to speak, recognize, and understand an indefinitely large number of novel sentences; his sense of structures and relationships (for instance, his awareness that in the sentence "the cow was found by the farmer" the word "farmer" is the logical subject of "found"—the farmer did the finding—where as in "the cow was found by a millpond," "millpond" is not); his understanding of *un*grammatical sequences, like "anyone lived in a pretty how town"; and his recognition of grammatical ambiguity, as in "I had three books stolen."[7] Moreover, a grammar must do these things in a way that is consistent with some central facts about the human use of language: notably, that although a speaker's linguistic capacity is in a sense infinite, his brain is of course not infinitely large, and that a child will learn any language with equal ease—that is, his capacity is not restricted to the language of the community he is born into.[8]

Grammars apparently work best to this end if they cope with syntax by means of two kinds of rules.[9] The first, called "phrase structure rules," are of a kind long familiar in principle to anyone who has parsed a sentence. Informally, they may be expressed like this:

> A sentence may consist of a subject and a predicate.
> A predicate may consist of an intransitive verb and a particle.
> An intransitive verb may consist of an auxiliary and a main verb.
> A subject may consist of an article and a noun.
> Nouns include "wind," hero," etc.[10]

And so on. Phrase structure rules can handily account for ("generate") very simple sentences like "A wind had risen up" (which the rules listed above go part way toward generating) and "The wind rippled the pond." But if one attempts to describe more complex sentences—and the ways they are understood—using only phrase structure rules, difficulties multiply, and it quickly becomes apparent that one is missing important structural features that every speaker is aware of.

A grammar also needs what are called "transformational rules" to supply this deficiency. They operate, not on single elements (as do the phrase structure rules), but on entire structures, and in various ways. They may add to the structures, delete from them, permute linguistic units, or substitute one unit for another. For instance, on the underlying structure of "the farmer found the cow," a transformational rule operates to give us the underlying structure of the corresponding passive, "the cow was found by the farmer." Transformations can apply one after another, altering further the original underlying structure, and perhaps combining it with another, as sketched in the following sequence:

(1). (Someone) found the cow.
    The cow was found by (someone).   Passive
    The cow was found.   Deletion of agent
    The cow's being found   Nominalization

(2). The accident was lucky.
    (The accident) which was lucky   Relative
    (The) lucky (accident)   Prenominalization

(3). (Something) was an accident.
    (Something) was a lucky accident.   By combination of (1)
       and (3)

    The cow's being found was a lucky   By combination of (1)
      accident.   and (2)

Though it may strain belief to say so, in the long run this form of derivation is far simpler and more revealing than the one equivalent to parsing.

One of the ways in which it is revealing bears directly on the study of style. Recall that a crucial requirement for a grammar is that it account for the way sentences are understood. A grammar that has transformational rules does this for complex sentences by indicating their "deep structure," as well as their "surface structure." For instance, in the surface structure of "the cow was found by the farmer," the noun "cow" is subject of the verb "found"; but plainly the true relationship between the two words is that of direct object to verb. That is, every speaker knows that the farmer did the finding, and that what he found was the cow, rather than the other way around. Our derivation represents this understanding by including, as deep structure, "the farmer found the cow." By contrast, in "the cow was found by a millpond" we do not suppose that the millpond did the finding. This sentence has a different deep structure—roughly, "(someone) found the cow by a millpond"—although its surface structure is identical. A grammar with transformational rules can easily represent such differences, which are utterly commonplace in language; one with a single level of syntactic analysis cannot.

Notice, now, that the active and the passive versions of a structure mean the same thing;[11] they may be regarded as a formal variations on the same content. Indeed, it makes a certain sense to say that all the content of a sentence is indicated by its deep structure, and that its surface structure is its form.[12] Here the bearing on style should be evident: since a given underlying structure, or group of underlying structures, may pass through alternative transformations, a language affords the possibility of presenting the same content in alternative forms—usually in a number of alternative forms. For instance, Burke's clause, "that he should never dream of beginning its reformation by its subversion," can become, "he should never dream of beginning to reform the state by subverting it," or it can take any one of numerous other shapes. Content is the same, form different. Now, the stylistic changes I made in Burke's sentence were nearly all of this sort; and every descriptive statement I made about his style can be put as a statement about syntactic transformations. By extension, I would argue that nearly all the major differences between Arnold's style and Burke's have a syntactic foundation, as do stylistic choices in general. Transformational grammar, in short, not only makes possible a coherent theory of style, but facilitates revealing descriptions as well.[13]

An answer to my other question—what importance do styles have?—follows from the hypothesis as to what they *are*. If stylistic choices operate among alternate formulations of propositional content, then a *pattern* of such choices—a style—implies a characteristic way of conceiving, relating, and presenting content. For an instance: I may write "the evil of inconstancy" or "it is evil to be inconstant." Both have in their deep structures the form "(something) + Be + evil" and the form "(someone) + Be + inconstant," and these two forms are similarly related. Hence "the evil of inconstancy" and "it is evil to be inconstant" have the same cognitive meaning; but there are two obvious differences in the way that meaning is conceived and presented. First, the version which is a complete sentence *states* something—ventures it as a proposition—that the noun phrase simply assumes. There is a rhetorical difference, plainly, which is also perhaps a difference in underlying feeling. The phrase belongs to a moral world more confidently perceived than the moral world of the sentence, one in which the questions of value need not be argued, but belong to a substratum of commonly held belief.[14] Second, by converting "inconstant" into a noun, the phrase seems to reify that quality, and confer upon it an ontological dignity it does not have in the sentence. As a "thing," it may act, be acted upon, cause events to happen, and so on. Regular use of nouns like "inconstancy" will suggest a reading of human nature as law-like, subsumable within fixed explanatory and descriptive categories.[15]

In sum, this paper builds on the premise that styles reflect habits of mind and feeling—conceptual and moral worlds—and that this is the main reason for taking a critical interest in style. By now the point has the ring, almost, of a theoretical commonplace, and I shall not argue it; my aim has been only to suggest its comfortable fit with a central idea of current linguistic theory. What follows is an attempt to mobilize both the commonplace and the linguistic theory in some reflections on the notion of Victorian style.

I

The passage from *Culture and Anarchy* ("Children of God," etc.) speaks in Arnold's voice. The earnestness, the appeal to good sense and common observation, the astonished indignation at a dissonance of ideal and actuality; these are recognizable Arnoldian modes. What, if any, are the salient features of syntax which create the voice? Let me begin with one that is fairly striking, once noticed: Arnold's exposure of smugness moves from point to point largely via the verb "Be."

His punctuation marks off six sentences, the first of which comprises three separate syntactic units. Of the eight units, six have as their basic structure N(oun) P(hrase) + Be + NP. This structure is evident in "it is an immense pretension," and slightly camouflaged in "And the work which we collective children of God do . . . is London" and "The word . . . is the *Daily Telegraph!*" Arnold's fondness for sentence fragments (sentences which, transformationally speaking have lost part of their structure through deletions) conceals the presence of the NP + Be + NP pattern at the base of two other sentences. "Children of God" is a truncated version of We + Be + children of God, which is a sub-part of the structure of the preceding sentence. And "London," the second time it occurs, is the surface token of the underlying structure, The work + Be + London, which is carried over from the previous sentence.[16] In short, five of the eight independent syntactic units in the passage turn on couplings of two noun phrases. Semantically, the most rudimentary drive of the passage is to bring concepts into relations of equivalence. This structuring of an argument typifies the movement of Arnold's thought; moreover, it is accompanied and supported by a number of other syntactic habits. To these I shall give some attention, but for the moment it may be well to consider the possibility of drawing a connection between this single stylistic feature and what we already know of Arnold's method.

One thing about Arnold strikes every reader: his insistent use of labels, epithets, and key terms generally. For many readers, indeed, these words and phrases stand as mnemonic surrogates for the complexes of idea and attitude which, in the original, they summed up. Some of Arnold's tags have led independent careers among people who have never read him; "sweetness and light" and "Philistine" have come unmoored from the firmness and fullness of their original meanings and have in this floating state affixed themselves to causes and ideas that Arnold might have deplored. Others—"high seriousness," "the grand style," "criticism of life"—have remained a sometimes unwelcome but certainly unshakable legacy to literary criticism, even during its anti-Arnoldian phases. Arnold stamped these terms into our vocabulary partly through sheer persistence, but partly by virtue of their aptness, their seeming to give *insight* into the phenomena they name.

He himself was fully conscious of the technique; he half-jokingly spoke of his "great achievement" in "launching phrases" with wide appeal. According to Howard Foster Lowry, "Arnold was used to putting quotations in his note-books and reflecting on them repeatedly. This habit made him attach to certain phrases overtones and connotations that escape his reader. . . ."[17] Whatever their sources, these phrases constitute a ready weapon in Arnold's stylistic arsenal. Lionel Trilling is right in calling their intent "magical": Arnold uses and reuses them almost as incantations.

He gives his key terms a tightly fixed range of applicability, as if they were proper nouns; but like names in Restoration plays, or among the American Indians, they *describe* as well as point. Ordinarily a noun or phrase either designates or describes, and proper names that begin by having meanings—"mender of pots and pans" or "son of John"—gradually lose their power to do more than refer to Tinker and Johnson. Arnold attempts to keep both sense and reference alive in his key terms, and thus to gain a special kind of clarity and economy: "Barbarians," for example, not only refers to an English social class, but conveys information about that class as well—tells in what sense, under what concept, and within what moral framework the aristocracy is referred to. Remorseless repetition of such terms merely buttresses the feeling of their being in some sense *the* names for their referents. They combine the inevitability of names with the semantic content of descriptions.

Arnold's more famous tags are not the only evidence of his preoccupation. A major part of his labor is to establish for things the fixity of being properly named. That he prefers not to let concepts, actions, properties, or groups of people drift in a limbo of namelessness is suggested by the way a perceptible release of tension, a sense almost of revelation, often accompanies the discovery of the proper word. A passage in which Arnold seeks to explain the failure of German higher criticism reaches resolution in this sentence: "But perhaps the quality specially needed for drawing the right conclusion from the facts, when one has got them, is best called *perception*, justness of perception."[18] The italics and the repetition underscore the feeling of newly acquired insight. Similarly, German scholars are specialists who lack "what we call *culture* . . ."; in "quickness and sureness of perception,—in tact,—they do seem to fall somewhat short."[19] To name the quality—tact, culture, perception—is to understand the failure.

Here, and often in Arnold, naming has consequences; a clause that labels or explains a label may be made the *causal* antecedent of another clause: "God is a father, because the power in and around us, which makes for righteousness, is indeed best described by the name of this authoritative but yet tender and protecting relation."[20] One description explains and supports another. Elsewhere Arnold makes description bear an even heavier freight; he moves from naming to activities not merely verbal:

> If culture, then, is a study of perfection . . . it is clear that culture, instead of being the frivolous and useless thing which Mr. Bright and Mr. Frederic Harrison, and many other liberals are apt to call it, has a very important function to fulfil for mankind.[21]

From a definition to something like a prediction, and by implication, from there to a recommendation, a suggested course of action. If the reader will only comprehend the nature of the thing (as in itself it really is!), he must then see the justness of this evaluation, the danger of this situation, the necessity of this program for improvement.

As with many writers, much of Arnold's argument turns on definition, but for him naming is not merely an instrumental device. He makes it an end in itself, and seeks the resolution of a difficulty not *through* naming but *in* naming. The main activity of *On the Study of Celtic Literature,* for instance, is the effort to specify the Celtic character, to circumscribe it with labels. And in *Literature and Dogma* Arnold is concerned to set up a religious terminology, building not on the work of theologians and metaphysicians, but on the language of those to whom religion was given as primary experience—the Hebrew people, Christ, his chroniclers, and his followers. This aim requires close reading of the Old Testament and the Gospels, in an attempt to recapture the import and the spirit of the Bible's words. Arnold wants to discover the true nature of Christianity by studying the original nature of Christianity (and thereby to confound the Bishops of Winchester and Gloucester). The book is a tissue of definitions, many of them rather well known:

> . . . the object of religion is conduct.
> . . . conduct [is] three-fourths of human life.
>   Eating, drinking, ease, pleasure, money, the intercourse of the sexes, the giving free swing to one's temper and instincts,—these are the matters with which conduct is concerned.
> . . . the true meaning of religion is thus, not simply *morality* but *morality touched by emotion.*
> . . . the *not ourselves* which is in us and all around us, became to them [the Hebrews] adorable eminently and altogether as *a power which makes for righteousness;* which makes for it unchangeably and eternally, and is therefore called *The Eternal.*
>   Wisdom and understanding mean, for Israel, the love of order, of righteousness.
>   The monotheistic idea of Israel is simply *seriousness.*
> . . . for science, God is simply *the stream of tendency by which all things fulfil the law of their being.*[22]

And so on. Nearly as common as the language of definition is the language of distinction, in which two things are named and set in opposition to each other or differentiated from each other:

Ethical means *practical*. . . . Religious also means *practical*, but practical in a still higher degree; and the right antithesis to both ethical and
religious, is the same as the right antithesis to practical: namely, theoretical.
The real antithesis to natural and revealed alike, is *invented, artificial*.
What we need for our foundation is not *Aberglaube*, but *Glaube*; not
extra-belief in what is beyond the range of possible experience, but
belief in what can and should be known to be true.[23]

Arnold draws these distinctions carefully in order to put down common
misconceptions and set the public language right. Many of the naming
passages are, in fact, quite integral to Arnoldian *moral* instruction, as
when he quotes from classical and Biblical writers a long list of pronouncements, calling some of them "morality" and some of them "religion."

It is no accident that the quotations from *Literature and Dogma* read
like a summary of the sections from which they come, for the book is
essentially an essay in naming, an attempt to establish an appropriate
religious lexicon. One thing necessary to this attempt is interpretation
of the Bible, not "through that process described by Butler by which anything can be made to mean anything,"[24] but by careful reading and sympathetic interpretation. Considering the pressure Arnold puts on the
"mistakes" of ordinary usage, the reader must view with some irony his
resolution to "use words as mankind generally use them";[25] but he does
at least make a serious case for

> . . . studying the Bible with a fair mind, and with the tact which
> letters, surely, alone can give. For the thing turns upon understand-
> ing the manner in which men have thought, their way of using
> words, and what they mean by them.[26]

Culture gives the power to understand words, the instruments of men's
thought, and thus gives access to "the history of the human spirit." We
cannot understand the religion of the Hebrews without understanding
the language in which they undertook to describe their religious experience. As Arnold seeks access to the past through language in *Literature
and Dogma*, in *Culture and Anarchy* he seeks to cope with the flux of
the present by giving things their proper names and by putting them in
their proper categories.

Through words to certain truth—that is the intellectual journey on which Arnold guides his reader. And yet, the truth he seeks is not tautological, not of the same order as the truth of "o = o" or "a square is a closed figure with four equal sides and four equal angles." The enlightenment that he expects from definition is insight into the way things are, as well as into verbal usage. This program is impossible, of course; he cannot have it both ways. But the philosophical confusion does not vitiate his method, I believe; for ultimately his aim is to encourage certain usages and certain attitudes—to build, for instance, a religious lexicon which will do justice to religious experience. The naming habit is a sign of Arnold's preoccupation with language, and the use of basic NP + Be + NP structures is a stylistic mark of this metalinguistic impulse.

The building of sentences on this basic pattern is not the only formal reflection of Arnold's persistent impulse to name and identify. I have noted five instances of the NP + Be + NP construction; in the deep structure of the passage there are seven more, which may be displayed in tabular form:

UNDERLYING STRUCTURE	SURFACE REPRESENTATION
1. we + Be + Children of God	we children of God
2. The work + Be + our centre	"work" in apposition with "centre"
3. the work + Be + our city	"work" in apposition with "city"
4. we + Be + children of God	we (collective) children of God
5. the word + Be + the voice	"word" in apposition with "voice"
6. the word + Be + the newspaper	"word" in apposition with "newspaper"
7. it + Be + time	it is high time

Nor does this exhaust the list of equivalences which are established by Arnold's syntax. The nouns in apposition with "work" have also an identity with each other, and with "London." I am not certain whether this relation would have a formal analogue in a complete transformational grammar of English (which, of course, does not exist), but it is distinctly implied by the construction, which imposes a scheme like the following one upon Arnold's nouns:

the work = our centre = our city = London
the word = the voice = the newspaper = the *Daily Telegraph*.

In the structure of the passage, in its rhetorical rhythm, and in its cognitive work, equivalence occupies a central position. The main intellectual business of the pasage, in fact, is to question the equivalence of "we" and "children of God," and to expose the presumably devastating equivalence of "work" and "London," "word" and "the *Daily Telegraph*."

The syntactic maneuvers that support this activity are not always evident; many of them are pretty well concealed in the complexities of deep structure. They are nonetheless one of the most dependable marks of Arnold's style: NP + Be + NP appears far more frequently in the underlying structures of his prose than it does in the prose of Carlyle, Newman, Ruskin, and Mill.[27] Appositives, likewise, which are one transformational variant of the structure, are somewhat more common in Arnold's prose.[28] And he relies much more heavily than do the other writers on a group of complement constructions, each of which covers an underlying occurrence of NP + Be + NP. For instance,

> we call ourselves children of God (we = children of God)
>
> by knowing Ancient Greece, I understand knowing her as the giver of Greek art (knowing Greece = knowing her as . . .)
>
> I regard X as Y (X = Y)[29]

These are particularly interesting because they bring to the conscious surface the activities of naming, equating concepts, seeing X as Y, and meaning X by Y.

I have stressed a particular cluster of stylistic facts, not with the intention of claiming that they *constitute* a style, but with the aim of tentatively locating them at the heart, and seeing other characteristics of his prose as closely related to the pattern of naming and identifying. For instance: the transformation that produces the relative clause is a common one with Arnold[30]—"works which we do," "words which we speak," "the voice which most hits our collective thought," etc.—and I would argue that relative clauses share one important function with equivalences. They serve to identify an object or a quality, to set it apart from others, to round out and deepen the concept Arnold is trying to establish.

Again, the appositive is only one of many structures that commonly interrupt the progress of the construction in which they are "embedded." Arnold is particularly given to embeddings of all sorts (though hardly more so than, say, Carlyle). When his interpolations do not label or classify, they usually add information, or they qualify, or they supply an additional vantage point from which to see the business at hand and grasp the manner in which it is maintained: "so I say," or "to use the words which Sallust puts in Cato's mouth," or "which I admit to express the most considerable effort after perfection that our race has yet made." These interruptions, in short, work toward *definition,* both in the sense already considered at length and in the sense of creating sharp outlines, completeness of delineation. Syntactic forward movement gives quarter, when necessary, in the service of this aim.

When a writer attempts clarity and fullness of concept, as Arnold does, his focal nouns are likely to multiply their grammatical relationships in the underlying structure; in this way the concepts they refer to gain definition by their links to other concepts. Arnold's prose is notable—especially considering his limited use of adjectives—for what I shall call "syntactic depth": that is, one word in the surface structure will often play several grammatical roles in the underlying structure. "Work" and "city" in the third sentence have four grammatical roles apiece; "organisations" in the last sentence has five; "criticism" in the first sentence of Mr. Holland's excerpt* has seven; and so on.[31] Arnold's sentences are like networks, with the crucial words at the nodes. Thus, for all his much-noted simplicity and condescension, there is a sense in which Arnold's prose is complex, though complex *in the interest of* conceptual clarity. Compare Burke: how much less effort he spends in regulating verbal or conceptual traffic, and how much more in saying what happens, or what will happen if . . . , or what should happen.

The networks of interrelation extend well beyond the confines of single sentences, of course, as Arnold presses for conceptual fullness. "Criticism" appears fourteen times, in all, in the structures that underlie Mr. Holland's passage, and twenty times in the next 150 words. This essay, like many of Arnold's, is virtually a set of variations on a single concept. And in noting this principle of construction, I have settled, finally, on one of the most obvious characteristics of Arnold's style: his notorious habit of repetition. But the foregoing discussion should suggest that the repetition of single words differs sharply from the reiteration of slogans, both logically and rhetorically. When a word reappears sentence after sentence, each time in a network of relationships, the concept it refers to is gradually being fixed, defined cumulatively—not simply reinforced

* See p. 326 [Mr. Ohmann and Mr. Holland, who read one another's papers, have cross-referenced their remarks out of mutual interest.—Eds.]

by habituation. Arnold's repetitiveness is the manner (not the mannerism) of a writer who sees life as exceedingly complex, yet at the same
time rationally structured in forms decipherable through the employment
of culture and right reason.

It is a long way from copulative basic structures to "syntactic depth"
and repetition, but I hope that the associations I have seen among a handful of stylistic features do not strike the reader as *free* associations. There
is, I think, something basic to Arnold's style and thought in this cluster
of idiosyncrasies. I have given it more than cursory attention not only
because it is a radical of his style, but because it seems to me responsive
to an impulse common among Victorian writers as a group: the urge to
overcome doubt and confusion in a period when the avenue to truth is
far from broad, straight, or public. Many Victorians are concerned not
merely to expose error and speak the plain truth (as is more nearly the
case with Burke, Johnson, Shaftesbury, and so on), but to create the very
climate of mind within which truth and conviction will become possibilities. Arnold and his contemporaries write in a society where no common
framework of feelings and assumptions can be taken for granted, and
their prose strains to provide the framework, in addition to the local truths
they are arguing. Yet at the same time they believe it not unlikely for
conversion to take place, for the culture to redeem its way of life; they
prod and insist and jostle the reader with dogged urgency to this end.[32]

Arnold's style is one answer to these very general apprehensions about
the decay of intellectual community, and one strategy for the restoration
of culture. It is the mark of a writer trying by main force to establish fixities in the ebbing sea of faith. He cannot, as Burke could, simply draw
his central, freighted terms from the public stock of language and count
on culture to supply adequate meanings. He must work to lodge both
terms and meanings in his audience's sensibility. Other characteristics of
his style, quite different from those I have dealt with, can profitably be
seen as contributing to the same endeavor. For instance, he relies heavily
on the constructions that English has for reporting speech and thought:
"I say that . . . ," and "our religious organisations, which *I admit to* express . . ." are two examples in the passage at hand. Usually these represent an attempt to put before the reader, not only an idea, but a judgment *on* that idea, or an attitude toward it, or a sense of the precise
strength with which it is maintained. Burke and Johnson could count
on ideas as a stable medium of exchange; Arnold must always be setting

the rates. On the other hand, he distinctly underplays the transformation, so common with Burke, that converts a predicate adjective into a nominal. To speak of "inconstancy" rather than saying that such and such a person is inconstant implies a faith in unchanging and universal qualities that was harder to sustain in 1868 than in 1790. And finally, the questions and imperatives that trouble the discursive flow of Arnold's prose may be partly an acknowledgment that basic accord is a delicate and elusive thing, and partly an attempt to jolt the reader loose from his complacencies.*

* How do these tentative conclusions fit with those to which Mr. Holland's psychoanalytic reading leads him? I cannot pretend to say with any great assurance, but the possible relationships between his analysis and mine are at least suggestive enough to warrant the attempt. First, the short passage he has chosen exhibits most of the stylistic tendencies that I have insisted upon: the focal emphasis in deep structure on a single noun ("criticism"), a series of relative clauses, interruptions, an apposition, a question, and a complement structure from the group I singled out ("what is called 'the practical view of things'"). Notably absent are NP + Be + NP constructions (only three in the passage), but there are twenty in the three hundred words immediately following. Arnold's syntax in "The Function of Criticism at the Present Time" is recognizably that of the man who wrote *Culture and Anarchy*. Furthermore, he is pursuing an intellectual activity of the same sort—exploring the nature of concepts, and rounding them out by setting them in proper relationship to one another. Two-thirds of the passage is an expansion of "disinterestedness," and the whole passage (in fact the whole essay) is an attempt to fix an idea of true criticism by detailing its relationships to the contemporary English scene.

Mr. Holland argues that Arnold's labeling and interrupting, as well as his hopes for criticism, have their "unconscious roots in a wish to avoid sexual touchings." Without saying yea or nay to this proposal, which takes us even more directly than do my own procedures to the genesis of the literary work, I am ready to allow a distinct and intriguing affinity between his conclusion and mine. Definition, boundary-setting, the discrimination of concepts—these are enterprises calculated to isolate, to prevent overlapping, or meshing, or blurring. They act out an intellectual fastidiousness which might well betoken a sexual drawing back. And certainly a great deal of Arnold's work urges the deferring of impulsive, partisan, self-seeking, and self-congratulatory action until thought has had its innings.

Against this reading of Arnold is the plain rhetorical intensity of his prose. He writes to convince, to exhort, and often to condemn. There is no refusal here to engage the audience as people; Mr. Holland notes the lively presence of a man speaking; a man, I would add, who is trying to change the lives of his readers, rather than to pursue ideas for their own sake. Perhaps Mr. Holland also points the way to a resolution of this puzzle: the person in Arnold's prose is there to

II

Arnold's style is far more complex than I have made it seem; any style is. A full account would naturally include features less easily subsumed in the single current of Arnoldian (and Victorian) thought and feeling which I have chosen to emphasize. But I have meant to be selective because my subject is neither style nor Arnold's style, but *Victorian* style, and it is convenient to notice that at least some components of Arnold's style and of the conceptual framework it reflects can be understood as deriving from the culture and period he inhabited. The question I want to address now is, how far can one press this familiar assumption?

Given the slant on Victorian style which I have proposed, instances from the other great writers of the period readily present themselves. Consider the paragraph which Mr. Holland quotes* from Mill:

> No society in which these liberties are not, on the whole, respected, is free, whatever may be its form of government; and none is completely free in which they do not exist absolute and unqualified. The only freedom which deserves the name, is that of pursuing our own good in our own way, so long as we do not attempt to deprive others of theirs, or impede their efforts to obtain it. Each is the proper guardian of his own health, whether bodily, or mental and spiritual. Mankind are greater gainers by suffering each other to live as seems good to themselves, than by compelling each to live as seems good to the rest.

Only one of the salient characteristics of Arnold's prose reveals itself here: the reliance on NP + Be + NP as a basic structure (in three out of the four sentences).[33] But if one thinks, not of particular features of

---

preserve decorum, to guarantee that the change in men's lives will occur through a change in their minds, not through revolution or apocalypse.

Perhaps. Whether Mr. Holland's reading and mine are finally compatible remains an open question. There is some evidence to suggest that they are; and, independently of the sketchy evidence of this study, it seems certain that a man's native conceptual impulses are in part the servants of his psychic needs and fantasies. But the attractive possibility that grammatical transformations have a near kinship to psychological transformations must remain only a possibility, for the present.

* See pp. 326-29—Eds.

syntax, but of the impulses *behind* the style, the passage falls in line. Mill, too, seeks fixity and clarity, though he does so by different means, many of them logical. Thus his paragraph bulges with determiners, the syntactic equivalents of logical quantifiers, in that they indicate what portion of a "class" is being referred to:

No society	Each (person)
none (= no society)	each other
the only freedom	each (man)

And many other locutions are devoted to specifying and relating classes. The five negatives in the paragraph all come from deep structures in which their function is to deny whole propositions,[34] as does the logician's "it is not the case that. . . ." Mill's verbs are in the timeless present tense, and he leaves unfilled the syntactic positions which might be given to indicators of time and place: logic is timeless and placeless. This abstractive tendency shows also in the transformational deletion and shifting of nominals marked as human. There are nearly thirty in the underlying structure, and only ten in the surface structure. And, of course, these ten are all non-specific: "we," "guardian," "Mankind," "each other," "the rest," and so on. It is easy to see, in the move toward class definition and generality, Mill's particular version of the Victorian struggle to provide a reliable common ground for discourse and to overcome doubt and uncertainty. Mr. Holland wishes to see through Mill's prose to a dependency on the father, and the idea is initially plausible. Whether or not the style seeks to supplant an absent, powerful someone, it unquestionably works to establish a reliable *something*: irrefutable and commonly agreed-upon truth.

A writer may look for stability in the abstract and general, as Mill does; or he may find it in the concrete. We require no linguistic apparatus to tell us that Carlyle is the most metaphorical of our prose writers, the extreme opposite of Mill in this respect. He is continually supplying an imagined concrete situation, or character, or narrative to accompany and interpret his ostensible subject. He is lavish also with the most particular references to the familiar—or the arcane—world: names of people and places, allusions, quotations. He peoples his prose in another sense, too, by creating a lively argumentative framework for the inquiry, assigning questions, objections, interjections, errors, and opinions to shadowy persons or ephemeral voices. Not only in the underlying structure (as with Mill), but also in the surface structure of his sentences, human nouns are prominent. And the specificity of person and object is matched by an equal specificity of place, time, manner, instrument, etc. There is an immense amount of qualification in his writing, as if he were inclined to provide a complete spatio-temporal setting for ideas, to make them material and visible. Like Arnold, Carlyle is a labeler; like Arnold, he uses appositives. But with a difference, it seems to me: the movement is toward *vividness,* rather than toward conceptual definition. In short, Carlyle's way of providing a framework for conviction is to turn always toward the external world— a zany and kaleidoscopic world, to be sure, but nonetheless reassuringly *there.*[35]

In Newman's prose the desired stability is that of reasoned judgment and just perception—he is close to Arnold in this, as in the syntactic measures of repetition and syntactic depth. A striking sign of his emphasis on judgment and understanding is his use, in underlying structure, of verbs that require human subjects. Most verbs in this syntactic class suggest mental acts, rhetorical acts, or ethical motions:

know ("knowledge," in the surface structure)

insist	accuse
advocate	pretend ("pretence")
detect	arrogate
observe ("observers")	praise
hope	

Put alongside these the verbs (again, in deep structure) with implied human indirect objects—"guarantee," "seem," "look"—and the large number of value-laden words to which Mr. Holland refers, and one begins to see an unusual emphasis on the *processes* of perceiving, deciding, and judging. The authority here resides as much in the reality of the presiding intellect as in the argument itself.

I might continue in this fashion: Ruskin, too, labors to validate his judgments; Pater (like Arnold and Carlyle) fills his prose with interruptions and interpolations. But to put the case for a Victorian style in this way is to sense that something has gone wrong. In sifting Victorian prose for this or that bit of grammar, one is no longer speaking of styles at all, for a style is a complex and highly organized working together of many linguistic patterns, not a handful of isolated devices. And the other stratagem I have adopted—appealing to the conceptual or emotional impulse behind the style—is scarcely more satisfactory. For at that level of interpretation one is speaking of something both nonlinguistic and non-literary. Writers in a given period may share large parts of a conceptual scheme and a large number of emotional needs produced by culture, without sharing a style. As Mr. Holland says, "the search for a 'Victorian style' will lead us away from purely linguistic considerations and toward the psychological issues a writer's syntax manages."*

In any case, even the feeblest intuition of style tells us that Arnold's is very different from Newman's, Newman's from Carlyle's, and so on. If we look for a fundamental pattern of syntactic organization shared by all these writers, and not, say, by a corresponding group from the eighteenth century, we will come up empty-handed. There are stylistic *tendencies* that divide Victorians from their eighteenth-century predecessors, but very few clear and pronounced indicators of one century or the other. I have made a preliminary syntactic inventory of prose samples by six major Victorians and six eighteenth-century writers;[36] out of 33 classes of basic structures and transformations, which constitute the fundamental machinery of English grammar, there are only three on which the two periods contrast significantly: the Victorians use more questions and imperatives; they use the transformation that converts nouns into adjectives less frequently; and—I am unable to account for this—they incorporate more basic sentences with intransitive verbs. Needless to say, these three differences scarcely add up to evidence for a theory of Victorian style. The truth is that in almost every stylistic dimension the Victorians differ nearly as much from each other as they differ from eighteenth-century writers.

Yet I have argued that style reflects conceptual framework, and critics like Houghton have amply shown that there is something worth calling *the* "Victorian Frame of Mind." How can the two points be reconciled? Fairly simply, I think. A man who occupies a given spot in history and culture is urged by his intellectual world to think and feel in certain ways; but the forming power of intellectual culture operates on a mind already formed, deeply and intricately, by a thousand subcultures, from the nursery on up. Style is responsive to the cut of a writer's mind, and that is only trimmed and decorated by intellectual culture, not created by it.

If this is so, as I imagine it to be, many of us have overestimated the

* See p. 335—Eds.

importance of historical periods to the description and understanding of styles.[37] Those of us interested in Victorian prose style will do well to study individual writers intensively, and with the best linguistic theory available, to discover the unique and intriguing shapes that mind and language take among the Victorians. We could take our direction from Newman's excellent comment on style:

> . . . while the many use language as they find it, the man of genius uses it indeed, but subjects it withal to his own purposes, and moulds it according to his own peculiarities. The throng and succession of ideas, thoughts, feelings, imaginations, aspirations, which pass within him, the abstractions, the juxtapositions, the comparisons, the discriminations, the conceptions which are so original in him, his views of external things, his judgments upon life, manners, and history, the exercises of his wit, of his humour, of his depth, of his sagacity, all these innumerable and incessant creations, the very pulsation and throbbing of his intellect, does he image forth, to all does he give utterance, in a corresponding language, which is as multiform as this inward mental action itself and analogous to it, the faithful expression of his intense personality, attending on his own inward world of thought as its very shadow: so that we might as well say that one man's shadow is another's as that the style of a really gifted mind can belong to any but himself.[38]

Reliable judgments about the history of style will come after an understanding of styles, and may be quite other than what the textbooks say.

NOTES

1. *Reflections on the Revolution in France,* as excerpted in *Eighteenth Century Poetry & Prose,* ed. Louis I. Bredvold, Alan D. McKillop, and Lois Whitney (New York, 1939), pp. 1024-5.

2. The linguistic framework that I employ (loosely) throughout this paper is that of generative grammar. The *locus classicus* is Noam Chomsky, *Syntactic Structures,* The Hague, 1957; a convenient place to consult more recent work in the field, by Chomsky and others, is Jerry A. Fodor and Jerrold J. Katz, eds., *The Structure of Language; Readings in the Philosophy of Language,* Englewood Cliffs, N. J., 1964. I have drawn heavily on the form of linguistic theory presented in Chomsky's *Aspects of the Theory of Syntax,* Cambridge, Mass., 1965. The present essay, however, is not a technical exposition, and I hope that the jargon I occasionally resort to will explain itself adequately in context.

3. All quotations of Arnold are from *The Works of Matthew Arnold,* Edition de Luxe, London, 1903. This one is from *Culture and Anarchy,* p. 27.

4. That Arnold was doing so is demonstrated by Michael Wolff in "The Uses of Context: Aspects of the 1860's," Supplement to *Victorian Studies,* IX (1965).

5. I have argued this point at length in "Generative Grammars and the Concept of Literary Style," *Word,* XX (December 1964).

6. True, of course, if the sense of the term "content" is attenuated to cover every last evocative flourish and connotative wiggle. But then the dogma becomes a near-truism, and loses interest correspondingly. As important as it once was for critics to stop thinking of style as embellishment, it is now perhaps at least as important for us to salvage the narrower and in some ways more helpful sense of "content": i.e. overt, cognitive meaning. Otherwise a distinction is lost, and criticism is the poorer.

7. Which can mean "someone stole three books from me," "I got someone to steal three books," or "I had stolen three books (when the police interrupted me)," depending on how its grammatical structure is perceived.

8. The upshot of these two requirements, it now seems, is that we will need a "universal grammar" after all, one which will form part of every particular grammar of a language and which must correspond to the innate human capacity for learning languages. It is impossible, and unnecessary, to spell out this intriguing likelihood here; interested readers should consult the first chapter of Chomsky's *Aspects of the Theory of Syntax* and the whole of his *Cartesian Linguistics,* New York, 1966.

9. A caution: in grammars of this sort, rules have nothing to do with prescription. They are formulas that express what a speaker "knows" of the structure of his language.

10. The customary way to write such rules is:

$$S \rightarrow \text{Subj} + \text{Pred}$$
$$\text{Pred} \rightarrow V\text{intr} + \text{Part,}$$

where the arrow means "may be rewritten as." Grammarians often represent the derivation of a sentence by means of a tree diagram:

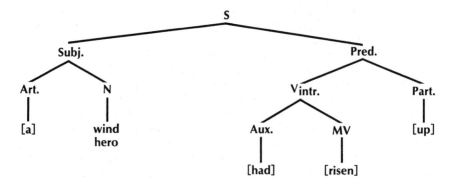

This one is equivalent to the rules written out in the text, except for the words added in brackets.

11. That is, have the same cognitive content. Connotative meaning changes, of course.

12. This point is argued technically and persuasively in Jerrold J. Katz and Paul Postal, *An Integrated Theory of Linguistic Descriptions,* Cambridge, Mass., 1964.

13. There is much to suggest that transformational analysis may illuminate even such matters as imagery, metaphor, and diction, insofar as they impinge on style. See my "Literature as Sentences," *College English,* XXVII (January 1966), and "Mentalism in the Study of Literary Language," in Thomas Bever and William Weksel, eds., *Studies in Psycholinguistics* (forthcoming).

14. This relation between deep and surface structure often holds: surface structure carries on the forthright business of persuasion, analysis, or whatever, while deep structure contains some of the presuppositions which color—and even license —the discourse.

15. The question often arises: "How do you know that? By what system of interpretation, generative or otherwise, can you make semantic inferences of that sort?" The answer, cheerfully given, is that I rely on what I hope are informed intuitions. In the absence of a full semantic analysis of English, the critic can do nothing else. But the procedure need disturb no one, since it is always subject to confirmation (or disconfirmation) by the intuitions of other speakers. One may lament the crudeness of some interpretations arrived at in this fashion, but not the fashion itself, which is merely a generally available way of reading English.

16. It may seem high-handed to say so. But consider how one understands "London, with its unutterable external hideousness. . . ." The whole construction is a nominal, and one therefore feels it to be playing the role of grammatical subject, direct object, predicate noun, or some other role open to nominals. Predicate noun is the natural choice, since the word "London" appears as a repetition of the predicate noun in the sentence before.

17. *The Letters of Matthew Arnold to Arthur Hugh Clough,* ed. Howard Foster Lowry, London and New York, 1932, p. 44.

18. *Literature and Dogma,* p. xxiii.

19. Ibid., pp. xxiii-xxiv.

20. Ibid., p. 35.

21. *Culture and Anarchy,* pp. 12-13.

22. *Literature and Dogma,* pp. 14, 15, 16, 20, 32, 34, 35, and 42, respectively.

23. Ibid., pp. 20, 50, and 378, respectively.

24. Ibid., p. 150.

25. Ibid., p. 21.

26. Ibid., p. 52.

27. In about 1500 words of the prose of each: Arnold, 51 times; Carlyle, 25 times; Mill, 23 times; Newman, 37 times; Ruskin, 29 times. This and the other counts are based on three passages of roughly 500 words from the works of each of the five writers. I have used my first passage from Arnold ("Children of

God . . ." and continuing on to 500 words); Hollands' passage from Arnold ("It is of the last importance . . ." and so on, to 500 words); Holland's passage from Carlyle ("How, then, comes it . . ." and on to 500 words); Holland's passage from Mill ("No society . . ." and on to 500 words); and Holland's passage from Newman ("It is well to be a gentleman . . . ," plus enough words before and after to make up 500). The other passages I used are all single pages in *Prose of the Victorian Period*, ed. William E. Buckler (Boston, 1958), as follows: p. 490 (from Arnold's "Literature and Science"); p. 126 (from *Heroes and Hero-Worship*); p. 163 (from *Past and Present*); p. 282 (from *On Liberty*); p. 337 (from Mill's "Nature"); p. 207 (from *The Idea of a University*); p. 237 (from *Apologia Pro Vita Sua*); p. 351 (from *Modern Painters*); p. 370 (from *The Stones of Venice*); and p. 396 (from *Unto This Last*).

28. Arnold, 10; Carlyle, 10; Mill, 7; Newman, 4; Ruskin, 7.

29. Arnold, 17; Carlyle, 6; Mill, 0; Newman, 2; Ruskin, 3.

30. Of relatives in "which" or "that," with the present tense — that is, those relatives which, by and large, do not simply add identifying detail, but say something about the nature of the main concept — Arnold has 16, Carlyle 3, Mill 4, Newman 6, Ruskin 1.

31. "Work":   The work is London
                We do the work
                The work is the centre
                The work is the city
   "city":   the work is the city
                we have a city
                we have builded the city
                we dwell in the city
  "organisations": we have organisations
                      the organisations are religious
                      the organisations express an effort
                      the organisations land us in a result
                      the organisations have an idea of perfection
  "criticism": the criticism is English
                 the criticism should discern (something)
                 the criticism has a course
                 the criticism ought to take a rule
                 * the criticism + avail + the criticism of the field
                 the field is opening to the criticism
                 the criticism + produce fruit

(* "Criticism" plays two roles in this underlying structure, so the total is actually eight.)

32. These generalities about the Victorian period are not, of course, my own: for views on which I am drawing, see especially Walter Houghton, *The Victorian Frame of Mind, 1830-1870*, New Haven, 1957; William A. Madden, "The Victorian Sensibility," *Victorian Studies*, VII (1963), 67-97; Jerome Hamilton Buckley, *The Victorian Temper, A Study in Literary Culture*, Cambridge, Mass.,

1951. The idea of conversion comes from Buckley's chapter, "The Pattern of Conversion," though I am thinking also of Houghton's discussion, "Optimism." The richest source for any point about Victorian rhetoric is John Holloway, *The Victorian Sage; Studies in Argument*, London, 1953; but see also, among others, A. Dwight Culler, "Method in the Study of Victorian Prose," *Victorian Newsletter* (Spring 1956), pp. 1-4, and Leonard W. Deen, "The Rhetoric of Newman's Apologia," *ELH*, XXIX (1962), 224-38.

33. Even so, although Mill uses the copula a good deal, he favors NP + Be + Adjective more than Arnold does, and his copulative constructions appear much less frequently in the *underlying* structures than do Arnold's.

34. See Edward Klima, "Negation in English," in Fodor and Katz, *The Structure of Language*.

35. Holland speaks of Carlyle as concealing a dangerous vision and displacing sight to something else. My argument, here, offers possible corroboration: Carlyle's overpopulated external world may be such a "something else."

36. A satisfactory report on this study would require far too much space, and must therefore be put off until another occasion. The writers, though, are Arnold, Carlyle, Huxley, Newman, Pater, Ruskin, Addison, Boswell, Burke, Defoe, Johnson, and Shaftesbury.

37. But at the same time, many critics have emphasized the individuality of Victorian writers—Holloway, for instance, throughout his book, and Houghton, p. 225. See also William E. Buckler's "Introduction" to the Riverside Edition, *Prose of the Victorian Period*, Cambridge, Mass., 1958; James Sutherland, *On English Prose*, Toronto, 1957, Ch. IV; and Holland's study in this volume.

38. *The Idea of a University*, ed. Charles Frederick Harrold, New York, 1947, pp. 240-41.

PROSE AND MINDS:
A PSYCHOANALYTIC APPROACH TO NON-FICTION

"Language most shewes a man: speake, that I may see thee. It springs
out of the most retired and inmost parts of us, and is the Image of the
Parent of it, the mind. No glasse renders a mans forme or likenesse so
true as his speech"—so Ben Jonson, translating Vives and Erasmus.[1] A
man walks a sidewise shuffle or an aggressive, duck-toed stride—we infer
his mind. He writes a florid hand or one that is crabbed and illegible
—again, we infer his mind, for proverbially, *le style est l'homme même.*
If we wish to do our inferring about *l'homme même* with some rigor,
some attention to specifics and to truth, we must resort to psychoanalysis,
for psychoanalysis is, so far as I know, the only psychology that enables
us to deal with the expression of a particular mind in particular words
and images.

There is, of course, no excuse at all for bringing psychoanalysis into
the chaste groves of literary criticism except to relate literary works to
some mind. In fiction, there are three minds possible: the author's, a
character's, the reader's. In much non-fiction, as in most lyric poetry, the
second possible mind becomes the author's persona; except in biography
and history, non-fiction has no characters as such, only a drama of
thought.

The first possibility, however, the writer's mind, persists in non-fiction
no less than fiction. A man's unconscious does not subside because he is
dealing with facts or opinions rather than characters and episodes. The
essayist, no less than the poet, has unconscious motivations for his being
a liberal or a conservative, new critic or old scholar, a spokesman for
cottage industry or candle saving or capital punishment. And these unconscious reasons will express themselves and co-act not only in his con-

scious reasoning but also in his walk, his talk, his verbal style—his very life.

For example, if we recall Edmund Wilson's analysis of Ben Jonson as an "anal character," we can see as part of his one unified self, his preoccupation with money, his irascibility, his explosive dramatic structures, and his collecting jargons and then pouring them out in his plays. His anality will show, presumably, even in such minutiae as his rendering Vives' *intimis nostri pectoribus recessibus* as "the most retired and inmost parts of us," omitting the phrase, *ubi verus ille ac purus homo habitat.* Vives' "breast" has slipped to a more fundamental area, losing purity in the fall.

Jonson's personality shows in both the form and the content of his translation, for form and content—so critics are fond of saying—are one. But they are one, I think, only in the sense both express personality, for, as transformational linguistics has shown, optional transformations change forms but not meanings. For example, a key sentence in Joyce's "Araby" is: "Gazing up into the darkness I saw myself as a creature driven and derided by vanity." Professor Richard Ohmann comments:

> Joyce might have written, "I gazed up into the darkness. I saw myself as a creature. The creature was driven by vanity. The creature was derided by vanity." Or, "Vanity drove and derided the creature I saw myself as, gazer up, gazer into the darkness." Content remains roughly the same, for the basic sentences are unchanged. But the style is different. And each revision structures and screens the content differently. The original sentence acquires part of its meaning and part of its unique character by resonating against these unwritten alternatives.[2]

True enough. I would add only that Joyce's choices cannot be purely for linguistic reasons. If he is a man, they must also serve psychological needs of both an expressive and a defensive kind: "Each revision structures and screens the content." The real bridge between form and content is the writer's mind, and the map to show that bridge must be not only linguistic but psychological.

Psychoanalysts themselves have long noticed such stylistic bridges in patients. The "verbal salad" of the schizophrenic marks an extreme in finding forms to express or defend against unconscious fantasies, but there are less pathological styles. Obsessional characters, in particular, customarily fend off emotion by using phrasings like, "There was a kind of anger inside me," instead of, simply, "I felt angry." Hysterics often perceive themselves as being acted upon rather than acting—linguistically, such an issue finds expression in passives, reflexives, or first person accusatives. The most courteous, complimentary person I know, much given to talk of humane values, also sprinkles his speech with military metaphors—am I wrong to infer aggressive impulses masked over?

Consider psychologically, then, this passage from John Stuart Mill's *On Liberty* which Professor Ohmann has already analyzed from a strictly linguistic point of view:

> No society in which these liberties are not, on the whole, respected, is free, whatever may be its form of government. And none is completely free in which they do not exist absolute and unqualified. The only freedom which deserves the name, is that of pursuing our own good in our own way, so long as we do not attempt to deprive others of theirs, or impede their efforts to obtain it. Each is the proper guardian of his own health, whether bodily, or mental and spiritual. Mankind are greater gainers by suffering each other to live as seems good to themselves, than by compelling each to live as seems good to the rest.[3]

How can psychological considerations relate the style understood in purely linguistic terms to the man himself?[4]

Ohmann notes that Mill does not qualify his verbs as to time or place; he is interested in the law-like and generally applicable. The style becomes abstract, rather markedly depersonalized. People become "mankind" or, even more abstractly, "society." The only specific people in the passage are "we" and "our" contrasted to "others" and "theirs."

Ohmann also points to the way Mill establishes a domain, then sets boundaries within it, as if to map a territory exhaustively. For example, contrast this sentence, "Pursuing our own good in our own way is the only freedom which deserves the name," with the way Mill actually wrote it: "The only freedom which deserves the name, is that of pursuing our own good in our own way. . . ." Logically, the content is exactly the same, but Mill chose a form that puts the strong assertion first. This choice of form is particularly obvious when Mill adopts the complicated double negative of the opening sentence instead of its more easily understood logical equivalent: "A society in which these liberties are not, on the whole, respected, is not free."

Bearing out Mill's initial assertiveness are his quantifications and qualifications: "whatever may be its form of government," "completely," "absolute and unqualified," "the only freedom," "so long as we do not attempt," "whether bodily, or mental and spiritual." Usually, these qualifications make the initial statement as extreme as possible. But sometimes, as in "on the whole," they weaken it a bit. Others are qualifications upon qualifications as when "so long as we do not attempt to deprive others of [their own good]," gets further specified: "or impede their efforts to obtain it." And sometimes these quantifications and qualifications shape the flow of the thought as a whole, as in the final comparative "greater gainers by . . . than by . . ." or in the opening pair of sentences which build from societies in which liberties are respected "on the whole" to societies which are "completely free."

Ohmann notes that the matrix sentences are all NP + Be + NP or NP + Be + Adj—that is, all copulative sentences. They put things into a class. In the surface structure, actions appear only as relative clauses, adjectivals, adverbials of manner, complements, possessive constructions, and so on. In the deep structure, though, there are many embedded sentences with active verbs. Similarly, there are nearly thirty nouns in the deep structure that would be characterized as human, but only one in the surface structure.

It is as though persons and actions could exist only if contained within the initial strong statement of class. Perhaps philosophy demands such a pattern of generality followed by logical segmentation, but, as a psychoanalytic critic, I am struck by the way this mannerism makes a high proportion of Mill's words dependent on others for meaning or even their very presence. Also, these dependent words are the ones that refer to acts and persons, while the matrix into which they fit simply *is*.

As is well known, this problem of dependency marked Mill's life as well as his style. He began by adopting totally and vigorously his father's Utilitarianism, even forming (at fifteen!) a little society of Utilitarians. But Mill ended by deeply qualifying his father's views, in effect, asserting his personality only within that matrix. No wonder Mill was deeply interested in the emancipation of women or that the two works of his we prize most are called *Autobiography* and *On Liberty*. As Mr. Howard R. Wolf notes:

> We can look to Mill's "On Liberty" as a work in which he found compensation for years of submission by giving expression to the need to

give "full freedom to human nature to expand itself in innumerable and conflicting directions." A political vision of freedom, valid in itself, was for Mill the working out of a neurotic conflict. Mill expressed in political philosophy the need for a freely chosen identity which had been denied to him in his own childhood. Still, like his father, he continued to serve the East India Company and only retired in 1858 after thirty-six years of service. The scant mention given to this "service" in the *Autobiography* is another example of his acceptance, consciously, of his father's professionally structured mode of life.[5]

In his life no less than in the content of his works, Mill's pattern was the establishment of an identity within the matrix of his father's thought.

Every adolescent faces the challenge of finding his identity, but the issue was complicated for Mill by the way his father presented himself as a somewhat overpowering teacher—in a sense, as the living embodiment of a doctrine. In his prose style, Mill seems to be responding two ways to the search for his own identity. First, he makes a strong assertion (which we can understand psychologically as his fusing with the doctrine he is stating and drawing his strength from it, as he did with his father). Then, he specifies acts and persons within the assertion (which we can understand psychologically as asserting himself within the doctrine from which he draws strength).

The pattern of identity-through-dependency shows in Mill's repeated rhythm of assertion followed by specification, but it comes through still more clearly in his striking use of pronouns. In 114 words, there are seventeen pronominal constructions, eight in the third sentence alone. On the average, in this passage, Mill is using one pronoun for every seven words. Arnold and Carlyle in the passages discussed below use one per fifteen and fourteen respectively. Nor does Mill (here) ever use "I" as they do.

The most interlocked of these constructions suggests their meaning: the antecedent of "themselves" is "each other" which in turn depends on the personal noun "mankind." "Depends" seems to be the key. A pronoun can stand alone, but, at the same time, it depends upon a noun for its meaning. A pronoun also replaces a noun. Am I being too far-fetched if I suggest that, at least for Mill, the noun was father to the pronoun? It is worth noting, I think, that every one of these seventeen pronouns follows the noun to which it refers. Mill does not write sentences like this: "Whatever may be its form of government, no society in which these

liberties. . . ." That very phrase, "these liberties," makes this entire paragraph dependent upon the preceding paragraph, as Mill's pronouns do.

The filial significance of Mill's pronouns shows quite clearly in his
account of that highly charged moment when his adolescent depression
lifted:

> I was reading, accidentally, Marmontel's Memoirs, and came to the
> passage where he relates his father's death, the distressed position of his
> family, and how he, then a mere boy, by a sudden inspiration, felt and
> made them feel that he would be everything, would supply the place
> of everything to them.[6]

Pronouns, I take it, "supply the place of" nouns. Notice, too, that Mill
builds the pronoun that refers to the son with an appositive noun phrase
("then a mere boy"), but the pronominal phrase that refers to the father
remains big and vague, "everything." And that same "everything" is to be
taken over by the son: "he would be everything." The son is active—
"He, then a mere boy" serves as the subject of four verbs. The father,
"all," is the object of a preposition and of "had lost." The father isn't
even allowed to die actively; he becomes an adjectival: "his father's
death" (transformed from "his father died").

I do not mean to imply that one could read back, without more data,
from one paragraph of a man's writing to his infancy. In the act of writing, prose style comes too far from the primitive, unconscious roots in
fantasy and much nearer to "higher" ego processes such as word choice
or obedience to grammar. For the same reason, I do not mean to imply
that a prose style very like Mill's might not serve different psychological
purposes for a different man. I do say, though, that Mill's relation with
his father, which affected so much of his life and thought, colored his
prose style as well. His use of pronouns, his propensity for assertion followed by grammatical dependency—these express his wish to be the
"everything" his father represented as much as his ideas do. *Le style est
l'homme même*, no less than his subject matter. I do not think this an
unreasonable conclusion to be reached by a psychoanalytic approach: to
show how a man's stylistic traits express and manage the traits and conflicts of his personality.

I do not, however, think it is the only kind of conclusion. A psychoanalytic approach to non-fiction prose style also offers the—to me—more
interesting possibility of understanding the dynamics of the experience

in the reader's mind. "Experience," may seem an odd word as applied to non-fiction. With a poem, story, play, or film, we "have an experience." Do we when we read a philosophical argument like Mill's? I suppose we do, but it seems awfully attenuated, a pale approximation of our rich response to fictions. Even so, we may be able to understand our experience of non-fiction by beginning with fiction and adding in the effect of the non-.

It has become possible in recent years to describe in considerable detail the dynamics of a reader's response to poem, story, play, or film. Essentially, at the heart of any literary work is a fantasy (or wish or drive or impulse). It may be the oedipal wishes of a Shakespeare or a Lawrence. It may be the anal wish to purge as with Ben Jonson or the wish to be purged as with Gerard Manley Hopkins. Or it may be the oral wish to satisfy a hunger (Marlowe) or to escape being devoured (Conrad). The variability is vast, but every literary work transforms such a nucleus of fantasy into social, moral, or intellectual meaning, and different aspects of the work play different roles in this transformation.

Plot typically expresses the fantasy, but also manages and controls it by such devices as omission, splitting, distancing, or resolution. Characters, too, typically express drives, though, often, minor characters act only to manage drives for us. Other aspects of literature, notably structure and language, serve primarily as ways of handling and controlling the fantasy. Poetic language, in particular, displaces our concern from the highly charged fantasy to a less charged, more purely verbal level where the words take on a life and logic of their own, based on sound associations that pretend to master the psychological issues involved. The critical cliché is, sound matches sense, but we would be more accurate to say, sound manages sense. Similarly, form and content, we say, are one, but I think we would be more accurate to say, form manages content, for the end result of all these transforming and managing devices is the shaping of a literary work to a "point" (or meaning, or thematic center) about which all its separate details come to a social, moral, or intellectual focus of mutual relevance.

This is a description of a medieval king:

> He could fight as well as any king going; and he could lie as well as any, except the King of France. He was a mighty hunter, and could read and write. His tastes were wide and ardent. He loved jewels like a woman, and gorgeous apparel. He dearly loved maids of honor, and indeed paintings generally.

At the level of fantasy, the passage deals with a powerful father-like man, portrayed as a creature of considerable power and appetite. In addition to "He dearly loved maids of honor," there is a faint hint of sexuality in the statement, "he could lie," (lie with), but more directly, in the am-biguity of "He loved jewels like a woman." Whatever anxieties such a powerful, sexual father might arouse, however, the passage allays (in the manner of psychological defenses) by its patronizing tone. Kings are ranked according to how well they fight—and how well they lie. Com-pared with the reader, kings are dumb enough so that merely to read and write is an accomplishment worthy of mention. And, as for this king's women, they are shoddy, merely "paintings," ultimately, then, fictions. Our response to the passage, I take it, is not anxiety, but wry amusement. We feel superior. We patronize what otherwise might have been a rather disconcerting father-figure. If we feel satisfied by the passage, our feeling comes from the mastery of anxiety by quasi-defensive means. Co-ordinate conjunctions have linked threatening aspects of this king to childish or feminine traits.

Now, there is no way of telling from the passage alone whether it is fiction or non-fiction. One might think, therefore, we would get this ex-perience of patronizing amusement either way. But we don't. I have found, trying this passage out on students, that they report different feel-ings toward the passage depending on what I tell them before they read it. If I say this is a description of Philip of Luxemburg from a history of medieval Europe, they report that, as they read the passage, they were asking themselves such questions as, "Were medieval kings really like this?" "Is this an accurate description of Philip of Luxemburg?" "Is this style right for a history book?" If, however, I tell them this is a passage from a Thurber fairy tale, no such questions arise. Instead, they report amusement (or annoyance) at the passage's cuteness. In short, though the words on the page are the same, the experience of them differs accord-ing to the expectation or "set" the reader brings. He has one kind of "set" for non-fiction, another for fiction.

Northrop Frye has criticized the distinction between fiction and non-fiction as unworkable; he attacks

> the view that the real meaning of fiction is falsehood or unreality. Thus an autobiography coming into a library would be classified as non-fiction if the librarian believed the author, and as fiction if she thought he was lying. It is difficult to see what use such a distinction can be to a literary critic.[7]

Frye's difficulty arises because he sees the difference between fiction and non-fiction as whether we believe or disbelieve. But the little experiment with the passage from Reade's *The Cloister and the Hearth* shows the issue is, do we apply criteria of belief or disbelief at all? We do if we think a given passage is history or biography, whereas we don't (usually) if we think it is part of a novel, play, or poem. For them, we "grant that willing suspension of disbelief for the moment which constitutes poetic faith."

In other words, the "set" or expectation we bring to a literary work imposes certain limits on the kind of experience the work can give us. If we come to a work expecting to test it according to our everyday notions of reality, we will have a less emotional experience than if we come to it not reality-testing. The reason is, reality-testing makes us more aware of ourselves. If we do not reality-test, we become less aware of ourselves; we become less aware of the division between us and the literary work; we half-consciously fuse with it so that the reworking of fantasy it acts out for us feels as though it is happening in our own minds. In non-fiction in particular, when we experience it as literature, we displace our commitment from the reality-issues it presents to the language for its own sake. If, on the other hand, we reality-test a literary work, we become more aware of our separate existence and its. We become spectators of rather than participants in the imaginative reworking embodied in the literary work.

Both fiction and non-fiction rework unconscious fantasies or issues into meaning. Fiction, though, usually pulls us toward feeling that transformation as though it were our own, while non-fiction tends to put us off into spectatorship.

Even so, the distinction is not hard and fast. With both fiction and non-fiction, there are degrees of involvement and disinvolvement. The secret to experiencing non-fiction prose as art lies not in the text but in ourselves: to the degree we can turn off our normal reality-testing, we can be drawn into non-fiction as a literary experience like our experience of poetry or fiction.

It is not always easy to do this. Some non-fiction asks rather directly that we take it in terms of the real world. For example, as I read that passage from Mill's *Liberty*, I do feel a sense of ringing self-assertion, coupled with a quite impersonal clarity and lucidity. Analyzing my reaction, I find that I feel freed by Mill's absolutes as he must have felt when he wrote them. A more mature me, though, is painfully aware of the consequences of laissez-faire economy and the kind of polity Mill advocates. To that extent, I find myself testing what he writes rather than being drawn into it; to that extent, I am repelled by the passage as I am by right-wing freedom-mongering. In other words, my experience of the passage gets limited because it advocates a doctrine and asks me to test it against my own experience as I would other doctrines I encounter.

Much less reality testing, however, is called for by such a passage as this from *Sartor Resartus*, and, as a result, I can respond to it more freely and emotionally than I can to Mill.

> How, then, comes it, may the reflective mind repeat, that the grand Tissue of all Tissues, the only real Tissue, should have been quite overlooked by Science,—the vestural Tissue, namely, of woollen or other cloth; which Man's Soul wears as its outmost wrappage and overall; wherein his whole other Tissues are included and screened, his whole Faculties work, his whole Self lives, moves, and has its being? For if, now and then, some straggling broken-winged thinker has cast an owl's-glance into this obscure region, the most have soared over it altogether heedless; regarding Clothes as a property, not an accident, as quite natural and spontaneous, like the leaves of trees, like the plumage of birds. In all speculations they have tacitly figured man as a *Clothed Animal*. Whereas he is by nature a *Naked Animal;* and only in certain circumstances, by purpose and device, masks himself in Clothes. Shakespeare says, we are creatures that look before and after. The more surprising that we do not look round a little, and see what is passing under our very eyes.[8]

I feel as I read it a kind of wry amusement, a whimsical tolerance of human foible, not the least such foible being Carlyle's mannerism of hurrying me along breathlessly. Now if, by examining the passage, I can find in it the transformation of fantasy that produces this reaction, I may be able to account for, not only my own reaction, but also the reactions of others, even though they may respond differently to the fantasy and its transformation. If so, then I shall be using psychoanalysis to relate the text to the third mind possible, the reader's.

Objectively, the most striking feature of the passage is its extensive use of what an older rhetorical tradition would have called *amplificatio*. For example, he sets his last four sentences as alternatives: between those who have looked into the obscure region and those who soared over it heedless; between man as a clothed animal and man as naked; finally, "Shakespeare says"—so why don't we? Similarly, he builds the opening sentence on appositives: "the grand Tissue of all Tissues, the only real Tissue . . . the vestural Tissue." According to Ohmann, the deep structure of the first sentence has fourteen kernels containing "tissue."

This tendency to build comes out most conspicuously in Carlyle's use of co-ordinate connectives—joining two grammatical equivalents, they automatically double the statement: "woollen or other cloth," or "wrappage and overall," or "wherein his whole other Tissues are included and screened, his whole Faculties work, his whole Self lives, moves, and has its being." I find seventeen such constructions in the passage, an average of one every eleven words. (The comparable figure for the Mill passage would be one per nineteen.) The effect of all this doubling, indeed, quadrupling, is a tremendous feeling of build-up. A simple idea—thinkers have not paid enough attention to clothes—becomes a wild concatenation of images.

Carlyle, notes Ohmann, uses "an immense amount of qualification." He is "inclined to provide a complete temporal-spatial setting for ideas." A psychoanalytic critic begins to suspect at this point that all this loquacity and concretization are covering up something. After all, *Sartor Resartus* does deal with coverings.

Carlyle's *amplificatio* most commonly takes the form of peopling his prose. Ohmann notes that his argument moves in questions, objections, or opinions assigned to hypothetical people.[9] The relationship found in Mill is reversed here, says Ohmann. Persons and active verbs in the matrix sentence, copulars in the insert sentences. Again, one senses a masking.

Carlyle uses metaphor and imagery extensively, the elaborate bird-metaphor of the second sentence, for example, but, of course, in this passage as in *Sartor Resartus* as a whole, clothing becomes an elaborated image for man's life. Carlyle is particularly strong in visual imagery: "overlooked," "owl's-glance," "regarding," "look before and after," "look round," "see . . . under our very eyes." And he uses the opposites of seeing, too: "screened," "masks." Words of seeing occur, on the average, once every 30 words; in the Mill passage of 114 words, there is at most only one visual image, "seems." Naming manages content for Mill as seeing does for Carlyle, or, more accurately, seeing-instead-of.

Carlyle manages the visual fantasy at the root of this paragraph by displacing our sight to something else, especially people. The sentences, first, show us the mask, second, peep behind the mask, then, third, rush our attention back to the mask again. In the following, I have italicized the words that refer to whatever is behind the mask:

> For if, now and then, some straggling broken-winged thinker has cast an owl's-glance *into this obscure region,* the most have soared over it altogether heedless; regarding Clothes as a property, not *an accident,* as quite natural and spontaneous, like the leaves of trees, like the plumage of birds. In all speculations they have tacitly figured man as a Clothed Animal; whereas he is *by nature a Naked Animal;* and only in certain circumstances, by purpose and device, masks himself in clothes.

How few are the words Carlyle devotes to the secret he is revealing! Notice, too, how they are buried or embedded between much more ample descriptions of the failure to see or understand this secret. What, then, is the fantasy at the heart of this paragraph?

The paragraph just before this one closed with "every cellular, vascular, muscular Tissue," references to the body. Now, Carlyle proposes to reveal "the grand Tissue of all Tissues." If we isolate the words that describe that special bodily tissue, we find (in order): "woollen or other cloth," "obscure region," "an accident," "Naked Animal," and "what is passing under." If I listen with the third ear, I hear about a "region" associated with nakedness, a woollen, obscure, animal region related to an accident, and with "passing under," in short, genitals. Carlyle enjoins us to "look round a little" but those who have "cast an owl's-glance" into "this obscure region" are "straggling" and "broken-winged"—evidently, to look at what Carlyle asks us to look at is dangerous. The passage defends again anxieties associated with its fantasy content (looking at genitals) by displacing our attention onto quite different sights: clothing, birds, thinkers.[10]

You may not wish to go so far with me. May we compromise and say that this passage shows the same displacement that pervades all of *Sartor:* Carlyle is about to show us some kind of ultimate secret; instead, he shows us a surface—clothing—and tells us, *that* is the secret. This repression, I think, leads to Carlyle's *amplificatio*—psychologically, he is displacing our attention from something we are curious about to something else, and he does it, as he says himself, "not without an apoplectic tendency." We feel hurried along, for he swiftly transmutes whatever helplessness we might feel as we are confronted with ultimate secrets to a safer helplessness—the overpowering rush of his prose. I, at least, feel amused, because, I think, Carlyle has reversed whatever inadequacies I might feel looking at "the grand Tissue of all Tissues," into looking down with impunity at important thinkers—Science, Shakespeare—*they* are missing something.

I feel amused. Others might feel over-managed and therefore bored. I can also imagine someone's feeling indignant or frustrated at Carlyle's constant withdrawal of the secret he promised. Whatever the reaction, though, the words of the passage remain the same. By understanding them psychologically, as, first, mentioning, then displacing attention from some secret animal thing, we define a range of appropriate responses. We become able to see how this fantasy and this defense embodied in the words might mesh or not mesh with any particular reader's patterns of fantasy and defense. We have supplied a psychoanalytic map of the relation between form and content, writer's mind and reader's.

The technique applies to gentler styles than Carlyle's:

> It is of the last importance that English criticism should clearly discern what rule for its course, in order to avail itself of the field now opening to it, and to produce fruit for the future, it ought to take. The rule may be summed up in one word,—*disinterestedness*. And how is criticism to show disinterestedness? By keeping aloof from what is called "the practical view of things;" by resolutely following the law of its own nature, which is to be a free play of the mind on all subjects which it touches; by steadily refusing to lend itself to any of those ulterior, political, practical considerations about ideas, which plenty of people will be sure to attach to them, which perhaps ought often to be attached to them, which in this country at any rate are certain to be attached to them quite sufficiently, but which criticism has really nothing to do with.[11]

Despite Carlyle's apoplectic peopling his prose, it is Arnold who really gives the feeling that a person is there. Carlyle's people come and go. Arnold sustains for page after page a single voice, urbane, balanced, sensible. Even at his most indignant, he seems somehow reassuring. Again, it is possible to account for at least my reaction psychologically, by understanding the sample as the interaction of a fantasy and a defense.

Ohmann points to Arnold's way of converting actions into nouns or nominatives. The first of these nominalizations comes at the outset, the long subordinate clause, "that English criticism should. . . ." But there are a number of others: "keeping aloof" from the kernel 'criticism keeps aloof'; "following resolutely" from 'criticism resolutely follows'; "a free play of the mind" from 'the mind freely plays'—a whole series of linguistic transformations that turn clauses with active verbs into modifiers. Arnold takes a condition or action and treats it as a fixed, manipulable entity, to be named and understood through its name.

Once Arnold arrives at a name that satisfies him, he not only repeats it, he uses it in multiple ways. 'Criticism' is the subject or object of about twenty underlying structures in less than a page. One word in the surface structure will play several grammatical roles in the underlying structure. Related to this tendency is Arnold's repeated us of "it" and "which." Having established in the second clause that "it" stands for "criticism," he uses "it" three times in the first sentence and three more times in the last. Similarly, in the last, having established "which" as "practical considerations about ideas" (a nominalization of an action, as, indeed, "criticism" itself is), he repeats the "which" four times. Again, once "them" is set to stand for "ideas," Arnold repeats that pronoun three times.

Partly as a result of this labeling tendency, Arnold has a propensity for forms of "to be." All three of the thought-units in this passage (sentences 1, 2, and 3-4) have the structure: noun plus a form of "to be" plus a predicate noun. Thus, "It is of the last importance that . . ." "The rule may be summed up . . ." "And how is criticism to show . . ." Forms of "to be" sometimes come in by way of passive verb forms, but others Arnold seems to introduce almost for their own sake: for example, "will be sure to attach" instead of, simply, "will attach"; or, "which is to be a free play" instead of "which is a free play." The effect is to attenuate the activity even of the active verbs Arnold uses.

Related, I suspect, to the extra "be's" are Arnold's variations upon ordinary sentence order. The last thought-unit, sentences 3-4, substitutes a rhetorical question-and-answer form for the ordinary word order: "Criticism is to show disinterestedness by keeping aloof. . . ." Similarly, the second sentence transposes ordinary, "One word, disinterestedness, may sum up the rule," into a passive, "The rule may be summed up in one word,—*disinterestedness*." The first sentence follows ordinary NP + VP word order, but only for the first clause. The second, subordinate clause interrupts the natural relation of object and verb with two longish purposive phrases. Most stylists, I think, would have written, ". . . English criticism should clearly discern what rule for its course it ought to take in order to avail itself of the field now opening to it, and to produce fruit for the future." Typically, the effect of Arnold's word orderings is to put the strong assertion at the end: "it ought to take"; "one word,—*disinterestedness*"; "but which criticism has really nothing to do with." Mill, by contrast, asserts first, then adds to his assertion. Arnold prepares us in the first part of a sentence for the assertion at the end. Arnold buffers his strongest medicine.

We can isolate, then, three characteristics of Arnold's prose. He tends to turn actions or conditions into nouns or pronouns which he then manipulates as fixed entities. Partly as a result of this naming, partly for the word's own sake, he tends to introduce "be's" even when not necessary. His word orderings present strong assertions only after considerable cultivating of the ground. Ohmann sees the naming as Arnold's "trying to fix conceptually an unstable world or one that threatens to become unstable"; the buffering as his "shying away from contact, direct expression of the physical." Certainly this is the tenor of Arnold's writing in this as in many other passages. His metaphors, however, suggest deeper roots for this intellectual attitude.

This passage has few metaphors, as such, and those are mostly idioms. Even so, I think it is possible to discern the unconscious fantasy that leads to Arnold's labeling and buffering. English criticism "ought to take" a "rule for its course." The rule may be "summed up." Criticism should be "following the law." I would call these metaphors (or idioms) of rule-following, perhaps even of navigating.

The second half of the passage has a number of expressions about spatial relations: "keeping aloof," "free play," "which it touches," "refusing to lend itself to"—the three references to attaching, then, finally, having "nothing to do with." All these relate to touching and keeping distance, and the idioms of navigation state as a purpose, keeping criticism from touching practicality. The only conspicuous metaphors occur in the first sentence and they concern that tabooed practicality: criticism is to keep its distance "in order to avail itself of the field now opening to it, and to produce fruit for the future." I take it they are (roughly) agricultural.

In short, the metaphors of the passage seem to say, criticism should navigate so as to keep clear of things and bear fruit that way. If I listen to such metaphors with the third ear, I hear as their very deeply buried fantasy content a wish for procreation without touching. Far-fetched as this may seem, I think the fantasy becomes quite clear later in this paragraph in a sentence whose unconscious content is revealed by a single deletion. Arnold is complaining of the present state of English criticism: "Our organs of criticism are organs of men . . . having practical ends to serve, and with them those practical ends are the first thing and the play of mind the second." As with some of Carlyle's phrasings, words like "organs," "ends," and "serve" have sexual connotations. I am perfectly sure Arnold did not consciously intend them—but he did choose the words he did.

If I am correct, Arnold's quite reasonable intellectual position, that criticism should eschew practicality, has unconscious roots in a wish to avoid sexual touchings. His prose mannerisms of labeling and buffering serve to put off or avoid some final active meshing in the sentence. From a psychoanalytic point of view, I would characterize Arnold's naming and looking and question-and-answering as defenses against or intellectual substitutes for words of action, action being felt as sexualized.[12] And it is this constant intervention of Arnold's that gives me, at least, the feeling "someone is there," someone who fends off whatever might disrupt balance, urbanity, or sense.

Another writer who asserts and argues is Newman, but I, at least, do not get at all the feeling of balance and reassurance that I do from Arnold.

It is well to be a gentleman. It is well to have a cultivated intellect, a delicate taste, a candid, equitable, dispassionate mind, a noble and courteous bearing in the conduct of life. These are the connatural qualities of a large knowledge. They are the objects of a University. I am advocating, I shall illustrate and insist upon them. But still, I repeat, they are no guarantee for sanctity or even for conscientiousness. They may attach to the man of the world, to the profligate, to the heartless, —pleasant, alas, and attractive as he shows when decked out in them. Taken by themselves, they do but seem to be what they are not. They look like virtue at a distance. But they are detected by close observers, and on the long run. And hence it is that they are popularly accused of pretence and hypocrisy, not, I repeat, from their own fault, but because their professors and their admirers persist in taking them for what they are not, and are officious in arrogating for them a praise to which they have no claim. Quarry the granite rock with razors. Or moor the vessel with a thread of silk. Then may you hope with such keen and delicate instruments as human knowledge and human reason to contend against those giants, the passion and the pride of man.[13]

If I try to state my reaction as precisely as I can, I feel involved in very strong, dogmatic assertions, but I also feel uneasy, as though I am somehow not "getting there," indeed, that the writer himself is not. Newman's style feels to me like a protesting too much or, perhaps more accurately, lik a self-directed *Schadenfreude*—he seems to court his own defeat.

I think I get so strong a feeling of assertiveness not only from Newman's assertions themselves, but also from the way he stacks his ideas in co-ordinate constructions. "It is well to . . . It is well to. . . ." There are five instances of such parallel independent clauses, and four of independent clauses joined by co-ordinate conjunctions. There are 19 instances of parallel joinings of other parts of speech, phrases, verbs, adjectives, or nouns. All in all, Newman uses a co-ordinate or parallel construction once every eight words in this passage. The corresponding figure for Arnold is once every 19 words, for Mill, once every 23. Carlyle also uses co-ordinate constructions frequently, but even he uses them only once every 11 words, and mostly between the smaller parts of speech: single nouns or modifiers. The effect in Newman's prose is to add his ideas as in a child's sum, an effect considerably reinforced by his rat-tat-a-tat use through 12 sentences of "they," "them," and "these" to stand for the long list of qualities sentences 1-2 set out.

Ohmann points to the way Newman uses a number of verbs with implied indirect objects: "They are no guarantee [to anyone]"; "They do but seem [to someone]"; "They look like virtue [to someone]." He also notes that many of Newman's verbs call for human subjects: "advocate," "insist," "detect," "accuse," "arrogate," "hope." Similarly, his vocabulary consists largely of value-words, with, again, a person implicit—the evaluator: "well," "cultivated," "delicate," "noble," "large," "sanctity," "attractive," "pleasant," "virtue," "praise," "claim"; and against those positives, "profligate," "heartless," "hypocrisy," "fault." Someone must be there to perceive such values, and, indeed, "I" is very much there, throughout the passage. Newman uses framing clauses that relate the real point to the writer and his discourse, for example, "I repeat." Then, he adds in "you" at the end of the passage, and, finally, "giants."

In short, Newman peoples his writing, both explicitly and implicitly.

Ohmann points to structures that apply an adjective predicatively to a nominalized sentence: thus, "It is well to be a gentleman" embeds [someone] + Be + a gentleman" in the matrix "NP is well." Persons are similarly embedded in the long series of phrases about "cultivated intellect," "delicate taste," and the rest. The repeated "they" and "them" (which even sound like personal pronouns) carry these embedded persons all through the passage. Ultimately, they become associated with the instruments used by "you" in the struggle against "giants."

Newman's metaphors suggest a motive for both his stacking his ideas and the quite extraordinary degree to which he peoples this passage. The qualities of a gentleman "look like virtue at a distance. But they are detected by close observers, and on the long run." "Quarry the granite rock with razors. Or moor the vessel with a thread of silk. Then may you hope. . . ." The first metaphor has to do with close observation, detecting the true state of affairs. The second pair of images has to do with physical control. I think we could put them together as both concerned with mastery, either physically or by observation. We might guess, then, that a basic issue for Newman himself and therefore indirectly for his reader is control or mastery. If so, then both his summing and his peopling of ideas act like a marshalling of forces for a struggle.

A similar mechanism shows in Newman's fondness for adjectives: he uses one, on the average, for every other noun. But interestingly, never for a noun or pronoun which is the subject of a verb—except once, and the particular usage rather intensifies than qualifies the subject: "Taken by themselves, they. . . ." Otherwise, the subjects of his verbs are simple and direct: "It," "These," "They," "I," "their professors and their admirers," "you." Again, the impression is one of assertiveness and force; qualification attaches not to the actor but to the complement or objects of the verb. The actor must be strong for the struggle.

Conventional criticism speaks of Newman's irony, meaning, I take it, his interest in negatives, that which is not enough. In this paragraph, for example, there is not one unqualified, positive statement. True, individual sentences, such as the first four, are unqualified, but their tenor and the tenor of the whole is that all the qualities of a gentleman, added together and stated forcefully and poised against even qualified and hedged predicates, are not enough "to contend against those giants, the passion and the pride of man."

Psychoanalytically, the issue is one of mastery. Newman's style acts out a struggle and defeat. His syntax says, in effect, asserting as strongly as I can is not enough. I am reminded that in the *Apologia*, he chose just two recollections of his childhood attitudes toward religion, "which are at once the most definite among them, and also have a bearing on my later convictions." First, "I used to wish the Arabian Tales were true: my imagination ran on unknown influences, on magical powers, and talismans . . . I thought life might be a dream, or I an Angel." Second, " 'I was very superstitious, and for some time previous to my conversion (when I was fifteen) used constantly to cross myself on going into the dark.' "

We can discern, I think, the same issue of mastery as in Newman's syntax. Against massive forces, one needs magical aids. The child saw his antagonists as outside himself; the man, wiser, sees them as the pride and passion within himself. But both the child and the man speak of marshalling magical forces for the struggle, the child, of "magical powers, and talismans," crossing oneself; the man, of religion. In either case, Newman speaks as though he were engaged in a struggle in which, even though he marshalls all his energy, he feels inadequate. Behind such a fear of defeat, I sense a wish for it, for every man's fear is also his deepest wish—so clinical experience says. Perhaps that is why I feel Newman courts his own defeat—in his prose; certainly, in his life, he sought a superior to whom he could submit.

In short, we can see how the style of Newman's writing reflects the style of his thought, which is presumably the style also of *l'homme même*. Then we, as readers, become engaged in his patterns of fantasy and defense. To the extent those patterns match our own, we tend to experience them as such. To the extent they do not, we tend to withdraw from the experience or modify it. But despite the great variations in subjective response, I hope this essay has at least opened up the possibility of relating our personal reactions to the writer's stylistic choices through a psychoanalytic understanding of non-fiction prose as an interaction of fantasy and defense.

We have seen that the basic difference between our experience of fiction and our experience of non-fiction stems from the difference in the amount of reality-testing each asks from us. Any given paragraph could be fiction or non-fiction—it is our different expectations from fiction and non-fiction rather than the texts as such that differentiate our degrees of involvement. Non-fiction usually asks us to do more reality-testing than fiction. The more we reality-test a work of literature, the more we become aware of the reality of ourselves as separate beings, and the less, therefore, we take the literary work into ourselves (introject it) and feel the psychological process it embodies as though it were happening in us. Thus, Carlyle draws us into an experience more than Mill or Arnold does.

The fundamental process, however, is the same in non-fiction as in fiction: the managing and transformation of unconscious or infantile fantasies into social, moral, and intellectual meaning. The ideas of non-fiction express a writer's or a reader's drives just as plots and characters do. But in a writing about liberty or gentlemanly qualities or English criticism, the distance between the underlying fantasy and the final verbal product will be much greater than in, say, *Hamlet* or *Oedipus*. There will be much more sublimation in the direction of meaning—another reason our experience of non-fiction is likely to be less emotional than our experience of fiction, a reason, too, my readings of these non-fiction passages probably seem more far-fetched than similar readings of poems, stories, or plays would.

Our expectations about fiction and non-fiction differ; fantasies are much less explicit in non-fiction. Given these two differences, however, the verbal texture operates in non-fiction just as it does in fiction. It manages (or adapts or sublimates) the fantasy at the heart of the writing. Pronouns or co-ordinate constructions or visual images can express and manage the underlying fantasy just as they do in a lyric or joke. In this sense, form will manage content just as in fictional works. Form and content can each be understood in terms of the other, if we look to the way they co-act in the writer's mind or the reader's.

We can, moreover, formalize a method for looking psychologically at the co-action of form and content. Figurative language provides the nearest thing to a royal road to unconscious content. Carlyle's visual metaphors, Arnold's *noli me tangere*, Newman's mooring and quarrying—each points to the unconscious fantasy, or at least the general kind of issue at the unconscious level. Second, the writer's biography may provide clues to the unconscious significance for him of the intellectual issues he discusses: Mill's liberty from his father or Newman's quest for supernatural strengths. Because non-fiction is more sublimate than fiction, biography is often more necessary.

More subtle and subjective than the fantasies are the defensive strategies for managing such unconscious materials in non-fiction: careful syntactic analysis (such as Ohmann's), an analysis of one's own reaction, most of all, a clinical awareness of typical defensive patterns—all may be necessary to see the way a man's verbal style manages the issues that have important unconscious meanings for him.

Style, then, if we limit it to syntactic patterns and the like, would seem to be more intimately related to the particular writer and his unconscious conflicts than to the period in which he wrote. Ohmann has asked, Is there such a thing as an "Enlightenment style" or a "Victorian style"?[14] Both his linguistic examination of these passages and my psychological one would seem to say there is not. Newman, Carlyle, Mill, and Reade, for example, all use co-ordinate constructions, but each uses them quite differently. The individuality of particular writers far outweighs the influence of their period.

On the other hand, most readers, I think, feel intuitively that there are some discernible differences between Enlightenment and Victorian writing in general; certainly between Elizabethan prose and Augustan. And perhaps it is possible to isolate these period differences. Reade's co-ordinate constructions join inappropriate nouns—the effect is one of mockery. Carlyle's co-ordinates build up a covering that obscures the real subject. Newman's marshal his forces against some antagonist. By considering something like co-ordinate constructions as psychological strategies rather than purely syntactic phenomena, we are led to look for the nuclear fantasy these strategies deal with. We then find that all five of these passages deal with a superior being or force, conceived in slightly different ways: as magically powerful or controlling by Mill and Newman; as sexual by Reade, Carlyle, and Arnold. Then each writer deals with this shared fantasy by his own idiosyncratic patterns of defense acted out in syntactic choices: Mill by dependence-independence; Reade by mockery; Carlyle by masking and unmasking; Arnold by retreat to the level of ideas; Newman by defeat in a struggle.

The differences stand out more than the similarities, but we nevertheless can find the similarities, and they seem to inhere rather in the unconscious issues than in the prose style *per se*. When Ohmann, for example, speaks of "the Victorian struggle to provide a reliable common ground for discourse and to overcome doubt and uncertainty," he is identifying a conscious, intellectual version of the unconscious issue, the attempt to deal with a superior being or force. Perhaps, then, the search for a "Victorian style" will lead us away from purely linguistic considerations and toward the psychological issues a writer's syntax manages. If so, then we shall be finding the linguistic expression of the basic psychosocial issues of Victorian culture, and we will be able to relate prose style to social patterns, as a linguistic anthropologist would.

Thus, behind the question, Is there a Victorian style?, lies a deeper question: To what extent do linguistic choices act out and express more pervasive phychological strategies? Do the kinds of particular sentence transformations modern linguistics reveals correspond to gross psychological patterns one knows from couch or clinic? Does a pronominal or relative or passive transformation act out psychological dependency? Does deletion act out denial or repression? Certainly, in each of the analyses above, linguistics has led us to one revealing trait: the introduction or removal of persons in the transition from deep to surface structure. One would expect from psychoanalytic studies of dreams that those persons would image the self and the parents (at their deepest level); adding or removing them would be of considerable importance.

It is good, in this connection, to remember that Freud often spoke of the dream-work as akin to translation. Even so, it seems unlikely that most linguistic transformations match psychological transformations in a one-to-one way. Rather, such transformations as subordination or co-ordination, nominalization or pronominalization, passive or relative, seem to co-act in combinations to express and manage unconscious issues (as, indeed, the quite precise and isolable strategies of dream-building do). Finding similarities will be subtle, but not impossible.

The twentieth century has been able to reconcile the microphysics of waves and particles with the macrophysics we inherited from Newton. Perhaps in the same way, we shall be able to reconcile the microlanguage of particular sentences and paragraphs to the macrolanguage of a man's whole life-style. And beyond the individual lie the patterns of his culture and epoch. The vista is a large and tempting one, and the psycholinguistic study of prose seems, at present, the most promising map.

NOTES

1. *Ben Jonson*, ed. C. H. Herford and Percy and Evelyn Simpson, Oxford, 1925-52, VIII, 625. The editors cite (XI, 270-72) Vives, *De Ratione Dicendi*, ii,

Opera, 1555, 103-5, and Erasmus, *Apophthegmata*, iii. 70, *Opera*, 1540, iv. 148, as sources for the passage.

2. Richard Ohmann, "Literature and Sentences," *College English*, XXVII, No. 4 (January 1966), 263. Throughout this essay, I am indebted to Professor Ohmann's linguistic analyses of prose style, not only this essay and others already published, but also the essay he has written for this volume as well as extended correspondence with him. He has been more than generous with his time and remarkable skill.

3. *On Liberty and Considerations on Representative Government*, ed. R. B. McCallum, Oxford, 1946, p. 11.

4. I shall be discussing five passages of prose. To make them easier to compare and refer to, it helps to cancel out individual variations in ways of marking off sentence-units (as by semicolon, comma splice, dash, and the like). Accordingly, I have repunctuated the passages to the extent of breaking them all into what Kellogg W. Hunt calls "minimal terminable syntactic units": "the shortest segments which it would be grammatically allowable to write with a capital letter at one end and a period or question mark at the other, leaving no fragment as residue." Each T-unit (as they are nicknamed) will thus consist of a single independent predication with any complements or modifiers that may be embedded in or otherwise attached to it. Chiefly this rewriting breaks two independent clauses joined by a co-ordinate conjunction into two T-units. Thus, "The dog bit, but not the boy" is a T-unit as it stands, while "The dog bit, but the boy didn't," would be rewritten as two T-units: "The dog bit. But the boy didn't." See Kellogg W. Hunt, *Differences in Grammatical Structures Written at Three Grade Levels, the Structures to Be Analyzed by Transformational Methods*, Report to the U. S. Office of Education, Cooperative Research Project No. 1998, Tallahassee, Florida, 1964, p. 27.

For the sake of my own style, however, I will refer, not to "T-units," but simply to "sentences."

5. Howard R. Wolf, "British Fathers and Sons, 1773-1913: From Filial Submissiveness to Creativity," *The Psychoanalytic Review*, LII, No. 2, 59-60.

6. This text is from *The Early Draft of John Stuart Mill's Autobiography*, ed. Jack Stillinger, Urbana, Ill., 1961, p. 121. The published text shows some interesting differences (italicized below):

> I was reading, accidentally, Marmontel's *Memoires*, and came to the passage *which* relates his father's death, the distressed position of *the* family, and the *sudden inspiration by which* he, then a mere boy, felt and made them feel that he would be everything *to them*—would supply the place of *all that they had lost*.

The especially revealing "everything" has been changed carefully to distinguish boy from father. Other changes result in the dropping of two personal pronouns, one of which (*"his* family") mixes up father and son as the "everything" did. Another change makes Marmontel relate not "how he . . . felt" but "the sudden inspiration by which he . . . felt." The changes, whether by Mill himself or his wife, all move away from direct expression of the son's wishes to supplant the father.

7. Northrop Frye, *Anatomy of Criticism*, Princeton, N. J., 1957, p. 303.

8. *Sartor Resartus: The Life and Opinions of Herr Teufelsdröckh*, ed. Charles Frederick Harrold, New York, 1937, p. 5.

9. If I may shift from the reader's mind to Carlyle's, it is worth noting, I think, this tendency to people ideas shows not only in Carlyle's prose style but also in his thought: his stress on biography, for example, in criticism and history; his wish to hero-worship. Drawing on Fichte, he tended to see the universe polarized into the Self and the Non-Self; he thought the business of the individual was to spiritualize the world of matter. Thus, in *Sartor*, the Everlasting No is depersonalization: "To me the Universe was all void of Life, or Purpose, of Volition, even of Hostility: it was one huge, dead, immeasurable Steam-engine . . . O, the vast, gloomy, solitary Golgotha . . ." (p. 164).

10. Again, to glance at Carlyle's mind, this pattern of masking-then-seeing-then-masking shows not only in the clothing theme of *Sartor*, but also in Carlyle's whole notion of historiography. " 'Stern Accuracy in inquiring, bold Imagination in expounding and filling-up; these . . . are the two pinions on which History soars,' — or flutters and wabbles," wrote Carlyle in his essay, "Count Cagliostro," *Works*, ed. H. D. Traill, London, 1896-99, XXVIII, 259-60. Similarly, Carlyle wrote about his own style to Mill: "I often think of the matter myself; and *see* only that I cannot yet see." *Letters of Thomas Carlyle to John Stuart Mill, John Sterling and Robert Browning*, ed. Alexander Carlyle, London, 1923, p. 74. The ambiguity in "matter" and especially in "that" acts out this fantasy pattern exactly. Is it a simple subordinating "that" or is it a "that which" or most intriguing of all, a "so that"? I have suggested elsewhere that a dominant—perhaps *the* dominant — mode in Victorian fantasy was the wish to see parents as a child would wish to see them, as non-sexual. "Psychological Depths and 'Dover Beach,'" *Victorian Studies*, Supplement to Vol. IX (1965), pp. 5-28. Carlyle instances the point amply.

11. Matthew Arnold, "The Function of Criticism at the Present Time," in *Lectures and Essays in Criticism*, ed. R. H. Super, Ann Arbor, Mich., 1962, III, 269-70.

12. I have suggested elsewhere that "Dover Beach" works out this same psychological issue. See above, note 10.

13. *The Idea of a University*, ed. Charles Frederick Harrold, New York, 1947, p. 107.

14. Richard Ohmann, "Methods in the Study of Victorian Style," *Victorian Newsletter*, No. 27 (Spring 1965), pp. 1-4.

THE COMPUTER APPROACH TO STYLE

LOUIS T. MILIC

WHEN CHARLES BABBAGE designed his Analytical Engine at the very beginning of the Victorian Age (in 1833), he thought of his accomplishment as one which would facilitate the performance of arithmetic operations. Although the Engine was in fact never built, it was in most respects very much like a modern digital computer, except that it was a mechanical rather than an electronic machine. The modern computer, however, is not used merely to solve mathematical problems. Because it is, in its nature, a device for executing instructions, it has been used in a very large variety of applications. Essentially a computer will do anything the user knows how to request. Therefore, it has been found useful, not only in the clerical tasks of business and the mathematical ones of science and engineering, but in the essentially qualitative problems of history, music, the fine arts, and literature.

To the person unfamiliar with the operation of a computer, it may seem as outlandish to program the study of a writer's style as to dissect the smell or feel of a rose petal. However outlandish it may seem, the study of style, with or without a computer, involves a number of discrete steps which can be separately described even though they are felt, when performed by a human scholar, as intuitive or unitary. The total response of a perceiver to an aesthetic or linguistic phenomenon can be subdivided into various parts. For the advantage of critical theory, this ought perhaps to be done more often. Thus, the tendency of critics of style to render their verdicts impressionistically, safe in some sort of organic cocoon, might be challenged and possibly curbed. This censure is not intended to signify that criticism of style is valueless without computers or an order of scientific objectivity, for there have been valuable stylistic studies which derive mainly from the critic's sensitive response to the writer's intentions, his intuitive grasp of the balance between the writer's meaning and the resources of his medium. But it is intended to call attention to the lack of methodology which characterizes most investigations of style.

I

To illustrate this contention and to make explicit some of the assumptions that underlie any investigation of style, I shall cite and examine briefly three studies of Victorian prose: Logan Pearsall Smith on Carlyle, G. S. Fraser on Macaulay, and Hugh Sykes Davies on Trollope.[1]

Smith's essay, "Thomas Carlyle: The Rembrandt of English Prose," incidentally raises the first question to be asked about a study of style: Is this really a study of the author's style? In actual fact, this essay is not a study of Carlyle's style, though nominally it claims to be. It contains the word *prose* in the title and some of what the author has to say concerns the manner of Carlyle's writing. Smith propounds the view that Carlyle was less a prophet and moralist than an artist, was more concerned with speaking in his peculiar original style than with the substance he was conveying. To substantiate this thesis, Carlyle is shown in his early retirement hatching his new style. And he is compared to Rembrandt, whose art though not beautiful either, was dramatic and full of contrasts. Despite what Smith implies about Carlyle's style, he makes very little comment about its quiddity. Smith's thesis postulates a change between Carlyle's early style and his late or famous style, and he gives examples from each period. His description of the early style, which Carlyle put behind during his crisis period, is limited to the adjective "elegant." The later style is never described in any detail, but there are a number of references to it in the essay, involving more or less description. This description taken as a whole gives only a vague sense of what Carlyle's late style actually is, whatever may be its effect on the reader, which seems to be what Smith is most concerned with.

The descriptive bits may be placed in three categories:

1. Frankly impressionistic, impossible to verify: "a richly coloured and resonant vocabulary,"[2] "the rich accumulation in the gloom of his great imagination of darkly gleaming words and images,"[3] "his prose had much of the splendour and music which makes English imaginative prose so magnificent an organ of expression."[4]

2. Subjective, but not impossible to verify: "he found or invented (and he was a great creator of new words) a vocabulary for its [his sense

for the mystery of existence] expression,"[5] "constant use of audible sensations in the phrases and metaphors of his writing."[6]

3. Objectively verifiable: "The difference between Carlyle's early prose, and the richness and resonance of his late style, is due partly to the immense vocabulary he had acquired, with its 'depth of fathomless adjective,' and the most far-fetched phrases of remote allusion, but, above all, as a needed corrective for this elevation, his use of idiom and spoken speech."[7]

These three types of statement are quite representative of the sort of thing that is usually said by writers on style. The first type is by and large only the emotional response of the reader, not an attempt at description. Reading Carlyle perhaps made Smith's mind dwell on images of rich piles of gold coins, darkly gleaming in the crypt of some religious edifice resonating to the sound of splendid organ music. Elsewhere, Smith was capable of this admitted kind of subjectivity. But as he was here writing a criticism of style, in which pseudo-description is normal, he was merely following the tradition.

Statements of the second type try to present objective reality, something which can be tested, proved, demonstrated, or shown to be true, at least in principle. If Carlyle invented a great number of new words, that fact should be demonstrable. If he used sense-imagery, that also should be demonstrable. The difficulty is partly one of definition: what is a new word, a sense-image? Is an obsolete word renewed a new word? Is the second statement true if everyone uses a great many sense-images?

The third type of statement, if it is possible to draw a finite line between Carlyle's early and late styles, may possibly be a contribution to the objective study of Carlyle's style. It distinguishes between the two on the basis of several testable criteria: vocabulary size, remote allusion, spoken speech. This last seems to be central, and Smith buttresses it with a quotation from Emerson, who praised Carlyle for not writing in the written language but for using the language of conversation. It does not matter much, from the viewpoint of methodology that these claims are probably erroneous. The claim that someone's style is conversational has very frequently been made in this century.[8] It is always taken as a compliment, whereas "he speaks like a book" is not. What is important is that statements of the third type are actual steps in the direction of a description of style whereas the other two are not.

To appreciate properly the significance of this examination of Smith's essay, it is essential to be aware that in large part a study of a writer's style must be a description of that writer's style or must be based on a known and accepted description. There may be subsidiary aims, such as the question of development, the reflection of philosophy or personality in the style and the like, but without a doubt a discussion of style without a description does not make sense. It is necessary to agree on what something is before we can decide how it has changed, how it may diverge from the norm, how it reflects various forces.

The difficulty of rigorously describing a linguistic phenomenon like style is surely one reason why so many scholars content themselves either with descriptions as vague as those of Logan Pearsall Smith or with references to a style as a known quantity which need not be described. Macaulay, criticizing the style of Johnson, said his faults were so well-known that there was no need to describe them. But he then proceeded to list them in a way that qualified for inclusion in my third category.[9] Many writers limit themselves to the first part of Macaulay's formula whether they are blaming or praising. A case in point is an article by G. S. Fraser on the style of Macaulay as an essayist. His main claim is that of all the great Victorian stylists—he cites Carlyle, Ruskin, Newman—only Macaulay has had a lasting influence, one which can be perceived in the prose of modern journals of opinion, in popularization, in political writing, and even in Bertrand Russell's non-mathematical works. Perhaps because of the audience he is writing for, which shares with him a certain kind of interest, education, and reading, he does not trouble to describe Macaulay's style except in inexact and allusive terms. There are only two passages even of such description: "the old machinery of allusion, point, and antithesis, of the periodic sentence coming down with a snap or bang at the end,"[10] "its dependence on point, balance, an abundance of not too recondite literary and historical allusion, periodic order, sharp antitheses . . . diverse exemplification and concealed repetition. . . ."[11] It can be readily seen that all the points of the first comment are included in the second. It seems as if Fraser thinks it would be superfluous to amplify the referential description he has given, because everyone knows Macaulay's style and because to be more precise might be tedious—it would certainly be time-consuming and difficult. Moreover, despite the title, the tendency of the discussion is to discover not what Macaulay's style is but what it is like, what it may be compared to. Thus Fraser stresses its kinship with modern historical and journalistic writing and its source in the quarterlies for which Macaulay wrote. But more important, "it is very much the style of an orator."[12] This assertion leads readily to the conclusion, buttressed by quotations from Matthew Arnold, that Macaulay's style was a rhetorical machine operating independently of the beliefs of the author. On the whole, this is very damaging criticism, but that is not the central concern of the essay. The concern seems to be the consequences of the style of Macaulay, rather than the style itself, which is supposed to be a bad thing.

The essay of Hugh Sykes Davies on Trollope's style, on the other hand, is an effort at rehabilitation. Davies observes that the critics of Trollope have denied his style any individuality, in fact, have denied him any style at all. Davies is concerned to refute this charge by asserting that Trollope had an idiosyncratic device of style—he calls it a "cadence" —and that many examples of it can be cited in illustration. The cadence consists of a tendency to produce anticlimax by the immediate qualification of a statement by means of adversative connectives and the skillful repetition of key terms. Davies cites, under five headings, a total of twenty-one examples taken from more than a hundred that he has collected.

Except for the bizarre desire to prove that Trollope does do something individual—the point is axiomatic because style is by definition the kind and type of individuality in a person's writing—Davies proceeds in a more objective way than the other two scholars that I have quoted. He stipulates a single device, describes it, illustrates it lavishly and resists the tendency to draw extravagant conclusions. Consequently, as a result of the detail with which he has done this job, his accomplishment seems less extensive than Smith's or Fraser's, who are really handling literary-historical problems under color of studying style. Because they do not itemize, they seem to be describing the whole styles of their authors, whereas in fact they merely glance at them. Davies, because he is detailed and illustrative, can only deal with a small bit of Trollope's style, one single device, which he believes, however, significantly to reflect Trollope's mode of thought.

Taken all in all, then, these three essays, which are quite representative examples of scholarly discussion of prose style, convey a general flavor of theoretical vagueness and a definite sense of methodological inadequacy. All three writers operate on the basis of unspoken and even unknown assumptions, some of which are mutually contradictory. Smith talks about Carlyle's style but mentions only his vocabulary, as if style were exclusively or mainly choice of word. Fraser discusses influence and attributes Macaulay's peculiar style to his Philistine outlook while insisting that Macaulay's style is not the man. Davies works hard to defend his author against a charge that could have been dismissed as absurd, that Trollope's style had no individuality.

The sort of essays these are would not have been written in their present form if their authors had had a sound theoretical framework for their efforts. Such a framework might take the following form, in the light of present knowledge and theory.

II

A natural language is an inefficient coding device, but it contains a number of safeguards against the loss through garbling of the messages it carries. These safeguards tend to take the form of repetition of information by several means, a process the engineers who developed information theory call *redundancy*. Inflections, word order, lexical compatibility, the use of function words, all together represent different ways of doing the same thing. According to one calculation, English is about 50 per cent redundant.[13] This characteristic of natural languages provides the speaker or writer with a variety of expressive possibilities. In expressing a given thought, he has the opportunity, in fact the obligation of making a number of choices, of which the best known but probably least important is the choice of word. This kind of choice is the basis of style. The language provides this basis; the individual's own quality determines his use of the opportunity it affords him.

Individual writers of a given language within a culture have a great deal in common: educational tradition, a body of values, standard reading, similar life situations eliciting the same kinds of linguistic behavior. Nonetheless, it is self-evident that the linguistic differences are considerable, if only because no two people grow up exposed to precisely the same linguistic stimuli. Everyone has an individual mode of expression, a style. Thus, each writer's linguistic repertory alone will differentiate him in a number of particulars from every other writer, and his way of writing (or style) is bound to reflect that peculiarity. The student of style has as his task the finding of peculiarity, not the solution of the question whether it exists, for exist it must.

The factor of individuality is a trap for the uninitiated. Some writers have an individuality that is highly visible and easily perceived, as eccentricity or as originality. Carlyle, Pater, and Ruskin might figure in such a group. Others, like Trollope, Stevenson, and Kipling, have styles that are less well-defined to the superficial eye. Their writings are stigmatized as styleless or described as lacking in color or neutral. Actually, the highly visible characteristics (mainly lexical), are not the only nor even the most important categories of style. In their effect on the reader, these highly individual styles may well be more striking. But in terms of their deviation from a standard norm, all these authors show more or less equal individuation. In other words, some forms of idiosyncrasy, such as syntactic, may be considerable yet not register on the average reader.

In addition, there is the factor of sample size, which gives individuality the room to assert itself. Two different persons, limited to describing an object in a single sentence, may well turn out the same sentence. It is improbable that they will turn out several identical sentences and virtually impossible that they will construct the same discourse. Given a large enough sample, the full set of their stylistic differences would presumably emerge.

It is necessary to have a clear idea of what is meant by "differences" in the sense used here. Most discourses are different from each other in that they are concerned with different meanings. Many suppose that the difference in meanings is a difference in style because of some confusion about the distinction between these two aspects of a discourse. That style and meaning are ultimately not to be completely separated is a view it would be futile to deny. But that they are the same or indistinguishable is a view contrary to all experience. Every writer knows that he must choose certain words or decide between alternate forms of expression before being able to proceed with his writing. He knows that he is not choosing between meanings but between forms. That part of the meaning which is popularly called "connotation" is included in style. One definition settles the matter this way: Meaning is what stays constant when the form of a sentence is changed. The question can be endlessly complicated but the simplest solution is to observe that unless style and meaning are separable, are different entities, style cannot be studied at all. Only if a given notion can be expressed in varying ways can the writer's choice of medium be explored.

Difference in another sense must still be considered. Smith's study of

Carlyle presents his style as two sets of differences. On the one hand, there is the early style and the late style. The examination of either is made against the background of the other and the differences between these two styles are emphasized. But when the style of Carlyle (or Macaulay or Trollope) is examined for itself, to bring out its peculiar uniqueness, then another background is needed. The average reader of prose has that background built into his mind in the form of a linguistic norm. The linguistic norm is theoretically the average speech of all speakers of the language, but it can be subdivided into the sub-norms of a period, a genre, a particular community, a written language. This norm does not coincide with any individual's use of the language, though any given reader's idea of it is doubtless influenced by his own linguistic repertory. As the average reader processes the linguistic input, he mentally matches it against his notion of the norm and observes deviations, which he notes as stylistic devices, tricks of style, elegance of expression, or, on the other hand, grammatical errors, jargon, etc. . . . There is of course a large gap between the items he perceives and those he can explicitly describe, much as music lovers can identify Bach's choral music without being in the slightest able to show what indicia guided them. There is also a gap between the items (in the sense of deviations from the norm) that he perceives and the ones that are there, ready to be perceived by a reader with a suitably keen sensitivity or an appropriate set of categories.

The unconsciousness of a great deal of the language-producing and perceiving process is responsible for a number of curious ideas about style. For instance, critics often speak as if a writer could change his style or could have several styles. No doubt a writer's style changes with time but even the most sophisticated writer has a very vague sense of what his own style really is like or what he does when he tries to modify it. In language production, the conscious attention of the speaker is on the meanings he is selecting, whereas the generation of appropriate sentence forms to convey them seems to be delegated to a subsidiary set of subconscious mechanisms. The same obtains when language is taken in: the emphasis is on the intake of meanings and not of forms, though the meanings are assigned by the forms. When the attention is concentrated on the forms, as in proofreading, editing, or stylistic investigation, it is very difficult to take in meanings at all.

Typically, in writing, an author selects with a certain degree of unconsciousness from his linguistic repertoire, which is a sub-set of the total resources of the language. By calling on differing portions of his sub-set, he may seem to be modifying his style. By increasing the degree of consciousness he exerts, he can achieve greater control over the manner of his writing and may even give a good imitation of another's style. Nonetheless, because writing can be pursued with even minimal efficiency only if it remains a largely subconscious activity, a writer's style is inevitably idiosyncratic in that it reflects the special and unique selection from the linguistic resources of a language which characterizes a particular human being. Certain consequences follow from this. (1) All writers have individual styles and no writer can lack style, unless by that is meant "good style." (2) However varied his writings may be, any writer's style will reveal some irreducible constancy. (3) The least conscious parts of the writing process will be the most likely to be constant over a wide range of genres. (4) The traditional categories of stylistic study (diction, rhetorical devices, imagery) are unlikely to be the most rewarding to investigate in uncovering the writer's basic style.

This last is really the crux of the matter, the categories which are the basis of the analysis of style. These are limited partly by the ingenuity of the scholar and partly by the characteristics of the equipment and techniques that he uses to prosecute his research (pencil and paper, file cards, collators, computers, or extra-sensory perception). The categories also impinge very importantly on the use that can be made of his findings, the interaction between the observation of peculiarities and their evaluation.

III

However loosely defined, categories in stylistic analysis are variables, in the sense that the value of x or y in an equation is a variable. Any statement in stylistics expressing a value for an author in any category is actually a quantitative statement defining a variable. Even Smith's vague remarks about Carlyle's tendency to create new words implicitly define a new-word variable with a high value for Carlyle. Whether Smith or the reader is aware of it, such statements are quantitative—vague, imprecise, and impossible to verify in their present form though they may be. Such statements, to be usable, must be converted to figures. Let us restate it thus: Carlyle's new-word index is x, which is the result of dividing his coined vocabulary by his total vocabulary. The resulting figure is a genuine quantity, but how useful is it by itself? We must know what values Macaulay, Newman, Ruskin, and Pater, for example, scored on that parameter. Once we have those figures, we are in a position to state whether Smith's statement is accurate with reference to a representative number of great writers of his time. With that empirical conclusion in hand, we could turn our attention to evaluating the observation. But results of this sort are arduous to procure, and it is certainly faster to describe one's feelings about a style than the style itself.

At any rate, how would one go about filling in values for the variable of new-word creation? Obviously someone would have to identify the new words in Carlyle's writings and count them, possibly making subtotals according to particular works or periods of time. The same procedure would be followed for samples of all the works of the various authors being used as a standard of comparison. When the results were collected, we might find that out of a total vocabulary (number of different words used in all his works) of 15,000, Carlyle had coined 500, which is an index of .0333. The others might have indices of .0205, .0150, .0010, and .0003.[14] Carlyle would clearly be the highest, but writers A, B, C, and D would all have some claim to be regarded as word-coiners. At that point, this would become a problem in interpretation.

As projected, the coined-word count upheld Smith's claim, though it might equally well not have. Neither event could be known, however, until the arduous task of counting was done. Possibly a computer would have helped. It is not difficult to describe the preparations required to permit a computer to perform this kind of task. But it is first necessary to have a general idea of how a computer works.[15] For all its outward complexity, a digital computer is based on one single characteristic: whether current is flowing or not. This is numerically equivalent to "1" or "0". Raised by several orders of magnitude and combined in special ways, this circuitry will perform a great many interesting and difficult tasks, all dependent on the binary structure. The basic simplicity of the machine gives it its enormous versatility.

A computer is a machine with four basic parts: input, storage, control, output. (There is also an arithmetic unit, but we shall ignore it.) The input is the means of introducing instructions and data into the machine so that it may act. The most common input is the notorious punched card, but paper tape, magnetic tape, typewriter, mark-sensing, optical scanning, and voice recognition are also real or soon-to-be-realized options. The control section is in charge of the operation and routes the flow of control so that the instructions are executed in the proper order. It ultimately activates the output and stops the machine. The storage (or "memory") is a set of cells, each of which contains a unit of information. This is "core" storage, where both program and data are stored. Information may also be stored on magnetic tape reels, which are usually shown as constantly in motion during a program run. The output, like the input, takes various forms, including an electronic music synthesizer, in addition to the input modes enumerated before.

This simple model is capable of very sophisticated results because of one feature that distinguishes a computer from a calculator, automation from automatism, a servo-mechanism from a machine. That feature is feedback. An ordinary machine does what it is told to do, then stops. It has no feedback, no means of examining the achieved result and comparing it with some expected result. The computer's feedback allows it to choose options, depending on the results of an operation it has performed. This self-correcting tendency is responsible for nearly all its sophistication, including its so-called decision-making power. A thermostat is also a feedback mechanism, of precisely the same type but far simpler. Once the temperature is set, it constantly compares the setting with the actual warmth and corrects any deviation by turning the heat source on or off. It is a very simple computer in that it has only one *bit* of information, one set of choices. Even a small computer has a capacity of thousands, even millions, of bits of information.

Information is what a computer deals in and that of two kinds: program and data. The program is the set of instructions. The data is what the instructions act on. Information is conveyed to the computer, via any input mode, in a symbolic code known as a "language." Computer languages are of several kinds, but none of them is very much like a natural language. The only code the computer is designed to respond to is machine language, which is numerical, highly detailed, and very complex. It is an efficient language, in that it has practically no redundancy. An error of a digit garbles the instructions. Programming in machine language is immensely complicated and time-consuming. Therefore, it is done no more than necessary. Consequently, symbolic languages have been devised, which are at a "higher level" than machine language. These languages—they have odd acronymic names like COBOL, ALGOL, FORTRAN, COMIT, SNOBOL, and PL/1—are really programs written in machine language which accept instructions in a less complicated symbolic code or language. In other words, before anyone could communicate with the machine in a high-level computer language, someone had to design a program in machine language which would translate from high-level to machine language.[16]

Such terms as *language, memory, information* are misleading if they imply an anthropomorphic view of the machine, a correspondence of functions between a computer and a human being. In popular usage, a computer is "told" or "fed" something; it "understands" or "remembers" or "stores things in its memory." After this, one "pushes the button" and it does what it has been told. There is an analogy between machine and brain function, but it is approximate and uninformative. The differences are more significant. For instance, a human being can be given instructions to perform certain operations on a body of data, which he can memorize until he understands the instructions or after, in something like the way that a program and a set of data are stored in a computer. The human being, however, may correctly interpret defective or incomplete instructions or he may bungle perfectly good instructions. He may forget the data or, on the other hand, he may develop new ideas owing to the interaction between the new data and what had been stored in his mind previously. This process may take place if he has only an imperfect recall of the stored data. In order to execute the instructions properly, he may need to be given illustrations, perhaps to be guided through a few runs, or he may even require extensive training. None of these contingencies is true of the computer.

If the program has been properly written, it will be executed without error. Illustrations or training would be superfluous and impracticable. The stored data will remain where it is,[17] impervious to decay, until called on. On the other hand, the machine cannot correct errors in the program or interpret the intention of the programmer. Nor will it come up with any new ideas, for among other things its memory is blank except for the new data. The computer always does what it is told, whether or not one has told it one's intentions. In the words of Lady Lovelace, the daughter of Byron and the first admirer of Babbage's invention: "The Analytical Engine has no pretensions whatever to originate anything. It can do whatever we *know how to order it* to perform."[18] Thus, in programming a literary problem, the scholar must conform his thinking to the level of the machine's own function. This means in practice that he must be able to define his problem explicitly in categories that can be fully formalized, that is, precisely described. Categories based on intuition cannot be used because the machine has no such capability.

These sound like formidable limitations, and they would be indeed if human minds were as limited as computers. Though the computer cannot accommodate to the scholar, the scholar can easily adjust to the computer's limitations. For instance, let us suppose that a student of English prose had formed the impression that sentences in older literature were longer than those in modern literature. He might state his belief in the form of a statement like this: "The English sentence has become gradually shorter." Under normal circumstances, such a remark might be left unsupported and unverified. But let us say that the originator of this view had an objective bent and was desirous of testing its accuracy. He might become aware that he had really said that sentence length is an inverse function of time and that there were thus two variables in his experiment which would have to be correlated. Actually, this is not a fictitious case: Professor Lucius A. Sherman, of the University of Nebraska, around 1885 became interested in this question and proceeded to test it by counting the length of sentences and computing averages for a number of authors at various times in literary history.[19]

It is interesting that in one account of his results, he concluded the hypothesis demonstrated by the results, whereas in another he attributed the variation in sentence-length to idiosyncratic factors, some kind of individual "sentence-sense." The difference is actually the result partly of his using different criteria of definition of "sentence" and partly from considering somewhat different sets of authors. Both his sampling technique and his experimental design were quite primitive.

Sherman did not spare himself, however, the onerous task of counting, for example, *all* the sentences in Macaulay's *History of England* and in his *Essays,* one word at a time, in order to discover that Macaulay's overall average sentence-length was 23.43 words and that this average would be approximated by nearly any group of 300 sentences in his writings. This was not a general rule, he found, for Macaulay showed remarkable consistency of sentence-length, unlike De Quincey, for example. It took Sherman several months to count all these words, record the figures, and compute all the averages. He might have saved himself some labor, as a critic of his work later pointed out, by counting lines, multiplying by an average word-per-line count and dividing by the number of end punctuation marks in the text.

In what way would a computer have been helpful to Sherman, supposing that he had designed his experiment in accordance with widely-known principles of sampling and experimental design, that is, supposing that he had defined *sentence* in some non-ambiguous way and that he had drawn samples of appropriate size randomly at stated intervals of time? His biggest difficulty would have been the same as that faced by anyone planning to process a large amount of text: converting the text into an input form readable by machine, say on punched cards. If he proceeded on the assumption that a sample of 300 sentences was adequate and he wished to cover four centuries at 25-year intervals, he would need 16 samples or 4800 sentences, a total of 168,000 words (taking an average sentence-length over the whole time of 35 words). Obviously, key-punching all these words on cards would be no faster than counting them.[20] There would, therefore, be no advantage in calling on a computer for this task if the laboriously compiled text were to be used only to measure this one parameter. Plainly, such a text would be valuable for an unlimited number of other uses; and it could, moreover, be made available to other scholars as well. But in case such possibilities were not relevant to this situation, there would still be another resource to draw on.

Whenever a scholar converts a text to machine-readable form, he preserves it even after he has completed the work, in part to save other scholars the duplication of effort necessary to key-punch large quantities of text. A consolidated list of such holdings is annually published. The current listing contains about two hundred entries, including texts in English, French, German, Spanish, Danish, Rumanian, Greek, Latin, Hebrew, Chinese, Japanese, Umbrian, Anglo-Saxon, Middle English, Old Norse, and others. The range of authors represented is equally wide.[21] An appropriate set of texts for the sentence-length measurement could be collected from this list, with the advantage that such a collection of 4800 sentences would become an independent corpus suitable for other investigations and for use by other scholars, possibly even some of those from whom the parts had been borrowed in the first place. The results of analyzing such a corpus could also be compared with a set of measures derived from an extant corpus of one million words of present-day English.[22]

Once this hurdle is overcome, and a uniform machine-readable text is available, the program must be written. For this particular measurement, the program would be very simple. In the SNOBOL language, it would require about a dozen instructions, and a processing time of perhaps fifteen minutes on a large machine like the IBM 7094.[23]

From this elementary illustration it may perhaps be inferred that some kinds of literary problems are efficiently handled by a computer, whereas others call for a disproportionate amount of preparation. Ideally, the text one wishes to study should already be in machine-readable form. Failing that, one's text should be short and need to be processed extensively (for a number of variables). In order to justify the expense of encoding a long text which one does not expect to process fully, it should be a text standard enough that it is probable others will want to use it, like the poems of Matthew Arnold, a play by Shakespeare, or any of the standard prose works of the great Victorians.[24]

Needless to say, if computers were able to perform tasks no more sophisticated than computing sentence-length, it would hardly be worth invoking their aid in the study of style. But in fact they can be used in more valuable ways, subject only to the skill of the user. A computer can scan a text for any category that can be defined. For instance, the total vocabulary of a writer can be counted if the canon of his works is available on cards or tape. In addition, the vocabulary can be saved and printed out in a variety of forms: an alphabetical list, a frequency list with the most common word first and the rarest last, a list with the adjacent words printed along with the key-word. All of these are exhaustive compilations amounting to the making of concordances or indices verborum. Texts may be searched for particular words, proper names, or combinations of words. The technique called "content analysis" searches texts for words which form clusters of associations around a given concept or group of concepts. Thus, for instance, a content analysis of one scene in *Hamlet* shows a number of words associated with the theme of madness.[25] Admittedly, this theme is hardly a secret, but similar studies could reveal semantic clusters whose existence might not be known. The application of such a technique to studies of imagery seems self-evident. The difficulty of the task, however, would not reside in the provision of a machine-readable text.

The extensive processing required for making a concordance is mainly a problem of programming. Unless the desired concordance has unusual features, one could use with suitable modifications existing concordance programs which their creators have made available.[26] Content analysis, however, is dependent on a program containing a thesaurus of ideas suitably linked. Although such programs are in existence, it is obvious that differences of opinion about relevance of connection between related ideas could occur among different scholars. Therefore, a program of this type would have to be tailored to individual texts. Such a program would be based on some theory of the interconnection of ideas, words, or images in the particular writers. In other words, in this more sophisticated use of a computer, the problem would have to be tentatively solved before the computer-assisted phase of work could begin. It is true that, in cases like these, a dialectic between the theoretical and the empirical usually takes place. The theory is tentatively formulated, and a small computer model designed to test it. The results are used to review and revise the theory, and a new model is constructed. This process is repeated until both theory and evidence are complete. This sequence of progressive complication also helps to make the program easier to design, inasmuch as it too develops in stages.

Categories of typographic units (words, sentences, letters) are, as we have seen, easily processed by machine. Ideas and meanings, as reflected in the actual words used by the writer, can also be handled, but with more effort. Grammatical categories can be impossibly difficult if the machine is to do the parsing.[27] But they can be much more easily processed if the text bears suitable grammatical indications, i.e. has been analyzed before processing. The difficulty can be illustrated by reference to my study of the style of Swift, compared with Addison, Johnson, Gibbon, and Macaulay.[28]

One purpose of this study was to establish the consistency of word-class categories (parts of speech) in different works of the same author. Instead of taking the standard text and trying to design a program which would analyze each word grammatically—a task of incredible complexity —the text was analyzed manually and only numerical equivalents for the grammatical class of each word were encoded. The input thus consisted exclusively of numbers and end punctuation. Macaulay's sentence, "his conversation appears to have been quite equal to his writings in matter and far superior to them in manner," was encoded as follows:

31 01 02 61 21 21 33 03 51 31 01 51 01 41 33
03 51 11 51 01

The program sorted each "word" of the text in one of the 24 word-classes and produced frequency tables for each sample and for requested sub-samples. Extensive analysis of the output showed that certain classes or groups of classes have high consistency because they are idiosyncratic variables for a particular author, others because they are linguistic constants. Other classes fluctuate widely with different genres or subject matters.

With the text encoded in the fashion described, it was possible to design programs which would extract other kinds of information. Sentence-length was easily counted, as each word was represented by a two-digit number with end punctuation preserved.[29] Word-classes and patterns appearing at the beginning and at the end of sentences could be collected and counted. Patterns of three successive word-classes were examined in the hope of finding individual syntactic preferences.[30] The results of that very elaborate search illustrate the serendipity of the computer. The same pattern was preferred by all the writers in all their samples, but the total number of different patterns, a figure requested almost as an after-thought, turned out to be significantly individual for several writers and consistent within each author's writings.[31]

Grammatical categories, to the extent that they are realized in describable forms, are well-suited to computer analysis. Rhetorical features of style fall into two basically different types: figures of arrangement and figures of thought or meaning. Figures that involve repetition of letters (alliteration, homoioteleuton), of words (anaphora, epistrophe, polysyndeton, epanodos), of phrases (epanalepsis, climax, ploce), or of grammatical constructions (isocolon), as well as those that require the omission of words or word-classes (asyndeton, brachylogia, zeugma) can be detected by formal means. Figures of thought, which involve the substitution of one kind of expression for another (decorated for plain, figurative for literal) are very much more difficult to find by machine. This is not to say that the problem is insoluble or ought not to be attempted, for it has repeatedly occurred that the consequences of trying to formalize an "insoluble" literary or linguistic problem for computer assistance has resulted in an increase of knowledge, a discovery of formal patterns previously unsuspected. But such attempts are not economical. Therefore, those to whom the computer is most attractive as a time- and labor-saver will prefer to avoid heuristic explorations and consider only the standard data-processing applications.

IV

Among those who doubt the value of computer-assisted literary study a favorite question is often asked: What kinds of conclusions does a computer make possible? A very informative answer by a linguist is in the form of a counter-question which makes use of a convenient analogy: Would the buyer of a car ask the salesman whether the car could go to Philadelphia?[32] Of course, the problem of interpreting the results of stylistic study is no different whether the results have been compiled by hand or by machine. The distance between observation and evaluation is basically always the same, though perhaps it is more important in stylistics and receives a heavier emphasis when the results have been gathered by a computer.

Traditional studies of style begin with a conclusion, which is conveyed rhetorically and ornamented with bits of evidence. Fraser's thesis on Macaulay's influence is an insight (whether right or wrong) deriving from the intuition of the critic. Hardly any attempt is made to prove the contention; the effort goes into making the thesis presentable. It would not be impossible to design an experiment to test Fraser's hypothesis. Such a test would require an agreed-on description of Macaulay's style and a definition of influence. Then presumably a great deal of modern writing could be searched for something like those qualities and perhaps be found to possess them. Before a conclusion, positive or negative, could be reached, it would be necessary to test for the influence of Newman, Ruskin, Pater, Carlyle, and others in the same body of writing. Whether the conclusion reached had been worth all the effort is not at issue; the fact is, that such a conclusion could indeed be made to follow the gathering of evidence.

Unlike traditional studies, computer-assisted studies usually generate evidence even in the absence of a covering hypothesis. This is frequently the result of the derivative nature of such studies, which are inspired by and perhaps based on the thinking (and programs) of other scholars. And it is this tendency to be empirical, actually to deal with the text, which makes such studies objective, not simply their association with machines. If one has observed what looks like a unique feature of style in a writer, carried out research which shows that it is indeed characteristic and unique within stateable quantitative limits, what then? The expectation is that one will interpret this finding in terms of the style of the author. This is much less easy to do responsibly than is commonly believed.

If the stylistic study is intended to reveal something about the writer, such as a trait of personality, the evaluation will be perforce speculative. Though one may suspect that an excess of modifying words, phrases, and clauses portends a cautious or a precise mind, there is only intuition to go on, for no studies have documented such a theory. The same is true for a variety of guesses concerning the personality equivalents of short sentences, various kinds of connectives, use of adjectives or the passive voice, and the like. Interpretation of this kind may be made to sound convincing by persuasive rhetoric but, at the present state of knowledge about the relation between personality and style, these are mere guesses. Careful examination of the prevalence of similar devices in other writers of the time and in examples of the same genre may reveal significant deviation on the part of the writer studied, which may permit certain kinds of inference not nearly so dramatic as those offered by Logan Pearsall Smith about Carlyle.

Inferences about the style of an author, in terms of his originality, for example, may go aground on the question of how much of his style is conscious design, how much the automatic language production of his unconscious. Every writer and reader likes to believe in the total control of the artist over his medium, but there is no question that the writer at any rate (whatever may be true of the composer or painter) is subject to a determinism deriving equally from the laws of language and the properties of the nervous system.

Stylistic studies that emphasize effects on the reader (the perception rather than the production) proceed almost equally in the dark. It is true that rhetoric, the science of effects in speaking and writing, has a much longer history than personality theory. To some extent, therefore, the discovery of certain rhetorical procedures may be evaluated in the traditional terms of rhetorical analysis. Repetition, for instance, is indeed a mode of emphasis, and elaborate figurative statement will attract more attention than plain literal statement. But much depends on the expectation of the reader, which is formed in part by the context. Elevated language in a context which requires it will make less effect than vulgar language. Rules, therefore, about the absolute efficiency of certain devices are likely to be inadequate. The best rhetoricians have always been aware, of course, of the relative nature of effect in ordered language, but until the recent surge in linguistic activity, technical means did not exist to describe it.

It is unfortunately true that the gap between observation and evaluation has still to be bridged with something solid. To some extent, the use of computers in literary work reflects a realization of this difficulty, for computers are evidence-generating not conclusion-reaching machines. In one branch of stylistic study, the attribution of disputed texts by internal evidence, there has been a renewal of interest during the past decade. Three classic authorship problems (the Junius letters, the *Federalist Papers*, and the Epistles of St. Paul) have been investigated by computer, and solutions announced. The notable aspect of these investigations is that they are wholly dependent on means of evidence gathered by computer and that conclusions are reached by means of well-known statistical criteria, not impressionistic evaluation. The collection of evidence about the styles of various authors, whether or not the material collected can be immediately evaluated, cannot help but tend toward the eventual solution of the problem of style. That an increasing number of scholars are finding the evidential basis of computer-assisted study of style attractive is now certain.[33]

In fact, a consciousness of this means of getting data was evident even in the work of Davies on Trollope discussed earlier. After presenting his examples, which were chosen from more than one hundred, he adds:

> . . . it can hardly be expected of any human being to carry such an inquiry further, above all at this moment of time, when electronic devices are within a few years of doing a job like this (including the actual reading of the books) and producing quite definite results, all in a tenth or a hundreth of the time that would be needed by a merely human student of stylistics in the mass. The machine, moreover, will with equal celerity produce the obviously needful comparisons between Trollope and his contemporaries: George Eliot, Dickens, Lytton, Kingsley, Lever and so forth.[34]

In time, the use of computers, not only for matter-of-fact processing but for heuristic purposes and even for imaginative reconstruction of lost texts and the generation of new ones in the style, say, of Milton or Keats, is not beyond possibility. The computer approach to style not only offers certain opportunities for investigation, it imposes responsibilities which must ultimately improve the status of this interdisciplinary branch of criticism.

NOTES

1. Logan Pearsall Smith, "The Rembrandt of English Prose," *Reperusals and Re-Collections* (New York, 1937), pp. 202-21; reprinted as "Thomas Carlyle: The Rembrandt of English Prose," in *Victorian Literature: Modern Essays in Criticism,* ed. Austin Wright, New York, 1961, pp. 113-27. G. S. Fraser, "Macaulay's Style as an Essayist," *Review of English Literature,* I (1960), 9-19; Hugh Sykes Davies, "Trollope and His Style," ibid., 73-85.

2. Wright, p. 116.

3. Ibid., p. 117.

4. Ibid., p. 120.

5. Ibid., p. 118.

6. Ibid., p. 118.

7. Ibid., p. 123.

8. See, for example, A. L. Rowse making this claim for Macaulay in *The English Spirit*, New York, 1946, p. 229; John Rosenberg for Ruskin in *The Darkening Glass,* New York, 1961, p. 219; J. R. Sutherland for nearly all the English Augustans in *On English Prose,* Toronto, 1957, pp. 69 ff.

9. "The characteristic faults of his style are so familiar to our readers, and have been so often burlesqued, that it is almost superfluous to point them out. It is well known that he made less use than any other eminent writer of those strong plain words, Anglo-Saxon or Norman-French, of which the roots lie in the inmost depths of our language; and that he felt a vicious partiality for terms . . . borrowed from the Greek and Latin. . . . His constant practice of padding out a sentence with useless epithets . . . his antithetical form of expression, constantly employed even where there is no opposition in the ideas expressed, his big words wasted on little things, his harsh inversions. . . ." *Literary and Historical Essays,* Oxford, 1923, I, 247.

10. Fraser, loc. cit., p. 9.

11. Ibid., p. 11.

12. Ibid. This is probably a version of the conversational style.

13. Warren Weaver, "Recent Contributions to the Mathematical Theory of Communication," *The Mathematical Theory of Communication,* Urbana, Ill., 1963, p. 104.

14. The figures cited are purely hypothetical and have no basis in reality.

15. Readable introductions to the subject are Jeremy Bernstein, *The Analytical Engine,* New York, 1964, and S. H. Hollingdale and G. C. Tootill, *Electronic*

Computers, Harmondsworth, 1965. The former is based on a series of articles in *The New Yorker;* the latter is a Pelican book.

16. The distinction between these two levels of language can be illustrated by comparing the high-level instructions given by the motorist to his garageman ("Change the oil") with the low-level instructions the garageman gets from his manual ("Find crankcase. Place drain receptacle under crankcase. Get socket wrench. Open bolt at underside of crankcase . . . etc . . .").

17. In computer jargon, *data* is always singular.

18. As quoted in Hollingdale and Tootill, pp. 112-13.

19. "Some Observations upon the Sentence Lengths in English Prose," *University of Nebraska Studies,* I (1888), 119-30; "On Certain Facts and Principles in the Development of Form in Literature," ibid., I (1892), 337-66.

20. A key-punch is an electronic typewriter which prints text on the upper edge of a punch-card at the same time as it punches the appropriate code of holes for each character in the column below it. The machine reads the holes; the human operator reads the printed characters to verify his text.

21. Gary Carlson, "Literary Works in Machine-Readable Form," *Computers and the Humanities: A Newsletter,* I (1967), 75-102. Copies of the list may be obtained from Dr. Gary Carlson, Director, Computer Research Center, C-73 ASB, Brigham Young University, Provo, Utah 84601.

22. The corpus is described in Henry Kucera and W. Nelson Francis, *Computational Analysis of Present-Day American English,* Providence, R. I., 1967.

23. See Appendix for a sample program in SNOBOL which would perform this computation. For a readable description of this language see Allen Forte, *A SNOBOL Primer* (forthcoming).

24. In the matter of the proper format for a literary text and for a more detailed exposition of some of the foregoing matters, see Robert S. Wachal, "On Using a Computer," in *The Computer and Literary Style,* ed. Jacob Leed, Kent, Ohio, 1966, pp. 14-37.

25. For a brief account of this study, see Sally Y. Sedelow, "Some Parameters for Computational Stylistics," *Literary Data Processing Conference Proceedings,* White Plains, (1965), pp. 211-29.

26. For further details, see the article by the programmer of the Cornell poetry concordances, James A. Painter, "Implications of the Cornell Concordances for Computing," ibid., pp. 160-70.

27. Witness the long struggles of Machine Translators and of linguists engaged in syntactic analysis.

28. *A Quantitative Approach to the Style of Swift,* The Hague, 1967, Ch. VI. A shorter account of the same work is to be found in "Unconscious Ordering in the Prose of Swift," *The Computer and Literary Style,* pp. 79-106.

29. Despite samples of less than the size advocated by Sherman, results for Macaulay matched reasonably well with his figures: two samples of 158 sentences drawn by random from the *Literary Essays* and the *Historical Essays* showed averages of 21.76 and 21.67 words, respectively, as compared with Sherman's figure of 23+ for the *Essays.*

30. The first three patterns of the example given above would be 31 01 02, 01 02 61 and 02 61 21. The concluding pattern is 11 51 01.

31. The preferred pattern is 51 31 01 (preposition, determiner, noun, e.g. "of the man"), and the next most common are variations of it. In 3500-word samples, Swift averaged 833 different patterns, Gibbon 468, Addison, Johnson, and Macaulay, 704, 724, and 712, each.

32. Sydney M. Lamb, "What Computers May Do with the Printed Word," *Computers for the Humanities?*, New Haven, Conn., 1965.

33. A list of computer-assisted work in various humane fields is given in "Computerized Research in the Humanities: A Survey," *ACLS Newsletter*, Special Supplement (June 1966). The section on Literature, which lists 88 different projects, is on pp. 23-38.

34. Davies, loc. cit., pp. 81-2.

APPENDIX

A SNOBOL3 Program for Computing Average Sentence-Length of an End-Punctuated English Text

```
(1)    START    CARD = TRIM(SYSPIT)
(2)             CARD = ''CARD''
(3)             CARD '******'                    /S(RESULT)
(4)    POINT    CARD '.' =                        /F(WORD)
(5)             P = P + '1'                       /(POINT)
(6)    WORD     CARD ''*WORD*'' = ''              /F(START)
(7)             W = W + '1'                       /(WORD)
(8)    RESULT   A = W / P
(9)             SYSPOT = 'TOTAL SENTENCES = 'P
(10)            SYSPOT = 'TOTAL WORDS = 'W
(11)            SYSPOT = 'AVERAGE SENTENCE LENGTH OF
                         THIS SAMPLE = 'A
(12)   END

(13)   JOHNSON AS MR BURKE MOST JUSTLY OBSERVED
(14)   APPEARS FAR GREATER IN BOSWELL'S BOOKS THAN
(15)   IN HIS OWN. HIS CONVERSATION APPEARS TO HAVE
(16)   BEEN QUITE EQUAL TO HIS WRITINGS IN MATTER
(17)   AND FAR SUPERIOR TO THEM IN MANNER. WHEN HE
(18)   TALKED HE CLOTHED HIS WIT AND HIS SENSE IN
(19)   FORCIBLE AND NATURAL EXPRESSIONS. AS SOON AS
(20)   HE TOOK HIS PEN IN HIS HAND TO WRITE FOR THE
(21)   PUBLIC HIS STYLE BECAME SYSTEMATICALLY
(22)   VICIOUS.
(23)   * * * *
```

The instruction on Line 1 reads in the contents of the first data card. Line 3 tests whether this card is the last one; when the program reaches this last card, it transfers to Line 8. Line 4 searches for a period and Line 5 counts each such occurrence. Line 6 searches for words and each one is counted on Line 7. When there are no words left on the card being read, the instruction on Line 6 fails and control returns to Line 1, which orders another card read. When all the cards have been read, the computation on Line 8 is made. The results are printed in three lines (9, 10, 11) and the program reaches its end. Lines 13 to 22 show the format of a small sample of data from Macaulay. Line 23 is the end indicator. For simplicity, this program is designed to process only one sample in one pass. The average truncates all decimals.

NOTES ON CONTRIBUTORS

WALTER F. CANNON is Chairman of the department of the History of Science at the Smithsonian Institution's Museum of History and Technology. He is Editor of *The Smithsonian Journal of History,* and a member of the advisory board of *Victorian Studies.* His research field is nineteenth-century Britain, and he has published articles on geology, biology, astronomy, theology, and the relation of science to other intellectual activities in that period.

A. DWIGHT CULLER is Professor of English at Yale University, where he has served as Director of Graduate Studies in English. He is author of *The Imperial Intellect: A Study of Newman's Educational Ideal* (1955) and *Imaginative Reason: The Poetry of Matthew Arnold* (1966).

ALAN DONAGAN is Professor of Philosophy at the University of Illinois. He has published *The Later Philosophy of R. G. Collingwood* (1962) and, with his wife, Barbara, an anthology *Philosophy of History* (1965).

G. S. FRASER is Reader in Modern English Literature at the University of Leicester and a member of the advisory committee of Leicester's Victorian Studies Centre. His publications include *The Modern Writer and His World* (1953) and *Vision and Rhetoric* (1959).

NORMAN N. HOLLAND is Professor of English and Chairman of the department at the State University of New York at Buffalo. He is the author of *Psychoanalysis and Shakespeare* (1966) and *The Dynamics of Literary Response* (forthcoming).

JOHN HOLLOWAY is Reader of Modern English at Queen's College, Cambridge. His *Victorian Sage: Studies in Argument* (1953) is a study of Victorian non-fictional techniques. He has published widely in many areas and has special training in the application of philosophical analysis to literature.

GEORGE LEVINE is Associate Professor of English at Indiana University and Editor of *Victorian Studies*. He has published an anthology, *The Emergence of Victorian Consciousness* (1966), and has completed a book-length study of the prose of Carlyle, Macaulay, and Newman, to be published in spring, 1968.

WILLIAM A. MADDEN is Professor of English at Indiana University. He was a co-editor of and a contributor to *1859: Entering an Age of Crisis* (1959) and has recently published *Matthew Arnold: A Study of the Aesthetic Temperament in Victorian England* (1967).

TRAVIS MERRITT is Assistant Professor of English at the Massachusetts Institute of Technology. He is editor of an anthology of essays (forthcoming) and is completing work on a study of attitudes toward English prose and prose style since 1750.

LOUIS T. MILIC is Associate Professor of English at Columbia University, Teacher's College. He is author of *A Quantitative Approach to the Style of Jonathan Swift* (1967) and compiler of *Style and Stylistics: An Analytic Bibliography* (1966). He is also the review editor of *Computers and the Humanities,* a new bi-monthly journal.

RICHARD OHMANN is Professor of English at Wesleyan University. He is the author of *Shaw: The Style and the Man* (1962). With Harold Martin, he wrote the widely-used textbook *The Logic and Rhetoric of Exposition* (1963) and edited the anthology *Inquiry and Expression* (1963). He is Editor of the monthly journal *College English*.

JOHN ROSENBERG is Professor of English at Columbia University. His publications include *The Darkening Glass: A Portrait of Ruskin's Genius* (1963) and an edition and selection of Ruskin's writings, *The Genius of John Ruskin* (1964). His selection of Swinburne's poetry is to be published in 1968.

G. ROBERT STANGE is Professor of English and Chairman of the department at Tufts University. He is author of *Matthew Arnold, the Poet as Humanist* (1967) and editor, with Walter Houghton, of *Victorian Poetry and Poetics* (1959). He is also a member of the advisory board of *Victorian Studies*.

MARTIN J. SVAGLIC is Professor of English at Loyola University in Chicago. He is editor of Newman's *Idea of a University* and of the Oxford English Text edition of the *Apologia pro vita sua*. He is a member of the advisory board of *Victorian Studies*.

GEOFFREY TILLOTSON is Professor of English Literature at Birkbeck College, University of London. He is author of books on the eighteenth century, of *Thackeray the Novelist* (1954), and with Kathleen Tillotson, of *Mid-Victorian Studies* (1966). He is currently working on the Victorian volume of the *Oxford History of English Literature*.

INDEX